AMERICAN PILOTS IN THE RAF

AMERICAN PILOTS
IN THE RAF
THE WWII
EAGLE SQUADRONS

by
Philip D. Caine

BRASSEY'S
Washington • London

Brassey's edition 1998
First published in August 1991 by NDU Press

Editorial Offices: Order Department:
22883 Quicksilver Drive   P.O. Box 960
Dulles, VA 20166   Herndon, VA 20172

Brassey's books are available at special discounts for bulk purchases
for sales promotions, premiums, fund-raising, or educational use.

Library of Congress Cataloging-in-Publication Data

```
Caine, Philip D., 1933-
   [Eagles of the RAF]
   American pilots in the RAF : the WWII Eagle Squadrons / Philip D.
Caine.
      p.    cm.
   Originally published: Eagles of the RAF. Washington, D.C. :
National Defense University Press, 1991.
   Includes bibliographical references and index.
   ISBN 1-57488-137-X (pbk.)
   1. World War, 1939-1945--Aerial operations, British.  2. Great
Britain,  Royal Air Force--History--World War, 1939-1945.
3. Fighter pilots--United States.  4. Fighter pilots--Great Britain.
I. Title
[D786.D33  1998]
940.54'4941--dc21                                       98-24964
                                                           CIP
```

First Edition

10 9 8 7 6 5 4 3 2 1
Printed in the United States of America

to
Doris

CONTENTS

FOREWORD

Although the United States did not enter World War II until the end of 1941, US citizens fought and died in the war long before the Japanese attacked Pearl Harbor. Among them were the pilots of the Eagle Squadrons, three fighter squadrons of Britain's Royal Air Force manned by young US flyers risking their lives in another nation's war.

In this book, Brigadier General Philip D. Caine, US Air Force, tells how the Eagle Squadrons were formed, describes their RAF experiences, and evaluates their contribution to Britain's defense. Unlike other accounts, *American Pilots in the RAF* is not simply a paean to the pilots as special heroes and "aces," though many performed heroically and some sacrificed their lives. Drawing almost exclusively on interviews with more than thirty-five surviving Eagles, on their letters and memoirs, and on official records of the squadrons, Caine shows who these men were and what drove them to endure the burdens of joining a foreign air force. We see them adjusting to life in a new country as they train, fly patrol and escort missions, and sit on alert in dispersal huts or airplane cockpits. We see their routine suddenly shattered by the momentary chaos and exhilaration of aerial combat.

The Eagles' story is a unique chapter in American military history; it deserves to be told as it happened—not as romanticized by Hollywood or nostalgic recollection. Beyond reliably telling the story, General Caine reveals much about why people enter the military, how military life satisfies or disappoints their preconceptions, and how at least some of them reacted to the realities of combat.

J. A. BALDWIN
Vice Admiral, US Navy
President, National Defense University

PREFACE

ONE OF THE REMARKABLE CHAPTERS IN THE HISTORY OF aviation concerns the 244 American airmen who fought against the Luftwaffe during the early days of World War II in Number 71, 121, and 133 Squadrons of the Royal Air Force Fighter Command, the Eagle Squadrons. Although several books have already been written about these famous units, those volumes have focused primarily on the combat adventures of the group. I have taken a different direction, my primary purpose being to write a history of the three units that will analyze their deeds, motivations, and contributions to the history of air power.

More than 80 members of these units are still alive and active in the Eagle Squadron Association. It is their experiences, as related to me during countless hours of interviews and in the documents that they have so graciously given me, that formed the foundation for my writing.

I began this study at the suggestion of Dr. Richard Kohn, former chief of the Office of Air Force History, and most of the research was done during a year as a senior research fellow at the National Defense University. When I first started my work, I did not know any Eagle Squadron members nor was I very familiar with the material that was available about the units. During the course of the nearly four years that I worked on this book, I came to know a number of Eagles, seeing them in circumstances ranging from their annual reunion to the living rooms of their homes. They shared their stories with me, we looked at their records and pictures, and I was generally taken wholeheartedly into their confidence and fellowship. That is perhaps the biggest reward to me—to have gotten to know a group of wonderful people both as pilots and as friends and to be part of the comradery of such a group. To all of those who helped me, I offer my deep and heartfelt thanks. I am particularly indebted to several Eagles—Edwin Taylor, Jim Gray, LeRoy Gover, Wilson Edwards, Charles Cook, Reade Tilley, and the late Chesley Peterson—who went the extra mile to aid me in so many ways. At the National Defense University, both Director of Research Fred Kiley and my editor, Tom Gill, were constant sources of encouragement and understanding. They both offered advice and generally shepherded this volume through its formation.

I also particularly want to thank Sam Westbrook and Joe Redden, very understanding bosses, for letting me have the time to write, and Jim Titus, Eric Ash, Larry Weaver, and Gerald Gustine for picking up a number of jobs that added to their already heavy workloads so I could concentrate on this volume. My secretaries, Jan Pieffer and Kathie Martin, were also inordinately understanding. Duane Reed, archivist at the Air Force Academy Library, official depository of the records of the Eagle Sqsuadrons, provided help, encouragement, and advice. The complete list of those to whom I owe a special thanks is far too lengthy to print here, so I simply say "thank you" to everyone who took the time to talk to me, encourage me, and aid me in this project. They did their best to arm me with the necessary information, and then let me do my work.

My family deserves special thanks. My daughters, Barb, Ginny, and Jennifer, are always an inspiration to me. I can never repay my debt to them for filling their role over the years as my understanding family. My father was the person who recognized a young boy absolutely consumed with airplanes and tolerated the days of models, the requests for help and money, and the excuses for not getting some of the jobs done around the house so the model planes could fly. Thanks, Dad. Finally, without my wife, Doris, this book would not exist. She lived every hour of the research and writing, spent days taking notes at interviews, asked the tough questions and made the suggestions that were so essential to the final volume. Most of all, she kept me working when it would have been easier to put it off and provided the home and love over the years that make life worthwhile.

US Air Force Academy, 1991

AMERICAN PILOTS IN THE RAF

1. PRELIMINARIES

ENGLAND WAS BEAUTIFUL IN THE SPRING OF 1940. THE fields were green with new crops, flowers were in bloom, trees were in full bud, and the entire countryside looked fresh. London, too, was green and blooming as if anticipating a wonderful summer. But the people of England did not share Mother Nature's mood. Things were not going well in Europe. Hitler had moved through Poland, Finland had fallen to the Russians, and everyone wondered what would happen next. The focus of life was not on the pleasures of the coming summer but on potential crisis. Few Englishmen fully realized, however, that in just four months their nation would be under siege, the lights of the towns and cities blacked out at night, their beautiful capital bombed day and night while the populace slept in the subways. Indeed, few could imagine that England would soon be fighting for its life, and just 700 or so airplanes and the men who flew them would tip the balance.

Across the Atlantic Ocean, spring was also coming to the United States. Washington, DC, among the most beautiful of all cities in the spring, was beginning to flower, and the Tidal Basin was lovely with cherry blossoms. In California the foliage had changed to its new, brighter summer hues, the beaches had begun to draw crowds, the hills of the Napa Valley were green, and the flowers of San Diego's Balboa Park were stunning. The mood in America, too, was hopeful in anticipation of the coming summer. The economy was continuing to recover from the depression, employment was better than it had been for over a decade, and things looked promising for most Americans. Yes, mad Hitler seemed intent on gobbling up Europe, but France had the Maginot Line to stop him and, anyway, he was Europe's problem, not America's.

In that spring, for young pilots all across the United States, many really still boys, the coming summer meant good flying weather and the chance to hone their skills, maybe even find a better job—a flying job. Little did many of them realize that before the year was over they would volunteer to fly in combat for England, a far-away nation most had never seen. Even less did any imagine that before the next spring some would give their lives for that nation in the skies above the English Channel or the blooming countryside.

In sharp contrast to the beauty of the spring countryside was the mighty North Atlantic. On a sunny day, the ocean seems calm and friendly. But when the clouds and wind come, it becomes a raging giant with waves over 50 feet high and water temperatures so cold that a human being without proper survival gear will lose consciousness in less than five minutes. By early 1940 this ocean had become even more hazardous as German submarine "wolf packs" ranged far and wide, sending ship after ship to the bottom and leaving countless sailors to the mercy of the waves. Certainly, the North Atlantic was not on the minds of young flyers in California, Illinois, Texas, or Washington as they looked to the sky that spring. But by the end of the year, some would face its dangers as they made the stormy crossing to England, a few even falling victim to submarine and sea.

The challenges of 1940, and indeed of the next few years, were exceptional, challenges that come with war. And those threatening England were met by "the few" of the Royal Air Force and its small Fighter Command. By the end of 1940, that unit would be manned by pilots from all over the world: Australians, New Zealanders, Canadians, South Africans, Czechs, Poles, Frenchmen, and Americans. All would be there to fly against the Germans. The members of the Commonwealth had no choice—they were defending the Mother country. For those from Poland or Czechoslovakia or France, the war was a fight against the nation that had conquered and ravaged their homelands and, for most, killed or imprisoned members of their families. But for the Americans it was different. The United States was not at war, and its law prohibited US citizens from getting involved. The Americans could have stayed at home and led normal lives. But instead, when most of their countrymen simply wished the British luck, these men were drawn, by both airplanes and principles, to England, to volunteer for the RAF.

This book is not an attempt to make these Americans heroes; some were and others were not. While in the RAF, they did not set records for the number of German airplanes they shot down. In fact, most did not shoot down any. They were not the heroes of the Battle of Britain—only seven even flew in that battle. No, not all were extraordinary combat pilots, although those who survived became the nucleus of the most productive American fighter group in World War II. But they all volunteered to fly two exceptional airplanes, the Hurricane and the Spitfire. These were the best planes in the world at the time—the "hot ships." That was the common denominator for all American RAF volunteers and subsequently Eagles. To be sure, they were patriotic defenders of freedom and democracy, but in the final analysis, it was the airplanes that made them sign up.

This is the story, then, of Squadrons 71, 121, and 133 of the RAF Fighter Command, from the activation of Number 71 in the fall of 1940 until the American pilots' transfer to the US Army Air Force at the end of September 1942. This is the story of the RAF Eagle Squadrons, hot ships, and brave boys.

What is it, though, about flying that would make those young Americans risk so much to get to fly those "hot" airplanes of the RAF? Just what is it about flying that so captures the minds of young and old alike? The first word that comes to mind is *freedom*. In flight, barriers to movement and travel seem to disappear. Fences no longer exist, nor do rivers, turns in the highways, cities, mountains, or any of the other normal impediments to earthbound movement. The airplane gives one the ability to transcend these restraints. This freedom is accompanied by an almost magical transformation of the countryside, as it becomes a patchwork of fields and forests, rivers and mountains. In the air, the pilot is in control and can climb and dive, fly right side up or upside down, twist and turn, and create thrills unequalled by any carnival ride. At the same time, flying can evoke a feeling of peace that can be experienced in no other way—through views of the sunrise or sunset over the clear, beautiful horizon, the blue of lakes and rivers on a sunny day, the miles of green in summer. At night the earth becomes a fairyland of twinkling, multi-colored lights. All this is the domain of the pilot. Little wonder that for as long as there have been airplanes there have been young people captured by the goddess of flight.

Another element that often captivates those caught up in the world of flight is the mystique of it all. Airplanes are mysterious machines, and certainly those relatively few who have mastered the skills of making those machines fly must be set apart. Because there are so few pilots, they can easily become idols for young men and women. A pilot has one way to be a "somebody" that is not available to most people: flying. Don Ross puts it well when writing about his first solo flight:

There is no way to describe the feeling of excitement, pride and a little apprehension as I took off all alone—looking out over southeast Los Angeles, watching the hazy horizon as I made my turns, . . . and down over the old airport restaurant and a good landing. . . . Then, taxiing back down the side of the field . . . and shutting down with an inner glow of knowledge that I was now a "true hero."[1]

These aspects of flight affected the young people who became involved in it in different ways. For some, like John Campbell, the reaction was immediate:

I started flying when I was 14 . . . and I was willing to hang around and do anything, gas airplanes, help strap passengers, wash airplanes, anything that would get me a little flying time. That's how I learned to fly.[2]

Ross Scarborough, killed in a flying accident in England in November 1941, couldn't get enough of either the airplanes or the flying environment. Before he was sixteen, he was "sleeping on an army cot and acting as night watchman at the field. . . . He always was paid in flying time rather than cash."[3] Lee Gover "washed parts, planes, cleaned up the area and hauled gasoline from a little service station, in five gallon cans" for the reward of an occasional flight from one of the aircraft owners.[4]

Flying was in Leo Nomis' blood because he had been around it since he was born. His father had flown in World War I and was a well-known stunt pilot in the 1920s and 1930s. Leo was really too young to participate much in the activity before his father died in 1932, but he soon found himself involved in flying on his own. Books, magazines, and airports were his standard fare, and he simply assumed that flying would be his vocation.[5]

Few young men were as completely committed to flying as Steve Pisanos. When Steve was fourteen, his father, a grocer in Athens, Greece, sent him to the airport with a load of vegetables for a British RAF squadron. In the course of that trip, young Steve saw his first airplane close up and he was hooked. Forgetting his delivery, he sought out the RAF commander and asked if he could learn to fly. A polite "No" was not what he wanted to hear, so month after month Steve wrote to the RAF, to the Greek military, to anyone he could think of, including General Joannes Metaxas, the Greek dictator, who granted the young man an interview. "If you ever want to be a pilot," he told Pisanos, "you will need more education than you have now." But to get the education needed to learn how to fly, Pisanos would have had to get into one of the military academies, which required that he come from a family with a high position in society, not be the son of a grocer. Then a Greek-American pilot whom Pisanos came to know offered a ray of hope. "If you really want to become a pilot," he told Steve, "America is the place to go. In America they have more aircraft than stars in the sky. Besides that, the schools are free to everyone in America."

In 1938 Steve got a job as a seaman to work his passage to the United States. He spoke almost no English, but an uncle sponsored him to stay, helped him get a job, and started him toward fulfilling his dream of flight. Every cent Pisanos could afford to spend from his wages as a waiter in Plainfield, New Jersey, went toward flying lessons. By 1940 he had earned his private pilot's license and was working toward commercial certification. "From the time I decided to leave Greece, I was committed to being a pilot no matter what the cost," he said.[6]

All of these young men, regardless of how they became involved in aviation, were seeing dramatic changes as the years passed after World War I, through the Roaring Twenties, and into the Great Depression.

The war produced a raft of heroes whose names became household words to the generations growing up in the 1920s and 1930s. Names Like Eddie Rickenbacker, Raoul Lufbery, Baron von Richthofen, Billy Bishop, and the members of the Lafayette Escadrille topped the list. These men's exploits during the war made fascinating reading and fueled the public's appetite for the new age of aviation. The war also provided stories for Hollywood movies about the exploits of wartime heroes and airplanes. Films like *Wings, Air Circus, Cloud Rider, Flight, Dawn Patrol, Lilac Time,* and Howard Hughes' epic, *Hell's Angels,* brought mobs to cinema box offices and further enhanced the image of flight in the American mind. For an adventurous young man, it was a wonderful age.

DEVELOPMENT OF FLIGHT

It was the barnstormer who really brought aviation to life throughout the United States. By 1920 there was hardly a county fair or summer resort without a visiting pilot ready to give rides for whatever price people would pay. Daredevils and innovators seemed always available to perform. Such stunts as the loop, figure eight, barrel roll, nosedive, and tailspin were soon standard, along with tricks like wing walking, transfering a man from one plane to another on a rope ladder, picking up someone from a speeding car using an airplane, and doing trapeze stunts from a low-flying plane, as well as the always included parachute demonstrations. Clyde Pangborn, Wiley Post, Frank Hawks, and Charles Lindbergh were all considered aerobats.

The daredevils and barnstormers weren't all that caught the public imagination. "Nearly every day there was a new headline or story about a spectacular accomplishment in flying," recalls LeRoy Gover.[7] For many, the tall, soft-spoken, "typical American boy" Charles Lindbergh, who completed his non-stop solo flight from New York to Paris on 21 May 1927, made the lure of aviation real. "The greatest influence on me," said Gover,

> was the race to see who would first fly the Atlantic solo. I stayed glued to the radio day and night when Lindbergh took off in May 1927. Then to see the pictures of his arrival in Paris, and the parade in New York on his return, that really clinched it for me. My mind was made up to be a flyer for the rest of my life.[8]

Lindbergh's accomplishment and others were enough to convince even the most doubting that flying was here to stay, and to many young men it was the vocation of the future.

9

The achievements of the 1920s were a testament as much to technology as to the individuals who flew the planes. The days of fabric and wire biplanes had vanished by the middle of the decade. The old standard Liberty engine had given way to the engine of the future, the radial, much lighter and more powerful than its in-line forebear. Because it was air cooled it was more reliable, and it opened up many new possibilities in aircraft design. A radial engine powered the *Spirit of St. Louis* on its epic flight. And as horsepower increased through continual redesign of engines, speed and altitude also increased. By the end of the 1920s, flight at altitudes of more than 30,000 feet was not unusual.

Design evolved rapidly, and the all-metal Ford trimotor became a common sight during the Great Depression. Efforts to safely fly in all kinds of weather assumed high priority, and the engineer-pilot began to be seen on the flight line. Among the first was Jimmy Doolittle, who had earned a doctorate from MIT. He was the first to fly totally "blind"—on instruments—in 1929. That flight also featured the first effective radio navigation. Seven years later, Major Ira Eaker became the first to fly completely across the continental United States, from New York to Los Angeles, on instruments.

Above all, it was speed that enticed young flyers in the years between the wars. The air speed record soared from less than 100 miles per hour to 193 miles per hour in 1920. Air racing soon became the feature sport of the day. Huge crowds would gather to see who would win the money put up by such publishing giants as the Pulitzers. These races proved to be the catalyst for many of the innovations that changed flying so quickly. In 1922 the first all-metal racing plane was clocked at 220 miles per hour. Speeds regularly exceeded 250 miles per hour for a closed course by 1930. Straight-line speeds also continued to soar: in 1931 the Supermarine S6B, a direct ancestor of the RAF Spitfire of World War II, was clocked at more than 340 miles per hour.[9]

Part and parcel of the advancements in civilian aviation were changes pioneered by the military. A number of the accomplishments that proved so significant were solely military ones. But whether the achievements were military or civilian was unimportant; it was the aviation feat itself that made the front page. Nonetheless, a brief look shows the significance of many milestones in military aviation in the United States, Great Britain, and Germany. It was these nations' air arms that largely determined how World War II was conducted, thus dictating the situation in which members of the Eagle Squadrons were to find themselves when they joined the RAF.

MILITARY ROLE OF AIR POWER

The end of World War I brought a two-decade debate in the United States about the role of military air power. On one hand, some believed the airplane was just another weapon in the military arsenal, like a tank or ship. To the diehard air power advocate, on the other hand, the airplane was a unique machine destined to change the nature of warfare. Of the many disciples of the airplane, none was more flamboyant or outspoken than General Billy Mitchell. This hero of the war in Europe rapidly became the primary air power spokesman. His battle with the Navy, the sinking of the *Ostfriesland,* and his subsequent court martial gained wide press coverage, bringing the issue of military air power to the public. In the end, both the Army and the Navy were authorized to have separate air arms. The Army's was for some time the more significant.

Mitchell and other Army air power advocates were convinced the bomber represented the future of air warfare. If, as commonly believed, any future US war would probably be fought outside the country, the bomber's strong offensive power was essential. Bomber advoctes were convinced that giant aircraft could effectively perform precise, high-altitude, unescorted bombing in daylight. Thus, US resources were directed mainly toward the strategic bomber, the B–17 "Flying Fortress" being the prime example when World War II began.

This devotion to the bomber dictated that the United States would lag behind in its development of fighters. Although some in the Army, particularly at the Air Corps Tactical School, strongly advocated the fighter or pursuit (a more acceptable word to the public) aircraft, they lacked resources. As a result, first-line American fighters, such as the P–40, were a notch below the best British or German fighters when the war began. It would take the United States until the end of 1942 to begin to deploy effective fighters to either the European or the Pacific theater.[10]

The British learned a very different lesson from World War I. Britain had been involved in the war nearly four years longer than the United States and had suffered many more casualties. German dirigibles and airplanes had bombed both the English countryside and London. It was clear to the British that air defense was critical. So in November 1917, even before the end of the war, Britain established a separate Air Ministry and created the Royal Air Force as one of the branches of its military. This proved a monumental step in the history of air warfare. While US advocates of air power had to work as subordinates within the Army and Navy, Britain's visionary Sir Hugh Trenchard, first chief of the Air Service, could operate as an equal of the Army and Navy chiefs. As they developed their air arm, the British focused primarily on air defense doctrine, including the use of fighter aircraft in conjunction with anti-aircraft guns. This philosophy also gave birth to radar research, which proved so essential to the British in World War II.

Critically important to the RAF's development was the January 1935 Air Ministry decision to build "a monoplane fighter capable of catching the fastest bomber and destroying it with two seconds of gunfire." The directive went on to specify that such an aircraft should include an enclosed cockpit, eight Browning machine-guns, a reflector gunsight, retractable undercarriage, and oxygen for the pilot. It had to be capable of flying at least 275 miles per hour, have an endurance of 1½ hours, and have a ceiling no lower than 33,000 feet. The results were the prototypes of the Hawker Hurricane and the Supermarine Spitfire, both powered by Rolls-Royce engines—the two planes that became the backbone of the RAF throughout World War II.[11] This development was further facilitated by the 1936 Inskipp Decision to form Fighter Command and allocate the primary resources of the RAF to building a comprehensive defense system using the technology of the day: radio, radar, control centers, and fighter aircraft.[12]

Meanwhile, despite provisions in the Treaty of Versailles virtually eliminating the German air force, by the late 1930s Germany had built the largest and most powerful air arm in the world. This swift buildup was the result primarily of German ingenuity and an unwillingness of the World War I victors to adequately police the German air industry. By 1931 the "nonexistent" German air force "was composed of four fighter, three heavy bomber, and eight reconnaissance-bomber squadrons."[13] When the Luftwaffe began operating in 1935, it was a separate service, equal to and independent of the army and navy, taking orders directly from Hitler.

The doctrine Germany adopted differed from America's strategic bombardment and Britain's air defense. After considerable debate, close air support of ground units became the German air force's primary mission. Most aircraft were therefore designed for that purpose: two-engined medium bombers, primarily the Heinkel 111 and the Dornier 17; dive bombers, such as the famed Stuka; and fighters, the primary one being the Messerschmitt 109. Many of the German aircraft were operationally tested in the Spanish Civil War of 1936–38.

When Germany launched its blitzkrieg attack against Poland on 1 September 1939, the German air force had 1,000 bombers and 1,050 fighters in operational condition.[14] That the German onslaught broke Poland's ability to resist in less than twenty days vindicated, in Hitler's mind, the decision to build an air force to support the ground forces. Hitler saw no need to build new types of aircraft or significantly increase production—an error that would prove fatal during the Battle of Britain.

THE TEST BEGINS

Hitler's annexation of Austria, the division and later complete acquisition of Czechoslovakia, and the bloodless invasion of Hungary, all in 1938 and 1939, set the stage for World War II. The victorious powers of World War I had neither the means nor the will to stop Hitler at that moment. With the German attack on Poland on 1 September 1939, the twenty years of peace ended: two days later Britain and France declared war on Germany.

Poland fell in less than a month. The Soviet Union, seizing its opportunity to capitalize on the chaos of the time, signed a non-aggression pact with Hitler and promptly invaded and conquered Finland. The western front was quiet for the rest of 1939, but on 9 April 1940 Germany invaded Denmark and Norway. The Germans followed a month later with attacks on Holland, Belgium, and, on 12 May, France. Before the end of May, both the Dutch and Belgians had capitulated and France was on the verge of defeat. The British, outflanked and outnumbered, retreated to the coast at Dunkirk, where more than 350,000 soldiers were plucked from the beach and ferried back to England. On 22 June 1940 newspapers throughout the world blared out that France had surrendered. Britain stood alone.

Although no one was sure just what Hitler had in mind after taking France, it stood to reason that he hoped Britain would make some kind of settlement with the Third Reich. But that was not to be. Under the dynamic leadership of a new prime minister, Winston Churchill, Britain vowed to resist the Germans no matter the cost. As Churchill so eloquently said, "We shall fight on the beaches. We shall fight on the landing grounds. We shall fight on the fields and in the streets. We shall fight in the hills; we shall never surrender."[15]

On 16 July 1940 the suspense ended, as Hitler issued orders for Operation Sea Lion, the invasion of England. The critical prerequisite for this undertaking was control of the air over the English Channel. To secure that air superiority, Gemany unleashed the 2,670 planes of the Luftwaffe against the 1,475 of the Royal Air Force. The Battle of Britain had begun.

THE BATTLE OF BRITAIN

The war in Europe had been front-page news in America since 1939, but the fall of France heightened American interest considerably. Isolationists feared it was only a matter of time before the United States entered the war, while millions of other Americans believed the nation *should* take sides. Officially, the United States identified with the British, making it clear that American aid to them would continue. With the onset of the Battle of Britain, the American press focused its coverage more sharply.

Britain, oldest and closest of America's friends, was fighting for its life. Every day, radio newscasters and newspaper front pages recounted the battle. And as Americans followed the news, the flyers of Britain's Fighter Command—the pilots of the Hurricanes and Spitfires—became heroes in households across the United States. To young men of the day, the epitome of grandeur was the RAF pilot.

Future Eagles Barry Mahon, Jim Gray, George Sperry, and Marion Jackson, typical of many other Americans, followed the battle daily. Stories of the stouthearted pilots of Fighter Command motivated Harold Strickland to approach the British embassy about joining the RAF. Edwin Taylor was also moved to try to become an RAF pilot. To them, as to pilots all across the United States, the Spitfire and the Hurricane were the best of airplanes—fast, deadly, beautiful machines. According to the press, they could out-fly and out-fight anything else in the world. And in 1940 the skies above England and the Channel provided the ultimate test of these machines and the pilots who flew them.

The Battle of Britain also convinced a tremendous number of young men that the United States would soon enter the war. To more than half of those who joined the Eagles, this conviction affected the decision to do so. Because they either lacked the prerequisites for entering US Army or Navy pilot training or had already washed out, they knew that if the United States entered the war they would be drafted as ground troops. Carroll McColpin expressed an attitude shared by many Eagles when he said, "I knew that the United States would soon be in the war and I would be involved. I certainly did not want to spend the war on the ground, so the RAF looked like the way to go for me."[16]

Germany had been launching bomber and fighter raids over the Channel and the ports of east and southeast England, directed primarily at British shipping and support facilities, for more than six weeks when, on 13 August 1940, the Nazis launched the first phase of what would prove to be a three-part air offensive against England itself. That Tuesday, code-named "Eagle Day" by the Germans, began the battle Germany intended to have drive the RAF Fighter Command from the skies—by killing or exhausting the British pilots and destroying their aircraft both in the air and on the ground. The Germans sent more than 1,500 aircraft to England that day, only a precursor of things to come. If they were going to destroy Fighter Command, thought the Germans, they had to do it in daylight, in full view of the world. For the British, the mission was just as clear: make the attacks so costly for the Luftwaffe that Germany would have to abandon its invasion plans.

It became apparent by the beginning of September that the Germans were achieving some of their objectives in this largest air battle in history. Both British and German losses were high, but the British were reeling from the attacks. Six of the seven airfields that provided air cover for London were severely damaged. More fighters were being lost than produced. In addition to aircraft reserves running low, pilot training could not keep pace with losses. Of the nearly 1,000 pilots of Fighter Command at the start of the campaign, fewer than 700 remained. Victory for the Luftwaffe seemed close at hand. A *Sunday Times* of London report on one of Prime Minister Churchill's visits to Fighter Command Headquarters reveals the desperation of the British predicament:

> On the radar screen [Churchill] watched the advance of the German bombers.
>
> As each wave approached, Air Vice-Marshal Park gave his orders to put in the British fighter squadrons. The Air Vice-Marshal was calm and businesslike. Mr. Churchill's nerves were taut, but underneath, his emotions were surging.
>
> Each attack was successfully repelled, but to the waves of German bombers there seemed to be no end. At last, unable to control himself, Mr. Churchill turned to Park. "How many more have you got?" he asked abruptly. Quietly the Air Vice-Marshal replied, "I am putting in my last."
>
> Their eyes fixed on the screen, the two men waited for the next German wave. It never came. The Germans, too, had put in their last. With tears in his eyes, Mr. Churchill got into his car.[17]

That experience inspired Churchill's 20 August statement that, in turn, so inspired the people of Britain and the free world:

> The gratitude of every home in our island, in our Empire and indeed in the world, goes out to the British airmen. Never in the field of human conflict was so much owed by so many to so few.[18]

These words, carried on radio and in newspapers throughout the United States, moved numbers of young American pilots who longed to fly fast airplanes and defend freedom.

Whether the German plan to destroy Fighter Command could have succeeded will never be known because, on 7 September, the Germans shifted their objective to London. Why the target changed has been the subject of much research and speculation. Whatever the reason, the attacks on London began with a vengeance that day and continued through 5 October. The size of the raids illustrates the earnestness of the German undertaking. On 7 September more than 350 aircraft attacked London's docks. More than 500 attacked on 15 September. That Sunday, the 15th, German losses reached the point at which the attackers could not continue the battle at its present pace. Although these were dark days for the people of London, who often spent entire nights and most of their days in air raid shelters or subways, they provided a respite for the RAF, enabling them to repair much of the damage from the previous weeks.

On 17 September Hitler postponed the planned invasion of England indefinitely and focused the aerial attacks almost exclusively on the people of London and other English cities. Because aircraft losses were unacceptably high during the day, the Germans began making almost all their raids at night. The mighty Luftwaffe had lost nearly 1,500 aircraft by the end of September, but had neither silenced Fighter Command nor broken the will of the British people.

There is not really a date on which the Battle of Britain ended, but historians generally accept that it was over by the end of October 1940. Night attacks continued in varied strength well into 1943, including some horrible raids such as the 14 November 1940 raid that burned Coventry and large raids on London on 29 December 1940 and 10 May 1941. By July 1941 more than 10,000 Britons were to have been killed in the Blitz, but by November 1940 the worst was over. Hitler turned his sights eastward, and by the time of his invasion of the Soviet Union on 22 June 1941, two-thirds of Germany's air power was on the eastern front.[19]

The Battle of Britain demonstrated that air power was essential to military success and brought the RAF transatlantic fame. But it also severely depleted the resources of Fighter Command. In addition to aircraft losses, the command had lost 515 fighter pilots killed and another 358 wounded. So the call continued to go out both to the Commonwealth and to other friendly nations for pilots to help fill the ranks of the RAF.

One potential source of help remained largely untapped: the United States. Only seven US citizens had seen action in the Battle of Britain. There were hundreds of potential RAF members in the States, but the strict neutrality to which the nation was pledged made access to those pilots difficult. Some people believed Britain could obtain help through just a little ingenuity. The same situation had existed in 1914, and yet Americans were serving in all branches of the French service shortly after World War I began. In 1916 the Lafayette Escadrille, one of the most famous of flying organizations, was founded, made up of Americans flying for the French. The achievement could certainly be repeated in 1940.

PRECEDENT: THE LAFAYETTE ESCADRILLE

"I founded the Eagle Squadron in May 1940, and I had in mind the Lafayette Escadrille which made such a distinguished contribution to the War effort in WWI," said Charles Sweeny, founder of the Eagles.[20] Sweeny picked the ideal unit to use both as the model for his new squadron of Americans and as an effective selling point for its formation. Not only did the Lafayette Escadrille have a brilliant record in the war, but it also was well known by flyers throughout the United States, its pilots boyhood heroes to many of the potential Eagles. Typical of many future Eagles, Jim Griffin "loved flying . . . and had wanted to fly military aircraft since I'd first read about the Lafayette Escadrille, about Eddie Rickenbacker, Bert Hall, and the Canadian, Billy Bishop, years before when I was a boy."[21]

Griffin's comment highlights a general impression that, in many ways, the Eagle Squadrons were the natural successor to the Lafayette Escadrille—a group of Americans volunteering to fly for their European friends in need. Several logical links span the 24 years between the founding of the two organizations. Both were composed of Americans with a great desire to fly who volunteered to join a foreign air force before the United States was at war; both units initially were seen as propaganda tools but eventually established distinguished records in combat; both eventually became part of the US Army. None of the members of either group appear to have joined for the meager pay that they received—in other words, they could not be termed mercenaries.

By the same token, the Eagles were by no means a re-creation of the French unit. A crucial difference lay in the matter of government support for the squadrons' formation. In the case of the Lafayette Escadrille, by 1915 prominent officials on both sides of the Atlantic were interested in the idea of an American squadron to fly with the French. Their efforts resulted in the formation in early 1915 of a Franco-American committee to function as the official advocate for such a squadron. By the end of the year, it appeared that the only real unsolved issue was American neutrality, which had precluded any official government sanction of the effort to form a squadron. When the US State Department refused to honor a German protest against Americans flying with the French air service in early 1916, the door was finally open for the establishment of the squadron. Not only was such US government interest and support lacking in 1940, but the Eagle Squadrons were established despite opposition, albeit sometimes passive, from the United States.

The makeup of the Lafayette Escadrille when it became operational on 16 April 1916 also contrasts with that of the World War II Eagles. Most of the Americans in the Lafayette Escadrille were rather well off financially and had excellent education but little or no flying experience. Most Eagles, on the other hand, had only high school education but considerable experience in and around airplanes.

The French scheme for employing the American squadron is remarkably similar to that of the British more than twenty years later. Commanded by a French captain and his French lieutenant, both experienced career officers, the unit was initially posted in quiet sectors of the front and kept out of combat because of its pilots' lack of experience and the overwhelming superiority of the Germans in the skies over Verdun. The French seemed content to use the Escadrille as a propaganda tool and not risk such a potentially valuable resource in combat. But the crisis at Verdun in late May 1916 changed all that.

With their backs to the wall, the French committed every unit available, the Lafayette Escadrille included. Fortunately, most members of the squadron had gained some combat experience in the past month, and the unit was strengthened by the addition of six pilots, including the legendary Raoul Lufbery. Thrown into action, the Americans acquitted themselves well. When the squadron was pulled from the Verdun sector nearly four months later, it had flown more than 1,000 sorties, been engaged in 146 combats with German aircraft, and scored 13 victories at the cost of one American dead and three wounded in action. The Americans of the Escadrille continued in the thick of combat throughout their service with the French. The heroism and dedication they showed became the standard for the entire French air service throughout the war.[22]

As it would in 1941 for the Eagles, American entry into World War I on 4 April 1917 raised the issue of the future of the Lafayette Escadrille. Although all parties agreed that the squadron should become a part of the American Expeditionary Force, no legal mechanism was available for commissioning the pilots and bringing them into the US forces. In addition, they were members of the French air force and had sworn to serve France for the duration of the war. Transfer or assignment of rank was also a problem. So for almost a year the Americans continued to fight as part of the French air force. Finally, a workable, although not popular, agreement was reached, and on 18 February 1918 the Lafayette Escadrille folded the tri-color and became the American 103d Aero Squadron, the first and only American combat squadron at the front.

Of the 38 Americans who served in the Escadrille, 9 were killed and 2 were removed from the ranks because of their wounds. The obvious question is, Why did these young Americans give up their careers, their homes, their families, in some cases their lives to fly and fight? Most authors believe that patriotism and a taste for adventure were the initial motivators for most members of the Escadrille. But it appears that, like the Eagles who would follow them, the majority finally decided to sign up because of their love of flying. Most, however, did eventually come to believe they had a moral obligation to be in France in the war.

The legacy of the Lafayette Escadrille impressed others aside from Charles Sweeny. In the fall of 1940, the Chinese, employing retired US Army Captain Claire Chennault, began to form US pilots into the famous Flying Tigers. This unit was by far the most well known and most publicized volunteer unit of World War II. A number of books tell the story of the Flying Tigers, and that story is not necessary here.[23] Although the Eagle Squadrons are frequently compared to the Flying Tigers, there is, for all practical purposes, almost no similarity.

The initial idea for capitalizing on the potential of pilots from the United States at the start of World War II, predating both the Flying Tigers and the Eagles, was aimed at aiding France. It was the brainchild of an American soldier of fortune, Colonel Charles Sweeny (uncle of the already mentioned Charles Sweeny), later co-founder of the Eagle Squadrons. The saga of finding those pilots, who would eventually become Eagles, reads like a detective novel. Before the squadrons were finally operational, the story involved not only the American soldier of fortune but also a retired British air marshal, members of the Lafayette Escadrille, an American heiress, a prominent British business family, an amateur golf champion, a well-known American artist and illustrator, members of the British Air Ministry and Parliament, the US Federal Bureau of Investigation, the US president, and countless other individuals, not to mention the more than 200 brave volunteers.

COLONEL CHARLES SWEENY

Colonel Charles Sweeny had a varied, exciting background. The son of a wealthy American entrepreneur, he became convinced early in his life that the profession of arms was his calling. After serving in the Army as an underage soldier during the Spanish-American War, Sweeny entered West Point in 1899, but he was unable to fit into the system and was dismissed. When war came to Europe in 1914, he joined approximately 30 other young Americans in the French Foreign Legion (enlistment in the regular French forces would have cost them their US citizenship) and soon found himself in charge of the small American unit. His exuberance was obvious as he drilled his American charges daily and prepared them for the coming fight.

Sweeny rose rapidly in the enlisted ranks of the Foreign Legion and, in 1915, found himself the first American commissioned in that body in World War I. That same year, he was wounded and given up for dead at a field hospital, but he recovered after several months. His sacrifice was not without reward, for he received both the Croix de Guerre and the Legion of Honor (the first American in World War I to receive the latter) for his heroism in battle. The US entry into the war prompted Sweeny to leave the Foreign Legion in favor of the US Army. He ended the war as a lieutenant colonel.

Because of his subsequent activity organizing various flying units and his propensity to take whatever credit came his way, Colonel Sweeny has often been credited with being one of the founders of the Lafayette Escadrille, and even with being a pilot with that group. Neither is true. The closest Sweeny came to involvement with the Lafayette Escadrille was drilling several future members of the unit after their joining the Foreign Legion before the famed flying squadron was formed. Sweeny was always a ground officer.

He continued his career as a soldier of fortune following World War I. In 1920, as a temporary brigadier general in the Polish army, Sweeny was involved in the Battle of Warsaw with a contingent of some 200 former American troops. In 1925 he heeded the Spanish call for aid in crushing the Rif Rebellion in Morocco. In 1937 he journeyed to Spain to observe the Civil War and assess the effectiveness of the airplanes France had furnished the Republican Army.

As war became imminent in 1939, Sweeny and an old friend, US Army Brigadier General Henry J. Reilly, conceived the formation of a division of American volunteers to fight for France. The French, using the World War I plan, decided to form the Americans into an ambulance corps to avoid the problems of US neutrality. But Sweeny continued to search for a more effective way to respond to the crisis his adopted homeland was facing. He evidently got the approval of General Armengaud, former commander-in-chief of the French air force, to try to form an American flying unit, a virtual re-creation of the Lafayette Escadrille. Given Armengaud's general agreement, Colonel Sweeny departed for North America late in 1939 to enlist pilots for his new venture.

Sweeny was very aware of the problems he would face in the United States. Congress had taken almost desperate measures to ensure the United States would not get involved in the war. In 1935 Congress had passed a strict neutrality act that, among other provisions, stressed that Americans travelled on belligerent ships at their own risk. Congress revised this act in 1936 and again in 1937 to forbid travel on belligerent ships or in a war zone. The Fourth Neutrality Act of November 1939, passed in response to the German onslaught in Europe, reaffirmed the congressional stance.

The 1939 act had been preceded in September by a presidential proclamation specifically forbidding any recruiting within the United States or any territory over which the United States had jurisdiction for service in the armed forces of a foreign government. The proclamation also included, unfortunately for Sweeny, a provision that it was illegal to hire someone to go beyond the territorial limits of the United States—to Canada, for example—to enlist in a foreign country's military. The president further proclaimed it to be against the law to use a US passport to get to a foreign country to enlist, to travel anywhere on a belligerent ship, or to travel on any ship in the North Atlantic. (Although remaining technically neutral, the United States abandoned enforcement of a number of the provisions of the neutrality acts, including the prohibition of recruiting, after France fell.) Under the circumstances, especially given his reputation for forming Americans into units to fight in foreign wars, Sweeny's activities immediately came under the close scrutiny of the FBI, and Sweeny remained under surveillance every time he came to the United States.

Canada, too, was suspicious of an American soldier of fortune trying to enlist Canadians into the French air force, especially since the Canadians knew the FBI was hot on Sweeny's trail for attempting to circumvent American neutrality. But Sweeny still managed to achieve results. He was able to enlist the aid of Edwin C. Parsons, a former member of the Lafayette Escadrille, to help his cause. Parsons, having connections with the flying business in Southern California, was able to provide Sweeny several leads. He himself also interviewed a number of potential pilot recruits. As a result of Sweeny's efforts, 32 American pilots arrived in France between 13 April and 10 May 1940, including three—Eugene Tobin, Vernon Keough, and Andy Mamedoff—who eventually became Eagles. Several other young men en route to France, including future Eagle commander Chesley Peterson, were stopped at the Canadian border because of the neutrality laws and sent home. Even Sweeny and Parsons fled Los Angeles only one step ahead of the FBI, escaping the potential penalty of a $1,000 fine and up to three years in prison for violating the neutrality laws.

All was not well in France in late April 1940 when Colonel Sweeny returned to assess the situation. At almost the moment of his arrival in France, Germany invaded Belgium, Holland, and Luxembourg. The French, therefore, had little interest in training new pilots, so Sweeny rapidly changed his focus, now trying to get interested French pilots, and his recruited Americans, out of France so they could fight for England. Sweeny himself just managed to escape to England, leaving his family behind. Of the 32 Americans Sweeny recruited for the French, 4 were killed, 11 were taken prisoner, and 5 escaped to England. The remaining 12 disappeared, presumably escaping through Spain and finding their way back to the United States.

On 22 June 1940 France surrendered and England stood alone. It appears that Sweeny, back in the United States, surrendered to some degree at the same time. He reduced his recruiting efforts and gradually ceased to be an active force in obtaining American pilots for duty in Europe.[24] Nonetheless, Sweeny did keep recruiting long enough after the fall of France to send a number of American pilots to England, where they were met by his nephew Charles Sweeny and eventually formed the core of the first Eagle Squadron. Colonel Sweeny also played an active role in selecting the first commander of the Eagles. When he returned to England with his other nephew, Robert, in late summer of 1940, he was made an honorary group captain in the RAF and assumed titular leadership of the Eagle Squadron. In that capacity, he occasionally visited the bases where the Eagles were undergoing upgrade training in the Hurricane and, later, appeared infrequently with Number 71 Squadron after it was operational. He also helped briefly with recruiting in the autumn of 1940, but he never really played any key

*Colonel Charles Sweeny (right), soldier of fortune and
co-founder of the first Eagle Squadron, inspects an Eagle
Squadron Spitfire.*

role with the Eagles. By 1941 Colonel Sweeny had returned to the United States and become involved in other
wartime pursuits.[25]

So although Colonel Charles Sweeny was not the
founder of the Eagle Squadrons or even responsible for
recruiting most of their members, he was a significant
force in their eventual formation and can certainly be
considered a co-founder. He was responsible for creating
the initial awareness in the United States of both France's
and Britain's need for pilots. He built an extensive
recruiting network and numerous contacts others would
use to bring pilots to Canada and England. He recruited
many members of the first Eagle Squadron through his
effort to find flyers for France and England. Through his
huge appetite for publicity, factual or fictional, he also
created in the press and on the airfields of the United

States an interest among Americans in flying in the war that would bring scores of volunteers into the RAF.

FOUNDING THE EAGLE SQUADRONS

The actual founder of the Eagle Squadrons was the younger Charles Sweeny, nephew of Colonel Charles Sweeny. Young Charles was the older of two sons of Robert Sweeny Sr., Colonel Sweeny's brother. (For clarity, from here on I will refer to the elder Charles Sweeny as Colonel Sweeny and to his brother as Robert Sweeny Sr.) Rather than pursue the less than conventional career of his brother, Colonel Sweeny, Robert Sweeny Sr. decided on business. After graduating from Notre Dame and Harvard Law School, he settled in London, where the Sweeny family had business interests, and became a well-known, wealthy member of British society. His two sons, Charles and Robert, play crucial roles in the Eagle story.[26]

Charles was raised in the traditional English manner despite the fact that his family was American. But instead of joining several of his friends in attending Oxford, Charles returned to the United States and graduated from Yale. He then went back to England, where he married and settled into the London business world. A patriotic American, but with his life centered in England, he was inspired to do something to help when World War II began. The Eagle Squadrons were the result. When the United States entered the war, Sweeny joined the US Army Air Force as a major and was assigned to Eighth Army Headquarters. After the war, Charles resumed his business career in London, where he is still active.[27]

Charles' brother, Robert, was a dashing man about town before World War II. After attending Oxford, he, too, settled into the family business of finance, but he also retained a great number of outside interests, including golf—he was probably the best known of the Sweenys because of his 1937 victory in the British Amateur Golf Championship. When the first Eagle Squadron was formed, Air Vice-Marshal (later Sir) Sholto Douglas, vice-chief of the Air Staff, personally chose Robert Sweeny as the squadron adjutant. Douglas thought Robert could "keep the Squadron in line." Robert left the squadron in late 1940 and went on to a distinguished career as a bomber pilot. At the end of the war, he settled in Florida and continued both his business and golfing careers. He was beaten by Arnold Palmer on the last hole of the US Amateur Golf Championship in 1954. Robert returned to England in 1970 and died there in 1983.[28]

When war broke out in Europe, both Charles and Robert Sweeny rapidly became convinced that US help was essential to defeating Germany, and both became dedicated to gaining that help any way they could. In 1939 Charles organized the First Motorized Squadron, a home guard unit composed of Americans living in London, despite the opposition of Joseph P. Kennedy, US ambassador to the Court of St James. Ambassador Kennedy's lack of support is interesting, because he also opposed formation of the Eagle Squadrons. It appears he was convinced that Britain could not win, or even survive the German onslaught, and that the Americans were only jeopardizing themselves by such efforts. But Kennedy was soon replaced by John Winant, who was very receptive to the idea of American participation, and with whom Charles Sweeny freely discussed his ideas.[29]

Charles continued to look for more ways to contribute. Because any successful crossing of the English Channel by German invasion forces would require German air superiority, the real hope for the British was the RAF, specifically Fighter Command. There were already several squadrons manned by flyers from the Commonwealth countries, as well as pilots who had escaped from France, Poland, and Czechoslovakia. So why not an American squadron in Fighter Command?

Certainly, plenty of young men in the United States were ready and able to join the ranks of the RAF. The aviation cadet program of the Army Air Corps had so many more applicants than it could accommodate that it had resorted to very high washout rates to keep the number of trainees manageable. This high washout rate, plus the requirements for two years of college and perfect eyesight, kept a number of experienced pilots out of the US Army Air Force. In addition, a visitor to any of the hundreds of airports across the United States would have been impressed by the number of young men hanging around waiting for a ride, a lesson, a job—any opportunity to fly. Charles Sweeny, keenly aware of these facts, was determined to form an RAF squadron composed of American volunteers. His real motivation was his conviction that

> the War could not be won without the assistance of the U.S., and I thought that everything that registered the efforts of the Americans in the War would help to bring the U.S. in on the side of the Allies.[30]

But building an American squadron would not be easy. First, Sweeny had to have the permission of the British Air Ministry to form such an organization. Second, he had to develop some system for recruiting the Americans. Third, he needed financing for the entire operation, at least to provide for each individual until he could be brought within the system of the RAF. And the details of squadron organization, including the choice of a commander, had to be worked out. This was a rather tough assignment, especially because the British, about to enter a fight for their existence against the mighty Luftwaffe, had more important concerns than helping Sweeny. But this very fight against Germany proved to be one of the factors that led to approval of the American squadron concept.

In June 1940 Sweeny contacted Lord Beaverbrook, then Minister of Production, with his idea for the squadron. Sweeny, of course, addressed Britain's need for pilots for its ever-growing air force, but he also stressed the idea that an American squadron would be good propaganda and might further the cause of American intervention. Lord Beaverbrook was amenable to the idea. He suggested that Sweeny talk to his good friend, Brendan Bracken, personal assistant to Winston Churchill. The idea intrigued the prime minister, and Sweeny was asked to put his thoughts on paper for use by the Air Ministry. A short time later, he was summoned to the offices of the Air Ministry, ostensibly to present his idea to Air Minister Sir Archibald Sinclair. Instead, he was brought before the entire Air Council to explain his proposal.

Sweeny was actively supported at that meeting by Douglas, who would head Fighter Command before year's end. Sweeny evidently made his points well, because on 2 July 1940 the Air Council approved his idea and told him to begin work, with the proviso that before the squadron could be organized there had to be 25 pilots and 25 reserves available.[31] Under Secretary of State for Air Harold Balfour voiced the only significant opposition to Sweeny's plan. Balfour feared that Sweeny's work would interfere with his own efforts to recruit pilots in the United States to work as instructors at the growing number of flying schools in Canada. Balfour finally agreed, however, based on Air Ministry assurance that all US volunteers for the Royal Canadian Air Force would be given the option of training in Canada or joining the Eagle Squadrons in England.[32]

As Charles Sweeny thought about his presentation to the Air Ministry, he also considered the need for an appropriate shoulder patch, or flash, for wear on the RAF uniform, one that would set the Americans apart from the rest of the service. Inspired by the insignia of the eagle on his US passport, he created a flash incorporating a similar eagle insignia. When his father saw the new flash, he suggested that the unit be called the American Eagle Squadron. Charles, in turn, took this idea to his old friend at the Air Ministry, Sir Hugh Seeley, and it was approved.[33] A *New York Sun* report described the insignia as "the American spread Eagle embroidered in white against a background of gray. Over the top of the spread Eagle are the three embroidered letters AES in white against a similar background."[34] (The *A* was eventually

Shoulder patch of the Eagle Squadrons.

dropped, *ES* remained across the top of the patch.) In addition to being worn on the Eagles' uniforms, the insignia was painted on a number of the aircraft flown by the Eagles over the next two years.

After the squadron was approved, Charles Sweeny faced another vexing problem—how to both finance the recruiting effort and sustain the flyers until they became members of the RAF. Colonel Sweeny had faced this same problem when he was recruiting pilots to go to Morocco in 1925 and to France in 1940. Because of the American neutrality acts, the new recruits would have to be transported to Canada before they could enlist, and then be provided for until they could be put aboard a ship for England. (After the fall of France, US authorities only occasionally enforced the prohibition against moving Americans to Canada so they could enlist in the Canadian or British forces.) The logical source of money was the Sweeny coffers, and they were again opened as they had been in 1925. Robert contributed about $40,000 to the cause, while his father put up an undisclosed amount. A good friend of Robert, Barbara Hutton, commonly known as the Countess Reventlow and heir to the Woolworth fortune, also gave some $15,000, while Charles donated an undisclosed amount. In all, about $100,000 was raised, a sum adequate to sustain the effort in first-class style.[35]

Charles Sweeny apparently anticipated that the recruiting process would remain similar to that established by his uncle, Colonel Sweeny, before the fall of France. In that operation, either Colonel Sweeny or an associate would make it known around one of the US airports frequented by young, eager pilots that they were looking for flyers to join the French. The qualifications were 250 hours of logged flying time, a current flight physical, and good character. An interview, often conducted in a very out-of-the-way place, would follow. If everything seemed in order, Sweeny would offer the prospective candidate second lieutenant's pay, a possible commission, and, if the candidate accepted the terms, transportation across the Atlantic.[36] When Charles Sweeny began recruiting Eagles, the US neutrality acts made it essential not only that the entire operation be conducted very quietly but also that those young men who became "Sweeny candidates" be routed through Canada in order to avoid legal penalties.

Those who did get to Canada had to be provided with accommodations, typically a few days' residence in a first-class hotel, meals, and five dollars a day for spending money, while the candidate took a flight check and accomplished some preliminary paperwork. Assuming the new recruit passed the flight check—and it seems all recruits did—he would then be put on a train for the east coast of Canada, where he would board a ship for the ocean voyage.[37] Such an operation would require a considerable amount of money, possibly the entire $100,000, in a short time. But circumstances changed shortly after approval of the American squadron in July 1940, and the Sweeny recruiting network was dissolved. Just how many members of the first Eagle Squadron were financed by the Sweenys is unclear, but certainly a number of them were.

One of Charles Sweeny's important early tasks was finding a suitable commander for the organization, preferably an American. Doing so proved easier than Sweeny expected. Colonel Sweeny and Charles' brother, Robert, both were in the United States and were able to contact former Navy pilot and family friend, William E. G. Taylor. After looking at Taylor's credentials, the Sweenys decided he would be ideal for the command role. Taylor eagerly accepted the offer and accompanied the Sweenys back to England in late summer.[38] The Air Ministry apparently approved of Taylor, and he was introduced as the commander when the squadron was officially announced, but a British commander was also named.[39]

Although the first Eagle Squadron dated from July, it was not until 8 October 1940, when the pilots were in place in England, that Air Minister Sinclair made that official announcement to the world of the squadron's existence. There had already been considerable media coverage of the Americans in the RAF, but this announcement produced a new surge of newspaper articles about the squadron and its members—showing an interest that continued until the United States entered the war. The US government had no official reaction to the announcement.[40]

The organization and formation of one squadron is as far as Charles Sweeny had anticipated the Eagles story would go. Though he never played any active role in the operation of the unit, he did meet some of the Eagle recruits when they arrived in England.[41] But overall, except for attending occasional social functions in the early days and setting up a welfare fund for use by the squadrons, he did not have any significant contact with the group. Many of the Eagles did not know that he was the actual founder of the squadron until nearly 30 years later when the story came out at an Eagle Squadron Association reunion. Before that time, all the credit had gone to his uncle, Colonel Sweeny. Certainly, Charles Sweeny did not anticipate that there would eventually be three squadrons, which would have 244 Americans and 16 Englishmen go through their ranks, or that these squadrons would form the core of the highest-scoring fighter group in the US Army Air Force in World War II. The surprising growth from the initial squadron resulted from an entirely unforseen change in both the system for recruiting RAF pilots in the United States and the environment in which the recruiters worked.

2. SIGNING UP

As the specter of war loomed larger in Europe, Colonel Sweeny and his nephews were not alone in envisioning the potential value of the pilot pool in the United States. The British government and the Canadians both became active in planning ways to use American pilots and airfields for training if the need should arise. The most important of these ventures revolved around an American artist, Clayton Knight.

CLAYTON KNIGHT

Clayton Knight was rather an unlikely person to mastermind a huge pilot acquisition program. Born in 1891, he embarked early on a career in art. Living in New York in 1917, Knight had been much troubled by the war in Europe for some time. Because of his early interest in airplanes, both as machines and as art subjects, he developed a keen interest in flying and a great admiration for the Lafayette Escadrille. By the time Knight decided to join the air service, the United States had entered the war, so he was trained as an Army aviator. After completing a six-week course in primary flying at Austin, Texas, he went to Europe as part of the early contingent of American flyers. Subsequently posted with the British on the front in France, on 5 October 1918 he was wounded when shot down behind enemy lines and taken prisoner by the Germans. He was released at the end of the war.

Knight returned to the world of art after the war and became one of America's best-known aviation artists and illustrators. (His work can be found in a number of volumes about World War I, and he and his wife co-authored several books on flying in both wars.) Attached to the office of the Chief of the Air Staff during the later stages of World War II, Knight did sketches of a number of historic events, including the surrender of the Japanese aboard the USS *Missouri*. In 1946 he was awarded the Order of the British Empire because of his conspicuous service to England's cause in both World Wars.[1]

One of Knight's real joys in life was the world of flying. He regularly attended the major air shows and races, as both an aficionado and an illustrator. Over the years, he made many friends and acquaintances in flying circles. Little did Knight know that his trip to illustrate the Cleveland Air Races in September 1939 would be interrupted by an urgent request for help from an old friend and World War I pilot, Canadian Air Marshal Billy Bishop. At Cleveland, Bishop asked Knight to put together an organization to supply Canada with flying instructors to train pilots for the RAF in case the war in Europe expanded. As the planes roared around the race circuit, Knight listened to Bishop tell him that when the war spread throughout Europe, which it would do, Americans would be ready to help just as they had in World War I. Bishop's scheme was to set up an official organization that could screen applicants and direct them into the proper area of service before they came across the border into Canada, preventing a repeat of the chaos early in World War I. Knight accepted the challenge, but was not called into action until Hitler invaded Denmark, Norway, Holland, Belgium, and Luxembourg in the spring of 1940. Before it was disbanded in late 1942, the organization Knight was to form would process nearly 50,000 Americans' applications for duty with either the RAF or RCAF. It would be responsible for enrolling more than

10 percent of American RCAF recruits and more than 80 percent of those who became members of the RAF Eagle Squadrons.[2]

As the war clouds had grown dark over the continent in 1939, the British had foreseen their need for large numbers of military pilots. It seemed unlikely that the needed airmen could all be trained in England. The up-shot of this concern was the high-level Riverdale Mission to Canada in late 1939. One of the topics of that group's discussions was the need to train pilots and aircrews in the Dominions, particularly in Canada, if England were drawn into the war. By the end of December 1939, a plan, labeled the Empire Training Scheme (sometimes called the Empire Training Plan), had been agreed on. Pilots and aircrews would receive their initial training in the Dominions and then be given advanced training in the United Kingdom. The forces so trained would become members of the RAF but would be identified as contingents from the particular Dominion that did the training. (For this reason, several Americans in the Eagle Squadrons were actually identified on RAF records as part of the RCAF.) In agreeing to join this undertaking, each of the Dominions—Canada, Australia, New Zealand, and eventually South Africa and Rhodesia—agreed to set up its own training organization to provide a set number of aircrew members to the RAF. This plan was followed throughout the war, most countries training not only their own nationals but also large numbers of airmen from the United Kingdom.[3] The Canadian program was the largest and eventually employed significant numbers of American civilian volunteers as instructors. It was on obtaining these instructors that Clayton Knight originally focused.

Knight was willing to devote his time and connections to the undertaking, but he needed an experienced administrator to help. Air Marshal Bishop was able to secure the aid of gregarious Homer Smith, who administered a large family fortune derived from the Imperial Oil Company of Canada. (Smith, incidentally, was a cousin of Charles Sweeny). He, like Knight and Bishop, had been a pilot in World War I and appreciated the problems that the emerging war would bring for England and all of the Western world. Smith suggested that he and Knight immediately travel across the United States to take the pulse of the flying business, determine the number of potential instructors, and get some idea of what it would take to successfully hire available pilots.

The trip was an unqualified success. Not only did the two men obtain dossiers on more than 300 interested American pilots, but they also built a corps of influential people, mostly previous acquaintances of Knight or Smith, who would help if the plan were ever put into operation. In all, eight major cities were listed as good sources of instructors. Within a few weeks, in April 1940, Knight found himself in Ottawa, volunteering his list and his talent to the top air officials of the British Empire. With little discussion, the group accepted his offer and, according to Knight, "Thus the Clayton Knight Committee was born, and I began living the most hectic two years of my life."[4]

There were still a number of problems to be addressed if recruiting was to be effective. The committee had to establish a headquarters, gain at least tacit approval of the US Army and Navy (since any pilots recruited by Knight might well be prospective pilots for the US forces), and obtain the consent of the US State Department so that the strict US neutrality legislation would not defeat the entire project. Overcoming these obstacles called into play all of the many connections Knight and Smith had established over the years. While Homer Smith worked on the headquarters, Clayton Knight went on the road.

Smith believed the best way to publicize the committee's effort was to locate in the best place and establish a first-class operation. So he engaged a suite at the Waldorf-Astoria Hotel in New York, hired a secretary, set up an accounting and administrative system, and awaited the go-ahead signal from Knight, whose tasks were more difficult. Fortunately, Knight knew both General Hap Arnold and Admiral Jack Towers, commanders of the Army and Navy Air Forces, from his work as an aviation illustrator, so he was able to contact them with little difficulty. Once they were assured that Knight's group would not attempt to divert men away from the US forces or hire pilots already on active duty, they agreed to not oppose the enterprise. Actually, the Knight group was unlikely to be competing with the US services for the same pilots anyway, since the British and Canadian physical requirements were for 20/40 vision correctable to 20/20 with glasses, while the US standard was 20/20 uncorrected. In addition, the Canadian age limits were more liberal and a person could enter pilot training if he were married, a disqualifier for the US forces. General Arnold proved prophetic when he remarked to Knight,

> According to the rules I'm working under, if a flying cadet gets fractious, goes in for low stunt flying, gets drunk even once or we discover he's married, we've got to wash him out. If I was fighting a war, they're the kind I would want to keep. I wouldn't be surprised if a lot of our washouts look you up.[5]

Knight perceived the State Department to be a tougher challenge, because he was not known in that arena. So he sought the advice of his old World War I commander, fellow flyer, and longtime friend Mayor Fiorello LaGuardia of New York. LaGuardia was an enthusiastic supporter of the Knight scheme and arranged for Knight to visit Foggy Bottom. Two problems arose during the meeting with the State Department. First was the anticipated issue of the neutrality legislation, which stated "hiring or retaining another person to enlist or enter himself in the service of a belligerent as a soldier or a marine or seaman on board any ship of war" to be illegal. Knight's solution was to not advertise or recruit but simply provide a center to advise volunteers and to facilitate their training and journey to Canada or England.

The State Department's second concern was a surprise—the issue of citizenship, which would plague some of the eventual volunteers well into the 1970s.[6] According to the Citizenship Act of 1907, "any American citizen shall be deemed to have expatriated himself . . . when he has taken an oath of allegiance to any foreign state." Unknown to Knight, this law had caused significant legal problems for many Americans who joined foreign military forces during World War I; according to the State Department, the same would hold true for recruits in Knight's undertaking. The solution Knight eventually adopted, supported by both the Canadian and British governments, was to have Americans who entered the RCAF and RAF simply swear to obey the orders of their commanders without swearing allegiance to the King. Knight was a pioneer in dealing with the restrictions of the neutrality acts, and his solutions are classics in the history of World War II undercover operations.[7]

The State Department, however, was not pleased with this solution. On 25 July 1940 the FBI investigated the entire Knight system, but found no basis for any legal charges and so did nothing to curtail the committee's operation.[8] The State Department continued a voluminous correspondence with the Justice Department concerning the subject of recruiting in general and the Clayton Knight Committee in particular. But although there were a number of allegations made about the Knight organization, neither the Department of State nor the Department of Justice ever took any action to curtail its activities.[9] The citizenship and neutrality issues were blurred considerably anyway by the American policy of not enforcing the prohibition of recruiting in the United States for foreign military forces after France fell in June 1940 (more on the citizenship issue in the next chapter).

Although Knight and Smith were worried about the State Department opinion, they were even more concerned with the situation in Europe. So they "decided to regard the State Department's wrath as a calculated risk and shove things up to full throttle."[10] Letters went out in large numbers informing the pilots on the Knight list of the "opportunity" to enter the Canadian forces. Letters of acceptance, requests for information, and men wanting interviews came to New York in larger numbers than anticipated, requiring an expanded staff. Knight and Smith were careful to select only the best individuals available and chose Harold Fowler, an ace with the British in World War I, and Pierpont (Pete) Hamilton, a banker, to join the group. Hamilton standardized office and interview procedures and was crucial in the forthcoming expansion of the Knight Committee's operations.

What were the requirements that those interested in flying for the Canadians or the British had to meet?

> Each man had to produce a high school diploma or its equivalent and a birth certificate. He had to be between 20 and 45 and if under 21, he had to have his parents' or guardian's consent. We wanted a man to have a minimum of 300 hours of certified flying time, a CAA license and be currently capable of piloting two-seater aircraft.[11]

When the Knight Committee began accepting applications for the RAF, it set an age ceiling of 31 and required that candidates be unmarried.

Despite the urgent need for pilots, the Knight organization was not so desperate that they took anyone who walked through the door. Every man who approached the Knight Committee first filled out a two-page questionnaire, including complete personal data, a narrative of flying experience, the number and type of his pilot's license, hours flown and type of aircraft, and any records of flying violations. Interestingly, the only information required concerning a pilot's physical qualifications was the date of his last flight physical, whether he had any waivers for physical defects, history of operations, and his own opinion of whether his eyesight was at least 20/40 correctable to 20/20 and whether he was color-blind. The questionnaire also asked for a work history and a list of references, and provided a space for other comments.[12]

If the application was accepted, the candidate had a one-hour interview to determine if he was officer material, since almost all the pilots who entered the RAF or RCAF through the Knight Committee were commissioned. During the meeting, the interviewer generally was very careful to explain just what duties could be expected and what the conditions of enlistment were. (In practice, a number of different stories and promises were made to candidates, depending on where they were interviewed.) If the interview was satisfactory, the committee had the Hooper-Holmes Agency of New York, a large private investigation firm, prepare a confidential report on the candidate. The committee wanted to be sure they were getting the type of person they believed they were. "We were especially anxious to avoid sending a 'plant'—a man with pro-German or pro-Communist sympathies," wrote Knight.[13] Amazingly, copies of most of this information ended up in German hands and served as a basis for interrogating Eagles who were shot down.[14] This entire process took from three to eight weeks. The rather detailed selection process served the Canadians and British well and certainly resulted in only the best candidates being accepted.

James Happel applied to the Knight Committee in June 1941 and was accepted on 18 September 1941. The job for which he was applying was described in a letter from the Knight Committee in which the effort to circumvent US neutrality legislation is obvious:

The employment referred to would involve your taking a refresher course lasting approximately eight weeks in this country. Upon successful completion of this course you would proceed to Canada and probably to the United Kingdom, engaged in one of the British Aviation Ltd.'s activities comprising check-testing of latest type service planes after overhaul, flight-checking of instrument and equipment installation, ferry work from factory to depot et cetera.

The *et cetera* was understood to mean flying fighters for the RAF. The letter to Happel further spelled out his relationship with the RAF:

> Employees of British Aviation Ltd. are given opportunity, after a reasonable period of satisfactory service, to join the Royal Air Force by applying for commission in the R.A.F. Volunteer Reserve as a Pilot Officer with the same rates of pay and allowances (fourteen shillings and sixpence per day plus quarters and rations and forty pounds, £40, uniform allowance) and identical chances of advancement with any other officer of the Royal Air Force.[15]

Over the course of its existence, from April 1940 until October 1942, the Clayton Knight Committee accepted only about 6,700 pilots from among nearly 50,000 applicants.[16]

The large numbers of volunteers led Knight to open offices in several major US cities. The first area for expansion was California, where Knight and Smith had already ascertained about one-fourth of the unemployed pilots in the United States lived. By the end of 1940 the Clayton Knight Committee had major offices in New York, Memphis, Cleveland, Chicago, Kansas City, St. Louis, Dallas, San Antonio, Oakland, and Los Angeles.[17] Apparently, there were smaller offices, or simply individual representatives of the Knight organization, in a number of other cities, such as Washington, DC, since several Eagles report having signed up in places other than the major cities listed. Each operation was as similar as possible to that of New York—headquartered in the best hotel in the city and staffed by efficient and, in the case of secretaries, attractive people. The head of each operation and the people who did the interviewing were, as much as possible, men who had been flyers in World War I. In the Oakland office, for example, internationally famous flyer Clyde Pangborn was the head, assisted by another flyer, H. L. Stradley. These two dynamos had sent 26 flyers to Canada by the end of August 1940.[18]

Pangborn was also actively involved in recruiting outside the Knight Committee. As early as 19 August 1940, William H. Byington Jr., chairman of the Advisory Committee of the Aviation League of the United States, Inc., of which Pangborn was a member, wrote to the State Department to ask a legal opinion on Pangborn's recruiting of pilots to join the British and Canadian forces. The State Department's answer to this inquiry was rather evasive, referring to the Neutrality Act as a guide but refusing to take a concrete position.[19] Here, again, the guidance, probably from the president, to not enforce the foreign recruiting provisions of the presidential proclamation of 1939 left the Department of State in a difficult position.

There appears to have been no direct connection between the Aviation League of the United States and the Clayton Knight Committee, but the presence of Pangborn as a key person in both organizations, along with their mutual purpose and the groups having key administrative offices within a few blocks of each other in New York, suggests that the two organizations were aware of each other's activities and that, apparently, several organizations were "unofficially" recruiting American pilots. Apparently, though, only two were recruiting *fighter* pilots for the RAF: the Sweeny organization, which focused on building an American squadron in the RAF, and the fledgling Clayton Knight Committee, representing the Canadians and seeking pilots to become instructors in the Empire Training Program. Both these groups were dedicated to helping the British, but they went about their work in very different ways.

While the Clayton Knight Committee ostensibly only helped volunteers get to Canada, the Sweeny group actively recruited pilots. Both the Knight and Sweeny operations apparently were well financed, but size and scope separated the two. While Sweeny was dealing in ones and twos in order to obtain 25 pilots and 25 reserves for one squadron, Knight was looking for hundreds, eventually thousands, to help man an entire training command. The

Knight group was working marginally within the law and in the open, while Sweeny and his men were staying under cover and actually violating the neutrality legislation. The two organizations were linked in at least one State Department document, in August 1940. On that occasion, Mr. Pierepont Moffat of the American embassy in Canada wrote to the State Department in Washington concerning complaints of illegal recruiting by both the Sweeny and Knight organizations.[20]

Because of RAF Fighter Command's loss of pilots during the summer of 1940, as the Battle of Britain began in earnest, the British Air Ministry determined that the RAF could use all the flyers it could get to help fill the dwindling pilot pool.[21] This decision significantly increased demands on the Empire Training Scheme and prompted the British to look to the United States for training facilities as well as more pilots. The logical organization to meet the demand, the British believed, was the Clayton Knight Committee rather than the Sweeny organization. Thus, in the fall of 1940, the Knight Committee became the principal agent for channeling American pilots into the RAF, and eventually into the Eagle Squadrons.

There are, however, two very different points of view on just how this change in the focus of Eagle recruitment took place. According to Charles Sweeny, the recruiting was subsumed by the Empire Training Scheme, working through the Knight Committee, after Sweeny called his father and brother in New York and asked them to come to England. They were to bring along Colonel Sweeny, so he could become the honorary commander of the Eagle Squadron, and W. E. G. Taylor, the squadron's official commander. When the group sailed for England in late summer, the formal Sweeny recruiting activity in the United States ended.[22]

Clayton Knight's view is somewhat different. He wrote that the Sweeny penchant for seeking newspaper publicity and for entertaining volunteers at champagne parties and in nightclubs alarmed the British embassy, which feared the entire pilot recruiting program in the United States might be jeopardized. So Homer Smith, Sweeny's cousin, came up with the idea of sending the Sweenys and their potential RAF pilots to England so London could properly censor their activities.[23]

The Sweeny account seems more probable because, as already described, the Sweenys were phasing out their program by the late summer of 1940. France was occupied by Germany, Colonel Sweeny had lost much of his enthusiasm, nearly all the necessary pilots for the first Eagle Squadron had been recruited, and in less than two months the unit's existence would be announced to the world. Whatever the reason, though, the Knight organization absorbed some of the Sweeny people, but none of the Sweenys played any active role in its operation or recruiting.

On 13 August 1941 the Clayton Knight Committee changed its name to the Canadian Aviation Bureau, for unknown reasons. The main offices remained in eight rooms of the Waldorf-Astoria Hotel in New York, and all the branch offices of the Knight Committee, as well as the 50 employees, remained. The change, it appears, was in name only. But it triggered an immediate request from the State Department for an FBI investigation of the new organization. The ensuing FBI report sheds considerable light on the nature of the Clayton Knight Committee and its operation.

The purpose of the new Canadian Aviation Bureau, according to Pierpont Hamilton, was the same as that of the Knight organization. It was not soliciting or recruiting men for the Canadian Air Force, but rather "performing the function of an Information Bureau, giving interviews and generally assisting any young men who might be interested to ascertain if they meet the requirements of employees of the Canadian Air Force." He further stated that the committee did no actual recruiting in the United States. Financing for the operation was "supplied by the Royal Air Force, the Canadian Government, and donations from private individuals."[24]

Clayton Knight reinforced these same points in an FBI interview on 30 December 1941. In that interview, Knight listed the major officers of the Canadian Aviation Bureau as Homer Smith, Director; himself and Pierpont Hamilton as Associate Directors; Mr. J. A. Smith, Treasurer; and Beatrice Thomas as another officer. Knight noted that all were American citizens except Homer Smith, a Canadian. In this interview, Knight referred to the entire operation, ever since its founding in July 1940, as the Canadian Aviation Bureau. FBI records, however, show it to have been officially the Clayton Knight Committee until 5 December 1941, and Knight's own account of his activities agrees. Whatever the real name of the organization was at any given time, all the members of the Eagle Squadrons who entered the RAF via that route refer to the organization as the Clayton Knight Committee.[25]

Another method of getting into the RAF, not involving either the Sweeny or Knight organizations, was simply to join the British or Canadian armed forces and try to get into a flying assignment. This was the least used method, but several Eagles, including William Dunn and Jim DuFour, did take this route. Having shot down two German aircraft from the ground as a member of the Canadian army, Dunn saw a notice on the squadron bulletin board that anyone with 500 hours of flying time could apply for the RAF. Dunn doctored his flight records to show 560 hours rather than his actual 160 and was accepted. His flight training took place in Canada and he arrived in 71 Squadron in early 1941. DuFour had joined the Seaforth Regiment of Canada, which was based in southern England. When he discovered that there was a chance to fly, he contacted the Air Ministry, which in turn referred him to the Clayton Knight Committee in the United States.[26] Those who reached the Eagle Squadrons in this way really did not join the British or Canadian forces in an effort to get into the RAF or the Eagles. They simply happened to have the opportunity and took it.

Another direct route into flying, taken by Eagles Jim Goodson, Walter "Wick" Wicker, Don Blakeslee, Reade Tilley, Bert Stewart, Gilmore Daniel, Jim Griffin, Richard Alexander, and Leon Blanding, among others, was to join the Royal Canadian Air Force with the hope of escaping instructor duty in Canada and eventually transferring into the RAF. The Empire Training Scheme created great demand for pilots to be instructors in the various countries of the British Commonwealth. These countries had to expand their own air forces, and they had been put on notice that they might well have to train large numbers of RAF pilots. The Canadians looked to the United States as a source of additional instructors. Jim Griffin reports, "everywhere you went in Canada in 1940 there were Americans in Canadian uniforms . . . in fact, there were so many Texans that wags often referred to the RCAF as the Royal Canadian Air Force of Texas."[27]

The basic ground rules were that the Americans would come to Canada as civilians, but some who went saw that doing so might give them a chance to fly with the RCAF. There were few openings for fighter pilots but many for pilots to ferry aircraft across the Atlantic to England. For those impatient Americans who did not know about the Clayton Knight Committee or Colonel Sweeny's program, joining the RCAF seemed like the best way to get into flying and the war. For some, such as Richard Alexander, it was also a way to keep from being drafted and spending the war in the infantry, while Gilmore Daniel, the youngest Eagle at 15, said, "I just wanted to fly."[28] Those who did volunteer for the RCAF received the complete Canadian Officers Training Program and Basic Flight Training, and then had to fight for a fighter assignment, which a few were lucky enough to get. A distinction of the RCAF enlistees who became Eagles was that most of them went into the RAF as sergeant pilots rather than officers, although all of those who lived long enough managed eventually to get their commission in either the RAF or the US Army. Some, like Wicker, were killed as sergeant pilots.

As noted earlier, the Knight Committee, too, which ended up recruiting nearly 90 percent of those who became Eagles, made use of the fact that the RAF needed ferry pilots. "We were told that we were being trained to ferry aircraft to Britain from Canada," said Vernon Parker. "However, the word leaked out while we were in Dallas that we would be commissioned in the RAF."[29]

The Knight organization used various methods to make their presence known, depending on local circumstances. The most preferred way of advertising, at least by 1941, was through key people and on bulletin boards at local airports. This system got the information to the young college students who were enrolled in the Civilian Pilot Training Program as well as to current pilots. Former Navy gunner Ervin Miller saw a bulletin board notice at the Oakland Airport and hurried to sign up.[30]

In some areas Knight also took out small ads in key newspapers. Eddie Miluck was attracted by a tiny ad in a Dallas paper that identified a hotel room where "pilots seeking adventure" could obtain further information.[31] Various regional flying magazines and newsletters also carried notices of the opportunity to join the RAF. When key members of the Knight organization, such as Knight himself or Clyde Pangborn, were interviewed by the press, they always pointed out how a pilot could contact them.[32]

There was even an RAF information booth located outside the gate at Maxwell Field to catch those who washed out of aviation cadet training. Don Smith summed up the feelings of most in this group by saying, "I wanted to prove to the US Army that they made a mistake when they washed me out."[33]

The most effective advertising, however, was by word of mouth. Douglas Booth was told about the Knight Committee by his uncle, a retired Army officer who worked for Clayton Knight. Art Roscoe was working at Los Angeles Metropolitan Airport when Tommy

McGerty, a Knight Committee trainee, made a forced landing and told Roscoe, who was working on his plane, how to sign up.[34] By one means or another, the existence of the Clayton Knight organization was well known in flying circles throughout the country by early 1941.

Knight Committee applicants were generally, though not always, told straight out what they were interviewing for and what the conditions were to be. They knew they would be flying in the RAF and would be paid as flight officers, about $85 per month. Many were told they would be fighter pilots, but not all. Several candidates, including George Carpenter, were recruited simply to fly, with no assurance or even mention of fighters. Carpenter was one recruit who really thought he could be ferrying aircraft across to England.[35] In many cases the issue of citizenship was also discussed and the applicant assured that he would not lose his US standing. In some cases, however, these rules were not followed. For example, John Brown was told by the recruiters in Chicago that the minimum requirement was 80 flying hours and successful completion of a flight check, and was assured before he signed up that he would be a fighter pilot, would fly combat, and would be paid $600 per month. Others from the Chicago area were under the same impression, and a few refused to fly when they found that their pay would be only 15 percent of that amount.[36]

Most members of the Eagles were not aware that the Knight organization also conducted the previously mentioned background check on each of them. John Campbell was one of the few Eagles who knew about his security check: a storekeeper in his native Chula Vista, California, asked him just what he was planning to do because there had been "the nicest British gentleman checking on you the other day."[37] This background investigation was one of the reasons a few candidates had to wait as long as three or four months before being accepted into training.

A 30-minute flight check, often conducted by a former instructor of the candidate, was also part of the acceptance process. When William Geiger reported for his check, Hank Coffin, his examiner, said, "I know you know how to fly, but the RAF paid for 30 minutes so just take the Waco and have fun."[38] I found no instance of a candidate failing this check ride.

PERSONALITIES

Who were the young men who decided to join a foreign air force to fight a war in which their country was not involved? (For a listing of the age, home state, education, and occupation of each Eagle, see appendix A.) They ranged in age from 15-year-old American Indian Gilmore Daniel to 37-year-old Harold Strickland. Most fell into the 19-to-24 age group. They came from all over the United States. LeRoy Skinner came from Missouri; Steve Pisanos joined in New York City, where he had lived only two years since emigrating from Greece; William Daley was from Texas; school teacher Oscar Coen and John Brown were both from Illinois.

A large majority of those who enlisted were from California, which was really the seat of flying and the aviation industry before World War II. Art Roscoe, William Geiger, John Campbell, and LeRoy Gover went to the offices of the Clayton Knight Committee and applied to enter the RAF. Chesley Peterson, Jack Fessler, Gus Daymond, and Gene Tobin, all working in California, were recruited by Colonel Sweeny and made their way into Canada with some difficulty. From Florida, Reade Tilley joined the Royal Canadian Air Force, as did Richard Alexander from Illinois, Don Blakeslee from Ohio, and Jim Goodson from New York (though Goodson reached the RCAF via the RAF, having joined up in England after being on an ocean liner torpedoed shortly after it left its English port).

According to the standards laid down by both Sweeny and the Clayton Knight Committee, all of these young men should have been very experienced pilots. The only ones who could legally sign up with little or no flying time were those who joined the RCAF, like Walter

Wicker and Leon Blanding, who had no flying experience, and Richard Alexander, with only 25 flying hours. Despite the theoretically tight standards, in reality the range of flying experience, particularly of those who entered through the Knight organization, was wide indeed.

A significant number of the young men who eventually became Eagles doctored their flying log books to indicate they had more hours than they really had— many of these pilots were willing to do almost anything to get into a Spitfire. Although there is no evidence to indicate that the Clayton Knight Committee knew this was going on, it is difficult to believe it was a secret, particularly since some of the efforts to change the flying record were blatantly obvious. Wilson (Bill) Edwards, for example, believes that most Clayton Knight applicants padded their log books as he did. But neither he nor any of the other Eagles knows of a case of an applicant being accused of padding his log book and being denied admission into the Knight system, and eventually into the RAF, for that reason.[39] A number of those who did falsify their flying records paid a terrible price in the end: the losses in training after the applicants got to England were very high, a result in no small part of the fact that the British assumed a level of flying competency based on documented flying experience. A number of young Americans in the RAF were put into flying conditions, especially in severe weather, that they could not handle, sometimes leading to fatal crashes.[40]

But the majority survived, with widely varying amounts of actual flying experience. Carroll McColpin had a legitimate 475 hours when he signed up, Robert Smith had nearly 800 hours, and Vernon Parker, a self-proclaimed barnstormer from Texas, had about 650 hours. Those with the average of 100 to 400 hours of real experience included engineer Joe Bennett from Idaho with 200 hours, Ernest Beatie, an 18-year-old Georgian who signed up with Clayton Knight in California, with 100 hours, and New Yorkers Ervin Miller with 200 hours and Douglas Booth with 150 hours. Some, like Roland

Wolfe with 1,000 hours and Jim DuFour with 1,500 hours, had experience in high-powered aircraft; others, including Joe Durham, a golf professional from Arkansas, had no more than 60 hours in the Piper Cub; and Bill Edwards, a college student from Santa Monica, had only the 35 hours he flew in the Civilian Pilot Training Program. It was this diversity of experience on the part of the applicants that made the British decide very early in the existence of the Clayton Knight Committee to send the Knight volunteers to a flight training program in the United States. This program, although it did identify those who could not fly and cause them to be sent home, was intended primarily to establish some common level of experience. Then when the applicants reached England and were sent to operational training, they could be placed into the existing RAF program with a reasonable hope for success.

When Clayton Knight was searching for the best source of pilots, he hit upon California because he determined that nearly one-fourth of all the unemployed pilots in the United States lived there. But, in fact, almost none of the men who signed up were unemployed. In addition, although more of the candidates were flying for a living than working in any other single occupation, more than two-thirds had jobs that did not involve any flying at all. The largest number were working in what are generally referred to as blue-collar jobs, that is, as skilled or semi-skilled laborers. Robert Priser worked as an aircraft mechanic in Tucson, Arizona. Alfred Hopson was a machinist in Texas. Don Nee worked for a wholesale electric company in California. Jim Griffin was a factory worker in New York. Many of these men were simply working at whatever job was available in the tough times of the late 1930s—and much of their pay was being spent on flying.

Outside of the blue-collar jobs, the list expands in all directions. Fred Gamble from Tennessee was a reporter. Gene Fetrow worked as an aircraft inspector for Douglas Aviation in Los Angeles, as did Chesley Peterson. Marion Jackson owned a bar in Los Angeles. James Nelson was a bank manager, Wendell Pendleton a draftsman, Dean Satterlee a druggist, and Ervin Miller a civil servant. Several applicants classed themselves as students, a category that covered all sorts of study in many different fields. Charles Cook was studying at California Polytechnic Institute, Jack Fessler was in airline pilot training, Don Ross was a high school student, and Walter Wicker had just left the University of Virginia.

Those who were pilots by vocation included Harold Strickland, an administrator for the Civilian Pilot Training Program; Coburn King, who had flown just about everything and had served a tour of duty as an instructor in Canada; LeRoy Gover, who had done all sorts of flying in his 800 hours; and William Geiger and Gus Daymond, who flew whatever jobs came along in Southern California. Several, too, including George Carpenter, Charles Cook, Don Smith, Chesley Peterson, and Paul Ellington, had been eliminated from the US Army aviation cadet program for one reason or another. Barry Mahon was in the Navy Reserve and had to get released to go into the RAF.[41]

Although many of the Eagles had some college education, very few were active students at the time they volunteered to join the RAF. There are several explanations for this phenomenon, but two stand out. First, most young men who had a college education and wanted to fly went into the very desirable US Army aviation training program. The Army required that applicants for the scarce slots in aviation cadet training have at least two years of college, and desired that applicants have a degree. A significant number of those who joined the RCAF and RAF would have preferred to have been in the American forces but did not meet the education requirement. A second explanation is that the organizations recruiting for the RAF sought experienced pilots. With the United States still in the throes of the depression in the late 1930s, a young man almost had to go to work directly out of high school, and he had to choose carefully how to spend his hard-earned money. For most with an interest in flight, flying lessons and hours generally won out over education. Many of those who could afford to go to college, like Reade Tilley and Wick Wicker, decided that the university did not offer the adventure they sought and that they would rather be flying.

As mentioned earlier, this educational characteristic of the Eagle Squadrons was one major difference from the Lafayette Escadrille of World War I. In fact, Colonel Charles Sweeny stressed this point in an interview with *The Washington Post* in April 1941, commenting, "The men in the Escadrille . . . were for the most part university men, sons of wealthy families. With them aviation was a sport." The Eagles were "professional fliers. They [had] worked as stunt pilots, as crop dusters, as freight carriers."[42] Although Sweeny was not very well-versed on the background of the men who made up the Eagle Squadrons (as the occupation listings in appendix A show), he was correct in identifying one factor that set the Eagles apart from the Lafayette Escadrille.

MOTIVATIONS

Just what motivated a man to give up a job, in many cases a good job, and volunteer to risk his life for a country that he had never seen and about which he may have known very little? Certainly, few of the Eagles spent their evenings studying about the British, their system of government, the Nazi regime in Germany, and the like. They spent their time thinking about flying or about their jobs, or going to a movie, or looking for a date. Yet it is this issue of why they joined that is one of the most significant of the entire story of the Eagles. Although flying was, without exception, a factor in their decisions, that really doesn't get to the heart of the issue. There were, after all, opportunities to fly, both for a living and for pleasure, in the United States. For each of the Eagles, flying occupied a somewhat different place in the equation and mixed with a number of other factors.

For the founder of the Eagle Squadrons, the explanation was straightforward. Charles Sweeny believed the Americans came to fly *the aircraft* of the RAF. Royce Wilkinson, an RAF ace who served as a flight commander in two of the Eagle Squadrons, concluded that those who signed up came over basically to fly. J. Roland "Robbie" Robinson, the late Right Honorable Lord Martonmere, not a pilot at all but a member of Parliament, volunteered for the RAF and found himself as the intelligence officer of the recently formed 71 Squadron, the first of the Eagles. One of the most perceptive members of the Eagles, Robinson believed

> the reasons why most Americans joined the Royal Air Force as volunteers are very varied. Some came for sheer idealism, others had the idea that they wanted to fight Hitler and get into a scrap while others because they thought they would like to emerge fully trained as fighter pilots.[43]

Chesley Peterson, the first American to command the Eagles in combat, takes a slightly different view, one more along the lines of Charles Sweeny's. "Everyone wanted to fly big, fast airplanes," he said, "and the only way to do that was in one of the services. Since most of those who joined the RAF did not have the necessary qualifications to join the US Army or Navy, the only answer that readily presented itself was the RAF." But that was not the only reason. Peterson continues, "Many also had a sense of adventure and were imbued with stories of flying in World War I and the actions of the Lafayette Escadrille. To them joining the RAF was the greatest adventure of all." Peterson had been bitten by the flying bug when a barnstormer had landed in his father's field in Utah and, in exchange for using the field as a base of operations, had given young Chesley a ride. From then on all Peterson's actions were directed toward flying. He even went to Brigham Young University just long enough to get the needed two years of college to qualify for the Army flying program. Unfortunately, he was underage and the Army eliminated him from aviation cadets.

Commenting on the issue of patriotism, Peterson believed it was a factor in a number of Eagles' decisions, although he noted, "most Eagles will not admit they had any deep feelings in this area until the US came into the war." But a telling point in the matter of fighting for freedom, he observed, is that no Americans volunteered to form a squadron and fly for the Luftwaffe.[44] Whether they would have if an organization such as Sweeny's or Clayton Knight's had been recruiting for the Germans will never be known. All the Eagles I have interviewed said they would not have joined the Luftwaffe because they didn't believe in the German cause.

Reade Tilley had always been the adventurous type and wanted to drive race cars, but when racing proved impractical, he determined to fly fighters. Turned down for flying by the US Army because he was too tall, he made his way to Canada and joined the RCAF, hoping to become a fighter pilot. Tilley had learned to fly through the Civilian Pilot Training Program while he was a pre-med student at the University of Texas. (He abandoned the pre-med course because it did not promise enough adventure.) Because of low marks on a mathematics test during basic training, he was ordered to duty as a gunner. But Tilley talked his way into a second chance on the exam, hired a tutor, and, after a week of hard study, passed and entered flight training. Posted to northern Scotland after graduation, he was assigned to an observer training squadron. On his first operational mission, Tilley rolled the plane onto its back, a forbidden maneuver, and was promptly hauled before the commandant. A frantic phone call to Charles Sweeny landed Tilley in Eagle Squadron 121 the next day.[45]

Bert Stewart went to Canada to sign up with the RCAF because he "didn't want to be a ground pounder." Upon completion of pilot training in October 1940, he was posted to New Brunswick as an instructor. While traveling to his new assignment, he found himself in the same railroad depot as several Eagles. He went with them and stowed away on their ship to England. When he arrived in England, Stewart became the subject of high-level negotiations, but finally was allowed to stay and was assigned to 121 Squadron just as it was forming.[46]

Jim Griffin had been reading about flying and adventure since he was a child. Flyers such as Charles Lindbergh, Wiley Post, and Amelia Earhart were his childhood heroes. He had to wait until 1938 to fulfill his dream of flight, however. As he notes, "an hour of dual flying with an instructor cost $12.00 at the time—solo flying was $8.00 an hour. A lot of money for a 20-year-old who had only recently acquired a steady job." But when the flight came it was something he would never forget. "There was hardly any physical sensation as the wheels of the Piper Cub left the runway and it soared gently into the air. . . . In spite of the steady drone of the engine there was a sense of peace and quiet and contentment." Griffin was hooked.

Concerned about the war in Europe, he had "no doubt . . . in the autumn of 1940, that the United States would soon be at war, and that I would soon be in the military. Of course I wanted to be a pilot, but realized that without a college degree there was no chance of getting into the USAAF (US Army Air Force)." So when several Canadians, representing the RCAF, came to the New York area in October 1940 looking for civilian flight instructors, Griffin talked to them. He was told, in strictest confidence, that if he went to Canada and enlisted in the RCAF he would have a good chance to become a military pilot. He and two friends crossed the border that October, enlisted, and entered flight training.[47]

Quite a different sense motivated Walter Wicker, member of a wealthy and important Chicago family and son of radio's then-famous "Singing Lady." Wicker's sense of adventure led him to take flying lessons, and as early as 1938, his sister recalls, their talks were dominated by great concerns about the war:

I remember very clearly our being in a movie theatre when a newsreel was shown of Hitler, making a speech with that terrible hysteria in his voice and gesticulating wildly. The audience was laughing. Wick was shocked and white-faced when he turned to me and said: "They shouldn't laugh. He is a dangerous man and will have us all in a war."

So it was that he went to Canada, joined the RCAF, and "did exactly what he dreamed of doing, to fly, to be a fighter pilot. He wanted exactly what he had, a place with a group he admired, fighting for a cause he believed mattered more than life itself." He died for that cause.[48]

George Carpenter, committed to flying in the military, found himself in Army pilot training at the Spartan School of Aeronautics in Tulsa, Oklahoma, in June 1941. Spartan was also under contract to train volunteers for the RAF, many of whom came from the Clayton Knight Committee. "I had nearly completed my primary training . . . when I fainted from a routine tetanus injection and I was washed out of the program and discharged from the (Army) Air Force." He learned of the opportunity provided by the RAF, contacted the Clayton Knight Committee, and was accepted. Carpenter sums it all up by saying, "the single most important factor in my decision . . . was the opportunity to continue flying. However, the adventure aspect certainly cannot be discounted as an important factor."[49]

Gene Fetrow joined simply because "it would give [him] the opportunity to fly the finest, fastest and hottest plane built."[50]

Several of the Eagles, including Art Roscoe, Bill Edwards, and Bill Geiger had been frustrated in one way or another in their desires for military careers. Roscoe had been reading and listening to people talk about World War I for as long as he could remember. Although no one in his family was involved in aviation, he joined a local youth organization in Southern California, sponsored by the Richfield Oil Company, called the Jimmie Allen Flying Club. The club gave him an opportunity to read even more, build model airplanes, and, at the age of twelve, have his first airplane ride. His interest progressed as he joined a quasi-military organization called the American Air Cadet Corps at the Los Angeles Metropolitan Airport at age fifteen and started to work for flying time. Through this group he got all his ground school and soloed when he was sixteen. "After that," he reminisces, "it was just a matter of where and when you could get flying time. I worked for it, swept hangars, washed airplanes—you lived at the airport."

When Roscoe got out of high school he went to work for Lockheed and, in company with two friends, bought an airplane and continued to fly. Roscoe tried to get into West Point but was turned down because of a slight astigmatism in one eye, so he took a job back at Los Angeles Airport and there found out about the Knight organization. For Roscoe, flying high-powered pursuit planes and being in the military seemed possible only through the RAF, and he signed up in February 1941.

Accompanying Art to the headquarters of the Clayton Knight Committee was his good friend Jack Weir, who had also been bitten by the flying bug and was working at the same airport. Weir was posted to 71 Squadron shortly before Roscoe arrived at that unit and was killed in a flying accident a few weeks after Roscoe joined the squadron.[51]

For Bill Edwards, the story was different. He took his first airplane ride on his sixteenth birthday while visiting his brother-in-law, who was the field manager for TWA in Wichita, Kansas. Edwards knew he had found his future, and he began to spend his free time around Jim Hart Flying Service at the Wichita airport, just to get an occasional flight. After finishing high school in Prescott, Arizona, he enrolled in Santa Monica City College and the Civilian Pilot Training Program. His objective was to finish two years of college, get his private license, and enter the Army aviation cadet program. Having passed all the Army exams at March Field, he was turned down because he was missing two teeth. Back in Southern California, devastated by the rejection, he continued college and worked part-time as a draftsman until he could no longer make ends meet. Realizing that US involvement in the war in Europe was not far off and sensing the draft breathing down his neck, Edwards decided flying was better than marching. So he sought out the Clayton Knight Committee at the Hollywood Roosevelt Hotel and signed up.[52]

William Geiger had little doubt about why he wanted to join the RAF. "I joined the Eagle Squadron for one reason," he said in a 1987 interview. "I wanted to make a career out of being a military pilot. I had wanted to fly ever since I was a little teeny boy." He had heard much about the Army from his uncle Spike, a graduate of West Point and an early flyer. After high school, Geiger attended Pasadena City College, where he learned to fly and earned his private license, courtesy of the Civilian Pilot Training Program at Alhambra Airport. He continued to fly during the summer of 1940, taking an aerobatics course, but the only way for him to get into military flying was through the Army program at Randolph Field, and his grades were not good enough to qualify him for that program.

Geiger was about to hire a tutor to help him qualify for the Army program when he heard about the Clayton Knight Committee through scuttlebutt at the Alhambra Airport. So off he went to the Hollywood Roosevelt Hotel, where he was told there would be an American squadron in the RAF flying fighters. He signed up without hesitation.

> At the time I signed up I wanted to fly . . . a military type of airplane and I wanted to be a career military officer and that was my real purpose in doing it. . . . I thought that I would benefit from the fact that when the United States got in the war, I would already have combat experience and so now I would be a plus . . . and have a leg up.

As far as being motivated by a desire to help the British, Geiger said, "To be perfectly honest with you, I don't believe that ever crossed my mind at that point in time." Bill Geiger's plans for a military career were shattered when he was one of the first Eagles shot down. He spent most of the war in a German prison camp.[53]

One of the oldest of the Eagles was Harold Strickland, who signed up at age 37. He summed up his reasons for volunteering this way:

> I think we were all motivated by the thought of high adventure, the excitement of combat flying, and a desire to help Britain. I hesitate to use the expression "romance" but it was there; it was the romance of highest adventure, a sort of trademark among flyers everywhere. Adventure could have been found in any of the British armed services where thousands of other Americans had volunteered, but we could *fly,* and the Royal Air Force offered fulfillment of all three or four expectations.[54]

Strickland had been bitten by the flying bug in 1915 while attending the Panama Pacific International Exposition in San Francisco. In an effort to get into military flying he joined the Army Signal Corps in 1921, but not until he turned 21, in 1924, was he eligible to compete for a spot as an aviation cadet. He arrived at primary flying school at Brooks Field, Texas, in March 1925, about the same time that young Charles Lindbergh was graduating from advanced flying training at nearby Kelly Field. After nearly 40 hours of dual and solo time in Curtiss Jennys, Strickland failed a check ride and joined the nearly 85 percent who were eliminated from the Army flying program in those days.

His subsequent work kept him in one aspect of aviation or another during the next fifteen years, and in mid-1940 he was appointed District Flight Supervisor in the Civilian Pilot Training Program of the Civil Aeronautics Authority. Because his work kept him driving from town to town, he had ample time to listen to the car radio. While listening, he was particularly struck by the news from London featuring Ed Murrow, or occasionally a talk by Winston Churchill. Probably the most moving talk he ever heard was Churchill's speech to Parliament on 4

June 1940, when he said that England would never surrender, but would hold out as long as need be until the new world came forth to rescue and liberate the old. Strickland was part of that new world. So, while flying across the Midwest on a spring day in 1941, Strickland made his decision:

> I would resign my successful, enjoyable, well-paying and exciting job and volunteer my services to the Royal Air Force as soon as it could be arranged. . . . I was sufficiently mature to know what I was doing. I did not discount the physical risks.

In May of 1941 he presented himself at the British Embassy in Washington, DC, and was directed to the Clayton Knight Committee in New York City. Because of his more than 2,000 hours of flying time and his record, he was sent directly to Canada, took a flight check, and was on his way to England before the end of June.[55]

Other Eagles had many other reasons for volunteering. Don Blakeslee, who was to become one of the legendary fighter pilots of World War II, joined because his Waco had been wrecked by a friend and, since he had no insurance, he decided the only way to get another plane was to join the RAF.[56] Ervin Miller said he "had no noble motives like helping defeat Nazism, or defending freedom. . . . All I wanted to do was get my hands on a really high performance aircraft."[57] "The papers were full of articles about the Battle of Britain, Hurricanes and Spitfires, and I wanted to be in combat as a fighter," wrote Leon Blanding.[58] Ira Eaker, who would become the commander of most of the Eagles when they joined the American Eighth Air Force, wrote, "They realized the Second World War would eventually involve the United States and that, in the meantime, they should do their gallant best to see that Great Britain survived."[59] The list could go on.

Although most of these examples are of those who joined through the Clayton Knight Committee, the same motivations held true for those who used the other means of entry. Without any question, the primary motivation for each of these men to leave home was the desire to fly the fast, hot ships that were available only in the military. Many had been frustrated in this desire by not qualifying for or being eliminated from the US Army program. Certainly, there was no universal element of uncommon valor or patriotism that drove them to join the RAF, although the press seemed to champion this view throughout the squadrons' existence. On 12 November 1942, *Life,* exercising considerable journalistic license, reported that the Americans went to Britain because "they found it morally impossible to stay out of the battle. They wanted even a small part of the biggest fight in history for the biggest stakes in life."[60] The war and the plight of those whom Germany had conquered was a factor in driving some to want to fight, but they were in the minority.

Such elements as love of freedom, adventure, romance, excitement, glamor, and the desire to be somebody, maybe even a hero, cannot be ruled out. After all, though several Eagles were already established in careers when they signed up, most did not have any career and no real prospects on the horizon. Many had known very little success and saw joining the RAF as a way they could make something of themselves, possibly even start a military career. For many there was also the conviction that the United States would soon be drawn into the war, and they wanted to fly rather than walk when that day came. Very few had any overwhelming desire to save England from the Nazi onslaught. But it is also true that, for most, England's cause eventually became their cause and England's war, their war. Most of the Eagles still have a strong feeling about England today; several, including Jim Goodson and Ervin Miller, live there.

Harold Strickland wrote that he understood there were physical risks involved in his decision to join the RAF. Many of the Eagles will say today that they understood the risks, although many others, like Gus Daymond, recall that they did not consider them at the time. Both positions seem likely. Certainly, few skills a man can master build more self-confidence than does flying. Confidence is one of the inherent traits a pilot must have if he is to be successful. There is no way to predict just what an airplane will do at any given moment or in any given situation. The pilot knows what it *should* do, but a sudden air current, gust of wind, slight change in airspeed or angle of bank will make the machine respond differently. And, of course, a significant malfunction, like an engine failure, a fire, or a structural failure, creates a real emergency when you are several thousand feet above the ground. Any pilot who is really a master at flying must have confidence that he can master any situation that might come along. You can not be afraid and be a successful pilot.

An inherent confidence was quite probably the major reason why most of the Eagles believed they could handle the risks. As for those who said they did not even consider the risks, that too seems plausible, not only because of their confidence as pilots but also because of the general naivete of youth. Young men are the most self-assured group of people in the world, and pilots are probably at the front of the pack. To most young people, injury and death are something that happens to the other guy. And most of the Eagles were young, under 25 years old.

But even those who claim they knew about the risks, considered them, and decided to go anyway probably didn't really understand what they were getting into. There was simply no way they could know. Almost none of them had seen war in any form and none had been in air-to-air combat. The reality of flying an airplane and having another pilot trying to shoot you down was beyond their realm of understanding. Combat is something a person has to experience to understand and appreciate.

Royce Wilkinson had fought over France, at Dunkirk, and in the Battle of Britain, and was already a highly decorated double ace when he was posted to command the Eagles. He believed that there was no way they could have realized the risks involved. In fact, some panicked and ran for home the first time the bullets started to fly. "They got very excited at first," he said, "but they quickly got over it and not one of the boys left for 'lack of moral fiber.'" He believed the Americans all were very brave men and served well.[61] Charles Sweeny and the late Lord Martonmere (Robbie Robinson) both agreed. Sweeny said they all seemed to have some idea of what they were getting into—mostly from newspapers, movies, and the like—when they agreed to fly fighters. He did not believe they appreciated the danger involved, but agreed with Wilkinson that they were a brave group and that all held up once combat started. Lord Martonmere wrote, "at first, many of them did not realize that this adventure might cost them their lives. Casualties, at times, were very high and the pilots quickly realized what the hazards were that they faced."[62]

And so they joined up, some through the Clayton Knight Committee, others after talking with Colonel Sweeny. Several went to Canada and joined the RCAF, and a few came into flying by other diverse routes. But all were to eventually find their way to England and the RAF.

Almost without exception, the main reason for joining the RAF was the desire to fly hot fighter aircraft, the Hurricane and Spitfire. But also, more than half believed that the war would soon involve the United States and, for various reasons, they wanted to be in it. Appreciating that there was some risk associated with flying in combat, most Eagles either did not think much about it or greatly underestimated the reality of injury and death. Some were good flyers, others weren't. Because of the great diversity of flying experience, they had to be brought up to some common level of flying proficiency before joining an operational unit. So training was the next step in their progress toward combat.

3. TRAINING FOR BATTLE

NO ONE IS EXACTLY SURE WHO WERE THE FIRST OF Colonel Sweeny's recruits, but among the first both to go to Europe and to become original members of the Eagles were Vernon Keough, Eugene Tobin, and Andy Mamedoff. Tobin and Mamedoff were both working in Southern California to support their love of flying. They were initially contacted by a Sweeny agent in March 1940 to fly for Finland. Intrigued by the idea, they quit their jobs, sold most of their belongings, and were ready to go when Finland surrendered. Sweeny came to the rescue by offering them the opportunity to fly for France. Each given a train ticket and five dollars, they were off to Montreal. They had been instructed to go to the Mount Royal Hotel, where they were to pick up additional money and further instructions. While waiting for the expected letters, the two met four-foot ten-inch Vernon Keough, another flyer and professional parachutist who had decided to join the French. A friend, it seems, had borrowed his airplane, wrecked it, and left Keough bankrupt.

The three were soon given tickets to Halifax, ten dollars apiece, and instructions that sound as if they were lifted straight from a spy novel: "You will take the night train to Halifax. Upon arrival, remain at the station after the other passengers have departed. Discuss flying in a loud voice so our agent can identify you." The agent appeared and led them through alleys and back streets to the top floor of a deserted building. There they were given pink identity cards and fifty dollars each, and were told to be at the ship the next morning to go to France. After a long voyage, the three arrived in Paris in the middle of May only to find that the hard-pressed French were not interested in training American pilots. Along with a number of other Americans Sweeny had recruited, they spent a month waiting for the call to fly, but to no avail. The French were more interested in fighting for their lives against the Germans than in training fledgling American volunteer pilots.

Finding themselves in danger of being captured by the Germans, the trio joined three Czech pilots in a scheme to steal an airplane and fly to England. Foiled in this attempt, during which the Czechs were mistaken for Germans and shot, the three became part of the mass of refugees streaming out of France. As luck would have it, they were able to find one of the last ships crossing to England, and they arrived in London about the same time France fell. Initially, their efforts to join the RAF also met little interest, but then the three were able to collar a member of Parliament. They told him their story and on 4 July 1940 passed their physicals and signed up as RAF flight officers ready for training. Coincidentally, they also met young Charles Sweeny the same day. Although the young pilots had been recruited by Colonel Sweeny, Charles apparently knew nothing of his uncle's efforts at that time. After dinner and an evening of conversation with Sweeny, the three went off to operational training units (OTUs).

After completing a three-week OTU program, they were posted to existing fighter squadrons, in which they were among the seven Americans who saw action during the Battle of Britain. They would meet Sweeny again in September when Tobin, Keough, and Mamedoff became members of the first Eagle Squadron. In March 1941, the experiences of these three pilots were serialized in *Liberty* magazine. This series of articles certainly helped publicize the Eagles as well as create a rather false air of heroism about their exploits. All three were killed before the end of 1941.[1]

A number of other young American pilots were coming to England in the late summer of 1940 as Colonel Sweeny, now responding to the urging of his nephew in England, took up his role as the recruiting agent for the first Eagle Squadron. Charles Bateman was working in the Los Angeles area, as were most of the first Eagles. He recalled,

> I got word from [the person] who was running Culver City Airport. All he had was a phone number which got me the address of . . . the meeting place, a contractor's office on Melrose Blvd. [Colonel Sweeny] asked us our qualifications as to flying time and told us . . . where to pick up our tickets and expenses to Ottawa. We were then referred to as "Sweeny Candidates," took a flight check and physical, and embarked on the SS *Duchess of Richmond* for Liverpool.[2]

Chesley Peterson, after a first unsuccessful attempt to cross into Canada, successfully negotiated the border and arrived in Ottawa. But having reached their first destination, he and the other "Sweeny Candidates" with him were met with another setback when they found that France had surrendered. It took considerable talking, and some stretching of the truth about their flying time, for Peterson's group to convince the Canadians that they should be sent to England to fly for the RAF. They ultimately succeeded, and in early July this first contingent of the future Eagle Squadrons set sail for England. The group included Peterson; Jim Moore from Duncan, Oklahoma; Edwin Orbison, Dean Satterlee, and Paul Anderson from Sacramento, California; Byron Kennerly from Pasadena, California; and Jim McGinnis from Hollywood, California. Anderson, incidently, was one of the first Eagles killed: a bomb hit a night club in London where he was attending a show.[3]

Gus Daymond was also one of the early Sweeny recruits. He was working at Warner Brothers in Hollywood, flying when he could, when he found out about Sweeny through talk at the airport. After following directions through the back streets of Los Angeles, he found himself at a contractor's shed (the same one where Tobin had first met a Sweeny agent); there he signed up with Sweeny to go to France. His experience in France was similar to that of Tobin, Mamedoff, and Keough, and he too was fortunate to escape to England. Also like Tobin, Mamedoff, and Keough, Daymond was unsuccessful in his initial bid to join the RAF but, when about to be sent home by the American embassy, found a sympathetic member of Parliament who intervened on his behalf and got him into the RAF. After completing a short training tour flying Hurricanes, he was sent to Number 71 Squadron as the youngest Eagle at the time, age 19.[4]

Two other Americans who saw action in the Battle of Britain and became members of the first Eagle Squadron were Philip Leckrone and Arthur Donahue. Leckrone was from Salem, Illinois, where he worked as a flying instructor. He apparently decided to come to England on his own after passing the RAF physical in Windsor, Ontario, on 23 July 1940. After a month at his first and only training base in England, where he arrived on 2 August 1940, he was posted to Number 616 Squadron of Fighter Command, where he saw action against the Germans. On 25 September 1940 he was transferred to Number 71 Eagle Squadron.[5]

Art Donahue arrived in England from Laredo, Texas, shortly before Leckrone. By the time this Minnesota native decided to leave his civilian occupation as a flight instructor and aviation mechanic, he had some 1,814 hours of flying time. He, too, took his physical in Windsor, Ontario, then he sailed to England and was commissioned as a Pilot Officer on 7 July 1940. He was sent to an operational training unit to "learn British fighting tactics and the behavior of British fighting planes."[6] When he completed his training, he was posted to Number 64 Squadron on 4 August 1940, six weeks after leaving home. There was no Eagle Squadron yet. The next day he saw action over the Channel, during which he damaged—possibly destroyed—one Messerschmitt. On 12 August he was shot down and severely burned. After only seven weeks in the hospital and on sick leave, he was posted to 71 Squadron. Donahue was only with the Eagle Squadron for a short time before requesting duty in a more active unit. He subsequently served in Singapore, then returned to England and lost his life over the Channel in 1942.[7]

The pilots who served with the Eagles received varying amounts of training after they arrived in England and before they were posted to an operational squadron. Most of those who arrived after mid-1941 were sent to pre-OTU at Bournemouth, where they received military training and familiarization with the RAF flying system before being assigned to an operational training unit. After November 1941, they were also sent to advanced flying training (AFT) for three weeks of refresher training that included night, instrument, and aerobatic flight before going to an OTU. But the early members of the Eagles, including those who arrived through June 1941, were certainly far from adequately trained when they joined their squadron. Art Roscoe, who went into the RAF in February 1941, summed it up by saying,

> Flight training . . . at OTU in England was good in the areas of aerobatics, formation flying and instrument flying. However, air-to-air and air-to-ground gunnery training was woefully inadequate, most of us learning these skills "on the job."[8]

The only flying in a fighter for this group was at the operational training unit and that was only for a month or less, using a fairly ad hoc curriculum.

There were two apparent reasons for this inadequacy of training. First, as mentioned earlier, the RAF assumed that the recruiting source had ascertained a pilot's ability to fly. Some of the Europeans—Czechs, Poles, Finns, and the like—had military training, but some were straight out of civilian life, as were the Americans. But the British assumed a level of proficiency equal to that gained by completing the RAF pilot training program, and advanced training was predicated on that skill level.

The second factor was simply time. The members of the first Eagle Squadron were arriving in England during the height of the Battle of Britain and there was simply not time to train them extensively. Whether the short time spent at OTU was sufficient was not the issue. Once a pilot was familiar with the Hurricane, which all flew in OTU, he could learn the rest at his operational squadron. And how much the pilot learned before combat depended on the location of his new squadron. Some, like Art Donahue, were put into combat right away. On the other hand, those who formed the first Eagle Squadron and had not been in another RAF organization had over six months of experience before their squadron saw any action.

FORMATION OF NUMBER 71 SQUADRON

By the end of summer 1940, there were enough American pilots flying in the RAF or completing OTU to make Charles Sweeny's all-American squadron a reality. Sweeny had already been in contact with a number of the American pilots and was convinced that they were of the caliber to form the nucleus of the squadron. Furthermore, his brother, Robert, and his uncle, Colonel Charles Sweeny, were on a ship bound for England with William E. G. Taylor, who Sweeny believed was slated to be the commander of the new squadron. It seemed time to make the organization official. According to RAF records, Number 71 Squadron of Fighter Command was formed at Church Fenton on 19 September 1940. Three pilots, Andy Mamedoff, Vernon Keough, and Eugene Tobin, arrived that day, "each with about 50 hours in Spitfires." On 29 September they were followed by Squadron Leader W. M. Churchill, whom the RAF had chosen, rather than Taylor, to be the commander, Pilot Officer F. H. Tann, adjutant, and Pilot Officer Arthur Donahue, out of the hospital after being shot down some seven weeks earlier. The first Eagle Squadron was now a reality and pilots could be posted to it as they came available. Early October saw several arrivals, including Flight Lieutenant George Brown, slated to be one of the flight commanders, and Pilot Officer F. N. B. Bennett, engineering officer. On 4 October Charles Sweeny's choice for commander, W. E. G. Taylor, along with Sweeny's brother, Pilot Officer Robert Sweeny, arrived. Group Captain (Colonel) Charles Sweeny must also have arrived at Church Fenton about that same time since there was a parade in his honor on 7 October. The squadron records obviously are not complete because, according to the record, there were not enough personnel assigned to the squadron on that date to have had a parade.[9]

The strength of the organization was sufficient, though, for Air Minister Sir Archibald Sinclair to summon the press on 8 October 1940 and announce the existence of the new squadron. Sinclair reported that the members of the group "joined spontaneously, following the glorious example set in the World War by the Lafayette Escadrille." At the same time it was made clear that the group would not be required to swear allegiance to the King, for fear of losing their US citizenship.[10] Listed as members of the squadron at the time of the press announcement were Gregory A. Daymond, Paul Harren, William Taylor, Paul Anderson, Luke Allen, Charles Batemen, Victor Bono, Byron Kennerly, Harry LaGuardia, James McGinnis, Richard Moore, Edwin Orbison, Virgil Olson, Chesley Peterson, Ira Sullivan, Dean Satterlee, and Eugene Tobin. In addition, the RAF officially lists Newton Anderson, John Agre, Arthur Donahue, Stanley Goddard, Oliver Holton, Vernon Keough, Stanley Kolendorski, Philip Leckrone, Michael Luczkow, Andrew Mamedoff, Peter Provenzano, Robert Sweeny, and Charles Whitehead as part of the original contingent of Number 71 Squadron. Very few of these pilots were actually present at announcement time. Most were still in training and were to arrive over the next several weeks. The squadron was also without airplanes on 8 October. More than two weeks later, October 24th "was a momentous day for three Brewsters [American Fighters] arrived."[11] Ironically, Pilot Officer Donahue had transferred out of the unit a day earlier because there were no aircraft.

The official announcement also included a description of the squadron badge as approved by the King:

> The badge consists of a spread eagle surmounted with the letters "E.S." These letters represent "Eagle Squadron," the pilots of which will all be American citizens who have volunteered for service with the R.A.F. They will wear the badge and letters on the right arm of their R.A.F. uniform.

All flying units of the RAF adopted both a motto and an emblem. For Number 71 the motto was "First from the Eyries"; the emblem featured a bald eagle charged with three nine-pointed stars. (See the facing page.) The symbolism is interesting. The eagle was shown as the spread American Eagle, representing the origins of the unit personnel. The "twenty-seven points on the stars are symbolic of the twenty six states to which it is known that personnel of this unit belonged, the extra point stands for the State or States which may have been omitted through lack of sufficient information." W. E. G. Taylor was listed as the new commander and Colonel Charles Sweeny as the honorary commander. (The official announcement also credits Sweeny erroneously with forming the Lafayette Escadrille.) A portent of things to come was the paragraph that noted, "There will be many other American pilots who will wish to follow the lead of the first members of the Eagle Squadron and volunteer for service in the Squadron itself or in sister squadrons which will be formed later." There was no mention of either Sweeny or the Clayton Knight Committee as agents for joining the RAF, but the announcement concluded by noting that information about entry could be obtained by "applying

Number 71 Squadron emblem.

in writing or in person to the Eagle Squadron, Royal Air Force, Mount Royal Hotel, Montreal."[12]

The announcement brought a barrage of media attention that was to last for a number of months. Nearly every major newspaper in the United States carried a lengthy article on the unit, and stories of individuals in the organization abounded. Young men who had been disregarded or thought to be rather foolish a few months earlier when they had signed up to join the RAF were now the heroes of the day. Chesley Peterson, for example, was the subject of scores of articles in the Salt Lake

City newspapers alone; William Taylor's biography became common national media fare.

The accounts in the press were to some degree misleading, however, because being declared an operational squadron and going into combat were two very different things. On 8 October 1940 Number 71 Squadron had no airplanes, nor were any on the horizon. The pilots, with only three weeks of training to bolster their civilian experience, were a very long way from being a real operational asset for the RAF. The New York *Herald Tribune* told its readers, "Much more training will be necessary before they are ready for combat."[13] It would be ten months before the Eagle Squadron would take its place with the other RAF units engaging the Germans over the English Channel. By that time the second Eagle Squadron, Number 121, would also be operational, and Number 133, the third squadron of Eagles, would be only a month from reality. Several of the pilots who were listed as original Squadron members would be either dead or transferred by the time the shooting really began. But *Life* magazine put this delay into perspective when it said, "Significant of England's comfortable margin of manpower is the fact that these Americans, all experienced fliers when they began, were given six months training before they were sent into action."[14]

The majority of Eagles did not rush through the brief training program of the early members, but arrived at their squadron reasonably well qualified to assume their operational role. Before considering the history of each of the Eagle Squadrons as they became operational, it is useful to look at the training programs nearly all the Eagles passed through: the US Civilian Pilot Training Program, the RAF training program in the United States, and the program used in Canada by the RCAF.

CIVILIAN PILOT TRAINING PROGRAM

The pilots who became members of the Eagle squadrons learned to fly from many different sources, but the Civilian Pilot Training Program (CPTP) provided initial flight training for over half of them. This program was designed to help civilian airport operators, who had been hit hard by the depression, and build a cadre of young Americans who knew how to fly. The initial goal of the CPTP was to teach flying to 20,000 college students. In the process, each would get from 35 to 50 hours of flying at a local airport, while the college or university the trainees attended would teach a 72-hour ground school. The total cost to the student was $40.00. In January 1940 the student base was expanded to allow up to seven percent of those enrolled to be non-college students.

The war in Europe completely changed the nature of the CPTP, the shortage of military pilots rapidly changing training priorities. The president's call for 50,000 planes annually from the American aircraft industry generated a great need for pilots. So the Civil Aeronautics Administration (CAA) announced that the training goal beginning on 1 July 1940 would be 45,000 in primary pilot training and 9,000 in advanced training. The number of volunteers was consistent with the goals: nearly 50,000 signed up by the end of the year. After the United States entered the war, the program changed even more. All the CPTP facilities were taken over by the military and the curriculum was revised to focus on military flying. The age limit for entry was dropped and uniforms became required for trainees, who were now billeted on the training base. By 1942, older volunteers were accepted to train as glider pilots, instructors, cargo pilots, and the like. The civilian training program reached its height in mid-1942 and was phased out in 1944 because the military no longer needed voluntary pilot enlistments.

Aside from the fact that many Eagles received their initial flight training with the CPTP, the program has an additional significance to the squadrons. Flyers who signed up after the initial cadre of volunteers was sent to

England by Colonel Charles Sweeny and the Knight Committee, were trained in the United States. The fields where they trained and the instructors who trained them were those that had been developed and employed by the CPTP. In fact, the future RAF pilots flew at the same bases, in some of the same aircraft, under some of the same instructors as were being used to teach future US Army and Navy pilots. Without the CPTP there probably would not have been a cadre of pilots for the Clayton Knight Committee to recruit nor airfields at which to train them.[15]

RAF TRAINING SCHOOLS IN THE UNITED STATES

Even before World War II actually began, British officials were considering the possibility of obtaining pilot training help from the United States. But in May 1940, when it seemed apparent that the British would be short of pilots by the end of the year, the suggestion was made that flight training might be done in either the United States or Canada using American airplanes and instructors. When the idea was broached to Ambassador Kennedy, he responded favorably and forwarded it to Washington, where the reaction was also positive. Further discussions led to an unofficial American position that it would be better, given US neutrality, to train RAF pilots in Canada with American planes and instructors. This arrangement was, in essence, a key part of what came to be known as the Empire Training Scheme.

The intensity of the Battle of Britain and its attrition of Britain's pilots led the British to reopen the discussion of direct training in the United States in August 1940. The American public was certainly pro-British and seemed to agree that some sort of aid, short of actually joining the conflict, might be appropriate. The main difficulty appeared to be lack of training aircraft, which were in short supply in both the United States and Britain. The alternative to military training was to use civil aviation school operators in the United States who were already doing training for the Army, but lack of aircraft was again a stumbling block.

Despite the aircraft shortage, the British succeeded in setting up three small schools, owned and operated by civilians who initially used their own aircraft, to provide refresher training for experienced American pilots. These schools became operational in November 1940. Their purpose was to give up to 150 hours of training to American volunteers, most of whom were signed up by the Clayton Knight Committee, before they were sent to England. Although the schools operated under the pretense of producing ferry pilots, they actually focused on training fighter and bomber pilots, many of whom would be bound for the Eagle Squadrons.

These schools were the Spartan School of Aeronautics in Tulsa, Oklahoma, owned by Captain Maxwell W. Balfour; the Dallas Aviation School in Dallas, Texas, owned by Major William F. Long; and Polaris Flight Academy in Glendale, California, operated by Major C. C. Moseley. Balfour, Long, and Moseley were all World War I pilots who had gone into the aviation business and established well-regarded flying operations during the 1920s and 1930s. All the pilots who signed up for Eagle duty after November 1940 were sent to one of these schools, as were many candidates for other units. Kern County Airport in Bakersfield, California, was added to the list in early 1941. The first students there came from the Dallas facility, which had become overcrowded. Bakersfield continued as a regular training location and eventually became the largest of the training facilities for Clayton Knight–recruited pilots.[16]

This small training system was far from what the British had in mind, so negotiations continued. On 5 March 1941 General Hap Arnold announced that as soon as the Lend-Lease Bill was passed the US Army would offer Britain 260 primary and 285 advanced aircraft to train British pilots in US Army schools. The training concept, known as the All-through Scheme, was adopted in April 1941. It called for construction of six

new schools, operated by American contractors, to produce about 3,000 pilots a year. The term *all-through*
referred to the fact that British pilots would complete all
their training, except the OTU, in the United States.
From the six new facilities, officially named the British
Flying Training Schools (BFTSs), graduates went to
three US Army basic schools and then to three advanced
schools. None of these schools trained pilots for the
Eagle Squadrons.

Establishment of the All-through system does not
end the RAF training story, but the details of the entire
British training system are beyond the scope of this book.
Suffice it to say that, despite much disagreement and
controversy between the RAF and the US Army over
curriculum, washout criteria, number of flying hours,
and the like, the system trained several thousand pilots
for the beleaguered RAF and was a successful partner-
ship by any standards.

But only the four schools at Tulsa, Dallas, Glendale,
and Bakersfield were involved in refresher training for
the Eagle Squadrons. These schools fulfilled their primary mission of getting the experienced Americans who
had been recruited through the Clayton Knight organization to a standard level of proficiency so they could enter
OTU in England.

For most of the fledgling Eagles, the schools introduced the reality of being in the RAF flying program.
Ervin Miller reacted typically when he went to the Spartan School of Aeronautics in Tulsa. "This was a terrific
experience," he said.

> Here there were 26 or 30 other civilian pilot volunteers who
> were as amazed as I that even though we were not yet at war,
> and were a declared neutral nation, here we were, paid by
> Britain and flying US Army PT–19s, Stearmans and North
> American AT–6s.[17]

The schools differed greatly in many respects, however,
and were not without their problems, four of which dominated the operation from the beginning.

The most significant problem was the lack of a standardized syllabus. This was partly a result of the initial students entering the refresher schools individually rather than as a class. Additionally, the contractors who ran the schools, all having been in the aviation business for many years, each had his own idea of just how to most effectively train a pilot and, from their World War I experience, what was required to be successful in war. Therefore, the overall idea was to match the training to the individual pilot's ability and experience. Because each individual signing up for the training had a different flying background, it was almost impossible to establish any common starting point or set curriculum. As a result, each student got different numbers of hours in different areas of training and finished pretty much when the instructor said he was proficient. So it was impossible to assume any standard level of competence upon reaching the OTU, a problem already mentioned and to be discussed more later.

At Dallas, for example, some students passed with only 3 hours of flying. Carroll McColpin flew about 30 hours and had 4 or 5 hours in the Link trainer before he was sent off to England to avoid being drafted. Marion Jackson reported between 60 and 70 hours and Leo Nomis flew about 80.[18] The training content also varied considerably. When Edwin Taylor entered the program at Dallas, there was no syllabus and the students "just played around." The same was true when he arrived at Bakersfield, where he received no instrument time and spent much of his 20 hours in the AT–6 "sneaking off to fly through the Grand Canyon."[19] On the other hand, by the time John Campbell, who entered Polaris in late 1940, departed for England in March 1941, he had about 100 hours of "good instrument, night, formation and aerobatic instruction." Art Roscoe's recollection echoes Campbell's.[20]

A good deal of this curriculum problem was addressed in March 1941, when students began entering the refresher schools in classes and going through their training on that basis. At the same time, the RAF began to establish a standard curriculum for each of the schools. The quality of training slowly improved throughout the remainder of the year. Nonetheless, there was never a uniform curriculum at all four facilities and the number of hours and types of flying continued to vary greatly. For example, in mid-1941 Gene Fetrow flew 6.1 hours in the Ryan ST, 30.3 in the Stearman, 18.2 in the Vultee BT–13, 1.3 in the AT–6, and 5.5 in the Spartan 7–W; his experience included 18 hours on instruments and 13 in the Link trainer. Six months later, Robert Priser had a typical 37 hours dual, 30 solo, 17 instrument, and 23 in the Link trainer.[21]

The second area of concern was the quality of instructors. By early 1941, every flying instructor in the United States was besieged with offers from various flying schools. It did not matter what the instructors' records were, so long as they had the required credentials to legally teach flying. This demand for instructors made it very difficult to obtain uniformly excellent instructors at the refresher schools, thus the quality varied significantly. The uneven quality of instruction compounded problems caused by the lack of a standardized syllabus. A marginally qualified pilot might be given an instructor with like qualifications and so be instructed incorrectly, but be given credit for satisfactorily completing a phase of training when he lacked basic proficiency, or even graduated from the course and sent to England without having mastered the skills for which he was sent to school. During an early 1941 inspection tour, the RAF found that at Glendale there was practically no syllabus and much of the instruction was incorrect. At Tulsa they found that *no* instruction was given well. To address this problem, the British began periodic proficiency checks in early 1941 to ensure that the quality of instruction met defined standards. Given the great divergence of experiences the Eagle pilots had at these schools, the quality of their training appears to have been a function mainly of the caliber of their instructors.

Before criticizing the refresher schools too harshly for this situation, however, we should remember that each of these schools either came into existence in only two to three months or was called upon to increase the size of its student body several times over in an equally short period of time. Lacking a training syllabus from the RAF, they had little choice but to just expand whatever they had been doing to train small numbers of private civilian pilots. Even as the RAF began to develop a syllabus, problems continued because the British wanted to make the instruction conform as nearly as possible to RAF requirements and methods while the Americans found it difficult to understand the reasons for some of the RAF demands. And in order to fulfill the terms of their contracts with the RAF, the school operators were obliged to take whomever they could get as instructors and then endure the consequences.

The third, albeit less serious, problem was the differences in aircraft flown at the four refresher bases, particularly in early 1941. Recall that one of the problems that initially caused the idea of RAF training in the United States to founder was lack of aircraft. When the individual contractors agreed to take on training the RAF candidates, they were required to furnish their own aircraft. This led to an interesting mix, from the simple Piper Cub to the powerful, advanced Staggerwing Beechcraft and Spartan Executive. Obviously, the type of aircraft used at the refresher school was a factor in the proficiency of the graduate and his ability to handle the more than 1,000 horsepower of the Hurricane and Spitfire. Edwin Taylor flew K5 Fleet biplanes and the Staggerwing Beech at Dallas, then, after moving to Bakersfield, spent his time in the AT–6. LeRoy Gover, a few months later, began his program at Bakersfield in the PT–17 and finished in the AT–6. At about the same time, Leo Nomis was flying a 1931 Stearman, the Ryan ST, and the Spartan Executive at Glendale.[22] As with the syllabus, as time went on the aircraft became more standardized: by the beginning of

1942 all the schools had the PT–17 and the AT–6, the same aircraft being used at US Army training facilities.

Finally, there was the problem of housing, feeding, clothing, and paying the students at the refresher schools. Here again, the schools were simply overloaded. None of the facilities contracted with by the RAF had any existing student housing, so they had to build what they could and find enough other suitable housing wherever possible. Students were housed in rather crude barracks at Glendale, for example, and ate in a mess hall. At Bakersfield, they lived in the homes of people in the community and ate at a cafeteria in town. In Dallas, both the Knight recruits and a group of mechanic students lived together in barracks, five to a room, and a mess hall provided the food. Uniforms were also a problem: students at Dallas wore bright blue flying coveralls, those at Glendale went to school in their civilian clothing.

The method of payment also seems to have varied during the early period of the schools' existence. Some students recall being given cash every week while others got checks at various intervals. Most of the Eagles I have interviewed did not know the source of the money they were paid or who was financing their training, nor did they care at the time. In contrast, Leo Nomis recalls that at Glendale it was well known that the funds were from the British, paid through the Cal-Aero Corporation, the parent organization of Polaris Flight Academy. Nomis even went so far as to say that he thought the funds were part of Lend-Lease.[23]

Despite the problems, the quality of the pilots completing the refresher courses, arriving at the OTU, and joining operational squadrons continued to improve throughout the existence of the Eagle Squadrons. This increasing pilot proficiency led directly to lower casualty rates in both training and combat and to a much more rapid transition into combat-ready status by individual pilots after joining the squadron.[24]

Members of an RAF refresher class at Dallas Aviation School, assembled in front of a Staggerwing Beech, an advanced executive aircraft used for training at the contract bases. Among the class members are several future Eagles, including (top row, left to right) Vernon Parker, Douglas Booth, Edwin Taylor, Thomas Andrews, George Sperry, Roger Atkinson, (bottom row, left to right) Roland Wolfe, Gilmore Daniel, and Harry Hain.

TRAINING IN THE ROYAL CANADIAN AIR FORCE

Nearly 20 percent of the pilots who became Eagles were members of the Royal Canadian Air Force (RCAF) when they arrived in England. Most of these flyers fell into two categories. First, there were those who joined the RCAF because they were eager to get into the war and saw that as the only avenue. Most of these individuals did not know about the Clayton Knight Committee or were not in a location where it was convenient to make contact with that organization. It was much simpler for them to go across the border and sign up. This action was not without risk, however. Because of the tremendous demands placed on the RCAF by the Empire Training

Scheme and the desperate shortage of qualified instructors, a great number of the young Americans who took this course of action ended up as instructors in the RCAF training system rather than as fighter or bomber pilots in the RAF. The second category of Eagles who were trained by the RCAF were those who simply found themselves in England or Canada at the beginning of the war and decided to get involved as rapidly as possible. Jim Goodson and Bill Dunn signed on in England and were sent to Canada for training.

The RCAF syllabus was very different from that pursued by the Knight recruits in the United States, and it probably prepared the student better for what he would face when he got to England. First, it was a complete training program that involved military as well as flight training. Reade Tilley enlisted on 10 June 1940 and spent until 16 September just in military training.

The second difference was that the RCAF had a complete and standard syllabus, which it held in common with the other participants in the Empire Training Scheme. This syllabus, designed by the RAF, ensured that pilots graduating from the Canadian program were fully ready to go to an operational training unit in England. In addition to the standardized syllabus, all the RCAF bases trained using the same type of aircraft. The instructor cadre was also more qualified, consisting primarily of Canadian flying officers (some of whom had experience in World War I), a large number of Canadian civilians who had been brought into the RCAF specifically to instruct, and a significant group of Americans recruited to come to Canada for the same purpose. Reade Tilley received a total of 52 hours flying basics, 25 dual, and 27 solo, and an introduction to aerobatics in the Tiger Moth at his Elementary Flying Training Squadron (EFTS) from 16 September to 17 November 1940. He then moved to a Secondary Flying Training Squadron (SFTS), where, between 19 November 1940 and 24 January 1941, he flew 80 hours in the AT–6, split about 35 hours dual and 45 solo, including 20 hours of instruments, 6 of night flying, and extensive aerobatics. He was then posted to England for operational training.[25]

A third significant difference was that those who wanted to go to pilot training with the RCAF had to first enlist and then apply for flying duty after completing basic training. This procedure involved numerous physical and aptitude tests as well as examinations in such academic areas as mathematics. Even after completing pilot training, they had to volunteer and be accepted for oversea duty in order to get to England. This process had two important effects for the Americans who qualified. First, it meant that when they completed pilot training and joined their operational squadrons in England, they did so as sergeant pilots, as opposed to those recruited through the Knight Committee, who were officers. Being a sergeant pilot meant living in separate barracks, having different facilities, and generally not socializing with the officers in the squadron. Although this difference in rank and status was forgotten or ignored while flying, it did delineate both relationships and conduct while on the ground and, in several Eagles' opinions, had significant consequences for effectiveness. Richard Alexander put it well, saying,

> The chief disadvantage that the Sergeants had was that they were isolated from the experienced pilots in the Officer's Mess. In all of the talk sessions in the lounge or in the bar, a young Pilot Officer could benefit from the knowledge of a Flight Lieutenant or Squadron Leader or Wing Commander. There were many lessons to be learned. The advantages to two-handed shooting, of trying to make your bounce from out of the sun, of learning to make tight right-hand turns because of the Me–109's inability to turn tightly to the right. . . . The Sergeants shared none of this, simply because by the time a Sergeant became a Flight Sergeant, he had either gotten a commission and moved up to the Officer's Mess or he was dead![26]

The American sergeant pilots were all integrated into the US Army Air Force as officers. A number of

Americans who enlisted, though, were never selected for flying training and served out the war in the RCAF as ground crews or in other support capacities. Still others decided not to volunteer to go to England, and so stayed in Canada or even returned to the United States. Clearly, for the young man who wanted to fly fighters, joining the RCAF was risky.[27]

Fourth, those Americans who joined the RCAF and then became members of the Eagle Squadrons remained members of the RCAF until they transferred to the US Army Air Force. Being an RCAF member in an RAF squadron was not unusual, for pilots from all the countries of the British Commonwealth served with the RAF. Nonetheless, those who entered the RAF through the Knight organization were classed as RAF officers while those who enlisted in the RCAF were carried on the rolls as members of the Canadian forces serving in the RAF. For example, when Flight Sergeant Walter Wicker was killed on 27 April 1942, notification of his death came from the RCAF and he was listed as a Canadian casualty.[28]

Finally, joining the RCAF also complicated the citizenship issue for several Eagles. In fact, the subject of citizenship warrants a separate discussion.

CITIZENSHIP

For several of the Eagles, citizenship was a vexing issue. The problem was really two-fold. First, the Citizenship Act of 1907 provided that any American citizen swearing allegiance to any foreign state or sovereign would lose his citizenship. The second issue, directly related, had to do with the US Neutrality Laws. These laws, passed almost annually from 1936 through 1941, were designed to prevent circumstances arising that could draw the United States into the war in Europe. Of particular significance regarding citizenship was the 1940 act, which specified that service in the armed forces of a foreign power without authorization and with a consequent acquisition of foreign nationality would also expatriate an individual. The preceding neutrality act had specified that travel through a designated war zone or on board a belligerent ship could result in a prison sentence of up to two years and/or a $10,000 fine. This restriction was compounded by a provision that joining the armed forces of a belligerent nation was illegal, and doing so carried the same penalty as did disobeying the travel provision.[29]

The collapse of France in June 1940 brought about the first significant modification to the citizenship penalty. In an 18 June 1940 telegram to the US embassy in London, the State Department noted,

> While the Department looks with disfavor upon service of American citizens in any military unit in any way connected with a foreign army, American citizens who while outside of the United States join a military unit as part of a foreign army or under orders of an officer of such an army do not in doing so violate the laws of the United States nor are they required to obtain permission to join such unit from any official of this Government. However, if an oath of allegiance to a foreign country is required, American citizenship would be lost under Section 2, Act March 2, 1907. While serving in such military unit citizens could not look for protection by the United States against legitimate consequences of their conduct.

This same telegram suggested that the issue of an oath be discussed with British officials.[30] Action was swift, whether or not any discussions ever occurred: the next day, 19 June, the British issued an Order in Council that specified, "oaths of allegiance to the Crown were no longer required of American citizens who entered the army or air force."[31] Such an oath had never been required for service in the British Navy. The commissioning document that resulted said nothing about an oath of allegiance but, rather, stated,

> we do hereby command them to obey you as their superior Officer and you to observe and follow such orders and direc-

George R.I.

George VI *by the Grace of God*, OF GREAT BRITAIN, IRELAND AND THE BRITISH DOMINIONS BEYOND THE SEAS, KING, DEFENDER OF THE FAITH, EMPEROR OF INDIA, *&c.*

To Our Trusty and well beloved   **Edwin Dale Taylor**   Greeting :

WE *reposing especial Trust and Confidence in your Loyalty, Courage, and good Conduct, do by these Presents Constitute and Appoint you to be an Officer in Our* Royal Air Force Volunteer Reserve *from the* Tenth *day of* July *19* 41 *. You are therefore carefully and diligently to discharge your Duty as such in the Rank of* Pilot Officer *or in such higher Rank as We may from time to time hereafter be pleased to promote or appoint you to and you are at all times to exercise and well discipline in their Duties both the inferior Officers and Airmen serving under you and use your best endeavours to keep them in good Order and Discipline. And We do hereby Command them to Obey you as their superior Officer and you to observe and follow such Orders and Directions as from time to time you shall receive from Us, or any your superior Officer, according to the Rules and Discipline of War, in pursuance of the Trust hereby reposed in you.*

GIVEN at Our Court, at Saint James's the Fifth day of August 19 41 in the Fifth   Year of Our Reign

By **His Majesty's** *Command*

Edwin Taylor's appointment as an officer in the RAF Volunteer Reserve. For most of the Eagles, this document was the prize at the end of long training and the voyage across the Atlantic. The text is carefully worded to avoid the problem of swearing allegiance to the King and thus losing US citizenship.

tions as from time to time you shall receive from us, or any your superior officer, according to the rules and discipline of war, in pursuance of the trust hereby reposed in you.[32] [See the illustration above.]

The public received notice of the reality of the situation when, on 20 November 1940, *The New York Times* reported, "The State Department . . . has decided not to take cognizance of questions of law which might be raised in connection with the service of members of the Eagle Squadron and other Americans with the Royal Air Force in England."[33]

Despite these rulings, a number of men who joined the British forces were required to take an oath of allegiance, thus expatriating themselves. These included Reade Tilley, Carroll McColpin, and Oscar Coen. It appears that this was a matter of when and where they entered the foreign military, since McColpin went into the RAF and Tilley and Coen enlisted in the Royal Canadian Air Force all at about the same time. Apparently several, like McColpin, were erroneously given the oath because they were in groups made up primarily of members of the British Commonwealth when they were sworn into the RAF. Efforts to resolve this situation began as early as February 1941 when, at the urging of Reade Tilley's father, Senator Claude Pepper introduced a bill to restore citizenship to those who, like Tilley, had joined a foreign force. In a letter to Reade Tilley Sr., Pepper pledged to bring about the passage of the bill as soon as possible, but he was unable to get the bill to the Senate floor because of more pressing matters and the coming of US involvement in the war.[34] The matter then languished until the late 1950s, when the Supreme Court was asked to rule on portions of the 1907 and 1940 laws. Further court cases followed, and in *Schneider v Rusk* (1964) the issue was decided, the court ruling that expatriation for residence in a foreign country was not constitutional if the individual involved was a native-born US citizen. The matter is further clarified in Title 8 of the US Code.[35]

Because of the issue's history, there is considerable question as to when various Eagles regained their citizenship. Reade Tilley erroneously believed he had his back when he went into the US Army Air Corps in 1943. Carroll McColpin, Oscar Coen, and others found in the late 1960s, when either they or members of their families applied for passports, that they were not citizens. Not until the early 1970s were all the expatriated Eagles safely back in the fold as US citizens. Compounding the strangeness of the situation is the fact that several of these Eagles served full military careers with US forces and retired, McColpin as a major general and Tilley and Coen as colonels, without being US citizens during part or all of their service.[36]

Probably the most unusual citizenship case was that of Steve Pisanos, who was a Greek citizen when he joined the RAF through the Clayton Knight Committee. In order for him to transfer to the US Army Air Force, he had to become a US citizen. Through the efforts of several embassy officials and his commander, Chesley Peterson, Pisanos took his oath of citizenship in England in 1942, a first, he believes, in the annals of American citizenship.[37]

Certainly, the citizenship problem offers one more example of the dedication of these young men who went to fly for the RAF during World War II. Marion Jackson probably summed up the view of most of the Eagles regarding the citizenship issue:

> The issue of possibly losing our citizenship was no secret. We were told that we would probably lose it but I don't think that bothered most of us. We were quite confident that the United States would get into the war and when they did we would all be taken care of.[38]

Jim Gray agreed.[39] Nevertheless, they were taking a chance when they joined the RAF. But most Eagles simply wanted to fly high-performance aircraft, and many believed in the British cause as well. Most would not have let any posible outcomes of the citizenship issue dissuade them.

VOYAGE ACROSS THE ATLANTIC

Whether or not they trained with the RCAF, almost all of the Eagles at least passed through Canada, because it was from Canadian ports that the eager young flyers departed for their adventure in England. It was the journey from the new to the old world that also brought many of them face to face with the realities of war and the commitment they had made. For the early recruits, such as Chesley Peterson, the trip to Canada was a challenging game of cat-and-mouse with the law. The detailed instructions issued to "Sweeny Candidate" Morris Fessler are illustrative of the system.

A lengthy letter from the United Kingdom Air Liaison Mission, dated 2 November 1940 and stamped as "Secret and Confidential," instructed Fessler to take a train from Union Station in Ottawa to Windsor Station, Montreal, where he would be met by an agent of the shipping company and taken aboard the *Duchess of Atholl*. He was to limit his baggage to 150 pounds on the train and 336 pounds on the ship. He was given seven dollars for expenses on board ship and another five dollars a day to cover expenses before departing for England. On arrival in England, he was to be met by another officer, who would get him on a train to London, where he was to report to the Air Ministry, Room 507, Adastral House, Kingsway, London. The letter concluded by reassuring Fessler,

> On arrival at the London terminus you should enquire for the Royal Air Force transport officer: if you find yourself in any difficulties at this, or any other time during your journey in the United Kingdom, you should report to a police officer who can be relied upon to help you. You should be ready to produce this letter to the authorities, on request, both on embarkation in Canada and at the port of arrival: it will be accepted as your authority for entering the United Kingdom.[40]

Charles Cook came into the United Kingdom via Glasgow, Scotland, with a much different entry instrument:

> The Bearer, *Cook, Charles Albert*, who states that he is of *American* nationality, is permitted to land at *Glasgow* on condition that he reports at once to the Air Ministry, London, and subject to such conditions as may thereafter be imposed.
>
> Signed _____ ,
Immigration Officer.[41]

I.B. 23.

The Bearer COOK, Charles Albert who

states that he is of American

nationality, is permitted to land at Glasgow

on condition that— *he reports at once to the Air Ministry, London and subject to such further conditions as may thereafter be imposed*

—

(Signed)

Immigration Officer's
Stamp.

21 AUG 1941

GLASGOW

Signature of Bearer

Charles Cook's authorization to enter the United Kingdom, one of several different instruments that were used.

By the time the Knight Committee pilots were making the trip, a routine had been pretty well established and the venture was no longer a clandestine affair. For most, it meant a long train trip to Canada, generally Ottawa, followed by various kinds of processing and then a further trip by rail to the port of embarkation.

Ervin Miller recalls that all the students in his class at Tulsa were given a final briefing on how to legally go into Canada before they left their training base.

> I was told to report to my draft board in Sacramento and inform them I intended to go on vacation to Canada for a week. This was a condition which draftees had to comply with because draft boards kept tabs on their charges at all times. When I crossed the border I would then be a pilot officer in the Royal Air Force and would not have to contact the draft board any further.

Miller then went by train to Monkton, Ontario, where he joined a group of his fellow trainees for the trip to Halifax, Nova Scotia, and the voyage to England.[42]

Don Nee joined his fellow trainees from Tulsa in New York City and went by train to Ottawa, which was the more typical route. With most of his fellow recruits, Nee spent a week there processing and seeing the town and then began a sporadic rail trip that eventually ended in Halifax, where they boarded their ship.[43] LeRoy Gover had a longer trip to Canada. He left Oakland, California, on the evening of 3 November 1941, stopped for a day in Ogden, Utah, and arrived in Chicago on 7 November. There he was joined by Don Young and embarked for Ottawa, arriving on Saturday 8 November. Upon arrival in Ottawa, they were "met by RAF representatives and checked in at Lord Elgin Hotel." On Monday he went to RAF headquarters and received his salary of $7.50, which was paid every day. By Wednesday, 12 November, he was on his way to Halifax. He departed for England on 21 November.[44]

At their first stop in Canada, some of the candidates, including George Sperry, were confronted with a flight check ride.[45] This flight appears to have been a random requirement and served as a spot check on the quality of instruction in the United States. Whether because of adequate skills or the desperate need for pilots, there is no record of anyone failing the check ride. It was also in Ottawa that most of the Americans were processed into the RAF, but evidently not given their commissions. Most were either told they were officers in the RAF when they departed Canada for England or else given an envelope containing their commission certificates when they boarded ship. Bob Smith received an envelope in Ottawa to be opened when he boarded ship. It contained both his orders to England and his commission in the RAF.[46] So, for most of the Eagles, the latter part of the trip to England was made as an RAF officer. One would never have known the young men were officers, however, since all were in their civilian clothes. They did not receive their uniforms until arrival in London.

The sea voyage itself was, for most Eagles, a major concern. There was probably no more hazardous body of water in the world during 1940 and 1941 than the North Atlantic. Convoys carrying essential war material were streaming from North America to England, and the German submarines were doing all in their power to prevent these ships from arriving at their destination. It was a voyage across that dangerous ocean that every one of the Americans who joined the RAF endured. The length of the trip varied depending on the type of ship and the tactics employed to avoid the Germans. Because of the great demand for shipping, and the losses to German submarines, the British were hiring into service any vessel that had a possibility of making it across the sea. Circumstances of the crossing, therefore, varied greatly. Every one of the Eagles I have talked with had vivid recollections of that voyage; for most, it was a trying experience.

George Sperry made the crossing on the SS *Bayano*, a converted banana boat, as part of an 80-ship convoy that went around the top of Iceland. The SS *Letitia*, which Ervin Miller described as "a very small tub," sailed in the northern group of a two part convoy; the portion of the convoy that took the southern route suffered very heavy losses. While some crossings took nearly a month, Don Nee's passage on a Dutch freighter, the SS *Maaskerk*, took only thirteen days. That voyage, as well as the eleven-day crossing by Harold Strickland on the Norwegian ship

SS *Olaf*, was made without the vessel being part of a convoy.[47]

Lee Gover's diary provides a vivid description of his voyage. He departed Halifax on 21 November 1941 and the next day reported that he was feeling pretty seasick. "Subs are reported to be near—can't see any other boats," he noted that evening, but the next morning he saw "boats all around us . . . I counted 44. There are two destroyers zig zagging out in front looking for subs." Although instructed to sleep in his clothes and wear a life belt at all times, on 24 November Gover "took off my clothes last night after I found the boat was loaded with live ammunition. . . . There are now just 37 of us— one tanker went down last night and three others just disappeared." His report on the 29th included the comment, "it is beginning to look bad now—40 minutes ago one of our tankers in the rear was sunk. . . . I'm not so worried anymore about subs, they either sink you or they don't." By the following Tuesday, he wrote, "the ship now stinks so bad you can't eat," and "the crew members are betting we never make it." Gover arrived at Liverpool on 6 December and disembarked the next day.[48] If Gover had fears about his cargo, Marion Jackson could take some reassurance in his old banana boat's "four Hurricanes lashed to the deck, 2,000–3,000 tons of bacon in the hold, and the remainder of the cargo Kotex [sanitary napkins]." His ship went so far north it was "like a floating iceberg and you could read a newspaper on deck at night." Jackson's total crossing time was 31 days, all of it in his California clothes.[49]

In contrast to most of the other descriptions of the voyage, to Robert Smith, who had always loved the sea, "it was marvelous."

> The North Atlantic in the middle of winter, on a 16,000–ton freighter, the SS *Beaverhill*, was one of the few experiences that lived up to what I had imagined it to be like. The bow of the ship disappearing beneath the waves and then coming up with green water cascading off and foam and ice, and the ship just clad in ice pushing through the mountainous waves.

COURTESY OF DON YOUNG

Don Young aboard the SS Emma Alexander *between Halifax and Liverpool. All of the Eagles had to brave the North Atlantic to reach Britain.*

> The bow of the ship I'd swear was like an elevator going up in the air 60 to 80 feet at a time.

Smith's ship was part of a convoy in which a number of vessels were torpedoed and sunk. The experience made Smith "realize this was for keeps. It wasn't just a story."[50]

A few of the Eagles were unknowingly reviewed by Prime Minister Churchill on the high seas when his battleship, *Prince of Wales*, overtook the convoy in which Charles Cook, Wilson (Bill) Edwards, and William Wallace were being transported to England. Churchill was on his way home from his August 1941 meeting with President Roosevelt that produced the Atlantic Charter. Little did these future Eagles know that the decision for the United States to enter the war on England's side had, for all practical purposes, been made while they were steaming to England.[51]

There is no account of how many flyers lost their lives during the crossing, but certainly it was a significant number. Because actual assignments to the Eagle Squadrons were not made until after completion of OTU, there is no way of knowing just how many potential Eagles were lost. Several accounts, however, speak of flyers trained at the RAF training facilities in the United States being lost at sea. At any rate, the young volunteers endured considerable hardship on the treacherous North Atlantic before they ever set foot on English soil.

ENGLAND AND INITIAL ASSIGNMENT

It is not easy to imagine the excitement the young American pilots felt when they first arrived in England. Not only had they completed a long, treacherous voyage, but they were now face-to-face with war and the cause they had come to support. The face of war and the reality of what the young men had bargained for became evident in various ways. "Upon arriving in Liverpool," remarked Carroll McColpin, "it didn't take us long to realize that there was very much of a war on."

> As the ship was being docked, air raid sirens sounded and everyone scurried below decks. Everyone except our group of crazy Americans. We had come to fight a war and we felt completely justified in seeing what it was like. Overhead, the misty afternoon became filled with whirling black specks and small ominous clouds of flak. Below, the ground shook as bomb after bomb found its mark. The horizon became singed with red and orange hues as block after city block erupted in fire and smoke. We paid little attention to this panorama of death and destruction. What we wanted to see were the flaming remnants of German planes twisting down from the sky. We weren't disappointed. I saw several shot down by Spitfires and another by artillery. That night we "calmly" continued on to London.[52]

For Marion Jackson, arrival brought not only his first air raid but also a trip to the shelter, where he and his fellow voyagers were an unusual sight in their California clothes, asking questions about what was going on. The

British, too, were trying to find out just what a group of young Americans was doing in Liverpool at the height of a bombing raid.[53] Most Eagles echoed Bob Smith's observation that, despite the destruction from bombing, the British people were generally cheerful and confident.

No matter where they disembarked, the Americans did not remain long at the port. Most were on the train to London within a few hours. The experience is vividly recalled by George Sperry. His first view of England

> was not reassuring . . . as we viewed the brick rubble that had once constituted the city of Bristol. . . . Later as we traveled across Southern England, the rolling hills and quaint farmland glided to left and right of the railway line, bathed in the late spring sunshine. We felt better as we neared London . . . meeting us was Charles Sweeny, official greeter and founding father of the Eagles.[54]

Bill Edwards' impressions, while not as vivid, are quite telling.

> I think after our seeing London . . . and the damage done by the bombing, reality started to sink in. We realized that this was for real and that we were involved in a war.[55]

In contrast, those who travelled at night saw nothing because the entire countryside was blacked out.

Most of the Eagles were not met by Sweeny, and a number of the Americans did not even know they were going to be Eagles when they reached England. Most of the new pilots went straight to the Air Ministry, no matter what the hour, where they were signed in and directed to one of several hotels, such as the Regent Palace for Ervin Miller or the Overseas Club for Lee Gover and John Campbell.[56] It was during that stop at the Air Ministry that Carroll McColpin and ten others were required, probably in error, to take an oath of allegiance to the King that cost them their US citizenship for more than twenty years.[57] After taking a very welcome bath, catching up on news from home via the mail waiting at the Air Ministry, the Eagle Club, or the London School of Eco-

EAGLE SQUADRON

MEMBERS OF THE EAGLE SQUADRON HAVE BEEN OFFERED
THE OPPORTUNITY OF BECOMING HONORARY MEMBERS OF:-
THE AMERICAN CLUB,

90, PICCADILLY, LONDON.

THE OVER-SEAS LEAGUE

OVER-SEAS HOUSE,

ST.JAMES 'S, S-W.1.

TELEPHONE.   REGENT 5051.

SQUADRON MEMBERS ARE ADVISED TO STAY AT THE OVER-SEAS
LEAGUE CLUB WHEN ON LEAVE WHERE EXCELLENT ACCOMMODATION IS
AVAILABLE AT VERY REASONABLE RATES.

WILL THOSE WHO WISH TO TAKE ADVANTAGE OF THE ABOVE,
REGISTER AT THE CLUBS AS SOON AS CONVENIENT.

* * * * *

SUGGESTED TAILOR:-

MOSS BROS. & CO.LTD., 20 KING STREET, LONDON W.C.2.
WHERE ADVANTAGEOUS TERMS FOR UNIFORMS HAVE BEEN ARRANGED.

* * * * *

THE HEADQUATERS OF THE SQUADRON WELFARE COMMITTEE IS:-

C/O THE FEDERATED TRUST,

20, COPTHALL AVENUE, LONDON, E.C.2.

TELEPHONE:- CLERKENWELL 8078/9

* * * * *

ALL INQUIRIES SHOULD BE MADE TO MR. CHARLES SWEENY
AT THE ABOVE ADDRESS OR THE DORCHESTER HOTEL, LONDON W.1.
TELEPHONE.   MAYFAIR 8888.

Notice apparently given to many of the Eagles when they arrived in London. Charles Sweeny is identified as the contact for the newly arrived pilots, so it must have been used quite early, during the organization of the units. The Eagle Squadron Welfare Fund referred to in the notice never fully became a reality, although some money was collected and benefits were paid to survivors of a few of the Eagles.

103

ESTIMATE FOR EQUIPMENT REQUIRED BY
R.A.F. OFFICERS.

2 Tunics @ £7 each...............................	14. 0. 0.	
2 Pairs Slacks @ £2.15.0	5.10. 0.	
Uniform Cap & Badge..............................	2. 2. 6.	
Field Service Cap & Badge......................	1. 6. 6.	
Greatcoat.......................................	10.10. 0.	
4 Shirts (each with 2 collars) @ 13/10d........	2.15. 4.	
4 Pairs Socks @ 2/9 Pair (or 3/-).............	11. 0.	
Regulation Shoes................................	1.16. 6.	
Tie...	3. 6.	or 4/3d.
Gloves..	11. 9.	

These Prices Include Purchase Tax.   £39. 7. 3.

OPTIONAL EQUIPMENT.

Raincoat..	3. 5. 0.	& £3.15.0
Web Gaiters.....................................	7. 6.	
Blue Web Equipment.............................	1.11. 6.	
Haversack.......................................	12. 6.	
Waterbottle.....................................	18. 6.	

NOTE:

PURCHASE ONLY ONE UNIFORM NOW.
7½%
A SPECIAL 7% DISCOUNT HAS BEEN AGREED ON ANY PURCHASE BY
EAGLE SQUADRON MEMBERS. THESE TERMS AND THE ABOVE
PRICES ARE TO BE OBTAINED AT MOSS BROS. & CO.LTD.
20 KING STREET W.C.2.

....

A 7½% DISCOUNT HAS ALSO BEEN ARRANGED WITH SIMPSON
(PICCADILLY) LTD. 202 PICCADILLY W.1.

An information sheet on obtaining uniforms, given to a number of Eagles when they arrived in London.

nomics, and manging a few hours' sleep, the future Eagles set out to acquire their uniforms and become a recognizable part of the RAF.

To be fitted for the needed clothing, most of the flyers went to Moss Brothers, regardless of the time of day or night. There they were outfitted with their complete uniform, except shoes, and also received their first recognition as pilots. (Issued items included a Class A uniform with tunic and two pairs of pants, a rain coat, an overseas cap, a billed hat, a great coat, two or three shirts, two ties, gloves, and black socks.)[58] On each of their tunics were the wings of an RAF aviator and a USA patch on the shoulder. Leo Nomis thought the experience was fantastic. He recalls that the group of new pilots must have been quite a sight, "walking around London feeling like a bunch of Generals, despite not knowing even how to salute." "We are all decked out in our new uniforms and really look swell," wrote Lee Gover. John Campbell "felt bashful and self-conscious, but the people were gracious and appreciative of our being there and I just hoped that we would measure up." When he received his first salute on the street from an airman, Campbell was so shocked that he nearly fell off the sidewalk.[59] It was during this process of getting uniforms that Bill Geiger came face-to-face with both war and the courage of the British people:

> I had to wait for some of the others to get fitted and was walking along the street . . . when I saw someone working in a hole that was barricaded off in the street. . . . I walked over and stood on the edge of the hole and looked down and watched this guy down there tinkering around. . . . I asked a Bobbie what the man was doing down there and he replied, "Sir, he's defusing a bomb." I thought they were rather cool and calm and collected about that, so I liked the British people right away. . . . You instantly developed an admiration for the British people who fought fires all night long and then went to work at their job all day long. They were very good at building your morale and it was always "thank God you're here and thank God you're helping."[60]

Most of the new RAF officers did not have much time to look around London, however, because they were generally on their way within a day or two either to Uxbridge Depot or to the RAF Reception Center at Bournemouth.[61] It was there that they received their flying clothing and equipment and were given a night vision test (but no other physical examination).[62] Posting to their first RAF assignment followed.

Most of those recruited through the Clayton Knight organization were already programmed into fighters, so they were assigned to a fighter OTU. Some went directly to that assignment within a few days while others were given a week or two of military training. Steve Pisanos was sent to a two-month military training program at the base at Casport before returning to Bournemouth for assignment to OTU.[63] The determination of initial assignment was goverened by the availability of spaces in the OTU and is discussed in the next section of this chapter. Those not already programmed into fighter slots, including some of the Knight recruits, simply took their chances. Ervin Miller recalls that everyone in his group was lined up and an officer said, "all those to my left—fighters, all those to my right—bombers. That was our selection."[64]

The experience at Bournemouth was trying for some and disappointing to others, but it did bring the Americans more in touch with wartime England. George Sperry reported that the town and base were bombed while he was there, and several Eagles noted that it was difficult to find their way around with everything completely blacked out. At the same time, Lee Gover wrote, "the English countryside is sure beautiful and the city of Bournemouth . . . is the most picturesque I've seen—with its odd English buildings and all the narrow, winding streets." There were also efforts to keep the troops entertained. Gover wrote of one entertainment, "went to parade and then had to go to a tea dance. They sure have some silly customs here. Sat around and looked foolish until about 5:15." When Gover was set up with a young

Pilot Officer Charles A. Cook, Jr. (left), in his full RAF uniform, and LeRoy Gover (above) in a formal portrait such as many of the RAF pilots had made to send home.

lady, he found an advantage in the blackout: "I didn't care for the one I had so as the town is completely blacked out, I just stepped into a doorway and was rid of her in two seconds."[65]

Whatever their experiences, for all the Eagles Bournemouth was the gateway to their dream, for it was from there that they progressed to their first involvement with flying and fighting, the operational training unit.

OPERATIONAL TRAINING UNIT

For the Americans who signed on with His Majesty's forces, arriving at their operational training unit, or OTU base made the RAF a reality. All the action associated with flying in a military environment was present everywhere, and it was at OTU that they first saw, touched, and flew the objects of their obsession, the Hurricane or the Spitfire. John Campbell recalls his initial thought upon arrival at OTU:

> Oh my God, here I am at last! I can remember wandering out on the field in the evening on the day we arrived there and looking at the Hurricanes. . . . This was the first time it really hit me because here were these things camouflaged and they didn't look like the pictures I had imagined. They were a bigger airplane than I had figured. . . . Almost suddenly, it was for real.[66]

OTU also introduced the realities of flying fighters, which really opened George Sperry's eyes:

> Prior to arrival in England my six years of flying experience had given me a well-rounded confidence in my ability to do anything that could be done in an airplane in the form of aerobatics. At Sutton Bridge (OTU) I very quickly discovered that my knowledge of flying added up to next to nothing. I knew how to fly, but I had a lot to learn about flying fighters, and the "why of flying." . . . Within a week after starting training in Hurricanes, I had changed from a self-satisfied pilot to a very deflated novice. Flying fighters called

Mainstay of the Battle of Britain, the Hawker Hurricane (above) was the first fighter most of the Eagles flew. Cited by many as the best fighter of World War II, the Supermarine Spitfire (below) won the hearts of all the Eagles. This Spitfire, flying over the English countryside, carries the markings of Number 121 Squadron.

for a cold, reasoned observation and assessment of maneuvers, so as not to exceed the design limitations of the aircraft, and a much more accurate piloting of the aircraft than normally required on weekend flying jaunts back in California.[67]

If there was a rude awakening for many of the flyers, there was also still a sense of confidence as they approached their training. "It was a challenge," observed Campbell, "because I had confidence in my ability and it didn't occur to me that I might fail."[68]

109

The OTU was the key to fighter pilot production in the RAF throughout the early part of the war. It was during this short period of training that the student made his transformation from someone who knew how to fly to a pilot who could make an airplane a weapon for use against Germany. It was also a rather harsh introduction to the British flying system for the young Americans. The RAF philosophy of flying was that a pilot could fly any airplane in which he found himself. Leo Nomis put it another way: "The British were more or less fatalistic about flying. At OTU the object was to get them [the students] where they could fly and get up and down in one piece."[69] Thus the standard program at OTU was two or three flights in a training aircraft, generally the 700-horsepower Miles Master, and then on to the Hurricane or Spitfire. Since these two aircraft were single seaters, there was no dual instruction—the first flight was the first solo.

Before flying the fighter for the first time, each student spent considerable time in a cockpit mockup to learn the location of switches, controls, and other necessities for flight. Edwin Taylor was also given several hours of practice in radio procedures while in the cockpit mockup. This training was realistic right down to having women as the radio operators, as they were in the operational RAF.[70] A blindfold cockpit check followed and, if all was in order, the actual flight was next. George Sperry's description of his first flight in a Hurricane is one of the most graphic I have found:

Receiving final instructions from Ground Control, I tried to remember everything my flight commander had told me about the aircraft, lowered my seat, and with clammy hands slowly opened the throttle. She leaped into the air like a scared jackrabbit, and while adjusting throttle and propeller control for climb, forgot all about my undercarriage, until I was 10 miles away and had 5000'. My God, she was quick on the controls—the slightest pressures with hands or feet made her buck like a horse. Not knowing quite where I was heading, I timidly tried a turn, eased the spade grip back slightly and hurtled to 10,000' with no effort at all. . . . all I wanted to do was learn to handle this brute, so . . . I got bolder and tried a few basic maneuvers—Christ, how she reacted. As my confidence grew, decided to see how she would go down hill, so eased the stick forward—she went from the normal IAS of 220 to 400 MPH in a matter of seconds—the ground seemed to be coming straight at me, and frightened by the speed, I eased her slowly out of the dive—my head was driven into my shoulders, the weight pressed my back and butt into the seat, my eyes blurred and I went out like a light—instinctively I released the pressure on the stick and as my sight came back I was hurtling straight into the sky—throttling back because she was still climbing, I called Ground Control for homing vector. Arriving back over the field, I . . . finally received clearance to land. . . . The ground flew at me with frightening speed—eased back on the stick, felt the wheels touch and with a slight bounce she was rolling on the ground real nice and easy. . . . By the time I had taxied back to the flight line, I had gained complete control of my emotions—To the members of my class crowding around the wing when I shut her down, my comment: "Hell, there's nothing to it, just another airplane."[71]

The objective of the operational training unit was to establish a basic proficiency in the aircraft and a familiarization with the duties that were to follow after the pilot went to his operational squadron. This is why the focus was on flying either the Spitfire or Hurricane. Included in OTU training were as much instrument time as possible, a rather brief experience firing the guns into the water or, later in the war, at a drogue chute towed behind another aircraft, formation flying, aerobatics, a small amount of night flying, and, of course, numerous takeoffs and landings. The assumption was that when a pilot was graduated from OTU he was ready to join the operational squadron and, in minimum time, become a combat flyer.

When the war began, there were only two OTU units, one at Aston Down and the other at Sutton Bridge, with a combined pilot production of 80 per month. By the summer of 1940, the demand of Fighter Command had jumped to more than 200 pilots per month for casualty replacement and 300 more for increasing the number of fighter squadrons. Many squadrons were actually having to take pilots directly into their organization, without OTU, and try to train them as best they could on operational missions. In an effort to ensure that all new fighter pilots had at least some training in fighters before entering their squadrons, the length of OTU was reduced from four to two weeks in the summer of 1940, coinciding with the onset of the Battle of Britain and the soaring demand for fighter pilots. Although the Air Ministry knew that the fourteen days of training was grossly inadequate, it was impossible to return to the longer OTU time. (The minimum training needed at OTU for a pilot from the British flying training system was 3 weeks and 30 hours of flying.) During the height of the Battle of Britain, the system was actually operated on an ad hoc basis with training ranging from 10 days to 3 weeks and 1 to 20 hours of flying time, mostly in Hurricanes.[72] Given this situation, it is little wonder that the Americans who went through the OTU system during the summer of 1940 were far from combat ready when number 71 Squadron was declared operational in October. The need for additional training was the major reason the unit was held out of combat until the spring of 1941.

The unsatisfactory OTU situation was addressed in several ways during 1940, but no workable solution was found. The system, which had been unable to handle all the training requirements in the summer and fall of 1940, was even worse off after November, so the Air Ministry decided to establish a total of six OTU bases immediately, with a target of nine by the spring of 1941. In conjunction with this move, OTU was to be lengthened to six weeks. Despite all efforts, however, there were only four OTU bases at the end of 1940 and pilots were still being turned out with only ten to twenty hours of training. The urgent need for some drastic action was illustrated in January 1941 when, of the 1,461 pilots in the first line of Fighter Command, some 300 were found not fit for operational duty.[73] A new system of linking OTU training priority to an individual pilot's anticipated duty was adopted in the spring of 1941. Further refinements continued, and by May all the bases had a standardized curriculum, average flying time had risen to 43 hours, and the pilot output was nearly 500 per month.

Obviously, the training was quite inconsistent. John Campbell flew approximately 50 hours in Hurricanes during a five-week OTU in April and May of 1941.[74] In contrast, when Don Young went to Spitfire OTU in late 1941, he got about 30 hours of flying and one opportunity to fire his guns into the sea. "Outside of simply flying," Young said, "the training was most inadequate."[75] Ernie Beatie, who went through Spitfire OTU in the fall of 1941, also flew about 30 hours and echoed Young's comments. But in what was the spirit of many Eagles, Beatie added, "but those were tough times—the English needed bodies more than anything else, and we filled in for them."[76] By autumn of 1941 there were eleven OTUs, each with 68 aircraft, 90 pilots in training, and a course of six weeks' duration which was increased to eight weeks during the winter because of the weather.[77] Robert Priser flew 58 hours in the Spitfire at OTU in early 1942, including "aerobatics, cloud flying, formation flying, climbs to 30,000 feet, air-to-air firing, low firing, cross country."[78] The washout rate for the program was approximately 10 percent, but I found no record of any pilot recruited to be in an Eagle Squadron being eliminated.

The next major evolution in the training system came in June 1941 with the establishment of the Personnel Reception Centre at Bournemouth as a pre-OTU. Previously, oversea arrivals, including Americans, were sent to the Uxbridge Depot and then to OTU. According to the Air Ministry,

> There was no refresher flying practice between the end of basic training overseas and the start of operational training

in the U.K., and a good deal of skill was lost during the voyage and the inevitable waiting periods. OTUs consequently had to give overseas-trained pupils a considerable amount of basic training and revision, over and above what they had to do generally.[79]

By the end of 1941, there were over 3,000 personnel at Bournemouth and the system was so saturated that incoming pilots were given a vacation while waiting for an OTU class. Barry Mahon was basically told to go do what he wanted for a week. Marion Jackson and Roland Wolfe were given even more surprising treatment. These two were sent to an estate in northern England, where they were honored guests for two weeks. They had the use of all the facilities, were served by a butler, were provided all they wanted to eat and drink, and were generally introduced to the life of the British gentry.[80] (In areas far removed from London, life continued at a somewhat normal pace during the war, although rationing and the need for manpower made significant inroads. A butler, for example, was probably a man too old for service in the British military.) Obviously, Jackson's and Wolfe's treatment was not the norm, and the opening of a second pre-OTU at Harrogate in March 1942 ended the need for forced vacations.

Expanding the personnel reception facilities also helped the RAF add military training to the syllabus for those pilots trained overseas. For most of the early Eagles, for example, the process of becoming a military officer consisted of being handed a piece of paper when boarding the ship in Canada and obtaining an officer's uniform at Moss Brothers after arriving in London. There was no instruction on military customs and courtesies, how to salute, or other military subjects. "One minute we were a bunch of motley civilians, and the next moment a smart group of flying officers in the Royal Air Force," observed Ervin Miller.[81] The new officers simply picked up military matters as they went along. Certainly, this situation did not help the early Eagle reputation for being less than stellar military officers. With the expansion of Bournemouth, a rather comprehensive military training program was instituted; marching, saluting, customs and courtesies, and other officer training subjects became required fare for new RAF recruits.

The search for more ways to raise training levels and cope with the influx of personnel led to the establishment of advanced flying units (AFUs) in November 1941. The original idea was to give the initial operational conversion training at the AFU for three weeks and then send the student on to an OTU. The AFU course was expanded to four weeks in early 1942, and the number of bases involved rose from one in November to six by the end of January and ten by the end of March 1942.[82] When Bob Smith went through AFU in late spring 1942, the system had been fairly well perfected. He received between 25 and 30 hours in Miles Master trainers and also spent several hours practicing on instruments in the Link trainer. The provision for the instrument trainer time was strong evidence that the experience level of pilots entering OTU was simply too low.[83]

It was at the operational training unit that the Americans began to recognize the real hazards of flying high performance airplanes in a wartime environment. Aside from the normal risks associated with making the transition into single-seat fighters, the added factors of varying experience and weather complicated the Eagles' training. Differences in experience were a much greater factor for those Americans recruited by organizations like that run by Colonel Sweeny, because these pilots received no training whatsoever before arriving at OTU and several had lied about the amount of flying time they had in order to get into the RAF. After establishment of the RAF flight training schools in the United States in mid-1941, the American recruits entered the British system on a par with their counterparts from other countries and were not handicapped by lack of experience.

Flying in bad weather was a real problem for almost every American who entered OTU, except for those who came through the RCAF. A good percentage of the

The "Link" trainer. Most Eagles spent many hours in this
machine perfecting their instrument skills.

young men signed up through the Clayton Knight Committee were from California, and most of those who were
not went to their basic flying course there. Southern California (and Oklahoma and Texas for that matter) has
relatively few days that require instrument flying. In England, on the other hand, instrument weather is the norm.
And despite the many hours spent in the Link trainer or
"under the hood" doing simulated instrument flying, the
proficiency level of the Americans was very low.

"While I had over 100 hours in training and found
the transition easy," noted Jim Gray, "I didn't have nearly
enough weather time. And the British just had no idea of
what California weather was like so they did not really
understand our situation." Once in the UK, the potential
Eagles were randomly assigned to OTUs, so they simply
became members of their particular class, and their flying
proficiency, including that on instruments, was assumed
to be the same as everyone else's. The result was more
than a few hair-raising experiences for the Americans
and, unfortunately, a number of casualties. Jim Gray believes that as many as 20 percent of the casualties in OTU
were caused by weather. Chesley Peterson said the figure
might have been as high as 40 percent.[84]

The problems brought on by the weather were compounded by the appearance of the countryside. "The entire countryside looked like a big green checkerboard," said Leo Nomis. "As soon as you took off you would lose sight of the base because everything looked the same. It took me about a month to get used to the terrain and feel comfortable that I could find my base easily."[85] This phenomenon was compounded by the fact that most of the British fighter bases were grass, so the runway, and the entire base, looked just like the surrounding countryside.

Lee Gover entered OTU in December 1941 and his diary gives a first-hand account of the risk involved. His first entry after arriving at the base, 17 December 1941, notes, "One fellow was killed yesterday. The accident rate here is about four out of ten in training and when you watch these Spits come in you don't wonder." The next day he wrote, "The first plane I watched land this morning crashed. Then this afternoon, two more crashed. They have such a narrow landing gear, the Spitfires, and land so hot that it is going to be dynamite." On Christmas he noted sadly, "One of the fellows [meaning those with whom he had trained in the United States] was killed yesterday, Bill Avery. He had a forced landing and broke his neck." His comments on the weather are also informative. His entry for 2 January 1942 noted, "only about one mile visibility and 1200 ft. ceiling, but that's considered excellent flying weather here, while everything would be grounded in the States."

Gover's experiences on 28 January 1942 would convince any doubter of the hazards these young men faced:

This must be my bad day, came within an inch of getting killed twice: The first time Jay was in the front on instruments and I was check pilot. A storm came in suddenly and we had to force land at another airport. Came in a little slow and a wing dropped out from under, and a big bomber right under us. I poured the coal to it and just skimmed over. Then this afternoon I was flying through cloud on instruments and she stalled into a spin and away I went. Got it out of the spin just as I came out of the cloud base, just about

500 ft up and going straight down. Pulled it out and just cleared some house tops. If the cloud base had been 100 ft lower I'd never know the diff.

On 19 July 1942, after he had been in a combat squadron for several months and just about eight months after leaving the United States, Gover listed the fate of the fourteen pilots in his basic training class at Bakersfield, California. Of the group, only he and one other were still doing operational flying. Seven members of the class had been killed, one was a prisoner, three had been sent home, and one was an instructor in OTU.[86]

It was at OTU that the potential Eagles first came in contact with the airplanes that, in some way, were a factor in each person's decision to join the RAF. These were the machines that had captured their imagination as fledgling pilots, about which they had read and heard for months or even years before deciding to join the RAF.

THE HAWKER HURRICANE

For most of the Eagles, the dream of flying a fast, powerful fighter first came true in the Hawker Hurricane. This flight generally came during the first few days at the operational training unit. For the pilots of the first Eagle Squadron, Number 71, this acquaintance with the Hurricane was much longer, because the squadron was equipped with them until late August 1941, for nearly the first nine months of the unit's existence. Although the Hurricane has always seemed to play second fiddle to the Spitfire, it was by no means a poor aircraft. In fact, it was the Hurricane and not the Spitfire that really won the Battle of Britain.

This tough fighter began its life in 1935 as the answer to Britain's need to build a credible fighter force. It went through several modifications before the final delivery of plane number 14,233 in September 1944. In their training, the RAF pilots were exposed to several types of Hurricanes, most of the training planes having been retired from active combat service, but it was the Hurricane

IIa that the Eagles in 71 Squadron flew. Whatever the model, the plane had a wingspan of 40 feet and was 32 feet long. Unlike the Spitfire, it was not an all-metal craft. Rather, the wings and front part of the fuselage were metal-covered, while the back of the body and the tail were covered with fabric. Power came from the famous Rolls Royce "Merlin" V–12 engine, which produced 1,280 horsepower in the Hurricane. Top speed was about 340 miles per hour, maximum altitude was 32,000 feet— obviously no match for the top German fighters.

Although it was considered a heavily armed plane early in the war, the Hurricane's eight 303 caliber Browning machine guns were no match for the later fighters armed with cannons. Nonetheless, with some fourteen seconds of ammunition for each gun and a small concentration of fire, the Hurricane was a deadly killer.[87] The Hurricane cockpit was relatively austere, and was unlined, which let all the smoke from the guns enter the pilot's area, necessitating flying with the canopy open much of the time. It featured the same "spade grip" stick as the Spitfire and also had the same gunsight, which could be adjusted for distance and type of aircraft that the pilot expected to encounter.[88]

The Hurricane was a wonderful airplane to fly. It was light and highly maneuverable with no bad habits. Its thick wing, which accounted for the relatively slow top speed, gave it an amazingly tight turning radius of about 800 feet at 300 miles per hour and made it more than a match for almost any German aircraft in turns. Its exceptionally strong wings would not bend or shake when the guns were fired, so it was a very stable gun platform, especially effective against the German bombers during the Battle of Britain. Royce Wilkinson, one of the Englishmen who served with and commanded an Eagle Squadron, maintained that the Hurricane was a better fighter than the Spitfire because it was so stable and so strong. He stressed that the Hurricane "was the only airplane in the war you couldn't pull the wings off of."[89] The Hurricane was easy to operate off the British grass fields because of its short takeoff run and relatively slow landing speed of 85 to 90 miles per hour. Although the Eagles flew the Hurricane for a relatively short time in combat, it seems to have won a place in their hearts simply because it was a good airplane and gave them a satisfying introduction to the RAF.

THE SPITFIRE

"My first contact with the Spitfire was at the air show in Brussels in 1938 as a member of the German Aerobatic Team," said German General Johannes Steinhoff. "At the end of the air show about four or five single seaters came dashing across the airfield. They were the first Spitfires I had seen and I said, "For God's sake, something is coming here." Still recalling his contact with the airplane, Steinhoff continued,

> I first met the Spitfire during the Battle of Britain . . . and if you met them at the same altitude, they were turning somewhat better than we so we would try to avoid a dog fight, turning around. If you had a chance to get behind him or attack from a higher altitude then you had him because early in the war their engines had carburetors and not fuel injection, and when they would try to dive their engine would momentarily cut out. Our tactic was to try to force them to dive and then you would have them. Later they got fuel injection and they could both turn and dive to get away. . . . As far as turning is concerned, the Spitfire had a much better wing than the Messerschmitt. Before they had fuel injection we were slightly superior; after they got fuel injection you had to be very careful for they were slightly superior, no doubt. Only if you could surprise them did you have the advantage. One time when my good friend Adolf Galland was talking to Goering near the end of the Battle of Britain, Goering angrily demanded, "For God's sake what do you need to win?" Galland replied, "Give me one squadron of Spitfires and I will show you what I can do."[90]

No matter what their differences in background, motivation, or ability, all the members of the Eagle Squadrons were united by being fighter pilots. Even a stronger uniting factor was the love of an airplane, the Spitfire. The thought that each shared to greater or less degree is best summed up by Edwin Taylor. The Spitfire was, he said,

> a finely tuned flying machine, mechanically complete. The first Spitfire I flew was an old, raunchy, ropy, war-weary dog. But it had an air of truth about it, and I realized immediately that all the other planes that I had flown before, in comparison, were complete turkeys. It started a romance for me, and at every opportunity I made it an instrument of pleasure, but on work days, it was an instrument of death and destruction.[91]

What was it that made this machine such a fantastic airplane that it would attract young men to become part of a war just to fly it? Perhaps it was simply the fact, as reported by most pilots interviewed, that it was the best all-around fighter they ever flew. Art Roscoe compared the Hurricane and Spitfire as the former being a Mack truck while the latter was a Mercedes automobile.[92] Certainly, the Spitfire's record is amazing.

The airplane started with the RAF on 3 July 1936 when a contract was let for 310 of the machines. That airplane could fly at 362 miles per hour, could climb at 2,530 feet per minute, and had a ceiling of 31,900 feet. Before the last of the 20,351 Spits had rolled off the production line, the horsepower had gone from slightly over 1,000 to twice that figure, the speed had increased by 100 miles per hour, it could fly and fight at over 44,000 feet, and it carried twice the firepower. It was the only Allied fighter in continuous production throughout all of World War II.[93] Bill Dunn summed up the Spitfire by saying, "In its day it was the best combat aircraft—a pure joy to fly."[94]

While there were a number of variations of the Spitfire produced during the war, the Eagles primarily flew the Spit Vb, although 71 Squadron initially had the Spit II and Number 133 was equipped just before their transfer to the US Army Air Force with the Spit IX. The latter aircraft was necessitated by the appearance of the German Focke-Wulf 190 early in 1942. The three Spitfires were practically identical, the primary differences being in engine horsepower, armament, and some modification of wing design. All aircraft had a wing span of 36 feet 10 inches, but the IX was from 13 to 15 inches longer. In normal operation, the II and V were about 750 pounds lighter than the IX's 7,500 pounds. The IX was also some 40 miles per hour faster at 408 mph and could fly nearly 12,000 feet higher than the II and 7,000 feet higher than the V, reaching higher than 43,000 feet. The IX was also more heavily armed, with four cannon as opposed to two on the older V. All three aircraft were equipped with the Rolls Royce "Merlin" V–12 engine, which was continually modified to produce ever more power throughout the war. The engine used on the II produced 1,175 horsepower while the Spit V's was rated at 1,450 horsepower and that on the IX ranged from 1,475 to 1,650. This increase in power, along with changes in propeller design, was the primary factor in gaining better performance from the Spit IX.

The accommodations for the pilot of a fighter are never spacious, and the Spitfire was no exception. In fact, a pilot over six feet tall or of heavy build could barely fit into the cockpit, as six-foot three-inch Jack Fessler could attest. The pilot sat on a Bakelite seat that was slightly inclined, using his parachute as a seat cushion. When in this seat, his head would almost touch the closed canopy and his shoulders would nearly rub the sides of the cockpit. Once settled inside, however, even a tall pilot like Fessler or equally tall Reade Tilley could lean forward to use the gunsight and really be quite comfortable. The instruments were basic for the time and could be easily read, with the exception of the compass, which was located near the floor between the pilot's legs. In order to see just who was on his tail when sitting in this armor-plated seat, the pilot looked in a mirror located outside the top of the canopy. Art Roscoe thinks "you just seemed part of the airplane when you were in the cockpit of the Spit."[95]

Control was by use of a "spade grip" stick that moved from side to side about half way up to allow better aileron control than the normal straight stick. The "spade grip" was a circular ring, about eight inches in diameter and an inch thick, on which was located the large brass firing button with a ring around it to arm the guns. (See the illustration on the next page.) There were two sets of rudder pedals. The first set, on the floor of the cockpit, resembled stirrups and had retaining straps that would enable the pilot to still control the rudder if he lost the use of one foot or leg. The second set of pedals, just under the instrument panel, were used during combat to pull the pilot's knees closer to his chest, thus making him more resistant to blackout.

Of particular concern to Spitfire pilots was the canopy, which closed by sliding forward on rails on each side of the cockpit. There was a small door on the left side that, in addition to easing entry, could be put in the slightly open position to lock the canopy open for takeoff and landing. If the pilot had to abandon his aircraft in flight, standard procedure was to release the canopy's two front catches, which would allow the air to lift it off and away. Despite this mechanism, plus a small crowbar in the cockpit as an emergency method for getting the canopy off, too many pilots were unable to leave their stricken airplanes because they could not get the canopy off rapidly enough to make a safe exit. After his transfer to Malta, Reade Tilley made a habit of flying with the canopy locked open, both for relief from the heat and to facilitate his escape in case he had to abandon the ship.[96] Because the main fuel tank was directly in front of the instrument panel, an incendiary bullet could make the cockpit a blazing inferno in just a few seconds.

Directly in front of the pilot was a reflector gunsight. The sight could be adjusted for distances from 50 to 600

The cockpit of a Spitfire, showing the spade grip control column and double rudder pedal.

feet, but most pilots kept it set at 250 feet, the distance at which the guns were bore sighted to concentrate their firepower. The sight was also calibrated for the wing span of any aircraft. Thus set, when the enemy aircraft was in the circle and its wings within the span line, the pilot knew his shots had a good chance of striking home.[97] In front of the gunsight was a windshield of bulletproof glass, while the sides and top of the canopy were plexiglass. It was in this small but efficient cockpit that the Eagles first sat as they prepared to fly the aircraft of their dreams.

And just how did this aircraft of the Eagles' dreams fly? The expletives are numerous; nearly all are positive. Aside from difficulty taxiing because of the narrow spacing of the landing gear, it was a wonderful aircraft with no bad habits. It was light and easy to maneuver, had a good rate of climb, and could turn tighter than any of the aircraft it engaged on the western front. On his first flight, which was solo since there were no two-seat Spitfires, the pilot found the plane lifting off the ground in less than 1,000 feet at around 100 miles per hour. It landed beautifully at about 85 miles per hour. These were good speeds since almost all of the runways were simply fairly level grass fields. Visibility in the Spitfire was quite good, especially compared to the German Messerschmitt 109, and most of the controls were well located. The airplane was also a good platform for flying on instruments, obviously a requirement given the English weather. Overall, the Spitfire was a plane that was as beautiful to fly as to look at.

After being introduced to these airplanes and completing OTU, each of the future Eagles was ready to join his operational squadron. Some went directly into one of the Eagle Squadrons; others joined various fighter units where they were needed and would not become Eagles for several months. No matter the squadron, each Eagle embarked on a dangerous, thrilling experience in the RAF, and each would become a part of English society in his own way. It is to the establishment of the second and third Eagle Squadrons, Numbers 121 and 133, and the Americans' experiences as members of the RAF that we now turn.

4. INTO COMBAT, 1941

THE OPERATIONAL HISTORY OF THE THREE EAGLE Squadrons falls into two phases. During the first phase, lasting until the end of 1941, the squadrons were in various stages of organization, training, and combat with the Germans. By the beginning of 1942, all three were posted in 11 or 12 Group and each was involved in the mainstream of RAF action against the Germans. This chapter covers the first phase, following the three squadrons through 1941, mostly focusing on one squadron at a time because of their varied activities.

TWO MORE EAGLE SQUADRONS FORM

By the time the first Eagle Squadron, Number 71, became operational in October 1940, recruiting in the United States for Americans to fly with the RAF was in full swing. The Clayton Knight Committee had expanded throughout the country and the scheme to train pilots in the United States, discussed earlier, was being formulated. The RAF, and Charles Sweeny, had realized that there were enough Americans volunteering to more than fill the requirement for reserves for Number 71 Squadron. So plans were made to establish a second Eagle Squadron, Number 121, as soon as the groundwork could be laid and sufficient trained personnel were available.

This time, there was considerable emphasis on *groundwork* and *training* that was not apparent with 71 Squadron. There would be no new Eagle Squadrons until the proper organization existed and the pilots were given sufficient flying training in the United States or Canada to make them viable candidates for OTU. Future Eagles would be equal to their British counterparts in ability before joining the squadron. The new squadron would be formed when enough volunteers met these criteria. The objective was, among other things, to avoid repeating the lapse of more than six months between 71 Squadron's initial operational announcement and its reaching combat ready status.

By May 1941 the necessary conditions had been met. On 14 May, the second Eagle Squadron, Number 121, was established at Kirton-in-Lindsey, a base formerly occupied by the first Eagle Squadron. In keeping with its policy that most squadron commanders be British officers, Fighter Command assigned Squadron Leader Peter Powell to command 121 Squadron, aided by Flight Lieutenants Hugh Kennard and Royce Wilkinson, the latter transferred from Number 71. Wilkinson's move to 121 established the policy that, as much as possible, transfers to fill vacancies in an Eagle Squadron—particularly voids in the senior leadership—would be from another Eagle Squadron. The RAF maintained this policy throughout the units' existence.

Number 121's first Hurricanes were flown into Kirton-in-Lindsey on 17 May; by the end of the month there were fifteen planes, enough for the squadron to begin operational transition flying in full force. By that time, there were thirteen pilot officers, including Nat Maranz and Richard Moore from Number 71, Lawson Reed, Collier Mize, Fred Scudday, Loran Laughlin (who would be the first member of 121 killed), Selden Edner, and Carroll McColpin. The sergeant pilots included Bradley Smith, Reade Tilley, Bert Stewart, and Earl Mason. Both aircraft and pilots arrived at a rapid pace through early June, bringing the squadron to full strength by the middle of the month. These additions included Pilot Officers Vivian Watkins, T. H. Tucker, Donald Geffene, John Campbell, Richard Patterson, Joe Durham, and Edward Miluck, and Sergeant Pilots John Mooney, Gilmore Daniel, and Thomas Allen. In July, 121 Squadron transitioned to the newer Hurricane II. On 8 August Pilot Officer Edner and Sergeant Pilot Mooney made the unit's first contact with the Germans when they scored a probable destruction of a Ju 88. By the middle of August, Number 121 Squadron flew daily sweeps over the Channel and into France and contact with the enemy was routine.[1]

Just eight days before Edner and Mooney's engagement with the Ju 88, on 1 August 1941, the third and final Eagle Squadron, Number 133, was founded at Coltishall, again under the command of an Englishman, Squadron Leader George A. Brown. Brown was transferred from Number 71, where he had been a flight lieutenant and one of the original flight leaders. The two flight commanders for Number 133 were Flight Lieutenant Hugh A. S. Johnston, another Englishman, and Andy Mamedoff, one of the original Eagles, who also transferred from Number 71 Squadron. Pilots arrived more slowly in 133 than they had in Number 121. Many of the initial members of 121 had been transferred from other operational squadrons in order to get the unit into combat ready status more rapidly. Number 133, on the other hand, was staffed primarily from the OTU bases, so the arrivals were more spread out. Not until the first week in September did the squadron begin regularly flying their Hurricane IIb's. By that time, Marion Jackson, Roland Wolfe, Walter Soares, Coburn King, James Nelson, G. W. Scott, William White, Roy Stout, Hugh McCall, and George Sperry from OTU, and Ross Scarborough from Number 71 were all in the squadron.

Because almost all of the pilots arriving in Number 133 Squadron were fresh out of OTU, Fighter Command determined that they would need additional training before the unit was ready to actively engage the

Germans. So after short stays at several bases in England, in October the unit was sent to Northern Ireland, where its pilots could cut their teeth on convoy escort over the Atlantic approaches to the United Kingdom while becoming more familiar with both their aircraft and the RAF system of combat. They were to stay in Ireland until the end of 1941.[2]

Enough American volunteers still were coming into the RAF to establish a fourth Eagle Squadron, and both Charles Sweeny and Jim Goodson believe planning was underway for such a unit. Apparently the idea was scrapped when most of the potential members were lost, their ship sunk on the voyage to England. Unfortunately, there is no official record at the Air Ministry of a fourth Eagle Squadron, and neither Wing Commander Laddie Lucas, a key member of the Fighter Command staff who was familiar with all Eagle activities, nor anyone at the Air Ministry knows anything of plans for such a squadron. Apparently, if such a unit was to have been formed, potential members that completed the voyage to England were either put in the pool of replacements for the existing Eagle Squadrons or assigned to other RAF units when the idea was dropped.[3] Most of the available US pilots replaced flyers lost or transferred from the existing Eagle Squadrons and, when the United States entered the war less than four months after the establishment of Number 133, recruiting for the RAF in the United States, for all practical purposes, ceased.

LOCATIONS AND DUTIES

Each of the three Eagle Squadrons moved a number of times during their existence, all three ending up at Debden in late September 1942 when they became part of the US Army Air Corps. (See appendix B for complete information on the units' locations.) Fighter Command's decision to move a squadron from one base to another was well thought out, not made simply for a change of scenery.

Because both the Spitfire and the Hurricane had very limited range, they had to be stationed as near as possible to the objectives of their missions. Those parts of Britain within range of German aircraft were divided into four group areas, numbered 10 through 13. (See map in appendix B.) The most action throughout the war was in the 11 Group area, which included London and the other cities that bore the brunt of Luftwaffe attacks. This area was also the part of Britain closest to France, thus the area from which most sweeps over the Continent originated. Every fighter squadron that wanted action yearned to be posted in 11 Group. Immediately north and including the cities of Coventry, Liverpool, and York was the 12 Group area. This area had periodic action against German planes, but most missions were convoy escort over the North Sea. Little action could be expected in the 13 Group area in the north or the southwestern area protected by 10 Group. A number of other bases occupied specialized locations throughout the United Kingdom, such as notoriously cold, damp Eglinton in Northern Ireland, from which convoy patrols were flown over the approaches to the British Isles. So a squadron could be excited or disappointed by a change in posting because the location gave a good idea of the missions the pilots would be flying and what the chances were for significant action against the Germans.

Fighter Command was reluctant to leave a squadron in the areas of the most action, such as around London in 11 Group, for too long because of pilot fatigue, so the rule was to move squadrons two or three times a year. This system also allowed the RAF to post new squadrons, or those with a large number of new pilots, at bases in 10, 12, or 13 Group, where they would see limited contact with the enemy until their proficiency reached the point where they could safely and effectively be used in actual combat.[4]

THE BASICS OF LIFE

Regardless of where the squadrons were posted and what kinds of missions they were flying, the Eagles had to satisfy their basic subsistence needs.

"We ate as well as could be expected under the circumstances," reminisced Edwin Taylor,

> and the British were very generous with all that they had. There was no choice of menu and we all had to eat in the mess at a certain time. The food was cooked by regular military cooks. We usually had fish, potatoes, brussels sprouts, which I still can't stand, treacle, which was a syrup-like substance for sweetening toast, and, of course, tea. There were hardly ever any eggs and almost never beef or pork. Fresh fruit was at a premium also. But no one really complained because we were eating as well as anyone else, although we all lost weight.[5]

Occasionally, there were breaks that brightened the normally dreary diet:

> We were all given ration stamps the same as any other British airman so we could buy food, if needed, clothes, and the like. One time we saved up our ration stamps and found a butcher with some beef. We got three of the largest steaks that the British had seen and took them next door to a restaurant to have them cooked. The cook's eyes bulged when he saw them but he did an excellent job of preparing our feast.[6]

Steve Pisanos remembers taking several of his Eagle buddies to a wonderful Greek restaurant in London. The resulting rave notices were such that the entire squadron went later and asked for the best steaks, which all thought were a bit tough but excellent. "No one really knew it was horse meat until I told them on the train going back to the base. There was very little Eagle patronage of that restaurant after that meal," remarked Pisanos.[7]

Living conditions varied from base to base. The older bases had fairly good quarters for officers, and most of the pilots thought they were fairly comfortable. Newer or temporary bases had more problems. Often there was not enough wood or coal for heating, so winter could be miserable. Reade Tilley got in a great deal of trouble for tearing down a wooden fence to burn for heat, while George Sperry recalls sleeping in his clothes many a night just to keep warm.[8] It was normal to live two pilots to a room, served by a British "batman" or similar servant. A batman is an enlisted soldier who acts as a servant to an officer in the British armed forces. The duties of the batman included waking the officers, bringing hot tea in the morning, maintaining the uniforms and the room, and generally taking care of his officers. "They were wonderful people," recalled Edwin Taylor, "and they really knew how to take care of you. We would give them cigarettes and maybe some tea and sugar sent to us from home if they did a good job."[9]

Transportation was also at a premium around the bases as well as into town. Edwin Taylor recalled,

> We had a bunch of bicycles in the Squadron. We rode them from the mess or our quarters down to the flight line and all over the base. We also had a Chevrolet panel truck with wooden seats on the sides which we took from base to base. Although we couldn't drive it, there was a driver who would take us almost anywhere we needed to go, including an occasional downtown rescue mission.[10]

Each of the squadrons had a doctor assigned, who would take care of minor problems as they arose and could, if needed, deal with emergency battle wounds. If an injury was more serious, the first stop for the wounded pilot would generally be a field hospital. Most of those who entered these facilities found them to be rather rudimentary, primarily because of the routine shortages of equipment, medicine, and other supplies. From the field hospital, the casualty was sent to one of the major hospitals for anywhere from a few days for a minor wound to several months for serious injuries (or, in Bill Edwards case, for treatment of spinal meningitis). Almost without exception, the Eagles reported that the treatment was excellent, comparable to that in the United States at the time.

Once a pilot was established at a base, mail went directly to that location. Most Eagles were very happy with the mail service, especially considering the hazardous conditions on the high seas. Mail from the States commonly took more than a month to reach the Eagles, since it had to come by ship, so it might well have taken nearly three months to get the answer to a question asked in a letter home. Some did complain about the amount of censoring that was evident. If the censor decided that what was written was inappropriate, the offending words, sentences, or even paragraphs were simply cut out of the letter. Mail often arrived in the United States almost in ribbons if the writer decided to discuss such topics as aircraft, possible assignments, base locations, or anything else involving sensitive information.[11]

Although letters were the primary means of communication with home for the Eagles, it was not the only one. Each week a British Broadcasting Corporation radio broadcast from London was aimed at the United States. Generally broadcast on Saturday night from the Eagle Club in London, it would feature an interview with one or more Eagles. The interview, aimed at reassuring the family back home that all was well, would focus on activities in London and during off-duty time rather than on combat-related stories. Several Eagles were also interviewed by Ed Murrow on "The Army Hour," another radio program beamed to the United States from England.[12]

Still another method of getting news to the folks back in the United States was through the various newspaper correspondents and the stories they filed. These stories ran in spurts, depending on the location of a squadron and the amount of action in which it was involved, but often American newspapers would carry a story the day after the action. Locations of bases in England and details of the action might be omitted—or highly inaccurate—but the names of the pilots involved were common fare, so the folks back home would at least know that their sons were in the action.

The Eagles also had access to American newspapers and periodicals, both in their squadrons and at such locations as the Eagle Club, but the news was of course dated. Probably the most up-to-date source of news about the United States was in *Stars and Stripes,* the American newspaper published in London for the US troops. This publication was not available for the early Eagles, however, since it was not published until after the United States entered the war.

WAITING FOR ACTION

For a while, news from home had to take the place of action. The glow that permeated the small group of Americans in Number 71 when the formation of their squadron was announced on 8 October 1940 was short-lived. The few pilots present in the squadron were there to fly, and several already had some combat experience. Those who were arriving almost daily were eager to get into action. Yet they were a fighter squadron without airplanes and understandably upset that no one could tell them when their Hurricanes would arrive. After all, they had left their jobs and defied US law to get to Canada, survived an arduous voyage across the North Atlantic, and completed their initial operational training with the sole purpose of flying in combat. The situation prompted Art Donahue to leave the Eagles on 23 October for his old RAF squadron, where he could see some action. The *71 Squadron Record Book* reports, "the entire personnel were completely 'browned off' because of the enormous lack of interest in the equipping of the Squadron with any aircraft." But 24 October, just a day after Donahue's transfer, "was a momentous day for three Brewsters (American Fighters) arrived and the pall lifted."[13]

The Brewster Buffalo, however, was hardly a satisfactory substitute for the Hurricane or Spitfire that the Americans had anticipated flying. The Buffalo was a short, stubby, unattractive mid-wing American fighter armed with four machine guns, "considered by all of us as too slow, ceiling limited, terribly vulnerable—one bullet in the wing and the aircraft either burned or needed a new wing—with little armament, no spares and hard to maintain," reported Chesley Peterson. In addition, "the inspection doors on the wing had a nasty habit of opening in flight and making the airplane almost uncontrollable."[14] A number of Buffalos had been destined for Finland and Belgium, but the defeat of these two nations left the aircraft available for the British, who used them mostly in the Far East. The aircraft was clearly inferior to the Hurricane and Spitfire, as well as to German fighters, and saw very limited duty in England. Some of the Eagles believe the Buffalo may have been sent to 71 Squadron because someone in the American embassy thought American pilots should be flying American aircraft, but there is no record of this idea having been officially advocated.

Clearly, something had to be done if the Eagles were ever to get their prized Hurricanes. So the squadron commander, W. M. Churchill, decided to take advantage of one of the Buffalo's bad characteristics, its tendency to ground loop if the tail wheel was not locked for landing. The Brewster craft was so short and its landing gear was so narrowly spaced that, if the tail wheel was allowed to pivot, the tail of the aircraft would swing uncontrollably, sending the aircraft into a circle on the ground. This spin usually ended with the airplane tipping onto one wing or even nosing over and breaking the wing off. Churchill simply instructed the pilots to land with the tail wheel unlocked, thus practically ensuring a ground loop and serious damage to the airplane. Within a short time, the three Brewster Buffalos were sufficiently damaged that they were not flyable; when the unit moved to Kirton-in-Lindsey in late November, the offending machines were left behind.[15] Whether related to the destruction of the Brewsters or not, in November, a month after being declared an operational squadron, the first nine Hurricane I's were delivered, and flying began in earnest. In December the unit flew 409 hours.[16]

The charge that Fighter Command did not want to equip 71 Squadron with proper aircraft is not valid. The RAF was still recovering from the tremendous aircraft losses from the Battle of Britain and there were simply not enough first-line fighters to fill the demand. At the same time, there was no real hurry to provide planes to Number 71 because the unit was not up to full strength and certainly had a long way to go before it would be a truly operational squadron. In addition, the British were reluctant to put the unit into combat before it was ready. The Air Ministry was concerned that premature action for the marginally trained Americans against the experienced Germans would result in tremendous losses of both pilots and aircraft. Such losses, the Ministry believed, could bring a backlash in American public opinion against the British and the war. Prime Minister Churchill was very anxious to get the United States into the conflict and saw the Eagles as one small but potentially effective tool for doing that. Therefore, Air Ministry interest in the squadron was high and the Eagles were not about to be put into combat against the superior Luftwaffe, with its very experienced pilots, until they were definitely ready.

Part and parcel of this British position was the conscious effort at publicity by both the Air Ministry and the press. The numerous visits of dignitaries to the Eagles, particularly Number 71 Squadron, and the frequent press days at the squadron were designed to build American consciousness about the war and help move US public opinion toward entry into the conflict.[17] Articles about the squadron became common fare in both the American and British press. *The Washington Post* ran a feature article about the unit in late October that included pictures of the Eagles flying in formation, while a San Diego *Tribune-Sun* article, "Americans Will Fly as Unit in Fighting for England," included a number of pictures of both Hurricanes and unit personnel.[18]

During fall 1940, Robert Low spent considerable time interviewing Eugene Tobin for a five-part series that appeared in *Liberty* magazine in April 1941 as "Yankee Eagle Over London"; the articles were exciting and sensational if not factual. On 19 November Hector Bolitho visited 71 Squadron to get material for a forthcoming piece in *The Saturday Evening Post*. The 23 October 1940 issue of the British publication *The Bystander* carried an illustrated article on the Eagles that noted,

> a number of American pilots have . . . joined the R.A.F. and will fight Nazi aggression with deeds. Under the Commanding Officer, the renowned Group Captain Charles Sweeny, they have formed a unit which is known as the Eagle Squadron. . . . Squadron Leader of the Eagles, W. E. G. Taylor, had been in action with the Fleet Air Arm since the beginning of the war.

This article contained the usual errors that characterized the press accounts of the day, namely that Charles Sweeny was the commander and W. E. G. Taylor was the Squadron Leader.

On 5 December Charles Sweeny, Chesley Peterson, and Stanley Kolendorski were guests of honor at a lunch at the Overseas League in London at which Captain Harold Balfour, British Under Secretary of State for Air, gave a toast to the Eagles. The New York *Herald Tribune* carried a summary of this luncheon under the headline, "U.S. Volunteer Flyers Saluted by Lady Aster."[19] Air Marshal Sir Sholto Douglas, new chief of Fighter Command, visited the squadron on 15 December and each Eagle met him personally, something that most other RAF pilots did not generally have the opportunity to do. Visits by other dignitaries were regular occurrences.[20] It is no wonder that the press frequented the Eagle Squadron. Not only was there the lure of Americans flying for the RAF, but there was also the attraction of fighter pilots. Any correspondent in London during the early days of the war, British or foreign, heard about the exploits of fighter pilots wherever he went.

The British publication *Everybody's Weekly* put the publicity issue in perspective when it noted, "When the squadron was first formed the American papers were full of distorted stories of their powers, until in the end the British pilots dubbed them the 'Glamour Boys of the R.A.F.'" This same article then goes on to do exactly what had caused the flyers of Number 71 early problems in the eyes of their RAF fellows:

> A few minutes later the machines flew overhead, proudly displaying to the visitors a magnificent formation. With interlocking wings the Hurricanes swept by. While rubbernecking at these, the party failed to notice a plane speeding towards them, flying a couple of feet above the ground. At something approaching two hundred miles an hour, the machine cleared the heads of the party by about three feet. Hats were lifted as if in salutation by the terrific blast of air as the plane zoomed over. . . . Next moment they were all ducking quickly as another machine swept over.[21]

The charge of excessive publicity and "glamour boys" image was not without basis and kept a number of Americans from even joining the unit initially. Many American pilots in other RAF squadrons felt particular animosity when they would return from a hard, productive mission only to find the radio or newspapers from back home talking about the Eagles, who had not yet been into battle. Most Eagles do not think the publicity adversely affected their relationship with other RAF squadrons but, rather, believe that the other squadrons were too busy attending to their own operational business to pay much attention. The problem with excessive publicity was not solved for the Eagles, especially those of 71 Squadron, until November 1941, when Chesley Peterson barred the press from the squadron because reporters' constant activity was hindering the operation of the unit.[22]

Most of 1940 was actually spent getting 71 Squadron organized and doing initial training. And, as already noted, there was much training to be done. Roland "Robbie" Robinson (Lord Martonmere) described the situation well:

> Most of the Eagle Pilots who came to the United Kingdom, though they could fly well, did not have any service training or the opportunity of any combat training. However, they all had plenty of guts and dedication to their job and the willingness to accept orders and to follow those who had experience.[23]

The three to four weeks and 30 hours of flying at OTU had hardly prepared the Eagles for combat against the very professional, experienced Luftwaffe. They needed to practice formation flying, high-altitude flying, air combat tactics, and firing techniques. What would be commonplace once they were in action was all new to the Americans during the early days of training. For example, high-altitude flying was uncommon enough that, for 16 November, the Squadron Operations Record Book noted that the pilots flew to 30,000 feet. The temperature at that altitude was often 50 degrees below zero, and the air was so thin that a pilot without oxygen could remain conscious for less than two minutes. But fighter pilots evidently received little or no training about hypoxia or the other hazards associated with flight at high altitudes while at the OTU.[24] The Eagles had much to learn.

The flying clothing worn by RAF pilots was generally issued during their stay at Bournemouth and included a light blue-gray uniform, lined boots, a heavy lined jacket, lined gloves, and a turtleneck sweater. What was actually worn when flying varied with the individual's preference but was generally about the same. "We didn't have any flight suits in the present sense of the word," commented Bill Edwards in 1989.

> I flew in my uniform almost all the time. I usually had my "Irving Jacket," which was a heavy lined jacket to keep warm and I often wore a pullover turtleneck sweater, especially in the winter, since the Spitfire and Hurricane had no cockpit

heaters. I always wore my lined flying boots but no extra pants. This would keep you warm except for the coldest weather. Also flying at high altitude there was always sunshine and it really got warm beating through the canopy.[25]

To this garb was added a parachute on which the pilot sat, a leather helmet to which was attached an oxygen mask and goggles, and, of course, lined gloves. To most of the Eagles, the biggest problem with the severe temperatures at high altitude was cold hands.

Another clothing requirement was some kind of neck protection, such as a scarf, fur collar, or turtleneck sweater. Because a fighter pilot is always turning his head from side to side, looking for enemy planes, without protection his neck would be rubbed raw in one mission.

There was actually very little change in dress when a pilot was not flying. A uniform with a tie was required at all times on the base, and that was also the uniform when venturing off the station. Wearing the uniform also made good sense, since recognition as a pilot in the RAF, and an Eagle as well, almost guaranteed outstanding treatment wherever the off-duty flyer went.

TACTICS

Of particular concern to every pilot was mastering the flight formations and tactics introduced at the OTU. The tactics used by Fighter Command tended to differ depending on the area and circumstances. The general formation used throughout the existence of the three Eagle Squadrons was the Malan's or line astern formation. In this formation, the squadron's aircraft flew in three lines of four, with each section or line spaced from 200 to 300 yards apart. The Eagles generally referred to these three lines of four, called flights, as white, red, and blue flight. The first aircraft in line, flown by the flight commander, would be called "Blue (Red or White) Lead." The following ship would be "Blue Two," followed by "Blue Three" and "Blue Four." The position a pilot was flying was generally his call sign for that mission.

*Harold Strickland, dressed in typical RAF flying clothes,
leaves his Spitfire. The bar on the door is in case the pilot needs
to pry open the canopy in an emergency.*

One advantage of this formation was that, when an engagement began, each four-aircraft section split easily into two fighting units of two aircraft each. But a number of Eagles echoed Don Blakeslee's criticism of the line astern formation because it normally put the most experienced pilot in the front and the newest member of the unit in the rear, where he had no one to help defend him. This formation was significantly modified by the RAF in Malta to the fours in line abreast formation, primarily because of the Germans' overwhelming numerical superiority. The key advantages to the line abreast formation were the greatly increased firepower that could be directed toward targets in front of the formation and the ability of each member of the flight to protect the others. (See illustration on next page.)[26]

No matter what tactics were employed, they were all based on the anticipated use of the aircraft in the battle. Fighter Command laid out in very clear terms the role of the fighter in the overall concept of airpower for waging the war. According to an Air Ministry pamphlet, fighters had five roles:

First, air defence of the United Kingdom for instant participation in which all operational fighter squadrons have, as a routine, at least one and normally two sections of aircraft at "Readiness," and possibly further sections up to full squadron strength according to the operational situation. These aircraft are required to be airborne within a maximum of five minutes of the order to take off. A flight of six aircraft is usually off in 2½ to 3 minutes, and a squadron of 12 in 3½ to 4 minutes. These aircraft are responsible for the defence of Britain and they work in pairs, flights, squadrons or wings of three squadrons—never singly. Second, convoy patrols. All coastal shipping round the British Isles is constantly patrolled by aircraft working in pairs, or stronger formations, from dawn to dusk, except in weather so bad that attack is unlikely. Third, bomber escort. These aircraft are solely responsible for the safety of bombers and are therefore tied down to them. Fourth, fighter sweeps. In these, strong forces of aircraft carry out offensive patrols over enemy territory,

Some Eagles preferred the "line abreast" formation (above) to the "line astern" formation (below) more often used in the RAF, believing the line abreast allowed greater concentration of fire and better protection of the formation.

seeking to engage enemy aircraft and shipping. Fifth, attacks on enemy objectives. These are undertaken by small forces, by day and by night, under cover of surprise or cloud.[27]

Regardless of the formation or specific mission, the real payoff for the fighter pilot was combat with his German counterpart. In that arena, the skill of the pilot and how he used his capabilities were paramount. Edwin Taylor gave this view on the most important skills and capabilities:

> In arguments concerning speed or maneuverability—to me speed was of the greater importance. Speed means conversion to altitude. It also enabled the pilot to overtake his adversary or to escape when at a disadvantage. In making a decision to attack, the number of enemy planes doesn't matter. The advantage of position, sun, altitude and direction of attack are the influencing factors. Attack at high speed and break up into the sun, make the break hard and gain back the altitude. Once you had an altitude advantage, you could keep it, dive for another firing pass and then use speed and power to pull back up.[28]

The entire arena of tactics for the fighter pilot is summed up in *Ten of My Rules for Air Fighting,* which was posted, in some form or another, in every squadron in the RAF.

1. Wait until you see the whites of his eyes. Fire short bursts of 1–2 seconds and only when your sights are definitely ON.
2. Whilst shooting think of nothing else; brace the whole of the body; have both hands on the stick; concentrate on your ring sight.
3. Always keep a sharp lookout. "Keep your finger out."
4. Height gives *you* the advantage.
5. Always turn and face the attack.
6. Make your decisions promptly. It is better to act quickly even though your tactics are not the best.
7. Never fly straight and level for more than 30 seconds in the combat area.

8. When diving to attack always have a proportion of your formation above to act as top guard.

9. Initiative, aggression, air discipline and team work are words that mean something in Air Fighting.

10. Go in quickly. Punch hard and get out![29]

THE WAITING CONTINUES

Not only did the pilots lack flying experience, they also arrived at Church Fenton with little, if any, military training and no appreciation for military customs and courtesies. One contemporary observer characterized it this way: "Old soldiers around the station were amazed at the behavior of these young Americans who, in some cases, were plain saboteurs of military tradition." They were noisy, they forgot military courtesy, they had horrible table manners and drinking habits. They were in the true sense civilians for whom military courtesy and discipline had no meaning. "I would say that 80 percent of the members of the Eagle Squadrons were a bunch of renegades anyway," said Fred Almos.[30] One of the tasks Squadron Leader Walter Churchill faced was to keep the Americans quiet and patient while he trained them before letting them go into combat. Although the squadron never reached the point of having typical RAF discipline, Churchill and subsequent commanders did a remarkably good job of making the Eagles into a military unit.[31]

Mentioning Walter Churchill as the commander of 71 Squadron raises another persistent problem during the unit's early days: the confusing command situation. When the existence of the first Eagle Squadron was announced, most press sources reported that Squadron Leader W. E. G. Taylor, an American friend of the Sweenys, was the squadron commander. These reports concerned the RAF, because the British, in keeping with the policy that foreign units would be commanded by Englishmen, had assigned Walter Churchill to the job. Actually, neither of these officers was the first choice of

Charles Sweeny, who wanted American RAF ace Billy Fiske to be the first commander. Sweeny had discussed the concept of the Eagle Squadron with Fiske, and the RAF had agreed to have him lead the unit. Unfortunately, Fiske lost his life in August 1940—the first American pilot to be killed in the Battle of Britain—and so the post was open.[32]

Churchill, universally liked and respected by the members of the squadron, was a veteran of the air battle over France as well as the Battle of Britain. Royce Wilkinson, one of 71 Squadron's original flight commanders, believed Churchill was the ideal man to be the first commander of the Eagles, and Chesley Peterson, who in less than a year would move into that position, agreed. Taylor, on the other hand, had diverse military and flying experience, mostly in the US Navy, but was a stranger to the British system as well as to command of a flying squadron. Clearly, he was less qualified than Churchill.[33] The assignment of two "commanders," Taylor as the figurehead to the world and Churchill as the real commander, was not workable. Taylor was therefore transferred to 242 Squadron for a short period, but then moved back to 71, where he continued to serve as the figurehead. The situation was not resolved until 22 January 1941, when Churchill was taken ill and put on sick leave. Taylor then became acting commander, a post he held until June 1941. Although all do not agree, most Eagles give Churchill the credit for getting the squadron off the ground and establishing the foundation for what would eventually become an outstanding fighter unit.[34]

If the pilots of 71 Squadron were not yet prepared for action against the Germans, they were certainly learning the ways of the British and rapidly becoming part of the English scene. After all, pilots, particularly fighter pilots, were the saviors of England. Winston Churchill had set the stage when he made his famous comment, "Never in the field of human conflict was so much owed by so many to so few." Royce Wilkinson, a seasoned veteran of both the air battle over France and the Battle of

Britain, was most emphatic in his accounts of the British view of fighter pilots. In his view—and his wife seconded this opinion—the British public felt that fighter pilots could do no wrong. Actions that might well land an ordinary human being in jail (though not actions outside the law) were simply ignored when performed by fighter pilots. The general British perception of a fighter pilot was summed up in an account of the Battle of Britain:

> These RAF pilots meant many different things to different people. To the world they were the "few." To the British infantry, they were glamour boys, to the Royal Navy, men still wet behind the ears. To Hitler, they were madmen who refused to admit defeat even after they had been licked. To the London taxicab drivers, they were the "wild ones" who had to be taken back to base after their "benders." To the people of Kent, who played darts with them in pubs, they were "Those nice boys who try so hard to act grown up."
>
> They were young. (At 26, a group captain was considered over-age.) They were sloppy to be "different." They flew six "sorties" a day and played darts in the evening. They were boys who gulped down pints of mild and bitter ales and smoked pipes which they didn't enjoy. On the ground, these men acted like boys, mimicking their aerial exploits with "zooming" hand motions.[35]

And wherever they went, the Americans in the RAF saw the evidence of that spirit. In early 1941, *Everybody's Weekly* reported, "On returning to the aerodrome and completing the days' work . . . did those boys celebrate? Their exploits . . . are still spoken of in awe in the local town."[36] And there can be no doubt that the Americans adapted rapidly to the English custom of frequenting the local pub, although their conduct is the subject of disagreement. Most observers agree with Royce Wilkinson. "The first Eagles were a spirited bunch," he said. "They were young and eager to get cracking. Not one of them lacked the moral fiber to get the job done. I never had any problem with any of them."[37] Although some of the other flight commanders

*A typically young pilot of the RAF, Edwin Taylor of Number
133 Squadron.*

did have some disciplinary problems, Brian Kennerly is
the only Eagle recorded as being sent home, and he was a
man whom Chesley Peterson believes was without any
standards whatsoever. Kennerly was later to write a book
about his experiences as an Eagle, *The Eagles Roar,* which
gained him considerable notoriety but, because it was a
total fabrication, also established many erroneous ideas
about the units.[38]

One key to the Eagles' ability to adapt to the British
and their customs were the several Englishmen in the
squadron. Aside from Wilkinson and Churchill, one of
the most influential was J. Roland "Robbie" Robinson,
the late Lord Martonmere, retired governor and commander-in-chief of Bermuda. Robinson had early contact
with the Eagles, although by accident. As a member of
Parliament, he had been asked to show three Americans
through Parliament one fall day in 1940. Little did he

know when he volunteered for the RAF a few weeks later that he would be posted as the intelligence officer of Number 71 Eagle Squadron and these same three Americans would be charter members. That coincidence began a very important relationship, for many Eagles were to spend weekends and holidays at the Robinson home and there learn the customs of their adopted nation. Robbie also bailed more than one Eagle out of financial problems and even gave the bride away at Chesley Peterson's wedding. "The Eagle Pilots settled down quickly and soon settled down to new customs and discipline," he wrote. "Their only real difficulty was probably that they were always 'broke' owing to the inadequacies of the Royal Air Force pay which was at a lower standard than American pay."[39]

The Eagles got the treatment accorded other fighter pilots, plus some. They were a unique commodity in those early days before the United States entered the war. Bill Geiger found that the British genuinely appreciated what he and the other Americans were doing. Grover Hall summed it up well:

The Eagles got a reception beyond anything accorded the Americans who followed in American uniforms. The sight of them . . . imparted substance to Mr. Churchill's ". . . carry on the struggle, until, in God's good time, the New World, with all its power and might, steps forth to the rescue and liberation of the Old." The Eagles became the darlings of London. They couldn't buy at pubs, got [free] theatre tickets.[40]

Hall's opinion is fully backed by Chesley Peterson. "We were looked upon by the British as allies come to the aid of the British Empire in its great time of need," he commented. "Many of the British public saw the Eagles as an indication that the US was ready, willing and able to help prosecute the war."[41] Bill Geiger agreed. "Very often," he said, "a bartender would say 'you don't pay for drinks here, Yank.' While other fighter pilots often got the same kind of treatment, the Americans got it more often."[42]

Joe Durham thought his American traits served him well.

My English flying companions appeared somewhat aloof on my arrival, but my persistent friendly persuasion and exaggerated Southern drawl soon penetrated their reserve. They could not be persuaded that a character such as I could be spawned anywhere except Texas, and I was quickly dubbed "Tex". . . . The English people in general welcomed us with open arms, and treated us in the same manner that they showed to their own servicemen.

Lord Martonmere summed up the British view: "British civilians appreciated having Americans serving in the Royal Air Force and always were very happy with their achievements."[43]

Bert Stewart found some Englishmen curious as to why the Americans had come over but without exception they were appreciative that the "Yanks" were there. Stewart told probably the most touching story of British appreciation:

As I was getting on the bus after an event during the 1976 Eagle Reunion in London, the escort officer called me. "Hey Stu," he said, "come on over here a moment." I went over there and there was a little lady standing there. She was in her eighties he told me. He said, "Stu, here is a little lady who has walked twelve miles just to say thank you to an Eagle." It grabbed me by the throat and still does. I said, "Ma'am, you don't have to thank us, we thank you for holding the line." She was so small I could have held out my arm and she could have walked under it. She said, "No, we thank you because you came when we needed you." I had her come on the bus and tell everyone what she had told me. She came up and made a few statements and there was not a dry eye on that bus, not one.[44]

The members of 71 Squadron began 1941 with a feeling of promise. Their morale remained high during their first holiday season in England, according to the Squadron Operations Record Book, and all looked forward to action in the new year. The promise seemed real. On 4 January the unit got its first call to readiness, but the enthusiasm was dampened the following day when they got their first taste of a death in the organization. An occasional gear-up landing or even a minor crash were not unusual, but the real dangers hit home with the death of Philip Leckrone, one of the first members of the unit.

Although seeing flying comrades killed was not new to any of the Eagles, the unit integrity fostered by squadron identity made death harder to deal with because of the closeness of the squadron members. On 5 January 1941, while flying in formation with Vernon Keough and Ed Orbison at over 20,000 feet on a training flight, Leckrone collided with Orbison and did not bail out despite Keough following him all the way down shouting through the radio for him to get out. Orbison was able to successfully land his damaged ship. The event's effect on the squadron, and to some degree their attitude toward training, was clearly voiced by the adjutant as he wrote in the Squadron Operations Record Book,

> If the death of one of the pilots can hold a Squadron . . . it will tend to impress on the other pilots the attention they must pay to detail in all these practice flights, for it is true of the Squadron as it is of most others, I believe, in the RAF that they are inclined to treat all of this practice flying as a bit of a bore.

Leckrone was characterized as one who joined the RAF "for the highest of motives—not for the glamour, if any, or the thrills, but to defend our way of life." His funeral, the first for the Eagles, was the next day.[45]

To make matters worse, the well-liked Walter Churchill was taken very ill late in January and the less popular W. E. G. Taylor was given command of the squadron. All of these changes would have been more tolerable if the Eagles could have flown daily and seen their skills readily improve. But Mother Nature also seemed to turn against them, and the snows of January translated into a number of non-flying days. Nonetheless, the squadron was declared combat ready in late January and began to fly operational patrols escorting shipping on the North Sea.

Escort patrol was considered a boring job in which contact with the enemy was rare. But it was a mission in which the hazards were very real. Among other dangers, patrol duty could easily tax the weather flying skills of the pilot to the maximum. Takeoffs and landings were often made in marginal weather conditions and the persistent clouds over the water blended into the gray sea in such a way that the pilot could easily lose track of both his altitude and aircraft attitude if he did not pay constant attention to his instruments. This condition, popularly referred to by pilots as "vertigo," can be both terrifying and fatal. This fact was brought home to the members of 71 Squadron just a month after the Leckrone accident when Ed Orbison, the pilot who had collided with Leckrone, apparently got vertigo and spun into the water from about 4,000 feet.

While the squadron was still recovering from Orbison's death in this accident, one of the very first members of the unit, "Shorty" Keough, was reported missing and later confirmed killed when his plane evidently "crashed into the sea at great speed." The effect on the unit is again reflected in the Squadron Operations Record Book: "The other boys have taken the loss of Pilot Officers Orbison, Leckrone and Keough philosophically but it does seem that the fates are being most unkind."[46] Whether related to the three accidents or not, Charles Sweeny visited the squadron on 19 February and "all were glad to see him . . . his efforts have made an enormous difference to the comfort and happiness of the pilots in so many different ways."[47] Overall, however, February 1941 was not a good month for the Americans.

March 1941 was a crucial month in the evolution of the first Eagle Squadron. Although it began poorly with the usual dreary weather inhibiting flying, a much greater pall hung over the organization. According to Chesley Peterson, word came to the unit that on his recent trip to England, General Hap Arnold, chief of the US Army Air Force, had been told by Air Marshal Douglas about the three recent accidents and the general impression that the Eagles were not making satisfactory progress as a squadron. Douglas reportedly added that the Eagles were "a bunch of prima donnas." The information the Eagles had on Douglas' comments was correct. In his book, *Global Mission,* Arnold writes,

> the afternoon, I . . . went to see the Eagle Squadron. . . . The British had some trouble with them—too many prima donnas. As a matter of fact, other RAF, Colonial, and volunteer squadrons . . . were now fighting . . . while the Eagle Squadron was still waiting to move up to combat duty. Douglas had just made up his mind that the American outfit was going to start operating immediately or else. I told him I thought it was a good thing—that it should either start fighting or be disbanded, and the men sent home. Douglas agreed with me.[48]

News of the exchange between Douglas and Arnold led to Peterson, as spokesman for the Americans, going to Air Marshal Hugh Sanders, 12 Group commanding officer, and demanding that 71 Squadron be moved from 12 to 11 Group so they could become part of the action. "If we were to be prima donnas, the squadron resolved to be the best prima donnas in the entire RAF, and the record certainly proved that we were," said Peterson.[49] Although not a result of Peterson's actions, but rather because of Douglas' decision communicated to Arnold, the squadron was moved to Martlesham Heath, in 11 Group, on 9 April and declared ready for action.[50]

THE WAIT FOR ACTION ENDS

And action was not long in coming. Just four days after the unit's arrival at Martlesham Heath, Churchill, Jim McGinnis, and Sam Mauriello chased a Ju 88, which got away by diving into the clouds. Four days after that incident, Gus Daymond got off the first gun burst at an enemy aircraft when he shot at a Dornier 17, but again, it got away because the emergency boost on Daymond's Hurricane was wired off. Nonetheless, the Eagles were now in the thick of the action and were soon used to standing alert, being scrambled after actual or threatened enemy formations. Not until 15 May, however, could the squadron claim damage to an enemy aircraft, although several had been sighted earlier by unit pilots. On that date James Alexander and John Flynn got into the unit's first real dog fight with three Me 109s. In the ensuing melee, at least one German was damaged and left the action trailing heavy smoke, but Flynn's aircraft was also severely damaged, partly from Alexander's bullets, and had to crash land—the first pilot in the unit to be shot down in combat.[51]

Still, the wait for that first elusive "destroyed" continued. Not until after a change in commanders, from W. E. G. Taylor to H. de C. A. "Paddy" Woodhouse, and a move to North Weald in late June, did the Eagles join the ranks of those squadrons having destroyed enemy aircraft. On 2 July 1941 the entire squadron was escorting Blenheim bombers to a target on the coast of France, duty which had become normal for the unit. If any type of mission was guaranteed to get the German fighters into action it was a bomber raid. And the Eagles were not to be disappointed. They were jumped by 25 to 30 Me 109s and the action began. Squadron Leader Woodhouse drew first blood as an Me 109 he engaged crashed, smoking, into the sea. Gus Daymond got a second when the pilot of the aircraft he was fighting abandoned his out-of-control ship. Bob Mannix got a number of hits on a third Messerschmitt, and when last seen it was diving, smoking, toward the ground. The only Eagle loss was Bill Hall who bailed out and was captured, the first Eagle to become a prisoner of war.

As a message of congratulations came in from 11 Group Headquarters, the Eagles could celebrate having proven they could fly and fight effectively. A rash of press reports of varying accuracy on the Eagles' action adorned US newspapers and periodicals in the next few days, the most colorful of which appeared in *The New York World-Telegram* under the title "American Eagles Claw Germans to Celebrate Fourth of July." On that July 4th, Sir Archibald Sinclair unveiled a tablet in the crypt of St. Paul's Cathedral in London to William "Billy" Fiske, who would have been the first Eagle commander.[52]

The change from Taylor to Woodhouse, a Battle of Britain veteran, as commander of Number 71 Squadron was significant. Although evaluations of Taylor vary, it is generally conceded that his command experience, his quest for public acclaim for the squadron, and his general reluctance to fly fostered some of the problems that precipitated Air Marshal Douglas' comments to General Arnold. Bill Geiger believes

> the squadron got a bad reputation of just drinking and not doing much for the war effort under Taylor. This gave the British the idea that we had to do something or we might as well be sent home. Paddy Woodhouse was made Squadron Commander as a result and said, "We're going to war." We followed him and that is what we did.[53]

Taylor, himself, claimed he was just keeping the unit out of combat until it was fully manned, which he says it never was during his command. Some Eagles say Peterson was the real flying commander during Taylor's official tenure. It was he, not Taylor, who went to Group Headquarters to demand a move for the unit in April. Whether related to Peterson's action or not, in late May, Taylor recounts,

> I was called over to Group to see Leigh-Mallory. He told me that I had overrun the number of operational hours permitted between my Navy and RAF time, and that at 36 I was too old to command a fighter squadron, so that Group had decided to make me a Wing Commander and put me in charge of a fighter training unit. . . . As both the US and British

navies had asked me to come back, I received my American Commission first and I was back in the USN again.[54]

Regardless of the quality of leadership provided by Taylor, the squadron did increase its proficiency significantly under his command and was prepared for combat when Woodhouse took over. Taylor departed the squadron on 7 June 1941 and by the end of the year was on Admiral Kimmel's staff when the Japanese attacked Pearl Harbor.

Aside from a few visits to Number 71 Squadron, Taylor's departure also appears to have ended Charles Sweeny's active role with the Eagle Squadrons. By June, Number 121 had been organized and the two units were line squadrons of Fighter Command. In the varied publicity that appeared during the next fifteen months, the rest of the Eagles' tenure in the RAF, there is little mention of the Sweeny connection. Apparently Sweeny was not concerned about Taylor's departure. Sweeney merely says that by the middle of 1941 his interests in the war had changed and he had little time for involvement with the Eagles.[55]

As with any flying unit, there was a constant turnover of personnel throughout the history of all three Eagle Squadrons. There was, however, more stability in Number 71 during the first nine months of its existence than at any other time during the war. This stability was primarily a product of the unique nature of the unit, the desire to get it up to full strength as soon as possible, and the absence of any combat losses. By the time the squadron was seeing daily action against the Germans, from the late summer of 1941, changes in personnel became commonplace, both because of combat losses and because of experienced personnel being transferred to the other two Eagle Squadrons to increase those units' experience levels.

On 19 April 1941 William Hall, Thomas Wallace, R. C. Ward, Oscar Coen, and Virgil Olson arrived in 71 Squadron from Sutton Bridge OTU. The Squadron Operations Record Book noted, "All fully trained having had over 35 hours on Hurricanes at Sutton Bridge. P/O

Olsen was in France with P/O Mamedoff and P/O Tobin trying to join the 'Armee de l'Air' and escaped from France in September." All were immediately assigned to flights. The fact that 35 hours in the Hurricane was considered fully trained tells something of the standards during those early days of the war. The first departure for another Eagle Squadron was on 8 May, when Flight Lieutenant R. C. Wilkinson was posted as a flight commander to the newly formed Number 121 Squadron, a move that resulted in Chesley Peterson being given the rank of flight lieutenant, the first American in an Eagle Squadron to be promoted above pilot officer. "This is a well-deserved reward for Peterson has proved himself an extremely capable officer in every way," noted the Squadron Operations Record Book. The second key transfer to another Eagle Squadron came on 31 July, when Flight Lieutenant George Brown departed to take command of the third Eagle Squadron, Number 133.[56]

Throughout the early months of 1941, the number of important visitors to Number 71 remained inordinately high, evidently at the urging of both Charles Sweeny and W. E. G. Taylor.[57] A large press event was arranged by the Air Ministry for 17–18 March, resulting in another rash of articles in both the American and British press about the organization. The articles in the American press were typified by a front page story in *The New York Sun,* "American Eagle Squadron Set For Air Action Against Nazis." Readers in the United States were informed that the Eagles "have taken their place in the front line of the Battle of Britain, standing regular watch with the RAF fighters." The same article added a glamourous touch, a never-ending burden to the squadron, by noting, "Today they are dashing cavalrymen of the clouds, impatient to do battle with the sky stars of the Luftwaffe."[58]

In another article, "Eagle Squadron Shows Skill of Fighting Pilots," J. Norman Lodge commented on the impressive show put on for the correspondents. "They went through all maneuvers and are now ready to take the air as fighters at a moment's notice." Significant coverage was given to W. E. G. Taylor as the commander.[59] *Life* featured a most motivational two-page spread that carried pictures of various squadron members in all sorts of activities, including Bill Taylor and Chesley Peterson being awakened to go on a mission. In July, *New York Times Magazine* carried a full page of pictures and narrative on the unit, while the *San Francisco Examiner* ran a picture of the squadron with a Hurricane, a photo that became standard fare for many newspapers.

The social life of the Eagles was also fair game. On 31 May the *New York Sunday News* ran a number of pictures of various RAF personnel, including one of Chesley Peterson and Audrey Boyes with the caption, "Engaged. Squadron Leader C. G. Peterson of Utah, who commands an American Eagle Squadron in England, strolls in London with his fiancee, Audrey Boyes, a South African actress. Peterson had downed several Nazi planes." (Typically, the information was incorrect in stating that Peterson was the squadron commander.)

These were but a few out of scores of articles on the unit throughout 1941. British publicity was no less plentiful than American. *The Aeroplane* portrayed the Americans as a

> fine body of men with the same merits as any RAF squadron. They have the same insatiable love of flying, the same confidence in themselves and in their machines, and much of it comes from their long and careful training and the preservation of an alert mind in a sound body.[60]

The significance of the unit was the theme of a piece in *The Illustrated London News*. Referring to the naming of the unit, this article reported, "they are called Eagles because they were among the first flights of that 'vast emigration of young eagles coming from the New World to aid the R.A.F. to search out, pounce upon, and kill their wretched prey.'"[61]

In addition to press attention, the list of visitors to 71 Squadron reads like a Who's Who. In April, Sir Archibald Sinclair and Sir Hugh Seeley; in May, Air Commodore Prince Bernhard of the Netherlands, Lord Trenchard, and Air Marshal Leigh-Mallory; in July, Noel Coward; in August, Air Marshal Sir Sholto Douglas and American Ambassador John Winant, Charles Sweeny on his final visit, and J. D. Biddle, the American ambassador to foreign governments in London.[62] These visitors, plus the news correspondents looking for a story day after day, made life difficult because the squadron was taking on an increasing share of the action and downing more enemy aircraft; unfortunately, losses were also starting to mount.

After the success of 3 July, engagements with enemy aircraft became routine as the Eagles were called upon for increasing numbers of patrols and bomber escort missions. On 19 July Victor Bono got an Me 109 probable destroyed, and on the 21st Bill Dunn shot down another Messerschmitt. The 568 operational missions flown by the squadron in July made Number 71 one of the more active units in Fighter Command. Adding to the new spirit resulting from increased activity was the news that Number 71 would soon get the aircraft that the Eagles had been waiting for, the Spitfire. Jack Fessler remembers,

> We just flew down and dumped the Hurricanes off and picked up the Spitfire. None of us had flown it before but they told us about the switches and controls so it wasn't bad. Both planes had the spade-grip control column and the brakes worked the same. The big thing was that the Spit was clean . . . and so it was hard to slow down, especially in formation. We tried to make a good show when we took the Spits and tried to take off in formation and show everyone what good boys we were, and we were see-sawing all over the place getting home.[63]

On 17 August the squadron flew its first combat missions in the Spitfire II. The pilots were Fessler, Charles Tribken, Andy Mamedoff, Charles Bateman, Gus Daymond, Bill Geiger, Chesley Peterson, and Newton

Anderson. Three days later the Squadron flew all its missions in the Spitfire. The Spitfire IIa was only a stop-gap, and just ten days after completing the transition into that aircraft, the squadron began receiving the Spitfire Vb. This aircraft, with 300 more horsepower than the II, gave the Eagles, for the first time, a real edge over the Me 109 and enabled them to compete with the best units of Fighter Command.

The members of the Eagle Squadrons had seen their friends or squadron mates injured or killed in aircraft accidents, either in training or after arriving at the squadron, but the real test came with combat. The risks increased several times over and each pilot had to consider that his number might just come up next. Royce Wilkinson saw some apprehension when the Americans were first exposed to combat. "For the first time they said, 'Those guys are shooting at me!' They were all brave boys and, although they got excited, not one of them left because he was afraid."[64] As Bert Stewart recounted,

> The first time I was shot at, I was scared to death for one thing! I got out of the way as fast as I could. But I never said, What have I got myself into? Nor did I ever think I would get myself killed because it was always going to happen to someone else, not me. If any combat pilot, when he gets into action and sees the flak coming around him and the enemy aircraft flinging around, says he is not at least concerned, he is just not talking straight. But I was never sorry that I volunteered.[65]

Morris Fessler commented on a different side of the experience:

> I was never afraid, in that regard, I was pumped up. You were pumped up when you knew you were going to do the mission but it was never a problem . . . once I started out. You were there to shoot them down and they were there to shoot you down, but there was no hate involved. I never hated the Germans.[66]

The immediacy of the prospect of being killed is reflected in the number of war-related deaths for the Eagles. Of the 260 members of the Eagle Squadrons, 109—more than 40 pecent—were killed during the war. During the three months after the Eagles destroyed their first enemy aircraft and suffered their first combat loss, the Squadron Operations Record Book records the reality of combat. On 5 August P/O William Driver was killed, followed by P/O Kenneth S. Taylor on the 9th. Ten days later, Virgil Olsen crashed into the Channel, and on the 28th Jack Weir died in a crash. On 7 September Hillard Fenlaw, William Nichols, and Eugene Tobin were reported missing; Nichols was taken prisoner, both Fenlaw and Tobin, another of the first Eagles, were killed. Ten days later, Bill Geiger became a prisoner and Tommy McGerty was killed. In October the list of missing or killed included Gilmore Daniel, who had been in the squadron for two weeks, Roger Atkinson, Lawrence Chatterton, Jack Fessler, and Oscar Coen, who bailed out over France, was aided by the Underground, and returned to the Eagles two months later. The list continues on for the ensuing months of the war.

Roy Evans believes that most pilots thought about death even though they didn't talk much about it.

> It bothered you when your friends got shot down and I thought about that a lot. But even then it was seen as the "luck of the game" or "the roll of the dice." Sure you hated to lose a friend but we all lost a lot of good friends. You hated to see it but . . . you just went back out and did the best you could.[67]

Jim Goodson thought there were many close friendships and describes his reaction to the death of one of his friends after a particularly difficult mission.

> I was eating dinner and I looked down at my plate and saw water on it. I looked up at the ceiling to see where the leak was but didn't see one. The suddenly I realized that I was crying. I guess it was just the desire to release my feelings

because I don't recall crying another time during the war. You were just so busy and you identified with the guy who got shot down and realized it could have been you. But death is always something that happens to the other guy.[68]

"As time went on", said Carroll McColpin, "you began to think of yourself as invincible. 'Perhaps,' you would say to yourself, 'everybody will get klobbered except me. I have this fighting down to a science.'" Edwin Taylor stated simply, "I never saw one of the Eagle pilots who didn't think that everyone else would be killed before he would get it."[69]

Scarcely two months after he assumed command, the popular "Paddy" Woodhouse was promoted to wing commander and departed North Weald and the Eagles. Not only had he come to be well liked and respected by the squadron, but he also was the catalyst for the unit's transformation from fledglings to full combat pilots. From the outset, Woodhouse, as well as Churchill, Wilkinson, and Brown, demonstrated time and again the wisdom of the RAF decision that non-British squadrons have battle-tested, regular RAF commanders. As squadron and flight leaders, these men had all been teachers who reined in the eager, inexperienced, often foolhardy Americans and patiently taught them the art of flying a fighter aircraft in war.

Woodhouse was succeeded on 13 August by Squadron Leader E. R. Bitmead, another Battle of Britain veteran. Unfortunately, Bitmead was physically and mentally drained from almost continual combat flying. So he was replaced after only a few weeks by the exceptionally well qualified Stanley T. Meares. Like his predecessors, Meares ⸱ ⸰⸰ ⸰ veteran of the Battle of Britain as well as Dunkirk, and possessed exceptional leadership qualities. Under his command, the pilots of Number 71 Squadron were able to refine their combat skills and become, as Chesley Peterson put it, "one of the best units in the RAF."[70] The facts back Peterson's statement, for in October 1941 Number 71 Eagle Squadron led all RAF squadrons in the total number of German aircraft shot down, nine. The New York *Journal American,* the New York *Herald Tribune,* and the Chicago *Daily News* printed stories of this accomplishment. These accounts were echoed across the country and led to a new rash of articles about all three Eagle Squadrons and their members, among them, one about Carroll McColpin downing his fifth enemy aircraft to make him an ace. "Former Employer Calls Pilot 'Coolest' He Has Ever Known" was the *Oakland Tribune* piece on McColpin.[71]

The Squadron repeated its October performance in November, but the accomplishment was clouded in tragedy when Squadron Leader Meares was killed, along with Ross Scarborough, in a mid-air collision during a training flight. "This was tragedy indeed," wrote Harold Strickland.

> We lost our highly admired, distinguished British Squadron Leader, a veteran of Dunkerque, the Year Alone, and the Battle of Britain, and our colleague Ross Scarborough, a very aggressive and skilled fighter pilot who had destroyed four enemy aircraft.[72]

The London *Daily Mail* carried a very meaningful tribute to Meares:

> Squadron Leader Stanley Meares, the Englishman who for months has led the first American Eagle squadron in their great offensive over the enemy occupied coast, has been killed in collision over Britain with a comrade-in-battle. In death Stanley Meares remains with the men who fought beside him; he is to be buried in the little cemetery devoted to members of the squadron who have already died in battle. . . . Just over a month ago Mrs. D. H. Meares watched the King pin the D.F.C. on her son's tunic. She asked why he had won the decoration. "For being a good boy," replied Stanley.[73]

Carroll McColpin, Chesley Peterson, and Gus Daymond at the ceremony where they each received the Distinguished Flying Cross, first Eagles to be so honored. Also pictured are (second from right) Air Marshal Sir Sholto Douglas and (far right) Charles Sweeny.

AN AMERICAN TAKES COMMAND

After Meares' death, recently decorated Chesley Peterson, one of the original members of the unit who, with Carroll McColpin and Gus Daymond, had received the Distinguished Flying Cross from the King on 4 October, was named to command. (The DFC was generally awarded for four aerial victories.) "The burden of command fell upon Pete at the age of 21 and everyone closed ranks behind him," wrote Strickland.[74] This was a momentous occasion, for it was a well-thought-out recognition on the part of Fighter Command that the Americans had come of age and an American could command an RAF unit.[75] Royce Wilkinson noted that one of the reasons Fighter Command was willing to give command to an American was Peterson's record and personality: "Peterson was a very good lad, level-headed and mature, who spent much of his time studying flying, fighting and command. That's why I recommended him for command."[76] *Time* magazine caught the spirit of Peterson's promotion and also the significance of the squadron in a 1 December article. After commenting on Peterson's assuming command of the unit and on his background, it went on to note,

> He has also seen most of his pals killed or captured. Of 32 Eagle casualties, 20 are prisoners of war and twelve are dead. To replace these, 28 others are in training besides 84 Eagles who are now taking part in operations in England [referring to the three Squadrons then in operation]. Of the original Eagle Squadron of 34 men, Peterson and Flying Officer "Gus" Daymond of Van Nuys, California are the only ones who remain.[77]

The new flood of press interest in his appointment to command, added to the usual constant flow of publicity, prompted Peterson to close the squadron to the press when he took command. He firmly believed, and most of his pilots agreed, that they wanted to be just another RAF unit recognized by what they did rather than who they were.[78] Peterson's assumption of command was accompanied by a demise of Englishmen in all the key positions in the squadron. Harold Strickland's report of his 8 December mission illustrates the American dominance.

> Another Ramrod (bomber escort mission) and close escort to Hurricane bombers. Also, my mission No. 10. Some of my veteran pals told me that anyone who lived through his first 10 missions likely would reach 20, maybe 25, which was very encouraging from my concept of fighter pilot longevity. Gus Daymond led the Red Flight (Daymond would eventually command Number 71), Pete again led the squadron, and Carroll McColpin (eventual commander of Number 133) led Blue Flight.[79]

One of the reasons Fighter Command was ready to place an American in command was the outstanding operational record compiled by Number 71 in October and November. Bill Dunn, Gus Daymond, and Carroll McColpin became aces during that time. The best day of the period was 2 October, when the Eagles destroyed five enemy aircraft without losing any of their own. Mc-Colpin, who shot down two, described his part of the action:

> I was in the lead when I saw the Me 109s climbing to inter-
> cept us. Stanley Meares and I started accelerating first, div-
> ing toward the enemy formation and we engaged the enemy
> first. While Meares was firing at the nearest 109 I overtook
> the same plane from below and fired a half-second burst
> from about 100 yards. It burst into flame. I broke away to
> port and found myself in position for an attack on another
> 109, so I gave him a burst. He pulled up and dived with
> smoke pouring out. I thought I saw a man bail out. The
> plane was seen to hit the ground. I saw another Me 109
> below, dived on him, and followed him down to 3,000 feet
> where I gave him a one-second burst. He never pulled out,
> and he hit the deck as I pulled up.[80]

Heavy action continued for the first Eagle Squadron through November and into December. By that time, Bert Stewart believes, England's war had become the Eagle's war and all the Eagles were focused on the survival of the United Kingdom with little thought of much else. The Eagles had seen their members killed and taken prisoner, as had most other RAF squadrons, and they had become one of the battle-hardened units of Fighter Command. Certainly, the last thought in anyone's mind after the missions of 7 December was the US entry into the war. But Harold Strickland describes the event that followed later that day:

> After the final mission over the minesweepers and dinner I
> turned in early and was reading in bed when the bat-man
> pounded on the door, entered and shouted "PEARL HAR-
> BOR HAS BEEN ATTACKED BY THE JAPANESE!" He
> told me that the news had just been announced by the BBC
> and added that most of our battleships had been destroyed. I
> jumped into my clothes (literally) and headed for the bar (in
> the officer's mess) where pandemonium was in progress.

Strickland summed up the reasons for celebrating and the significance of the disaster for the Eagles.

> We knew that it was now only a matter time until thousands of American warplanes would arrive in Europe; hundreds of thousands—millions—of fighting men and the equipment to back them up. Now there was no question in any of our minds that we had been fighting for the United States as well as Britain.[81]

Chesley Peterson had also gone to bed early to get rested for the next day's missions when his roommate, Robbie Robinson, brought the news. Both men hurried to the mess and viewed the same pandemonium that Strickland saw. The booze flowed as toasts were drunk by the Eagles to their new allies and seemingly every pilot on the base found an excuse to celebrate their new comrades-in-arms. "I never saw the Eagles so hopped up and full of fight in my life," one pilot was reported as saying.[82] Besides the celebrating, plans were made to get into the war against Japan as soon as possible. In both 121 and 133 Squadrons the reaction was similar as the Americans realized they were now part of both England's and America's war.

Number 133 was still based in Ireland, but the phone lines between 71 and 121 were hot. They decided to each have two representatives go to the American embassy the next day to volunteer the squadrons for duty in the US forces. Squadron Leader Peterson was also to ask that 71 Squadron be transferred to the Far East to fight the Japanese directly. "The First Eagle Squadron was worried," noted the press, because "its members signed for the duration and perfected their fighting technique as a unit. They say that no matter what happens they want to stay together and wondered if they could transfer to the United States as a group."[83] The delegates from 71 and 121 Squadrons presented their case to Ambassador Winant, who assured them that they would be brought into the US Army Air Force in the near future. Armed with this assurance, and the firm denial by Air Marshal Douglas of their request for Far Eastern duty, the Americans resumed their duties as members of the RAF and allies in the war against the Third Reich.[84]

Although few Eagles probably gave it much thought at the time, Pearl Harbor and the declaration of war against Germany by the United States that followed on 8 December etched the significance of the Eagles in history forever. Now they were not just a bunch of foolish or heroic young men who had gone off to fight in a foreign war—they were the initial cadre, the first of what Winston Churchill referred to as the New World coming to save the Old. No wonder the Eagles are a proud group.

To Chesley Peterson, the significance of being an American in command of an American RAF unit was probably best demonstrated during the second week of December. In keeping with Fighter Command policy, Number 71, having been in the thick of the action since June, was ordered to rotate to Kirton-in-Lindsey, a more quiet base in 12 Group, to rest. Peterson's squadron was up in arms at the decision and the young squadron leader went directly to Air Marshal Leigh-Mallory, commander of 11 Group, to plead his case. The argument fell on deaf ears, so Peterson, in what he acknowledged was both unprofessional and improper, went over Leigh-Mallory's head to Air Marshal Douglas, Fighter Command commander. Douglas reversed Leigh-Mallory's decision and 71 was moved to Martlesham Heath, still in 11 Group and the main combat zone, while Number 121 Squadron transferred to North Weald to begin their tour of extensive action against the Luftwaffe. The Kirton-in-Lindsey opening was filled by 133 Squadron.

This appeal was not the only occasion when Peterson, or another Eagle commander, took advantage of the fact that they were Americans—a significance evidently not lost on the RAF. "I never hesitated to bypass Wing to request things from Group or even bypass them all and go directly to Fighter Command. This was unheard of in the RAF," Peterson said. "For that reason the Eagles got a lot of things, including base postings, that they wanted."[85] Carroll McColpin agrees with Peterson. He believes the British never really quite understood or knew just how to treat the Yanks, so the American commanders could get away with making requests, moving outside the chain of command, and the like, which a regular RAF officer could never do. Both Peterson and McColpin took full advantage of this situation during their tenure as commanders of Eagle Squadrons.[86]

During the last half of 1941 Number 71 Squadron had come of age in the RAF. They saw extensive combat, acquitted themselves well, and ended the year anticipating a continuation of the action. On Christmas, Harold Strickland had a "wonderful Christmas dinner with other RAF officers at beautiful Bigham Hall with Lady Black and the Misses Black." Three days later, Oscar Coen returned after evading the Germans for over a month. During his evasion Coen had been dressed as a teenage boy by the French Underground and taken through German lines without any significant trouble. So Strickland's entry for 31 December gives an idea of the Eagles' mood:

> Dense fog outside and denser inside, plus "Happy New Year Oscar!" parties everywhere within a 75 mile radius of London. All of which brought us into January 1942 with the fog still prevalent outside but lifting inside the Officers Mess at Martlesham Heath.[87]

SECOND EAGLE SQUADRON TAKES WING

While the first Eagle Squadron was rapidly moving, under the glare of the press, toward heavy action and eventual recognition as one of the best units in the RAF, the second group of Eagles, Number 121 Squadron, with their motto of "For Liberty" and emblem of an American Indian Chief's head adorned with a headdress of eagle feathers, was being formed, equipped, and trained at Kirton-in-Lindsey, a generally quiet base near the coast in 12 Group. (Number 71 had used this base for part of its initial operational training.) Number 121's formation, on 14 May 1941, was significant because it moved the concept of the Eagle Squadrons beyond what either Charles Sweeny or the initial Air Ministry proponents of an American unit ever intended. Their idea had been for one squadron to serve as an American presence until the United States entered the war.[88] Very successful recruiting by Clayton Knight, producing large numbers of volunteers, forced the entire concept of the Eagles onto another tack. By May 1941 there were so many Americans in the pipeline that either a second American unit had to be formed or even more Yanks had to be spread out among other RAF squadrons, which many veteran observers believed could lessen both those Americans' operational efficiency and their potential as a publicity tool.

To ensure a relatively rapid transition to genuine operational status for 121 Squadron, the RAF adhered to the policy established with 71 Squadron and picked a veteran squadron leader, Peter R. Powell, and two experienced flight commanders, Hugh Kennard and Royce Wilkinson, to lead the Americans. Powell, Kennard, and Wilkinson were all veterans of the Battle of Britain. Powell was credited with destroying seven German planes before his assignment to lead Number 121, while Wilkinson wore the DFC with bar and was reputed to be one of the best shots in the RAF. Hugh Kennard's thought when he found he was going to be assigned to an Eagle Squadron was, "it will be a most interesting posting with a new type of people that many RAF officers had not dealt with before." He was delighted.[89] The three leaders proved to be wise choices, because in just two months, on 21 July 1941, 121 Squadron was declared operational and began flying regular missions out of Kirton-in-Lindsey.[90]

There are several reasons for 121 Squadron's rapid progression compared to that of its predecessor. Of most significance was the planning that had been done by Fighter Command before organizing the squadron. With Number 71, there was no real planning and little thought had been given to just how to equip and use the unit. This lack of planning was evident in the initial assignment

Number 121 Squadron emblem.

of Brewster Buffalos to the squadron and their replacement with war-weary Hurricane I's. Once they received the Hurricane IIb's, nearly eight months after being organized, the squadron's progress to real combat-ready status was more rapid. By contrast, 121 flew the old Hurricane I for only two months, during initial training, before getting the combat effective IIb. According to Hugh Kennard, most squadrons were initially equipped with the old Hurricanes because they were expendable, while the Spitfires were not.[91]

There had been no initial plan for how to use Number 71, so progress was slow while the employment plan was hashed out. Whether to use the first Eagle Squadron in the area of heavy combat had also been in doubt because of possible losses, and not until spring 1941 was the decision made to push the unit into the heat of battle. By the time both 121 and 133 Squadrons were organized, the eventual use of the units and their ability to effectively fly combat had been proved by the Americans in Number 71, so the new Eagle Squadrons were designated to assume a combat role as rapidly as possible.

Personnel was also a factor in the newer squadron's more rapid development. The initial cadre in Number 71 did not have uniform training or qualifications, so much more time was needed to even establish a common proficiency base from which to begin operational preparation. Then, too, several pilots in 71 were really more in search of adventure, glamour, and the mystique of the fighter pilot than seeking serious operational flying against the Germans. For them, training was something to be endured and they did not necessarily put all their effort into it. "At least fifty percent of the first boys in 71 would go anywhere and do anything," said Royce Wilkinson. "In many ways, they were soldiers of fortune."[92] This was reinforced by the tremendous amount of publicity that accompanied 71 Squadron in whatever it did.

Both of these elements were generally missing with Number 121. The pilots had all been through a training program in the United States or Canada to ensure their common proficiency and "all were as well trained as their British counterparts."[93] They were also generally sheltered from the extensive publicity of Number 71, which, although it sometimes made the pilots of 121 jealous, generally helped them focus on the business of becoming proficient. Both Royce Wilkinson and Carroll McColpin believe that the 121 Squadron flyers were more mature than the initial cadre of Number 71. Most knew that they would be in the war sooner or later and had thought out more clearly the significance of joining the RAF. They had spent much more time in flight training and generally took what they were doing more seriously. For example, the tendency to party excessively was much more prevalent in the early days of 71 than in 121 or 133, and the few Eagles to be sent home by the RAF because of conduct were from among the early pilots in 71. In fact, several American pilots who ended up in 71 Squadron had initially requested not to go to that unit because of its general reputation, which had changed considerably by the time the squadron was in the heat of battle, in fall 1941, and becoming a first-class fighting unit.[94] Chesley Peterson's awareness of 71 Squadron's reputation was one of the major reasons he barred the press from the squadron when he took command.[95]

A third element that contributed to 121 Squadron's development as a combat unit was experience. A number of pilots from 71 Squadron were sent to 121 and several more pilots came to the unit from other RAF squadrons. The new flyers in the squadron were able to learn from this experienced cadre, helping the entire squadron pick up the "tricks of the trade" much more rapidly than had Number 71, which lacked such an experienced nucleus. This experience factor is also critical in the progress of 133 Squadron.

Nevertheless, the formation of 121 Squadron did not make it ready to begin effective flying. Although the unit began receiving Hurricane I's only three days after formation, most of the planes were not operational. But flying began on 19 May and at the end of the month unit strength was reported as 13 officers, 4 sergeant pilots, 134 enlisted men, and 11 serviceable aircraft. What a contrast to the seemingly endless wait for personnel and planes in Number 71!

Most of the Americans coming into the new unit expected to see action against the Germans fairly quickly. This expectation was compounded by the presence of the pilots who had been moved from other units, such as Royce Wilkinson and Richard Moore from Number 71, Bob Reed, Collier Mize, and Fred Scudday from Number 43, and Loran Laughlin and Carroll McColpin from

Number 607. The dedication of the pilots during those early days is well described by Hugh Kennard:

> They were all serious about why they had come and they were keen to go [into combat]. Most of them were well trained in flying and, while not ready for operational flying, they were enthusiastic and anxious to learn.[96]

June was spent completing the manning of the squadron, honing the skills of the pilots and ground crews, and generally working toward operational status.

There was no specified schedule for a squadron to reach operational status. A new RAF squadron would set up a formal training program depending on the needs of the pilots as perceived by the commander. Kennard explained,

> One didn't get into an airplane and take them over to wherever to begin with. You did special climbs and formation flights, dives, shooting and that sort of thing. I had to say when the squadron was ready for operations. I was given no special instructions because they were Americans. They were treated as any other newly formed squadron. . . . We also had to do training for landing in bad weather conditions. . . . You took very much what the Flight Commanders said about their people. You would do a lot of Squadron formations yourself to check on tactics and so forth. You had to feel comfortable . . . with their formation tactics before they were ready [for combat].[97]

The rapid transition of Number 121 to operational status and employment in meaningful combat-related duty is a testament to the effectiveness of the RAF planning for the squadron and the seriousness of the personnel.

Hurricane IIb's began arriving on the 4th of July, and the squadron flew a special formation in honor of the American holiday. Transition into the new aircraft was rapid, and on 21 July the unit took its place on the rolls of Fighter Command as an operational squadron. Within days, the squadron was being regularly employed in convoy escorts, very necessary missions but ones that squadrons flew either during their initial period in operational status or while being rested from the intense action in 11 Group. According to John Brown, "you brought her back to 1,600 rpm and about 155 mph going around convoys . . . round and round for 2 hours and 45 minutes. That was the longest I ever flew."[98] But on 8 August the unit's first contact with an enemy aircraft while on convoy patrol marked full combat status. Jim Griffin did his share of convoy patrol while with 121 Squadron and remembers it vividly:

> Jack Mooney (who had got the squadron's first shot at an enemy aircraft on August 8th) was turning in the wake of the last ship in the convoy. We were flying at an altitude of nine hundred feet, just beneath the clouds, and had been circling the ships for a half-hour. It would be another hour before we'd be relieved by four other 121 Eagle Squadron pilots.
> . . . The weather was always treacherous, and there was never anything between the ships and enemy territory but a stretch of open water. . . . Convincing yourself that flying endlessly between a hostile sky and deadly sea was boring was better than listening to the nagging voice of your subconscious reminding you of the unpleasant features of such a patrol: the fact that survival time in the icy water below would be a matter of minutes; that engine failure beyond gliding distance to land would leave you with two grim choices: ride the Spit down to what should be a quick merciful end . . . or bail out, knowing that even if there was enough altitude for your chute to open and lower you gently into the sea you would probably perish before help could arrive. Neither the other pilots, nor the crews of ships whose decks and rigging were covered with thick layers of ice could do anything, and there was little chance that Air-Sea Rescue could respond to a Mayday quickly enough, even if their motor launches and seaplanes could handle the strong winds and cope with the rough seas.[99]

Recalling the conditions Griffin describes, John Brown said, "It was times like these when you appreciated the quality of your maintenance people."[100]

GROUND CREWS

Ask any pilot who is really responsible for his success in the air and chances are he will tell you about his ground crew. The Eagles were no exception. Reliability of the squadron's aircraft when the time came to scramble on an enemy or to spend the very hazardous two hours over the frigid North Sea on convoy patrol was the ground crews' responsibility. The primary crew was a rigger and a fitter, who were responsible for the airframe and the mechanics of the aircraft, respectively. These teams ensured that twelve Hurricanes or Spitfires were available for every mission and that battle damage was repaired as rapidly as possible. There were other members of the ground crew, responsible for rearming the guns and refueling, but they were generally assigned to a group of aircraft, so they did not become as well known by the individual pilots. The most important ground crew member was the fitter, because he was responsible for maintaining the aircraft's engine. The complexity of his job is suggested in a story told by Kenny John, a fitter with Number 121 Squadron:

> It was at RAF Southend . . . that all Spitfires were grounded to raise the emergency engine boost pressure from plus 14 to plus 16 pounds per square inch . . . because of the advent of the enemy Focke Wulf FW 190. This important modification consisted of removing the entire boost control unit from the engine . . . blanking off the eighth inch bleed hole with a suitable rivet and substituting a smaller and more restricted sixteenth inch bleed hole.[101]

The fitter and rigger, plus other ground personnel, were also responsible for keeping the engines warm on aircraft standing alert. The procedure was to run the Merlin engine about every 30 minutes for long enough to get it to operating temperature. This warming of the engines was necessary because when the alert aircraft were scrambled they had to be in the air in less than two minutes, which meant applying full power to the engine immediately after starting it. Doing so with a cold engine would generally ensure engine failure before the pilot could even get airborne. It was while running an engine to get it warm that Kenny John had one of his most exciting moments:

> I was just about to pull the engine cut out to shut down when I was bounced by two Heinkel 111's. The ground alongside the port mainplane suddenly erupted as though hit by a high speed plough, the two enemy aircraft overshot and into a tight port turn to come round for a repeat attack. Meantime, I had signalled chocks away . . . opened the throttle . . . and taxied across the grass and tarmac, towards the hanger. Only just in time because the two Huns plastered the spot where we had been standing. . . . I suppose they assumed that a pilot might be ready for take off and decided to "rub him out" before taking further action against us.[102]

The tales of heroic deeds by these dedicated men require a separate volume. Reade Tilley vividly remembers watching the ground crews refuel his Spitfire on Malta with bombs falling all around and German aircraft making an occasional strafing attack.[103]

There seemed to be a natural affinity between the ground crews and the Eagles, and the relationship was the source of many a story around the bar after a day's flying. Natural comedy sometimes arose because of the different words the British and Americans used for certain items. For example, a windshield to the Americans was a windscreen to the British, gas was petrol, and an airplane a kite. Edwin Taylor remembers once, watching his fitter working on the airplane,

> He asked me to hand him a "spanner." I had no idea what that was but was not about to demonstrate my ignorance so I told him there wasn't one in the tool box. He insisted that there was so I told him he would have to get it himself. He came down, picked up an open ended wrench and we both had a good laugh because he knew I didn't know what he wanted when he first asked me for it.[104]

Shown above are Jim Daley and his ground crew of Number 121 Squadron. Below are Kenny John (second from left), also of Number 121, and his friends with the Spitfire he taxied to safety during a German attack.

Whenever a squadron was transferred to another base, the entire maintenance section moved along with the pilots and planes, so it was possible for a pilot to have the same ground crew for a very long time. This association helped the quality of maintenance, because the ground crews got to know the individual aircraft and could more rapidly diagnose a problem, repair it, and get the fighter back into the air. A number of the Eagles developed strong friendships with their fitters and riggers that have endured over the years.[105]

INTO ACTION WITH 121 SQUADRON

By mid-August 1941, Number 121 was being called upon to fly to bases in 11 Group area and stage from there as escorts for bombers on missions over France. "While actual air-to-air action was minimal," said Carroll Mc-Colpin, "everyone thought they were doing an essential job and it did get the unit into action early in their service. I think most of the pilots got all the flying they wanted to get."[106] The squadron flew 980 operational missions in August, a heavy load indeed. Hugh Kennard was also impressed with the squadron's attitude throughout his time with Number 121.

> When the weather was misty or foggy and not suitable for other operations, my Eagles anyway would say "what the hell are we doing today? We can't sit on our asses all day today, what shall we do?" This used to infuriate me because I could get the day off but they wanted to go and do something. We used to get permission to go off the coast of Holland . . . and shoot armed trawlers. . . . They needn't have gone anywhere . . . but they wanted to go do something all the time. And we lost a few doing that sort of thing. That activity was not typical of most RAF squadrons.[107]

As with their comrades in Number 71, the members of 121 saw early the real hazards of the duties they were performing. Just five weeks after the squadron was formed, the first casualty came: Pilot Officer Loran

Laughlin crashed on a low-altitude formation flight. On 26 July,

> while flying over Lincoln, Sgt. Pilot Shenk and Sgt. Pilot Smith collided and were forced to bail out. Both machines were a total wreck. Both pilots were alright; death, however, was caused to civilians and damage to the premises done in Lincoln owing to the planes falling on them over the city of Lincoln.[108]

August was accident free, but Pilot Officer Earl Mason was killed on 15 September when he did a slow roll too near the ground and crashed. Although these deaths had a real effect on the squadron, they were not the result of enemy action. It would be several months before the Germans would be able to claim their first member of 121 Squadron shot down.[109]

While 121 Sqadron was seeing no action with the enemy during September, several members of the unit were transferred to Number 71 Squadron to offset that unit's combat losses. Fighter Command had decided that the Eagle Squadrons would remain all-American as much as possible; so as long as there were operationally ready US pilots to fill the gaps in Number 71, they would be used. Carroll McColpin and Donald Geffene were transferred on 9 September and Edward Miluck and Bert Stewart followed on the 21st. The transfer of experienced pilots out of both 121 and 133 Squadrons would plague those units for the rest of 1941. Losing 4 of 24 experienced pilots in just two weeks strained the squadron. These transfers had to be replaced by inexperienced pilots coming straight out of the OTU, who needed at least a month to get up to speed so they could be considered fully combat ready. Generally, the flight commander or one of the more experienced pilots would take the new flyer under his wing and spend the month training him, further draining the unit's manpower. The process, though, was just a fact of life in all RAF squadrons, since any loss would precipitate this chain of events unless an experienced replacement was immediately available.[110]

The rather frequent movement of pilots into 71 Squadron has led to a general misconception about the relationship among the three American units. A sense developed that in some way Number 71 was the premier unit of the three, primarily because it was the first to be organized, received the most publicity, and got into combat with the Germans first. Some people see significance in the fact that 71 never had any sergeant pilots as did the other two American units. The relationship remains an item of contention among the Eagles, but most of those who served in 71 and one of the other squadrons tend to dismiss the issue as insignificant. Carroll McColpin, who was one of only two Eagles to serve in all three squadrons (Gilmore Daniel was the other), said that the transfers to Number 71 "were not because 71 was the premier unit but to fill the battle losses and keep the unit an American one. Seventy-one was in the thick of the battle and sustaining losses while the other two were not."[111] Royce Wilkinson, who was a flight commander in 71 when it was formed and then transferred to 121 to serve the same function, does not see any pecking order among the units.

> The Squadron you are in is always the best. Several of the pilots in 71 were transferred to 121 when it started as well as to other squadrons throughout the RAF. This was common practice. I don't think that anyone thought 71 was the premier Eagle squadron.[112]

The sergeant pilot issue is also insignificant. When 71 was formed all the pilots were officers: that was part of the recruiting package agreed upon by Charles Sweeny and the Air Ministry. Therefore, the unit did not have the facilities or organization established to accommodate sergeant pilots with separate quarters and a separate mess.

The line between pilot officers and sergeant pilots was very significant within the RAF, however, and the two groups seldom fraternized except when flying. Nearly all the Americans recruited through the Clayton Knight Committee were brought into the RAF as officers, but those who came through the Royal Canadian Air Force, including Reade Tilley, Bert Stewart, Gilmore Daniel, Jack Mooney, and a number more in 121 Squadron, entered as sergeant pilots. These individuals were all commissioned in short order, Tilley and Stewart by mid-August, but until they were officers there was no effective method of moving them to Number 71. In reality, there were almost no sergeant pilots in any of the Eagle Squadrons by the end of 1941.

There was little change in the mission profile of 121 Squadron during the last three months of 1941. Missions consisted primarily of the unpopular convoy escort, local training when there was no operational mission to fly, occasional scrambles to intercept enemy aircraft that seemed to never be there, some escort duty staging from other bases into France, and a few "Balboas," flights in which the fighters served as decoys to bring up the German defenders while bombers went to their targets a few miles away. But those three months of October through December still saw over 1,500 missions flown by the approximately twenty pilots in the squadron. In October the squadron's aircraft were changed from the Hurricane IIb to the Spitfire IIa; then, in November, to the Spitfire Vb, the newest fighter in the RAF. This change of aircraft resulted in an increase in the number of training missions the pilots flew, but did not curtail the operational status of the squadron. And acquisition of the Spitfire really told 121 that they would soon be in the main theater of action. The changeover also helped demonstrate to the pilots the caliber of leadership that the RAF had placed over them. "On the 19th of October," recalls John Brown,

> I went to Digby to fly one (Spitfire) back to Kirton. I'd never flown one before and didn't know much about them. They talked to us and told us what to expect when the flaps went down and the wheels, the little idiosyncrasies of the bird.

There was a lot of wind and it was a hassle. . . . We didn't know much about our Squadron Commander (Peter Powell). He didn't say a word, he just got in the Spitfire and I have never seen anything like it. He came over the field at about 200 and probably 1000 feet, dropped the nose down and came down to about 500 (feet), went up and did three slow rolls, two flick rolls, a tail slide, and we just stood there and looked at him. We couldn't believe it. You talk about building confidence in people, this guy really did it.[113]

Although not true in all cases, generally each pilot had an aircraft he considered his. "I always had aircraft MDV," said Charles Cook. "No one else could use it unless I wasn't flying. If you were new in the Squadron you probably would have to share a plane with a more senior member and sometimes you had to take turns with a particular ship."[114] Often, a pilot would paint a special insignia on the front of his plan, by the cockpit, or just put his name along the side. A number of Eagles used the insignia designed by Walt Disney of a cartoon Eagle wearing boxing gloves; others used an insignia like that on the Eagle patch or personalized their designs. (See facing page illustrations.) LeRoy Gover named his plane "Sondra-Lee," and Duane Beeson, from Idaho, called his the "Boise Bee." There was no guarantee that each time a pilot flew he would have the same ship, but he did get assigned the same aircraft as much as possible. "This [association of a pilot with one airplane] was an important thing to do in a combat situation," said Edwin Taylor. "The more you get to know a particular aircraft and its idiosyncracies, the better job you can do when you are in battle."[115] "I would work hard to get my aircraft set up the way I wanted it," remarked Carroll McColpin, "and I wanted to have that plane whenever I flew. I even had the guns zeroed at a different distance than some of the other pilots."[116]

Having your own plane was also valuable because when it was not scheduled for maintenance or another mission and you didn't have to fly or stand alert, the craft could be used for training or practice. "We used to take

COURTESY OF EDWIN TAYLOR

Walt Disney designed the "Fighting Eagle," shown above on Wendell Pendleton's Spitfire, early in the war for use by the Eagle Squadrons. The Eagles used the design extensively on aircraft, bulletin boards, and posters; members of the Eagle Squadron Association still use it today. A number of the Eagles, including Mike Kelly pictured below, painted the Eagle Squadron shoulder patch insignia on their aircraft.

COURTESY OF JAMES GRIFFIN

185

the new guys up in formation and teach them tactics and some of the tricks that would keep you alive," said Edwin Taylor. "Of course the new pilots would have to use any plane that was not being flown. If you did fly another man's ship you had to be careful since no one was very happy if their airplane got damaged."[117]

On 16 November, Harold Marting reminded 121 Squadron that they were still in the action when he badly damaged and probably destroyed a Ju 88 while on a patrol mission. In the middle of the month, three more squadron members were transferred to Number 71, and on 26 November the squadron had one of its infrequent open houses for the press.[118] Among the articles that resulted was one by Joseph Evans, Jr., in the New York *Herald Tribune.* Noting that this was the first time journalists had been permitted to visit the second Eagle Squadron, he included short biographies of several of the pilots. "The members of the Squadron were eager to get into combat after four months of patrol duty," he wrote, "and they will soon be transferred to a location to join the sweeps across the Channel." (Evans was evidently unaware that the unit had been conducting such sweeps from staging bases for two or three months.) Evans went on to relate that "the members of the Squadron had voted to demand an assignment that would give them action and if they didn't get it they had agreed to ask for transfers to other RAF Squadrons." The capstone of the article was a picture of 121 Squadron Spitfires flying past an American flag at Kirton-in-Lindsey.[119]

The Squadron Operations Record Book makes no mention of Pearl Harbor, but the members of 121 were certainly overjoyed at the US entry into the war, which caused a celebration that continued far into the night. Royce Wilkinson remembers the activity in the mess when the official word came over the radio. "Everyone cheered and drank a toast, 'Yanks, you're in it now.' No one wanted to leave the RAF, however. They all wanted to keep their Spitfires." Most of the members of the squadron, along with their fellows in 71, voted to request transfer to the Far East to fight the Japanese.[120] The requested transfers were not granted, but more action was soon to follow.

The "Balboas" of early December had produced two casualties, Richard Patterson and Kenneth Holder, but no German aircraft to show for the losses. So the squadron was overjoyed when they were transferred to North Weald, in 11 Group, on 16 December. There is speculation that the transfer was actually arranged by the squadron intelligence officer, Michael Duff Assheton-Smith (later to be knighted). Owner of a magnificent estate in North Wales, which was frequented by Eagles from 121, Assheton-Smith arrived at his posting in a Rolls-Royce. When he went to London, he often gave his address as Buckingham Palace, for the Queen was his godmother. Whether he spoke to his contacts about moving 121 will never be known, but Air Marshall Leigh-Mallory evidently showed no hesitation to move 121 to North Weald to take the place of the departing 71 Squadron.[121] It is interesting that the RAF picked prominent, wealthy English gentlemen to be the intelligence officers of both 71 and 121 Squadrons. One of the objectives, according to Charles Sweeny, was to imbue the Eagles with some of the culture and refinement expected of RAF officers. It was for the same reason that Robert Sweeny, brother of Charles and a prominent businessman and golfer, was also assigned to number 71.[122]

The entire 121 Squadron buzzed with anticipation after the move to North Weald, for now they were in the center of the action and engagements with the Germans were sure to follow. Their new station commander made them feel welcome by going to Harrods in London and buying a five-gallon tin of peanut butter because he knew the Americans liked peanut butter. "He told everybody else in the mess 'this peanut butter is for the Yanks. I don't want to see anybody else touch it,'" recalled John Brown.[123] Aside from standing alert and flying some convoy patrols, however, the squadron spent the remainder of December in practice and continued familiarization with their new aircraft.

THE THIRD EAGLE SQUADRON FLIES

In late August 1941, the members of the third Eagle Squadron were called together by their commanding officer, Squadron Leader George A. Brown. "Gentlemen," he said, "no Englishman is more appreciative than I to see you American Volunteers over here to assist us in our fight. It is going to get a lot tougher as time goes by—so, take a good look around this room, because a year from now most of you will be dead." George Sperry recalls, "His opening statement left us rather thunderstruck. We all glanced around at one another, all with the same thought in mind—'You poor ignorant bastards, you've had it.'"[124] Unfortunately, Squadron Leader Brown's words would prove to be very accurate.

Number 133 Squadron, with its motto, "Let us to the battle," and emblem of a spread eagle in a field of stars, had been announced by Fighter Command on 1 August 1941. Unlike Number 121, there were few veteran pilots in 133. The squadron had been designated to take new American recruits and bring them into a combat-ready status. Therefore, its progress was designed by Fighter Command to be slow compared to that of Number 121. The squadron spent the first two weeks of its life at Coltishall, where Brown began to build his organization. On 16 August the initial cadre of the new unit moved its Hurricane II's the few miles to Duxford. It was there that Number 131 came up to minimum operating strength. Most of the pilots who were greeted by Brown with his prophetic message were fresh out of the OTU at Sutton Bridge. The group included Marion Jackson, Ronald Wolfe, Walter Soares, Cecil Meierhoff, Coburn King, William White, George Sperry, Roy Stout, James Nelson, L. S. Loomis, Hugh McCall, and Robert Pewitt.[125]

The short stay at Duxford was devoted to practicing formation flying, learning air discipline, and becoming

Number 133 Squadron emblem.

familiar with the missions the unit would undertake. It was also at Duxford that the unit got its first taste of death, with which they would become all too familiar, when Walter Soares and Charles Barrell collided while turning onto final approach after a practice mission and both were killed. The human element of this crash was brought home in an *Oakland Tribune* article that noted that Soares' fiancee received the notice of his death just one day after she got a letter suggesting that she come to England to marry him.[126] Starting on 6 September, the unit was introduced to the monotony of convoy patrol in the North Sea as well as making "low level tours along the

Dutch coast hunting for German E boats" under the supervision of the flight commanders and commanding officer.[127]

The quality of commanders picked for the new squadron could not have been better. The commanding officer, Squadron Leader George A. Brown, was transferred from 71 Squadron because of his experience with Americans. He was another decorated veteran who understood Americans and how to get the most out of them. The two flight commanders were equally qualified. H. A. S. Johnston, the "A" Flight commander, was a combat veteran who worked hard with his pilots to continue to train them as a unit, stressing air discipline and individual proficiency as the keys to being an effective fighter pilot. "B" Flight was commanded by Andy Mamedoff, one of the few Americans who flew in the Battle of Britain and an original member of 71 Squadron. The RAF continued the tradition of assigning the rich and famous as intelligence officers by posting Flight Officer J. M. Emerson. George Sperry remembers him as a

> millionaire cattleman from Argentina, playboy, polo star, not too bright, but a fabulous character . . . who would often buy a bottle of bourbon or scotch from his own pocket for the troops after a rough mission. He was nuts about flying . . . but had no more talent than a fire plug.[128]

Having come up to minimal operational strength at Duxford, in September the unit moved the few miles to Colly Weston, then, about two weeks later, to Fowlmere.[129] The members of the squadron got the impression that Fighter Command was trying to decide just what to do with them, and they were correct. The issue the RAF faced really had little to do with the nature of 133 Squadron itself, but was driven by the situation in Number 71.

By September 1941, the first Eagle Squadron was in the thick of the battle and its losses were starting to mount. Fighter Command had decided that the unit would remain an all-American squadron and that replacements had to be as experienced as possible. Therefore, they had to come from the two other Eagle Squadrons or from Americans assigned to other RAF units. Number 121 lost a number of such transfers throughout the fall, and on 8 September Ross Scarborough became the first from 133 to go to Number 71. Later in the year, Gilmore Daniel and Harold Strickland followed. Transfers were even worse for Number 133 than for 121, because the cadre of experienced American pilots that had helped form 121 was not available for 133 and, with 71 and 121 Squadrons in the thick of combat, most of the newly trained Americans coming into Eagle Squadrons were sent to 133.[130] The problem created is well articulated by Eric Doorly.

> Our training for combat in OTU was lousy. . . . So when we got into any kind of action I just didn't know what to do. The scary part was that I didn't know who to ask either. You see we were all green pilots put together and you didn't have the cadre of experienced people who could take the younger ones on and say, "Look, if you want to live more than two or three days you better learn these few things." Of course this changed over a period of time but until we got to Biggin Hill . . . we were a uniformly green squadron and it showed.[131]

Thus the decision was made in early October to transfer the squadron to Eglinton, near Londonderry, in the inhospitable climate of Northern Ireland, to complete further training and to fly the unpopular but critical convoy patrol duty over the North Atlantic. Atlantic convoy patrols were necessitated by the Germans' use of observation aircraft to report to waiting German U-boats on the position of British shipping approaching Ireland. The flight to Eglinton proved tragic for the unit in more ways than one. While letting down in bad weather to refuel on the Isle of Man, a portion of "B" Flight hit a mountain and all were killed; several other planes in the formation missed the top of the hills by only feet. Those killed included veteran Eagle Andy Mamedoff, who had recently become the first of the American flyers to marry an English girl, William White, Roy Stout, and Hugh McCall. Two more accidents, which took the lives of George Bruce and Gene Coxetter, occurred less than two weeks after arriving in Ireland.[132] In less than two-and-a-half-months the unit had lost eight pilots without seeing any action against the enemy. George Brown's early words had been far too accurate and, to some, Number 133 had become a "hard luck" squadron.

The effect on the squadron, in Edwin Taylor's view, was devastating. "The reaction to the pilots' running into the mountain was chaos; it was a terrible thing," he said.

> Not only the devastating impact of losing four pilots at one time and the need to replace them, but the loss of experience with Mamedoff, the loss of the airplanes, which were so scarce—we never really recovered from that crash until we were at Biggin Hill.[133]

Fighter Command did try to replace some of the lost experience by sending Ed Bateman from 71 Squadron to take Mamedoff's place as flight commander, as well as several other Americans from other RAF squadrons, including Edwin Taylor, Hiram Putnam, S. H. Crowe, Carter Harp, David Florance, Fred Scuddy from 121 Squadron, Karl K. Kimbro, Gilmore Daniel, James Coxetter, and Charles Cook. Other arrivals during November and December, all from OTU, included Carl Miley, Denver Miner, Hugh Brown, Wilson Edwards, Carl Bodding, and Robert Brossmer.[134] By near the end of the year the unit was at full strength. The availability of American pilots to join 133 late in 1941 gives graphic evidence of the effectiveness of the Clayton Knight Committee and just how many Americans were in the RAF by that time. Edwin Taylor, for example, had wanted to go to an Eagle Squadron when he completed OTU in mid-1941 but was told he would have to wait until there was an opening.[135]

The arrival of the squadron at Eglinton was not heartening. They were greeted by clouds, rain, snow, cold temperatures, and six inches of mud. Eglinton had

The slow march to the cemetery became too familiar for all of the Eagle Squadrons. The honor guard here is Richard Alexander, Carter Harp, Carl Miley, Walter Wicker, Gilbert Omens, James Nelson, and Karl Kimbro of Number 133.

been built as a coastal command base for large reconnaissance aircraft and bombers, and was not well suited for fighters. Not only did the Eagles have to become accustomed to the climate at Eglinton, but they also were billeted in cold, drafty barracks, heated by a small coal stove in each room and more than a mile from the mess, which made both meals and entertainment a chore. It was nearly another mile to the bathing facility, where the supply of hot water was always marginal. On the bright side were the black market steaks, hams, eggs, and butter, friendly pubs, and hospitable citizens of Londonderry to which the squadron became attached. Having withstood a diet of fish, cabbage, bread, and brussels sprouts in Eng-

Form 260.

Cash ~~......~~ ....for month of.....................19 . Vr. No..........

ROYAL AIR FORCE ROUTE.

It is His Majesty's pleasure that you do cause the Air Forces under your command, in so far as authorised by the King's Regulations and Air Council Instructions, to proceed, from time to time as occasion shall require, by such routes as you may judge expedient, to or from such place or places as shall be necessary in the performance of their duties.

Wherein the Civil Magistrates, and all others concerned, are to be assisting in providing Quarters, impressing Carriages, and otherwise, as there shall be occasion, according to Law.

Given at the Air Ministry, this 3rd day of July, 1940.

By His Majesty's Command,

Archibald Sinclair

To Officers Commanding
whom it may concern.

Serial No............ ....

By virtue of the foregoing authority, the following move is authorised for the service specified :—

P/O. Cook. ....with.....................officers,.... ....warrant officers,
(Rank and Name)
.... F/Sgts. and Sgts...................airmen,..............women,...................children,
is ordered to proceed from*..... Sutton Bridge. ....to...... Eglington.

Duty on which proceeding.................... Posting.

No. and Date of superior authority, if any.................. H.Q.F.C. Signal F.304. 3/10.

Date	Departure time	Depart from	Arrive at	Arrival time	Mode of Conveyance	No. of Rly. Wt.*
		To arrive at R.A.F. Station Eglington on 16th October, 1941.				
		on completion of 7 days' leave.				
		APPLY TO R.T.O. FOR ROUTE.				

UNIT STAMP.	Additional Instructions (if any) :— CERTIFIED THAT THIS OFFICER HAS BEEN ALLOWED RATION ALLOWANCE UP TO AND INCLUDING DATE OF ARRIVAL.

Given at Trg Wing, No.56,O.T.U. this 6th day of October, 1941.

Signature..... *Jt Seton* .... Rank.......... P/O.

NOTE. If a route is issued for an escort to conduct a prisoner, an order must also be given to the escort in terms of Form T (see Third Appendix to the Rules of Procedure (Air Force) 1933).

*Where other than the cheapest and most direct route is authorised, railway warrants must be endorsed in red ink alternative route and initialled by the issuing officer.

[P.T.O.]

RAF transfer order sending Charles Cook to Number 133 Squadron.

land, George Sperry likened himself to "an overgrown bear" by the time he left Ireland.[136]

Rather than try to replace the Hurricanes lost by the squadron through accidents, more than half of the original fifteen, Fighter Command decided to make the transition into Spitfires. On 28 October the first Spit II's arrived, and within a few days the aircraft were being flown on operational missions.[137] The unit continued with both Hurricanes and Spitfires until their move to Kirton-in-Lindsey at the beginning of 1942, when they received new aircraft, although by the end of November the Hurricanes were getting very little use.[138] (Having the squadron's pilots flying two different types of aircraft did not present any problem to the RAF, given its philosophy that a pilot could fly any aircraft that he was given.)

In addition to acquiring new aircraft, 133 also received the scrutiny of several high-ranking people. The first was Air Marshal Sir Sholto Douglas, who visited on 24 October, the day after Pilot Officer Bruce was killed, and the Duke of Kent, who with his wife, was the sponsor of 133 Squadron.[139] Whether connected with the number of accidents and these visits no one knows, but the unit got a new commander when George Brown was transferred to Fighter Command Headquarters, his place taken by Eric Hugh Thomas. This transfer was significant, for Thomas is given credit by many of the squadron members for really whipping the unit into shape so it would be ready to assume its position in 11 Group when the opportunity came at the end of the year. Thomas was an experienced flight and squadron commander coming to 133 from Number 611 Squadron, which flew Spitfire Vb's. The citation that accompanied the award of his DFC tells much, not only about Thomas but, again, about the caliber of officers the RAF picked to command the Eagle Squadrons.

> This officer has been actively engaged in operational flying since August 1940, when he fought in the Battle of Britain. He has participated in 60 sorties over enemy territory since the beginning of 1941, and has destroyed at least three enemy aircraft and shared in the destruction of another.[140]

Even more of a strict disciplinarian and perfectionist than Brown, Thomas' basic concept of fighter tactics was teamwork, not individual heroics, so he devoted a great deal of time to perfecting the unit's formation flying and air discipline. He developed a strong attachment to the Americans and continued to wear his Eagle patch even after leaving the unit to become the wing commander at Biggin Hill.[141]

To augment the dreaded convoy patrol, 133 used the last two months of 1941 for intense training as well as providing air defense for Derry and the northwest approaches to Ireland. In the latter capacity, they were scrambled a number of times to intercept suspected hostile aircraft. No action resulted from these missions, however. Walter Wicker's log book gives a good example of the missions flown by the squadron for just three days in late December. These included convoy patrol, practice interceptions, a gun-camera dog fight, air firing, local reconnaissance, dusk landings, cloud flying, an aircraft test, a battle climb to 25,000 feet, aerobatics, and formation flying. All of the missions were flown in Spitfires.[142] Fortunately for the unit, November and December were free of fatality, although one aircraft crashed when Ronald Wolfe got lost in the weather, ran out of fuel, and had to bail out. Unfortunately, he landed on the wrong side of the Irish border and was interred in the Irish Free State until he escaped in 1943.[143]

By the end of November, 133 was getting restless, eager to join their fellow Eagles in 11 Group and get a taste of the real action. Rumors were rampant by the first of December that the anticipated move would soon take place and that it would be accompanied by a switch to new Spitfires. The attack on Pearl Harbor certainly reinforced the anticipation. While there was a big party in the mess—"we never passed up the opportunity to have a party," said Edwin Taylor—the Americans were mainly interested in any news or information about the events. Denver Miner describes the scene:

> I was listening to BBC . . . when a calm voice broke into the middle of a number and . . . stated that the Japs had bombed Pearl Harbor and now the United States was in the war. I let out a yell that could be heard all the way to Derry . . . I gave them the news I had just heard. . . . That was

The dispersal hut at Eglinton in Northern Ireland, with the Eagle Squadron insignia on the hut and the American flag flying overhead.

the start of a bash to end all bashes—with unashamed tears running down their cheeks and patting each other on the back and buying drinks for each other. . . . The next few days a pall seemed to fall over the guys. Gone was the horseplay of the past. I suspected, like myself, they were doing some soul searching and thinking of the short distance from the Hawaiian Islands to our cities on the West Coast and evaluating our worth at this crucial time in our lives.[144]

At first blush, it may seem odd that the Americans in all three Eagle Squadrons celebrated Pearl Harbor, with all the loss of life there. But their attitude becomes understandable when placed in the context of what the Eagles were doing and the fact that the attack brought the United States into the war. This reaction is probably one of the best indications that Britain's war had become the Eagles' war as well. There was open discussion about transfer to the US forces and a tremendous enthusiasm that the chance would soon come for the squadron to make a difference.[145] Walter Wicker conveyed the mood in a letter to his father.

All of us being Americans we could feel the tremendous change almost in the first dispatches. It's as though you and I were arguing with each other and a couple of guys came up and piled into us: it would not take long to get together.

You should hear the quiet in the Sergeants' mess when we get a Roosevelt speech. The RAFs have learned it's as much as your life's worth to make any noise. Most of them want to hear anyway. We get a queer feeling sitting over here listening to talk about our ships getting sunk and Manila flattened because of inadequate fighter protection. Anyway, we feel that we're doing something in [the] right direction.[146]

The rumor of leaving Ireland became fact when a replacement squadron arrived at Eglinton in December to take over Number 133's mission of convoy patrol. The occasion produced one of the unit's most memorable social functions. The new squadron

had just arrived back from Russia where they had spent some months training Soviet pilots on the Hurricane. The new boys found some difficulty in settling down and . . . in the mess a "free for all" developed and the Station Commander Dickie Bain . . . came down just in time to catch all members of both squadrons involved in a game which seemed a cross between rugby, soccer and American football.[147]

George Sperry continues the narrative: "Surveying the wreckage he [Bain] slightly lost his temper, and let the cat out of the bag about the rumors of our return to England."[148] This news prompted yet another celebration, but since Bain had closed the mess, "the personnel piled into cars and taxis and made their way to Derry where they took over several pubs and continued the party!"[149]

The end of 1941 had a special meaning to 133 for on 31 December they left Eglinton by train for Belfast, thence by ship to Scotland, and finally by train again, arriving at Kirton-in-Lindsey on 2 January 1942. The aircraft were all left behind with the squadron given a promise of Spit Vb's awaiting them at their new base. When the travel-weary crew arrived in Belfast near midnight on New Year's Eve, there were no facilities for the nearly 120 officers and men in the party. They eventually were ushered into an empty mess hall and served bully-beef, bread, and hot tea. Not to be deterred in their celebration of the New Year, they

> made believe that the cold meat was roast turkey, the bread chocolate cake and apple pie, and the tea the finest vintage champagne, we toasted and sang in the New Year . . . our British Army hosts just gawked at us figuring that those "Yankee bastards are really off their rockers."[150]

The arrival of 131 Squadron at Kirton-in-Lindsey began a new chapter in the squadron's history, for they were now ready to enter the action against the Luftwaffe. All three of the Eagle Squadrons were classed as combat ready and, although they were not yet in the 11 Group area, the pilots of 133 knew they had taken a giant step toward really being so.

5. IN THE THICK OF THE ACTION, 1942

FOR ALL THREE EAGLE SQUADRONS, JANUARY 1942 WAS a disappointing month indeed. All had viewed the coming year with great anticipation: Number 71, of more months leading Fighter Command in enemy aircraft destroyed; Number 121, of being posted in the heart of the action at North Weald, with the accompanying opportunity to show just what they could do against the Luftwaffe; and Number 133, of finally being located where some action could be expected to offset the tremendous losses they had suffered without contacting the enemy. But anticipation soon gave way to a dreary spirit that matched the English weather. None of the squadrons did much flying because of the weather, and what flying there was proved to be boring: convoy patrols, often in marginal weather, and more training. From 27 January through 17 February, Martlesham Heath, 71 Squadron's base, was unserviceable because of mud, snow, water, and ice.

But disappointment and frustration did not mean complete inactivity. For 133, it was a time of transition. There were the new Spit Vb's with which to become familiar, so a good percentage of the squadron's flying was aimed at becoming proficient in that aircraft. This training was doubly challenging because the new aircraft were having wing problems, requiring that each be modified with a tab on the elevator. Ed Bateman was replaced as flight commander in 133 by Carroll McColpin, who transferred from Number 71. And unfortunately, the squadron's losses continued, as Pilot Officer Hugh Brown crashed on a patrol over the North Sea and was killed. Number 121 also had a change of command. The unit celebrated Peter Powell's promotion from squadron leader to wing commander but reluctantly bade him farewell as he departed to become the commander at Hornchurch. Hugh Kennard moved up from his flight commander assignment to take over the unit as the last British commander it would have. Number 121, too, suffered a casualty when Pilot Officer Jack Gilliland "mistook the fog for cloud and crashed at tremendous speed" in a street in Ipswich.[1] On the same day that Gilliland was killed, Harold Strickland took off with a ceiling of 50 feet and visibility a quarter-mile. His experience illustrates the problems associated with such weather.

> A one-hour and 40 minute minesweeper patrol with Carroll McColpin over the North Sea started with low, but ample, ceiling; but on return to Martlesham Heath in tight formation, broken fog came in which lowered the ceiling and reduced visibility. Mac descended extra carefully through the soup and broke out with minimum ceiling. After Mac broke out and began dodging trees, etc., I moved from the echelon wing position into a line astern position. . . . This was my first experience with the winter coastal fogs and . . . it seemed to me that the danger of collision would be lessened if I pulled up into the soup. At the worst I could climb up and bail out. At best I could call Fighter Command and be vectored . . . to some base where there was more ceiling and visibility. . . . At this point I still had only about 13 hours of actual instrument flying . . . so . . . I went into an instrument climb . . . punched D for Drink and called: "This is Brawler Blue Two—Emergency homing, please!" Immediately a calm voice responded: "Brawler Blue Two. Steer ten degrees magnetic for Coltishall." It was a girl's voice, which compounded the miracle. I might add here that

I had never heard of radar, but undoubtedly I had been under radar surveillance and IFF identification ever since I pulled up into the clouds. . . . Fighter Command vectored me down through the clouds in stair-steps as I watched my altimeter getting closer and closer to the sea level altitude of Coltishall. Then they "suggested" that I lower the wheels and flaps and suddenly, despite the awful visibility, just over my nose I saw the most gorgeous, most beautiful flarepath in the world. All I had to do was reduce airspeed, ease back on the stick, land, and roll down the long runway. . . . Later we received information that Gilliland, 121 (Eagle) Squadron was killed during a landing in similar weather.[2]

Reade Tilley's description of an approach to Kirton-in-Lindsey after convoy patrol illustrates the challenge the pilots faced even when they could see:

You would get right down on the deck over the water and then fly a course until you got to the railroad track. As soon as you crossed the track you made a 90 degree turn to the right, maybe a little more so you could fly right down the track. You would fly down the track until you came to a pattern of tracks going off to the west and then you would know where you were. You would turn left, get back over the tracks and try to climb to maybe three or four hundred feet. You flew time and distance down the tracks for about four minutes, you were generally flying about 160 miles an hour, keeping a watch to the left, and you would see three smoke stacks. As soon as you saw the smoke stacks you would turn to such and such and let down the gear and the flaps, start to descend, and there was Kirton-in- Lindsey.[3]

Hugh Kennard remembered the procedure for landing when the field was covered with low clouds or fog.

You used to ask for a bearing to the airfield . . . and then the control tower would tell you when your engine was overhead. Then they would put you in a spiral and bring you down. They might also fire a rocket up through the clouds and you could then spiral down on that location. The conditions at North Weald were diabolical. One complete side of the field was surrounded by 50 to 100 radio towers 300 feet high. . . . Initially they relied on the leader to get them home anyway. We would have a landing stream and one would follow the other one in.[4]

The weather took another Eagle, William Inabinet of 71 Squadron, when he crashed into the North Sea while on convoy patrol.[5] But the general personnel shuffle that each of the units had been through in late 1941 stopped: only three new pilots arrived as Eagles in January.

February began with a new duty for both 121 and 133 Squadrons—shoveling snow.

The Station Commander ordered every able bodied man and woman (this included all the pilots) onto the field to start shoveling snow, working around the clock, two hours on, four hours off—so four days later we had a runway through the snow.[6]

The shoveling paid off for 133, for on the next day, 5 February, they got their first action with the Germans and their first Luftwaffe aircraft destroyed.

An average winter day as might be expected in Lincolnshire at this time of year. Cloud base was at 2000 ft., cloud 10/10ths, and visibility of 3-4 miles. 133 Squadron had its *first* series of combats and chases with e/a [enemy aircraft]. The first was a Ju.88 sighted by F/Lt Johnston at 09.30 hours. . . . The real fun began in the afternoon between 15.00 and 15.30 hours, when F/Lt Johnston with P/O Jackson as his No. 2, and F/Lt McColpin with Sgt. Wicker as his No. 2, were on patrols of convoys. . . . F/Lt. Johnston and P/O Jackson had combats with one or more Do. 217's who were trying to bomb the convoy. . . . it was confirmed at 15.30 . . . that a Do. 217 was seen to definitely crash into the sea. . . . F/Lt McColpin had still more fun, returning to base with all his guns empty and a Do. 217 damaged to his credit.[7]

This engagement was of tremendous significance for the Eagles of 133. They had worked as a team, had kept a convoy from being damaged, and almost every pilot had fired his guns at a German aircraft for the first time. And although the unit saw no action against the enemy for the rest of the month, the excitement of the 5th remained. The head of RAF Fighter Command, Air Chief Marshal Sir Sholto Douglas, visited later in the month bearing a telegram of congratulations from the King as well as the news that 133 would be moved further south in the spring. This visit was of special importance since Douglas' last visit to the squadron had been after the ill-fated flight to Ireland amid questions about the viability of the unit. The event also prompted another unit party, much like the one in Ireland when news of the transfer to Kirton-in-Lindsey was received.

While Number 71 remained out of operation because of the weather, 121 joined 133, once their runway at North Weald had also been shoveled by all the base personnel, in attacking the Germans.

> Eight of our pilots took part in large scale operations over the Channel today [12 February]. . . . Our job during these operations was to get and maintain air superiority while the bombing was carried out by Hurricane bombers, Stirlings, and Beauforts. The targets were the German battleships *Gneisneau* and *Scharnhorst* and the cruiser *Prinz Eugene*. It is believed that no great damage, if any, was done to these three ships.[8]

This action, though without great result, presaged a number of "Rhubarbs" (two-ship, low-level missions to destroy trains, trucks, and other enemy targets) into France during the remainder of the month.

Besides the Rhubarb, the fighter squadrons undertook several other types of missions, each with its own identification name. A "Circus" was a large-scale combined fighter and bomber operation designed to bring the enemy fighters into action. On a "Ramrod," fighters escorted a force of bombers with the primary objective of destroying a target. A "Roadstead" was similar to a Ramrod, except the targets were ships either at sea or in harbor. A sweep by a group of fighters over enemy territory without bombers was a "Rodeo," similar to a Ramrod but larger. An "Escort" mission detailed the fighters to give direct protection to bombers.[9]

BECOMING AN ACE

The importance of having someone actually see an enemy aircraft destroyed, as described in the record of 133 Squadron's 5 February action, was very important in the RAF to the overall claim of each pilot. An RAF pilot's claim of destruction of a German aircraft had to be confirmed by actual sight of either the plane hitting the ground or water; major parts, without which the plane could not fly, such as a wing, coming off in the air; or the pilot bailing out. Without one of these confirmations, the aircraft was classed as either probably destroyed or damaged. So if an RAF pilot severely damaged a German plane but it went into the clouds and was not seen again, it could not be claimed as destroyed. For this reason, RAF pilots generally claimed fewer enemy aircraft than their US Army Air Force counterparts. The Eagles might well have shot down several more enemy aircraft than they are credited with destroying.

In the American forces, the criterion was simply that an aircraft be sufficiently damaged so that it probably could not continue to fly. An aircraft on fire or one that appeared to be out of control could be counted as destroyed. So an enemy aircraft could have been claimed by both a fighter pilot and a gunner on a bomber when the machine was probably not destroyed. For example, the Messerschmitt 109, because of its fuel system, would belch black smoke when rapidly turned upside down. Because one of the German tactics when attacking a bomber was to roll inverted at the completion of the pass, many were claimed destroyed because smoke was seen coming from the aircraft when, in reality, the aircraft had not even been hit.[10] This difference in criteria must be kept in mind when comparing the productivity of the three

Eagle Squadrons in the RAF with their record after they became part of the US Army Air Force.

The same consideration must also be kept in mind when crediting a pilot as being an ace. To the British, there was no such thing, nor did any special status go with the number of enemy aircraft destroyed. With American forces, there was great significance attached to being an "ace." In the Army Air Force the definition of an ace was a pilot who could claim "five or more [enemy aircraft destroyed] either in the air or on the ground, but a combination of air and ground to make five or more, each of which is less than five, does not constitute an ace."[11] Although "in the U.S. Air Force the designation 'ace' has no official status," in reality, lists were kept, and still are today, of the fighter aces of the Air Force. So it was very important to the American Army fighter pilots to get credit for as many "kills" as possible in order to achieve the coveted title. There are only fourteen Eagles on the list of American Fighter Aces, partly because of the difficulty of getting credit for an enemy destroyed in the RAF and because most Eagles left combat flying shortly after transfer to the USAAF. Several Eagles also lost claims of aircraft destroyed upon transfer. For example, Bill Dunn, probably the first American ace in World War II, never really received timely credit for his accomplishment since his victories were while he was in the RAF and accurate records were not kept.[12]

In the Eagle Squadrons, relatively few individuals accounted for most of the German airplanes shot down. When asked what makes an ace, every fighter pilot will probably have a different answer. Reade Tilley, who became an ace in Malta, said,

> Not everyone was gung-ho, nor was fighting as important to everyone. Some pilots, like Don Blakeslee (who most Eagles the author interviewed said was the greatest fighter pilot of World War II), lived to fight. If he was not fighting the enemy he was fighting his friends. . . . Shooting down enemy planes was a combination of motivation, vision, flying ability, marksmanship, aggressiveness. Everyone had these

things to varying degrees. I knew a couple of pilots who were lousy aviators . . . but they could shoot real good and they shot down a lot of enemy airplanes, but I sure wouldn't want to ride with them in the back seat. Others, like Blakeslee and "Red" McColpin, who was a superb aviator, combined all these qualities. . . . Those who got the aircraft were not better shots but better hunters . . . able to stalk their prey and anticipate his next move. Fighting another airplane is a matter of seconds or tenths of seconds. You do it in one second bursts when you have the enemy in your sights because that's all the longer he is there. And a one-second burst is a long, long burst. Remember, we only had from seven to ten seconds of ammunition in the Spitfire.[13]

The real fighter war, though, was fought just as hard by those who were not aces as it was by those who ended up with that honor. Edwin Taylor put the matter into the proper perspective:

In this tragedy of errors that is called war in a fighter squadron, the big news isn't always the pilots you hear about every day. It takes leaders and followers. Some of the most interesting people are the other pilots that are rotated from day to day to make up the rest of the squadron. Of the 12 pilots that make up a full squadron flight, probably eight of them you never hear from or about, but they are the ones that insure the air happening to be a success. They are the interior linemen, but they are absolutely necessary on every squadron mission. It takes loyalty, faith and discipline of all involved to make an all out cooperative effort. On any given day these individuals can be caught in the act of just being themselves. They are always available, good formation flyers, dependable and always do exactly as they are programmed to do, and in a wide open dog fight will pull their own weight every time. Even though these characters appear colorless and without glamour, they jump to the same beat as the other few without the need to beat their own drum loud and long after the action is over and has been declared official. Even at this late date some still remain quiet and keep their stories and experiences intimate and canned, but you can't remove the memories even as they grow old.[14]

THE DAILY ROUTINE

The two terms that dominated the vocabulary of each of the Eagle Squadrons during March were weather and patrol. The weather was warmer than February, but it certainly was not more conducive to flying, so each squadron spent a number of days sitting on the ground and trying to find something to do. "Aerodrome and weather as previous day. Section still on readiness in the Mess. Several pilots put in time on the Link trainer," lamented the adjutant of 71 Squadron.[15]

Every day, the commander at each of the RAF bases would publish "Daily Routine Orders," which detailed the various duty officers, which fire party (fire-fighting company for combating both enemy air raid damage and aircraft emergencies) had duty and when, and similar information. Fire companies were on duty for shifts ranging from five to eight hours, depending on the anticipated workload. The orders also contained other items of interest. For example, those published for Kirton-in-Lindsey for 12 July 1941 included rather elaborate black-out instructions under the heading, "Discipline." They also contained an announcement that any airwomen who were qualified could apply to be Link trainer instructors and a notice that there would be a cricket match at 1830 hours that evening. The black-out instructions noted,

> Personnel are reminded that black-out precautions are just as necessary now as in the winter months. Care is to be taken that when offices etc. are secured for the night, all lights are extinguished. Personnel entering rooms at night are to ensure that black-out curtains are drawn before switching on the lights. With regard to Barrack Blocks and Married Quarters, it is stressed that lights must not be switched on after "Lights Out" (22.30 hours) except in emergency. There is no excuse, therefore, if lights are exposed after black-out times and disciplinary action will be taken against

offenders. Personnel who remain out of camp until their Permanent Passes expire must be prepared to undress in the dark.[16]

For the flying squadrons on the base, the basic rules were the same but their routine was strictly governed by their unique mission. "Our day really depended on what sector we were in," reminisced Bill Edwards,

> and what the squadron commander could get sector to agree to. The commander would have to provide so many officers to do this or that duty from the additional duty roster. . . . Most of the days would be about 12 hours long depending on the time of the year and the amount of daylight. You would generally report to dispersal about an hour or so before alert time started and check out your equipment, go out to the plane and look it over, put your parachute in place, talk to the crew chief and just make sure that everything was ready to go. . . . Almost every day we would have programmed lectures on such subjects as identification of aircraft because there were so many different types of airplanes in the skies. . . . The flight chief would come in sometimes and talk about aircraft systems, there would be talks about gunnery and all sorts of subjects.[17]

Additional subjects remembered by Edwin Taylor include military courtesy, conduct in uniform, out-of-control drinking, security consciousness when talking about job-related material, spies and infiltrators, and the Geneva Convention and conduct if you were captured by the enemy.[18] Eric Doorly also remembered some sessions on survival if you bailed out in the Channel, and Charles Cook attended a lecture on the proper use of oxygen.[19] As noted, the Link trainer also got considerable use and time was spent on such practice missions as air-to-sea firing and formation flying.[20]

Different squadrons worked days off differently. Combat flying is very fatiguing business, so the commander must guard against anyone getting too tired. Generally, flyers had two days on and then a day on spare or off. If someone was getting too tired, he could request time off and get three to five days. Every squadron had a different day off, the entire unit had a stand down day, and then individuals had a few days leave on top of that. "You didn't get tired," said Jim Daley in a 1942 interview. "Most of our boys wouldn't even take leave. They wanted to go on these shows."[21] Bill Edwards remembers,

> When you did have time off, you wouldn't hang around the base much. When you did there was an awful lot of pool played and snooker, you spent time at the club. There were some of the older lads who wouldn't go into town much, but the young bucks like myself went whenever we could. We might take in a movie, there were a lot of dances to go to, and we would see if we could take the gals away from the Army privates. Most of the towns we were around while I was an Eagle were small villages . . . and we were well received in all of them.[22]

Staying on the base did not necessarily mean a dull time. Some of the most memorable social occasions enjoyed by the Eagles took place at the officer's mess. John Brown described one scene:

> The ante room in the mess at Kirton-in-Lindsey was a large rectangular room, about 100 to 150 feet long and 50 feet wide, with a large fireplace at one end, double doors in at least two spots on the sides, furnished with large leather, overstuffed chairs, sofas, and generally a piano. Number 616 Squadron was leaving, which always brought on a party. At this one we had a tank battle. You turn the big leather chairs upside down, one squadron gets on one side and one on the other and you push them trying to get one to the opponent's side of the room. The loser pays for the drinks. In the course of the battle clothes get ripped off and torn up; it is crazy. At this party Jimmie Daley was standing by the fireplace doing a fan dance with the shovel and brush from the fire tending set. The WAFs in the room thought it was great. Johnny Johnson and Reade Tilley ended up in the center of the room battling like crazy, with Johnson having a scissors

around Tilley's head and Reade couldn't speak or breathe or anything. Suddenly there was a scream in this room with all the people and Johnson let go his grip as Tilley, in desperation, had bitten him. Eventually everyone would stagger off to bed and the batmen would straighten the place up. Overall, our conduct was not out of character with that of the British.[23]

There was also an opportunity to gamble, day or night, and some of the Eagles were quite successful. Of course, for every winner there was also at least one loser. One of the perpetual winners was Carroll McColpin, who always seemed to find a game. "All someone had to do was suggest a game of poker or dice," said McColpin, "and there would be a half-dozen waiting to get in."[24] Along with the gambling went a reasonable amount of drinking, but not any more than the Eagles' British counterparts did. "We did most of our drinking in the mess," remembered Edwin Taylor. "We just didn't have enough money to drink much in the pubs."[25] When they did decide to go to the pub, Eagles often found themselves being treated by their British cousins. "They were always buying drinks for us and telling us how glad they were that we had come over to help," recalled Art Roscoe.[26]

LONDON AND THE BRITISH

While almost any town would do when the decision was made to leave the base, the most popular destination was London and the diversions of the city.

> In the early days of the war the British did not refer to the Americans as "overpaid, oversexed and over here" as they were to later on. The Eagles were members of the RAF and part of the team of "the few." Many elegant homes were opened to them on the weekends or when they had days off and Quintan Reynolds kept a suite at the Savoy Hotel with plenty of whiskey and attractive girls to entertain the Eagles while they were in London. They tended to frequent the Embassy, the Savoy, the Strand Palace and the famous Wind-

mill Theatre in Soho which won a decoration for aiding the
morale of the troops by never closing during the war. The
young Americans were also new, different, and very popular
with the British girls. Several of the Eagles, of course, married English women.[27]

"If you had a day off or if the Squadron was standing
down for the entire day because of weather or the like,
then it would be off to town or to London, if you were
close enough," remarked Edwin Taylor.[28] "When we
went into London on a 24-hour leave, we'd head straight
to the Eagle Club to see if any of the fellows from other
squadrons were in town," said Lee Gover. "After catching
up on the news, we would proceed from there."[29] The
Eagle Club, run by two Americans, Mrs. Francis Dexter
and Barbara Blake, was located at 28 Charing Cross
Road, just off Piccadilly Circus. There, the Eagles could
catch up on the other squadrons, get any stray mail, get a
hamburger and a coke, and find out what social opportunities were available for the day or weekend.[30] None of
the Eagles know how the club was paid for; a membership
card was required but it came without cost.[31] According
to Charles Sweeny, his group had nothing to do with
either establishing or operating the club.[32]

The Eagle Club was a welcome resort for the Americans, and provided another basis of distinction for these
foreigners in England. "The Eagle Club was very good
for us," reminisced John Brown.

> We were able to read periodicals from home and get the
> news from the US. The people there were just very kind. I
> was there reading the paper one Sunday morning . . .
> when the door opened . . . and I looked right into the face
> of the King. He introduced me to the Queen and said
> "Didn't I meet you at North Weald?" He had been there
> some months before and I had met him, but his memory was
> absolutely remarkable. Who would remember one of a num-
> ber of pilots he had met some months before? Remarkable![33]

The entrance and lounge of the Eagle Club in London. Many of the Eagles made this friendly, attractive club their first stop on a trip to the city.

COURTESY OF JOHN BROWN

COURTESY OF N. D. SINTETOS

From the Eagle Club, the Americans headed almost any place where something interesting was happening. Often it was simply a movie. Sometimes there were tea dances, where Barry Mahon remembers seeing British Princess Margaret Rose but not dancing with her.[34] Cracker's Club and the bar at the Regent Palace Hotel were favorite hangouts for finding friends and catching up on the news, but also, more important, for finding some female companionship for dinner, a party, or just a quiet evening. For many of the pilots, a time in London could mean a night of partying and pub crawling ending only in time to catch the milk train back to the base and get ready for the day. "If the party got too wild at one of the local establishments, there was always the squadron station wagon to take everyone home," recalled Charles Cook. "Then we would just go to 100 percent oxygen when we flew the next morning and most of us would feel fine."[35]

For some there might be tea, or even an invitation to spend a weekend, in the country at an estate. "Lady Francis Rider took several of us to her house for tea," recalled Edwin Taylor. "I didn't know how to handle this with all the equipment (silverware). But I had always been reminded not to be a pig since there was such strict rationing, so I got along just fine."[36] Actually, about any type of activity was available; the choice simply depended on the mood of the individual.

Naturally, these entertainments sometimes led to consequences beyond the weekend or the next day. Ervin Miller remembers,

> Gene Neville and I were visiting London—taking in all the sights and pub crawling to our hearts' content. One evening we called into a small private club . . . where we found it very cozy, with a huge log fire blazing away. . . . Sitting by the fire having a quiet drink, we became aware of the arrival at the bar of two attractive young ladies. . . . Conditions being as they were, we made the customary approach and arranged respective dates for later that evening. . . . There was quite a get together later—dancing, soft music, and good companionship. . . . Gene and I extended our leave and the next day attended a party with our dates at some flat or other. . . . Our relationship and affection grew, and when I was eventually posted to Biggin Hill we decided to marry. . . . arrangements were made at the Burnt Oak Registry Office, and that was that.[37]

Mrs. Miller continues.

> On the 20th of August, 1942, Ervin and I were married. It was a typical war wedding—for me it meant saving up precious clothes coupons to buy a new dress and some undies,

etc. The ceremony took place in the morning and then we went to a nearby hotel for a reception. Press photographers took pictures and we eventually went back to my sister's house to say goodbye to my family. There were some telegrams of congratulations, but among them was one saying to Ervin "Return to base forthwith." Ervin and I took a taxi to Soldier's Green station and then from there to Charing Cross. We bought a *London Evening Standard* there and saw our wedding picture (I still have the cutting). We parted there and Ervin went on to . . . Biggin Hill. . . . It was days before we saw each other again to have a few days belated honeymoon.[38]

For most of the Eagles, who had never been to a city the size of London, much less to Europe, the metropolis itself offered many wonders.

All the historical sights we saw. . . . The Sunday Officer's dance at the famous Grosvenor Hotel Grand Ballroom where on one Sunday I rubbed elbows with the likes of King Peter of Yugoslavia and General DeGaulle of Free-France. And the great feeling of pride sitting in a jam-packed crowd at the London Palladium stomping our feet to the swing music of Benny Goodman as played by the RAF Squadronaires led by Sgt. Jimmie Miller. . . . I think back to all the beautiful girls we met and the bars we frequented such as the Chez-Cup Bar of the Regent Palace Hotel. . . . We had our serious sides too. Such as access to H.R.H. the Duke of Glouster's Grand Tier Box #17 at the Royal Albert Hall to listen to the London Philharmonic orchestra. Then there was the big thing we all got to do and that was meet and have tea with the Royal Family. It was the custom at the time to select groups from other countries such as South Africa, New Zealand, Australia, Canada and, in our case, Americans. We were ushered into the room and were presented to the King and Queen and the two Princesses. They would ask us such questions as what city we were from and I like to gone thru the floor when, in my answer to what city I was from, I said, "Racine, Wisconsin" and the Queen said, "Oh yes, Johnson's Wax."[39]

All of this activity took place in an environment that made the young Americans feel most welcome. Although their experiences with the British varied, there is no question in the mind of any Eagle that the English people liked them, welcomed them, and appreciated them having come. Many of the kindnesses shown toward the Americans were very practical. John Brown remembers,

> As part of our issue we were given a turtleneck sweater—they were very nice wool sweaters but they came down to your knees. I just happened to mention to my batman one night, "why do they give us these sweaters when they come down to your knees?" That's all I said and about three or four days later laying on my bed was this sweater which fit perfectly. His wife had taken and unraveled that darn thing and knitted a new bottom on it. That to me is a perfect example of the English people.[40]

Charles Cook also recalled that the Irish women would knit turtleneck sweaters for the members of 133 Squadron when they were stationed at Eglinton.[41] To Roy Evans, "it just seemed like they couldn't do enough for you. They gave you the best they had, the best food, the best equipment even though some of it was old. Under the circumstances, I could not have been more pleased."[42] George Sperry found a similar attitude.

> Whilst we absorbed the genteel art of becoming fighter pilots we got to know and understand our British cousins and so became the darlings of London. We could not buy a drink in the pubs,—theatre tickets, dinner invitations and well-stacked females were for free. Several thousand miles from our homes and facing a rather questionable future over the skies of France made us slightly high-spirited. Our unbridled celebrations and uninhibited acts gave those that did not know us the impression that we were not too well housebroken. We acted like we owned the whole of England—didn't we?[43]

The real basis for this kind of spirit was captured by Carroll McColpin, when he said,

From the first until the last day that I was in England, I knew that the British were going to win the war. Why? They told me so. They were, without a shadow of a doubt, the most courageous people that I have ever known. Although their cities were in shambles and Hitler was poised to finish them off, I never heard one Briton lose faith. To them, it was only a matter of time before the Third Reich would be finished.[44]

All the kindness and consideration displayed toward the Americans were even more evident when it came to food. Eating with a British family often presented one of the greatest problems. It was customary for the British to go out of their way to show their gratitude, and they might well short themeslves in order to set a plentiful table for visitors. Although the Eagles were not supposed to accept food because of the severe rationing in England, it was often impossible not to. One solution was for the Americans to save up their own ration coupons and give them to a British family if they were invited to dinner. "My Mother sent one English family that had been particularly nice to me sugar, tea, and other items that were so scarce in the UK," remembered John Brown.[45] For Bert Stewart, the British opened their food stores as well.

> Bert Stewart and Oscar Coen were able to obtain ration coupons for two weeks before they went to London on a 48 hour pass. They went to a butcher shop that was noted for having steak available and shortly came out with a huge package of meat. It seems that their uniforms with the Eagle patch had caught the eye of the shop owner who had a son in the RAF. He had cut them beautiful marbled steaks from his precious supply because nothing was too good for the two young men who had come across the sea, voluntarily, from a foreign country, to help.[46]

Roy Evans was so impressed with the way the British went out of their way to help the Americans, despite shortages and hardships, that years later he asked his Eagle friend, Jim Goodson, a very popular speaker in

Britain, to say thank you to the British sometime in a speech. At a reunion of Bomber Command, Goodson read Evans' thank you letter to a packed house and received a standing ovation, so much did the audience appreciate Evans' gesture.[47] Interviews with members of the squadrons are filled with stories of the kindness and generosity of the English people, the appreciation felt by the Eagles, and the enduring friendships that came from contact during the war. Gene Fetrow summed it up: "Most of the British were just glad that we were there."[48]

BACK INTO ACTION

Many Eagles also took advantage of opportunities to see the English countryside but were never far from the action. "While I was on leave I visited Oxford University and Churchill Hospital with Lulu Hollander and John Flynn," wrote Harold Strickland. "During the leave we learned that Sam Whedon had been killed in 133 Squadron."[49] Whedon's death illustrates well how cruel fate often seemed to touch the Eagles:

> Sam Whedon was forced to bail out after a very minor mid-air collision. . . . As we circled down, he opened his chute and waved to show he was unhurt and OK . . . but after the rest of us had landed at Kirton, learned that Sam had been killed . . . the gusty and strong wind on the ground had caused him to lose his footing as he touched down, and he inadvertently fell backwards hitting his head on a rock. . . . Sam was not only a good friend, but one of the most popular and admired pilots in the unit . . . we all felt his loss more than any could express.[50]

Number 121, from its station at North Weald, saw the most action during March. The Squadron's massive support of the "Repulse" operation on 1 March, a rehearsal for an amphibious ground raid on France, proved to be a portent of things to come. No one in the squadron knew the purpose of the exercise, during which they were deployed to various staging bases, but they would find out a few months later when called upon, along with 71 and 133 Squadrons, for extensive support of the Dieppe invasion. A week later, on a twelve-plane sweep over France, P/O Daley damaged an Me 109, and two weeks after that, on 23 March, P/O Mooney shot down an FW 190; these were the first enemy aircraft destroyed by 121 Squadron. The next day another sweep, vigorously opposed by the Germans, resulted in a probable destroyed by Reade Tilley. Hopes ran high that the rest of the month would bring a real surge in the action. But such was not the case, and the unit ended the month flying formation over London as part of that city's War Weapons Week program.[51]

No matter what the weather was, the requirement to fly convoy patrol over ships in the North Sea remained constant. All three Eagle Squadrons, along with most of the other fighter squadrons posted in southeast England, flew their share of the more than 150 sorties required each day. One of the most hazardous duties was that of making the weather test to determine if it was even possible to fly convoy patrol. The *Squadron Record Book* for Number 133 summarizes the hazards of this duty in the 16 March entry.

> F/Sgt. Harp & P/O Brown were ordered to make a weather test in the swept Channel . . . with a view to finding out if it was possible to patrol convoy. . . . F/Sgt. Harp called up P/O Brown, telling him that he was going to climb as visibility was practically nil. There was no answer, and it was assumed that P/O Brown crashed into the sea at that moment or a bit before.

The lack of action during the first three months of the new year was gradually taking its toll on the Eagles. They were anxious to be in the fight, especially the pilots of 121 and 133 who had really not tasted battle to any degree. The upshot was that several pilots requested transfer to a scene of more action.

A few Eagles had previously transferred into other RAF units for the same reason, including Art Donahue from Number 71 almost immediately after its formation, and John Campbell, who left Number 121 on 7 October 1941 for 258 Squadron and duty in the Far East. Both ended up in Singapore, where Donahue was severely wounded and Campbell was shot down by the Japanese. Donahue returned to England, where he recovered, once again entered combat, and was shot down over the Channel and killed in September 1942. Campbell spent the rest of the war in a Japanese POW camp, the only Eagle to do so.[52]

For those pilots who really wanted action, however, the place to go was Malta. That island bastion in the Mediterranean was continually under siege, attacked daily by the Luftwaffe and the Italians. Successfully obtaining a transfer in early 1942 were Art Roscoe, Leo Nomis, and John Lynch from 71; Douglas Booth, Donald McLeod, Reade Tilley, James Peck, Bruce Downs, and Richard McHan from 121; and Fred Scudday, Hugh Johnston, and Hiram Putnam (who was killed in April 1942) from 133.[53] Their experiences in Malta will be discussed later.

Finally, the flowers of April 1942 brought with them a significant increase in the activity of each of the Eagle Squadrons; some of their most challenging flying was yet to come. But before considering the Eagle Squadrons' final six months, we should discuss their adversaries, the Luftwaffe, and the fighters they flew.

THE GERMAN SITUATION

Shortly after the end of the Battle of Britain and Hitler's decision to abandon an invasion of the United Kingdom, a large part of the Luftwaffe was detailed to the coming invasion of Russia. From mid-1941 until the Allied invasion of Europe in 1944, the major operation of the war from the German perspective was in the east. And though the Germans had the largest air force in the world, that force was spread quite thin by the demands of combat on two fronts. By mid-1941 only two German fighter wings, totaling about 180 aircraft, were stationed in France.[54] This reduced force necessitated a change from the Germans' offensive spirit of 1940 and early 1941 to an increasingly defensive posture, because of the need to conserve both aircraft and pilots. It also meant that, as the British had been able to do in the Battle of Britain, the Germans were now engaging the enemy, the RAF, far from its bases and choosing the time and place of battles. So one Eagle mission might make no contact with the enemy while the identical mission a day later would meet heavy fighter resistance. But although Germany had a small number of fighters posted in France, it continued to send both its best aircraft and some of its best pilots to that theater.[55] The aircraft and pilots the Eagles fought during their service in the RAF were among the best the Germans had to offer—significantly better, incidentally, than those they would encounter after their transfer to the US Eighth Air Force.

Leo Nomis, a member of 71 Squadron and a student of fighter warfare, wrote about the significance of the quality of German pilots.

It is a matter of record that there were no terrifically high scoring individuals in any of the Eagle Squadrons during that period 1941–1942 and one reason in my mind was the extremely efficient quality of the Jerry pilots in North France at that time. Due to their commitment in Russia the Germans had to leave the defense of the West to more widely distributed but elite units. . . . I think it's probably to everyone's credit in the Eagles, who produced a hodge-podge of pilots with varying experience and skills (some of whom, sadly, should never have been in the skies over the Western Front—and some who were extremely good), that the record stands as it does. I know I asked myself, when the initial impact of reality dawned upon me, what the hell I was doing there. I felt in that early phase, and correctly so, that I was sadly lacking and, in effect, a ridiculous figure in a tragic situation.[56]

German bases in the west were massed in the relatively small area from Antwerp, Belgium, on the north to the Normandy Peninsula of France on the south. The heaviest concentration was in the area of Dunkirk, Calais, Lille, and Abbeville, less than 50 miles from Dover and less than 150 miles from London. (See the map in appendix B.) Even these relatively short distances, though, were significant for both the German and British fighters, for their range at normal cruise was only about 400 miles, and this range was cut considerably if any fighting occurred or if the mission required a long climb to high altitude. For the RAF to stay within fuel limitations and allow optimum fighting time, the ideal place for combat was over the Channel. Increasingly in late 1941 and early 1942, the Germans waited for the RAF to get over France before engaging them, forcing the British often to break off the combat for lack of fuel, just as the Germans had to do over London in 1940. The frequency of combat over France also meant that when an RAF pilot was shot down, his chances of being captured were increasingly high.

Once they were engaged in aerial combat, the Eagles could pretty well predict German tactics. Since the Me 109 and the FW 190 could climb faster and higher than their British counterparts, and because the Germans had less distance to fly, they were generally above the British aircraft when contact was made. The Germans also tried to stay in a position so the RAF pilot would have to look straight into the sun to find his adversary. The Luftwaffe aircraft would generally attack by coming down and through the British formation at very high speed, generally in formations of four or more aircraft. It was often after this first pass that the RAF would be able to get close enough to the German aircraft to engage them. The effectiveness of this German tactic was somewhat negated when the RAF got the Spit V and later the Spit IX, which were able to fly as high as the German craft and could climb to engage them. British pilots often claimed that the Germans flew in a bunch without any real formation, but retired German General Johannes Steinhoff, who shot down 176 aircraft during the war, said that the Germans did indeed use formations but they got less precise as the war progressed because of the decreasing experience level of Luftwaffe pilots. So as the British, and later the American, pilots continued to become more experienced, the Germans became less so because of their tremendous losses and increasing shortages of resources.[57]

MESSERSCHMITT BF 109

The aircraft that the Eagle pilots engaged most often during their duty with the RAF was the Messerschmitt Bf 109, commonly called the Me 109. It was an older aircraft than the Spitfire, having first flown in 1935 and having seen combat in the Spanish Civil War in 1937. It was the most widely used German fighter, flown by no fewer than fourteen different countries during World War II. By the end of the war nearly 35,000 had been built. Its popularity is understandable: the Me 109 was small, fast, reliable, carried excellent firepower, and was reasonably cheap to build. As with almost all fighters, it had very limited range—one hour and forty minutes at maximum—which, in the end, led to some very costly defeats because of improper employment by the Luftwaffe.

Although there were as many versions of the 109 as there were Spitfires, the one most seen over the Channel and France was the G model. It was about the same length as the Spitfire, but its wing was narrower and four feet shorter, which helped account for both its higher speed and its inferior turning ability. Weighing about the same at its British counterpart, it was powered by a Daimler-Benz inverted V–12 engine with horsepower varying from 1,475 to 1,800, slightly more than the Spitfire. The biggest difference in the engines was the fuel injection system on the German engine, which prevented

The aircraft that performed the majority of Luftwaffe fighter duties throughout World War II, the Messerschmitt Bf 109 was the plane the Eagles engaged most often over the English Channel and France.

it from cutting out under negative "g" loads, a fault that plagued the Spitfire during the early part of the war.

In combat, speed is critical, and there the edge went to the 109 by about 35 to 40 miles per hour. The Messerschmitt could also climb about 2,000 feet higher than the Spitfire, another significant advantage. In addition, the 109 had faster climbing and diving speed. It was every bit a match for the Spitfire early in the war, and clearly superior to the Hurricane, except when turning. In turns, both the British aircraft had a distinct advantage, an advantage that won many an air battle. The armament of the Me 109 was formidable and varied, with as many as three cannons mounted in the fuselage and one in each wing. As the war progressed, the Germans were unable to modify the Me 109 enough to keep up with improvements in the Spitfire, and by the late stages of the conflict the German aircraft was clearly inferior.

Inside the German fighter, the pilot found himself in a less hospitable environment than that of his British counterpart. The 109's very austere cockpit was even narrower than the Spitfire's, and the German pilot in his metal seat, sitting on his parachute, found his head against the canopy and his shoulders against the cockpit sides. In fact, a pilot over 5 feet 8 inches tall had to fly slumped down to keep from continually bumping his head on the top of the canopy. There are many stories of German pilots returning from missions with severe headaches caused by hitting their heads on the canopy. In addition, the canopy was so narrow that it was nearly impossible for the pilot to turn his head far enough to see what was behind him, making the rear-view mirror mounted on top of the canopy crucial for survival.

The instrumentation was similar to that of the Spitfire except that there was neither an artificial horizon nor a gyrocompass, which made flying in bad weather an extremely challenging task. Control was through a standard stick, which controlled both pitch and bank, while rudder pedals with straps to hold the pilot's feet controlled the yaw movement. The straps served the same function as the stirrups on the Spitfire, allowing the pilot to still control the rudder if he lost the use of one leg or foot. The firing button for the cannons was on top of the control stick. As in the Spitfire, the gunsight was located at the top of the instrument panel right behind the eight-inch-square bulletproof windshield. The guns were set for optimum firepower at about 250 feet. The canopy on the Spitfire posed a potential problem for in-flight escape, but that of the Messerschmitt was even worse. The entire affair was hinged on the right side and it had to be raised to facilitate entry and exit. This arrangement made it impossible to fly with the canopy open at all, and although there was a lever to jettison the canopy, if that failed it became almost impossible to bail out.[58]

The flight characteristics of the Me 109 were not nearly as similar to the Spitfire as were the aircraft dimensions. The landing gear was even narrower on the German plane and the engine torque made the aircraft tend to swing violently on takeoff or landing. At about 60 miles per hour on takeoff, the fighter had a tendency to roll violently to the right, which caused many an Me 109 to crash on takeoff. The landing characteristics were often described as being "malicious." Lateral control at high speeds was also a problem. In a tight turn the leading edge wing slats, designed to facilitate shorter takeoff and landing, would open to prevent a stall, but they ruined the pilot's aim.

In summary, while the Spitfire was graceful, easy to fly, and praised by all who flew it, the Me 109 proved to be a lean, mean fighter that had to be controlled if it was to be effective, demanding constant pilot attention and skill. One of the pilots at today's Confederate Air Force headquarters in Texas reported that the Messerschmitt was the only aircraft he had ever flown that he was afraid of.[59] But taking everything into consideration, if there were ever two fighters in a war that were evenly matched, they were the Spitfire and the Me 109.[60]

FOCKE-WULF 190

Although the aircraft engaged most often by the Eagles was the Me 109, the German plane that concerned the RAF most was the Focke-Wulf 190. Very fast and heavily armed, it was first seen over France in early 1941 and immediately became the topic of conversation among British pilots. Jim Griffin recalled one of his squadron's sergeant pilots telling him, "'I saw this aircraft coming up behind us. We were in a dive with maximum boost. It was climbing and catching us—an aircraft with a radial engine, if you can believe that.' . . . The radial-engine aircraft the sergeant pilot reported as climbing faster than we were diving was a Focke-Wulf 190."[61] The reasons for the FW 190's reputation are easy to find. Compared to the Spitfire V, it was faster, smaller, more maneuverable, and more heavily armed. In the eyes of most RAF pilots it was a more formidable foe than the Me 109, and to some it made the Spit V seem almost obsolete. And rightly so, given the fact that the 190 was at least 20 miles per hour

Fast, powerful, deadly—a superb fighter—the Focke-Wulf 190 became a frequent opponent of the Eagles by the middle of 1942.

faster than the Vb at all altitudes, could climb and dive at a significantly higher rate, and was much more maneuverable except in a turn. As time passed, the FW 190 was found to be beatable, but it was certainly a formidable challenge. It led directly to the development of the Spitfire IX, which was about its equal in all respects.

The FW 190 was not a new airplane in 1941. It had been flown before the war and had seen combat on the eastern front. Its introduction into France in 1941 seems to have been an effort by the Germans to make up for both the apparent deficiencies of the Me 109 in air-to-air combat and the transfer of many aircraft to the eastern front. The FW 190 was a smaller, more powerful plane than either the Me 109 or the Spitfire. It had a wingspan of only 34½ feet and was just 29 feet long. The rather compact airframe and its blunt nose gave it the appearance of a mean bulldog to Eagle Bill Edwards, who also thought it was a harder aircraft to see than the Me 109.[62]

Powering that small airframe was an 18-cylinder two-row radial engine of 1,700 horsepower with a boost capability of 2,100 horsepower, some 500 more than that available on the Spit V. Top speed was about equal to that of the Me 109 but nearly 40 miles per hour faster than the Spitfire, and the FW 190 had a ceiling of over 37,000 feet, 1,000 more than the British aircraft. Because it was heavier than the Spitfire it could go faster in a dive. Like the Me 109, though, the FW 190 could not turn as tight as the British fighter.

The FW 190 also excelled in armament, sporting two 13-millimeter cannons above the engine, two 20-millimeter cannons in the wing roots, and two more cannons, either 20- or 30-millimeter, in the outboard wing. The cockpit was larger than that of the Me 109 and featured a fairly large canopy that greatly aided the pilot's visibility. The very wide-track landing gear made it a much easier plane to handle on both takeoff and landing, which also increased its versatility.

If the Focke-Wulf was apparently such a superior airplane, the question arises, Why did almost all of the German aces fly the Me 109 with all its shortcomings? There doesn't seems to be a good answer to the question. One can speculate that, because the Me 109 had been around longer, most of the older pilots were more familiar with it and just felt more comfortable with it. The Me 109 was also easier and cheaper to produce. General Steinhoff claims that the FW 190 was not as good an aircraft against fighters as the Me 109, and that it was introduced into the western theatre in large numbers because it was superior against bombers: it carried greater firepower and its air-cooled engine could take more damage than the liquid-cooled one in the Me 109. Whatever the reason, it seems curious that the Germans did not curtail the Me 109 in favor of the FW 190 until you realize "Goering wanted numbers and the Messerschmitt was easier and faster to build."[63] Still, some 20,000 of the FW 190 were built during the war, and in several versions it saw action in many different missions, including close air support and bombing.

The FW 190 also appeared in a version known as the "long-nosed 190" in 1943. This version was powered by an inverted V–12 engine of nearly 1,800 horsepower that could achieve over 2,200 on boost. When introduced, it was the fastest fighter on the western front. When the Eagles encountered this plane they were members of the US Army Air Force and were flying American P–47s.[64]

RENEWED ACTION IN THE SPRING

After three months of cold, damp, cloudy weather, constant convoy patrol, almost no contact with the Germans, and continual loss of pilots in accidents, all three Eagle Squadrons were more than ready for the promised better weather of April and the assumed increase in action. For several of the Eagles, this was their second spring in England, but for most the anticipation of the season was enhanced by having survived their first English winter. But as if expressly to dampen the new enthusiasm and anticipation, the word in the alert shack as April began remained patrol and more patrol. The weather on the continent was better, however, which meant that there would be more opportunity for sweeps over France as well as more enemy aircraft over England.

For 133 Squadron, located farther north than the other Americans, nearly the entire month of April was spent on that monotonous duty over the ships in the Channel and North Sea, broken only by an occasional sweep into France. On the 26th there was finally contact with enemy aircraft and Carroll McColpin, already an ace in 71 Squadron, shot down the Eagles' first FW 190. The next day William Baker and Robert Pewitt each got a probable destroyed against FW 190s, but the enthusiasm was dampened when 19-year-old Sergeant Pilot Walter Wicker failed to return from a mission over France. His body washed up on the English shore two days later. Contact with the Luftwaffe continued through the last days of April as 133 Squadron closed out its operation at

Kirton-in-Lindsey and moved to Biggin Hill, in the heart of the action in 11 Group.[65]

The reaction to Walter Wicker's death was probably typical of that to most Eagle casualties and illustrates the number of people and agencies involved. Because he was a member of the RCAF, the notification of his death came to his mother, Mrs. Victor Hammer, from the Canadians. It read,

> Deeply regret to inform you advice has been received from the Royal Canadian Air Force casualties officer overseas that your son . . . Flight Sergeant Walter Charles Wicker was killed on active service on April twenty seventh nineteen forty two. More complete details will follow in a letter from your son's commanding officer. Your home chapter of the American Red Cross will be glad to advise you and to help you in every way possible. Please accept my profound sympathy.
>
> (Signed)
> Chief of the Air Staff[66]

A few days later, Squadron Leader Thomas, the 133 commander, wrote to Wicker's mother, concluding, "Your son's death comes as a great blow to us all. The whole squadron and myself would like to express our profound sympathy with you in your sad loss."[67] Further letters of condolence came from Lewis Clark, the American consul in Canada; Glenn Abbey, his counterpart in London; the Air Council of the RAF; and the King of England, who wrote, "The Queen and I offer you our heartfelt sympathy in your great sorrow. We pray that your country's gratitude for a life so nobly given in its service may bring you some measure of consolation. (Signed) George, R.I."[68]

As with most Eagle losses, a rash of newspaper articles also appeared. Typical was one in an unidentified paper that noted, "Irene Wicker, radio's 'Singing Story Lady,' has lost her only son in the people's war for freedom. Walter Cass Wicker, Jr., age 19, was shot down in a

fighter plane on April 28, over the English Channel."
Others talked about Wick's courage, accomplishments,
and dedication, as well as that of the Eagles in general.[69]

Of particular interest, given the citizenship situation
of most Eagles, is the "Report of the Death of an American Citizen," a State Department form used to record
death from any cause while in a foreign country. The first
copy, prepared in London on 1 June 1942, notes that
Wicker was "believed to have been an American citizen
although there is no record in the citizenship files of this
office of his status." The lack of a record in the citizenship files was not surprising since the Eagles did not join
the RCAF or go to England with the State Department's
blessing. A second copy of the same form, prepared at
the American embassy in Ottawa, dated 23 June 1942,
states, "on enlistment the deceased exhibited a true copy
of the certificate of his birth in the United States and
declared his willingness to serve but took no oath of allegiance. No evidence of American citizenship was received." The comment about the oath is critical because
it establishes the fact that Wicker had not lost his citizenship by joining the RCAF.[70]

Years later, in 1985, Wicker's sister, Nancy, penned
a tribute to her brother and all Eagles:

> No cause could be more American in nature. Two hundred
> and forty-four very young men with foresight, incredible
> courage, and that special kind of American integrity and
> initiative made their way to Canada . . . and then to Eng-
> land to fight in a war they knew would enmesh the world.
> . . . They served in the RAF receiving the same pay . . .
> living and flying under at least as difficult conditions as those
> of their RAF comrades. Those who survived until August of
> 1942 went on to fight with their American comrades in the
> Eighth Air Force. They distinguished themselves both with
> the British and later with their compatriots. They brought
> early respect and honor to America. . . . Two hundred
> and forty-four very young men began . . . the American
> Eagle Squadrons, one hundred and eight had survived by the
> end of the war. Please, let us never forget them.[71]

For the Eagles of 133 Squadron, the transfer to Biggin Hill in May brought the sun out both literally and figuratively. What they had longed for since their formation nine months earlier they now got almost daily— action against the Germans. The combination of warm, sunny days, frequent missions over France, and contact with the enemy made each of the unit members feel he was finally part of the first team of the RAF. The reaction among other personnel at Biggin Hill was also enthusiastic, for 133 was the first American squadron to be stationed there.

> The decorations were quickly changed, the "pin-ups" and Esquire girls giving place to advertisements in mouthwatering colour of Virginia hams, California oranges and steaming, juicy steaks, for Britain's war-time rationing was a sore point with American volunteers in the Royal Air Force.[72]

The action began with 133's first mission as part of the Biggin Hill wing, when they escorted bombers over Belgium on 7 May, and continued almost daily. On 10 May "No. 133 ran into a bunch of Me 109's at 21,000 feet, but e/a [enemy aircraft] put their noses down and made for the deck as fast as possible."[73] But a week later, the German aircraft did not get away.

> The Biggin Wing made another Fighter Sweep over the Abbeville area, and this time the Squadron succeeded in stirring up the Hun's nest! F/Lt McColpin and P/O Morris both had combats 5 miles N.W. of Le Treport as a result of which McColpin claimed an M.E. 109F destroyed and another "probable," and Morris claimed a "probable." Neither they or any of the remaining pilots suffered any damage.[74]

The action that continued for the next two days was the most intense yet experienced by the unit. On 18 May both Squadron Leader Thomas and George Sperry got shots at German aircraft, and on the 19th Moran Morris, Carter Harp, and Sperry all had combats with Me 109's and claimed enemy aircraft damaged—but the mission cost the lives of Pilot Officers Davis Florance and Robert

Pewitt. Just four days later Marion Jackson severely damaged another Me 109. Finally, on the 31st, Edwin Taylor damaged an FW 190, but both Moran Morris and William Ford were shot down and killed.

For many of the pilots, May brought the first exposure to intense combat. Charles Cook's reaction to one of his encounters illustrates just how challenging combat can be. He found himself

> caught in a whirling maelstrom of aircraft at one minute, and then . . . suddenly, terrifying, alone. Searching for the rest of 133 he ran into a whole squadron of Me 109's. "Come over here," he yelled, forgetting all R/T (radio/telephone) drill in his excitement. "I've got 'em cornered like rats." "How many?" inquired another pilot, the only one to hear "Cooksie." "Eight or ten of the _____ ." There was utter silence in reply. Cook returned to Biggin Hill badly shot-up and furious. "Hell," was the other pilot's comment. "You had them covered. I reckoned you could take care of yourself." [75]

If 133 wanted action, they got it, quickly making up for lost time. The *Squadron History* for 1 June 1942 speaks of one good day's work.

> The Squadron took off with Nos. 72, 124 and 401 at 1030 for a Fighter Sweep over the Hardelot, St. Omer, Calais area. They flew at 25,000 feet. The Hun was not playing, however, so there were no combats. All landed safely at 1140.
>
> They took off again at 1250 and flew as escort cover wing to 8 Hurribombers who were detailed to bomb Bruges Harbour and docks. All went like clockwork! No e/a interfered and there were no casualties. All landed safely at 1425.
>
> At 1550 the Squadron with 72 and Gravesend took off and landed at Martelsham to refuel. At 1750 they left Martlesham flying as escort wing to 12 Bostons who were detailed to bomb Flushing. Everything went to plan. No e/a came up so there were no combats. 133 landed safely at

1925, well satisfied with the day's work of 3 operational sweeps.[76]

This account, describing a day of activity not unusual for any of the squadrons in Fighter Command, graphically illustrates the need to take much more than enemy aircraft damaged and destroyed into account when evaluating the contributions of the unit to the war. The fighter squadron has done its work well if no enemy aircraft rise to challenge the mission. And the flyers knew they faced the same dangers on every mission. Edwin Taylor described his feelings as a pilot taking part, day after day, in a routine like that described for 1 June:

> For openers I would like for it to be known that we were engaged in a pursuit where the game was played constantly on the outer edge. Any show could develop into a confrontation where you would be called on to go to the absolute limit. That being the case it wasn't hard to get psyched up. Getting psyched down was something else to think about. . . . If you gave much thought to what was happening in a dog fight or on an attack on something, you might come completely unglued. Later when you put together what had transpired it was hard to get psyched down. I have heard and read about the high other people get from their activities . . . motor racing, football, World Series win, thoroughbred jockeys, swimming, etc., but when the situation is one on one . . . and the winner lives and the loser dies, that is the absolute end in high feelings. . . . Combat flying is the ultimate. Making a mistake didn't mean being penalized, punished, or having a replay, or making an ass of yourself in some manner, it would more than likely be terminal. German fighter aircraft were superior in almost all areas until midyear 1942. It was always beyond my capabilities of understanding why some of these brave pilots got themselves into this game. . . . There were all kinds of devious methods used to get into the RAF. Some of these people had 150 hours of flying time or less when they were fully operational combat pilots. They were not prepared to be apprehensive about being hurt or killed, they just didn't even think about it. Even so,

we all knew that some of the people that we worked, played, and lived with would be killed. In my little world I was almost out of touch with everything except flying, the air war, and day to day existence. The only way to lift the curtain on tomorrow is to wait for it.[77]

The following day the squadron was out of bed early and took off at 0630 for another escort mission over France, on which no enemy aircraft were seen. Another mission was flown during the day. This pattern was repeated by 133 almost daily throughout both June and July, except for bad weather days and a training period for a week during the middle of June. No matter how much combat the unit was involved in, the RAF periodically would take a squadron off the alert or mission board for practice flying to keep them in top shape. Whether a factor or not, the Germans were unable to enjoy this luxury to nearly the degree that the British and later the American pilots were. The Luftwaffe pilots could count on flying in combat almost every day, with no appreciable training time because of the shortage of fuel and the deteriorating quality of their airplanes. In the five years between the Battle of Britain and the end of World War II, the number of hours that an Me 109 engine could be run without major work decreased from 100 to 10.[78]

Weather again took its toll during the early part of July, but by the middle of the month, 133 Squadron was again flying over France daily. On 26 July the 900th German aircraft to be destroyed by Biggin Hill fighters was duly celebrated at the mess, where it seemed almost any accomplishment, including the arrival of new squadron members, was an occasion for some kind of party. Certainly, June had offered plenty of reasons to socialize, because of the arrival of more new squadron members than in any month since the unit's founding—eleven, including Don Blakeslee and Don Gentile, who were to become among the most famous pilots of World War II after they transferred to the American forces.[79]

The action promised Number 121 Squadron when they were posted to North Weald had finally become a daily routine in April. Although a number of pilots departed for oversea assignments, mostly to Malta, a number of new arrivals, both from OTU and from other squadrons, where they had been awaiting a chance to become Eagles, kept the unit at full strength. The encounters began on 12 April when Hugh Kennard, the commander, Barry Mahon, and Leroy Skinner each claimed a damaged FW 190 and Thomas Allen got one probable destroyed and one damaged. The high level of action continued for the next week, a week that culminated in a visit by Sir Archibald Sinclair, the secretary of state for air, on the 18th. Key British officials regularly visited various squadrons, but Sinclair's presence reinforced the perception in Number 121 that they had finally proved themselves as an effective fighting force. The last confirmed victory of the month was described in a rather picturesque manner:

> On the way home [on April 24th] . . . P/O Daley and P/O Skinner saw a JU 52 and jointly attacked it. . . . The result of these attacks . . . were clouds of white smoke, and bits were seen to fly off the enemy aircraft. . . . Quickly after this it was seen to fall in the sea with a great splash.[80]

The total of 740 operational missions during April was a record for the squadron but did not come without cost, as the unit lost Frederick Austin and Carl Bodding while Leroy Skinner joined many of his squadron mates as a prisoner of war. Just one week later, Ralph Freiberg and Robert Brossmer were also killed.

The high level of activity that 121 Squadron had throughout the early spring continued as summer approached. Members of the squadron saw combat against the Luftwaffe almost every day as they flew sweeps or escort missions into France. One of their more unusual accomplishments occurred at the end of the month when the squadron sank a German ship. Don Young remembers the mission, for it was only his second operational flight with the unit:

As we approached the enemy coast three small coastal freighters were spotted just off shore. They were immediately attacked. . . . After some maneuvering for position and spacing I followed Gunner Halsey on a broadside strafing run on the largest boat. As I pulled up over the boat I . . . started a climbing turn to the right for a look at the boat. As the boat came in sight over my right shoulder I saw a Spitfire firing at the boat in a broadside wave height attack. About two hundred yards from the target the Spitfire struck the water, broke free and pulled up over the boat, passing out of my field of vision. . . .

In about thirty seconds a voice on the radio said "this is Hawka Blue One. I hit the drink but will try to make it home. My engine is shaking badly." About a minute later, a voice said, "This is Hawka Blue One. I'm going in at a hundred miles an hour." Those were the last words spoken by Flt. Lt. Tommy Allen.

Of the three boats which were attacked, two were beached to prevent sinking and the other sank. The Wing loss for the show was Tommy Allen. This was my first combat mission with 121 Eagle Squadron.[81]

There had been few personnel changes in 121 during the winter, but by spring the losses from combat and transfer to other units necessitated a number of replacements. During May and June alone, there were seventeen additions to the squadron. One of these was Donald Willis, who

arrived this morning [June 2] . . . from 61 OTU. He joined the Finnish Air Force during the Finnish Russian War [Reade Tilley had tried to do the same], and later joined the Norwegian Air Force during the invasion of that country by the Germans. After escaping from Norway, when it was forced to surrender, he eventually made his way to this country and joined our air force a little less than a year ago.[82]

Also arriving was Ernie Beatie, who remembered,

I'll never forget the thrill of being assigned to the 121 Eagle Squadron because you didn't have to go in an Eagle Squadron, they could assign you anywhere they wanted. . . . You did an awful lot of flying training with the old heads there . . . but you were never assigned a mission . . . you had to volunteer for your first mission. Someone told me that in the barracks one night. Our barracks were in an English manor house, the most beautiful thing you have ever seen, just gorgeous. Anyway I volunteered for a mission. Not long after that . . . I went on a Rhubarb. On a Rhubarb you flew over, right on the deck to stay under the radar, and shot up canal barges. We shot up these barges and George got hit, he got hit real bad. . . . I pulled up beside him and what had happened was his cockpit had got shot up and he was hit in the fanny, the leg and his hand, and his throttle and several instruments, including his airspeed indicator, were gone. I flew beside him . . . gave him his airspeed and we got him home. Anyway that was my first mission. Now that's a thrill and I remember thinking "Good God, this is hairy! It's not a wonder they were losing a lot of pilots!"[83]

The unit moved from North Weald to Southend on Sea on 3 June. The mansion-barracks Ernie Beatie spoke of were at the new location, and the crews used their Chevy van or bicycles for transportation. By 9 June, 121 was back in the thick of the action. On that day Barry Mahon and John Mooney each got two FW 190s, but just one week later Mooney was killed on a Rhubarb over Belgium. Reported to have been strafing a train, he evidently crashed into it.

June was a busy month for all the members of the squadron, reported Don Young. "I flew twelve missions, did convoy patrols, scrambles and numerous training flights."[84] But it was 31 July that stood out in the minds of many members of 121, for that was their record day for destroying German planes. As were many of the missions that involved intense action, this one was an escort duty over Abbeville, France, the home of one of the crack German fighter units. In the melee that occurred, six German planes were destroyed, two each by Selden Edner and Barry Mahon and one by Hugh Kennard and Sgt/Plt William Kelly, and there was one more probable.

Norman Young was shot down and killed and the squadron commander, Hugh Kennard, was wounded, forcing him to relinquish the squadron to W. Dudley Williams, an Englishman who would lead the unit until its transfer to the US Army Air Force.[85]

No matter what was going on in the squadrons, there was always time for memories from home. The *121 Squadron Record Book* noted on 19 June,

> In the evening a dinner was held in the mess, after which an album of names signed by the citizens of Amarillo, Texas was handed to P/O Daley by the C.O. This album was made to commemorate the DFC being conferred on Daley.

The next day Daley, who had been in the squadron since September 1941, was promoted to flight lieutenant. He was in command of the squadron when it became part of the US forces in September 1942 and was killed on a mission near Paris in 1944.

Communication to and from home was important to these young men who faced death so often. The speed with which death could come, as well as German fighter tactics, are well illustrated by the fate of Ben Mays. Number 71 got off to a slow start in April; it looked like a repeat of March: lots of patrol and some standing down because of weather. On 10 April, though, the spring activity finally began with "the Squadron . . . airborne on a rodeo operation. This was," reported the squadron *Record Book*, "the first time some of our pilots had been over France."[86] One of those relatively new pilots was Ben Mays, who had joined the unit in January. On a 12 April mission Mays was flying fourth in a line of four. "As we approached the target area," wrote Harold Strickland,

> I checked my rear-view mirror [and] noticed that Ben was more than 50 yards astern and I called for him to close up. I believe that, like myself, Ben was flying one of his very first missions. Holding a position in a high-speed formation in the thin air at altitude is more difficult than at sea level. . . .
> When I rechecked Ben he was narrowing the gap probably

240

about the time that the Hornchurch and Debden wings were attacked by Me 109's and FW 190's diving at terrific speed out of the sun, firing from long range, then either zooming upward back into the sun . . . or else escaping with the superior speed in the dives. Then, when I rechecked Ben again, he was gone. . . . The sudden, deadly attack upon Ben again emphasized to me that many actions and reactions which fighter pilots talk about, write about, and read about, occur in or under about one second. When a pilot calls out: "Bandits! Six O'Clock!" perhaps two seconds have passed. Sometimes that can be too late.[87]

Leo Nomis, also of 71 Squadron, in commenting on the tactics employed by the Germans, noted that the German pilots

were vague and sinister shapes in aircraft that always seemed to be faster and higher than ours. . . . Research of certain individual tactics which Novotny (a German fighter pilot) employed certainly points to this. In this case it was simply a single FW, gaining superior speed from above and way behind, dropping down and then pulling up under an entire squadron of 12 aircraft [71, led by Peterson] and hanging briefly in a vertical position; pumping various rounds into a No. 4 . . . who in this case [Mays], never saw him and in all likelihood never knew what hit him, and then half rolling out and away. . . . I remember I was a bit shaken and felt a real sadness at Mays' departure because he was one of those Texas people who quietly had a somehow soothing philosophy for everything. . . . This occurrence of getting blasted without seeing the enemy happened more frequently than one might imagine, especially with pilots on initial combat runs or those with the inability to re-adjust the eye for various ranges.[88]

Almost every fighter pilot, including the Eagles, thought seriously about death. John Brown summed it up best:

When you see a friend crash, that's when it starts but the realization doesn't become evident in your own life until you are being shot at. At North Weald we were flying three or four missions a day. You would come in for lunch and in the formal gardens around the Officer's Mess it was amazing the number of people out walking and not saying one damn word. No doubt a number were wondering if they would be back to smell the flowers that evening. . . . You develop a sense of urgency to absorb as much as you can in a short amount of time because you are never certain what lies ahead. . . . I think we were all wearing facades . . . and that may well be why we would have parties and the like. . . . You did become tense . . . because life was fragile . . . but we had made a commitment and we were determined to fulfill it.[89]

Leo Nomis describes poignantly what these thoughts meant:

There was John (Long John) Flynn of 71 and if there was a Gary Cooper type he fit it. . . . Long John went out on a sweep on a real bright April day when spring had rolled around for 1942 and like so many at that time he just never came back. . . . But I remember the day before because Flynn and I had gone pheasant hunting in the fields around Martlesham. . . . It's funny but the most vivid thing I remember about it was that he had killed a big pheasant on the fly and when I walked over to him he was gazing down at the dead bird with a sad preoccupied expression on his face. That night he bought a bottle of wine from the Mess bar and we had the service cook prepare the pheasant for us and he and I . . . dined on it. And the dinner itself, in the Mess dining room after everyone else had left, had a strange depression about it. I remember we ate in silence and then the next day he was gone and it was such a delightful spring day that no one could believe it. That evening I missed Flynn more than I could remember missing anyone but it was the fashion in those days to keep such things to one's self.[90]

George Sperry tied the reality of death to the daily activities of many of the Eagles when he said,

We saw so many of our friends die that we soon developed a defense against any betrayal of emotion and refused to sentimentalize friendship and parting and death. To many, therefore, we were without loyalty or deep feeling. We trained for air warfare in England during a time of great tension and war nerves, when liquor, carousing and wenching provided a means of escape from grim realities.[91]

The risks were certainly real for the Eagles in spring 1942. By the middle of April, Number 71, as well as 121 and 133, was flying almost daily over France. Most missions were escorting bombers or conducting fighter sweeps, and, happily for the pilots, they led to contact with large numbers of the enemy. For Number 71, 27 April was the biggest day since the first of the year. On a bomber escort mission over St. Omer, the Germans came up in force—and paid a price. Chesley Peterson, the squadron commander, destroyed two enemy planes, Oscar Coen and Mike McPharlin destroyed three between them, and other members of the squadron damaged three more. Again, though, the Eagles also paid a price, as John Flynn, one of the unit's most experienced flight commanders, was shot down and killed. After flying 661 missions during April, Number 71 moved from Martlesham Heath to Debden, still in the 11 Group area, on 2 May.[92]

For the pilots of 71, the move to Debden, "which had a wonderful runway and beautiful accommodations," was a welcome change. The extra hours of daylight as summer approached, combined with Debden's location, produced long days of flying and a greater diversity of missions, as the squadron *Record Book* entry for 6 May illustrates:

At 0800 hours the Squadron was called to readiness in preparation for a circus and at 0910 hours were airborne. They landed at Biggin Hill at 0940 hours, taking off again at 1115 hours for their target over Caen. . . . Returning the Squadron landed at Ford. . . . The Squadron were airborne again at 1415 hours landing at base at 1505 hours.

The Squadron was then put on 30 min. [alert] until 1630 hours when they were called to readiness. At 1745 hours they were airborne again on another bomber escort to Calais. On the return journey the Squadron landed at Manston to refuel and returned to base as 2030 hours after which they were released.[93]

The weather did not hold up, however, and there were a number of days when the unit did not fly at all. Although the days of standing down were not particularly welcome, at least there was no convoy patrol, which was always good news. Most of the unit's work now was escorting bombers over the coastal regions of France—activity that had produced occasionally fierce German reaction in late April but brought little in May. Of significance, though, was Harold Strickland's observation that the number of FW 190s was increasing. On 31 May the squadron was called out to help in a massive search and rescue effort concentrating on bomber crews lost the previous day, when more than 1,000 bombers had raided Cologne and 44 had been lost. Even that duty was not without its hazards: just three days later, Frank Zavakos crashed into the sea and was killed on just such a mission.

The most action of the entire month of June for 71 came on the 1st when, as part of a four-squadron sweep, 71 was attacked by FW 190s. In the ensuing melee over Belgium, in which George Teicheira was shot down and killed, the squadron got one destroyed, two damaged, and one probable. Number 71 was fortunate, however, because the total loss for the four squadrons for the day was nine Spitfires and eight pilots. But the end of June saw Newton Anderson, the current squadron commander of 222 Squadron and a former member of Number 71, shot down over France.[94]

ALERT

For part of June, the 11th to the 19th, Number 71 did no operational flying because of poor weather but was required to keep several pilots on alert to fly if the need

arose. Although any operation would be extremely hazardous in poor weather, if the threat was severe enough
the RAF would send its fighters out in almost any
weather. Every RAF fighter pilot, especially early in the
war, spent a great deal of time on such alert duty, ready
to scramble to the defense of the English cities in case of a
German attack. For Carroll McColpin,

> There are many words you can use to describe alert duty. In
> war, there are not enough words to go around. After a while,
> I could count every board and nail in our alert shack. As a
> matter of fact, for the first eight months I never knew what it
> was like to have time off. Pulling alert was, for all practical
> purposes, like an actor waiting to go on stage or a fireman
> for the alarm bell. For us, it was waiting to go on the defen-
> sive or offensive mission.[95]

Speed was of the essence if the squadron was scrambled. McColpin recalls one morning when a city 40 miles
away from the base was attacked by the Luftwaffe:

> Two pilots were on 5 minute alert, the rest of the squadron
> were on standby sleeping in their barracks. It took less than
> 10 minutes from the time the alert sounded for 12 of us to
> be in the air and on our way. In those days, it was standard
> operating procedure to be wheels-up within five minutes af-
> ter the first gong. The Eagles, I am happy to say, usually did
> it in less than three and at one base held the record scramble
> time of 1 minute and 20 seconds flat.[96]

There were generally three different classes of alert,
although exact procedures varied from squadron to
squadron. Cockpit alert meant that the pilot was either
strapped in the aircraft or else sitting on the wing or very
near the plane, with the external battery power connected so he could start the engine and give it full power
immediately when a red flare was shot into the air. During this very boring alert duty, the pilot would run the
engine every 30 minutes or so, depending on the
weather, so it could take full power as soon as it was
started.

LeRoy Gover wrote about the experience of sitting cockpit alert.

> When you are on cockpit alert here, you sit in your Spitfire, all strapped in and on the edge of the field ready to go. We fly with two aircraft on cockpit alert. When a red flare is fired into the air, you have to be in the air in 30 seconds. We start the engine every 30 minutes so the engine is always warm enough to be given full throttle immediately upon starting. When airborne, radar control will give you a heading to fly and tell you to climb to angels 15, or whatever altitude the Germans are. Angels being a thousand feet of altitude.
>
> Was about to doze off when a red flare sailed into the air. I started the engine and firewalled the throttle. Was given a vector onto a Heinkel 111 that had just dropped 8 bombs on the city of Poole, which is real near the grass strip we operate from. . . . I climbed to 15 thousand feet, but still in cloud. Operations called and advised me I was near the enemy aircraft, but about mid-channel I was recalled and vectored back to base.[97]

In the next lower phase of alert duty, the pilot remained in the alert shack or dispersal hut on the flight line, dressed in flying clothes with the Mae West, his inflatable life vest, on. In this alert, the pilot's parachute was on the wing of his plane, his helmet on the control column. When the scramble signal was given, generally by telephone, the pilot would have from two to three minutes to get airborne. Here again, the engines were kept warm, but by the ground crew. Life in the dispersal hut was somewhat less boring than on cockpit alert because there were books, cards, and company, as well as chairs and a couch. Tea and crumpets or bread with jam were also availble to stave off hunger until release from alert.

The final category was 15- to 30-minute alert. In this case the pilots could be in their quarters or the mess, where they could play cards, shoot pool, read, write, and participate in various sports activities. The requirement

COURTESY OF CHARLES A. COOK

A Spitfire on alert, pilot's parachute on the wing, at Biggin Hill (above). Inside the dispersal hut, pilots meet the challenge of passing time while on alert duty. Three—(left to right) Ben Mays, Mike Kelly, and Tom Andrews—are on 5-minute alert; Harold Strickland, on 30-minute alert, is not wearing his Mae West.

COURTESY OF EDWIN TAYLOR

was that the pilot would have to be able to get to the flight line in the allotted time, generally to take the place of an alert crew that had been scrambled. Some of the ground school classes, such as aircraft identification, were also conducted in the mess during this more leisurely alert status.[98]

INTO SUMMER

For some days in late June, there had been rumors in Number 71 of impending significant action for the squadron, so when they packed up on 30 June and moved to Gravesend, East of London on a bluff overlooking the Thames, speculation ran high that some kind of commando raid on France was in the offing and the squadron would be the air support. Because of a lack of proper barracks at the base, the unit was housed at the estate of the Earl of Darnley. If the squadron had to wait and wonder, there were far worse places to do it than in this beautiful setting of spacious grounds, pools, luxurious rooms, and the like. After a week in this "hardship" environment, having never been informed why they had moved to Gravesend, the squadron was sent back to Debden. Upon arrival at Debden, they were immediately declared non-operational pending a move to the Soviet Union.[99]

For several months there had been RAF squadrons in the Soviet Union training the Soviets to fly both the Hurricane and the Spitfire. It was the return of one such squadron from the Soviet Union to Eglinton that caused such a problem in the mess with Number 133 shortly before Christmas 1941. In early July, Number 71 was chosen to go to the USSR and train the Soviet pilots in Spitfires as well as aid in the defense of Stalingrad. The planes, all new Spitfires, were being transported by sea to Murmansk. While still at Gravesend the pilots were interviewed by Squadron Leader Peterson to determine which ones would volunteer for "oversea duty" to an unknown location. Most of the squadron agreed to go.

Upon arrival back at Debden they were told the duty was in the Soviet Union. The unit received several inoculations against dreaded diseases, hurriedly packed, drew oversea equipment, and on 10 July held a formal farewell dinner attended by a number of distinguished guests. All was in readiness until the German navy intervened by sinking the transport carrying the Spitfires to Murmansk. With the planes at the bottom of the sea, on the 13th the mission was cancelled and the unpacking began.[100] Actual combat missions did not resume for 71 until 20 July, and then action was light; no enemy were engaged for the remainder of the month. During the entire month of July, because of their movement and pending transfer, Number 71 flew only 73 operational missions.[101]

Because of interest in the US entry into the war, the unwillingness of the Eagle Squadrons to let the press into their units, and frequent combat keeping the units busy day after day, the first half of 1942 saw considerably less publicity in America about the Eagles. July, however, brought what was to be the greatest publicity event to date for the Eagles. A Hollywood-produced movie, *Eagle Squadron*, premiered in London on 30 July 1942 to a house full of dignitaries as well as all of the Eagles in the area. Although the members of 71 Squadron were not consulted about the picture, they were led to believe that it would have a *March of Time* type format that would accurately depict the squadrons in action and their contribution to the war. The previous year, while 71 was at North Weald, they were visited by several film crews who took various background footage as well as filming some specific stories. Art Roscoe remembers,

> They were taking some shots around, us getting in and out of airplanes, I guess it was background footage. William Geiger and I were to be in one scene together and every time they would go to take it the two of us would start giggling and they would have to cut. This went on for several times, then they switched to something else and they never did get back to us so we weren't in the film at all. . . . I never did see the film until after the war. [Roscoe transferred to Malta

WORLD PREMIERE
at the
LEICESTER SQUARE THEATRE
THURSDAY, JULY 30, 1942
At 6.45 p.m.
in aid of the
WELFARE FUND
of the
A.T.C.

EAGLE SQUADRON

COURTESY OF EDWIN TAYLOR

Invitation to the premier of the Hollywood movie, Eagle Squadron.

in early July 1942; Geiger was the third Eagle to become a prisoner of war, shot down on 14 September 1941.][102]

The movie was to begin with an introduction narrated by Quentin Reynolds, a long-time correspondent in England, who was liked and trusted by most of the Eagles. What the crowd saw, however, was far from what had been advertised. The movie, which starred Robert Stack, Diana Barrymore, Jon Hall, Eddie Albert, Nigel Bruce, Leif Erikson, and John Loder, began faithfully enough with the very well-received Reynolds introduction but then became a typical Hollywood war hero romance that completely departed from the reality of the Eagle experience. There were some good flying scenes but, by and large, the film was a disappointment, enough so that many of the Eagles retired to a nearby pub before the film had run its course. Some, however, remained until the end because, as Edwin Taylor said, "I came all the way into London to see the thing, I thought I would stay and see how it ended." "My folks and girl friend received complimentary tickets to that farce they called a movie, *The Eagle Squadron,*" said Fred Almos. "The movie made me so mad that I couldn't stand it."[103] Those Eagles who elected to leave the movie early were joined later in the pub by those who stayed until the end, to talk about, laugh about, ridicule, and lament the film well into the night.

Reviews of the movie varied. The *New York World Telegram* thought it had good flying scenes and an excellent introduction by Reynolds, but that the story line, acting, and love theme ruined what could have been a much better film. *Time, Newsweek,* and *Life* all generally agreed. What praise they gave was based on the action shots and Reynolds' work. *Life* even called it a "stirring experience" because it preserved the reality of the documentary aerial combat shots.[104] While the title and combat theme gave the film a short popular run in the United States, it soon disappeared from US theaters.

There was to be no long weekend in London for most of the pilots, however, as action was fast and furious for both 121 and 133 the following day. On 31 July Number 133, led by its new American flight leader, recently arrived Flight Lieutenant Don Blakeslee, who was soon to take Squadron Leader Thomas' place temporarily when Thomas was promoted to wing commander, was escorting Bostons to bomb the heavily defended Abbeville Aerodrome. The *133 Squadron History* describes the action:

> Just before crossing the coast on the way back a number of F.W. 190's made their appearance. Combats followed in which 1 F.W. 190 was destroyed by P/O Baker, 1 F.W. 190 destroyed and 1 Me.109F damaged by P/O Taylor. Our casualties were not light—F/Lt King, P/O Harp and F/Sgt Eichar did not return.[105]

Edwin Taylor's recollection is more vivid:

> When we were jumped by the Germans, I immediately latched on to an FW 190 and shot him down. At the same time there evidently was a German on my tail. My wing man, Carter Harp, called to warn me but I never did hear him and he was shot down at the same time. I was hit badly with a bullet grazing my head, which blinded me, one through my foot and others all over the airplane. I pulled up figuring that I would stall and when I felt that, I would get out. Amazingly my eyesight came back and I went down on the deck after three other Germans. I shot an Me 109 which was having a terrible time staying in the air and I am sure it crashed before getting back to France. Down on the deck I engaged two more FW 190s and, although I did not see them crash, Squadron Leader Thomas and William Baker saw the two crash. By that time I was out of ammunition and I headed for England, was put in the hospital and operated on and that was the end of my Eagle and RAF career. One reason that I never got official credit for all these aircraft was that my gun camera quit working before I ran out of ammunition.[106]

Taylor's three destroyed and one probable was a record for the squadron and combined with Baker's one destroyed to make the unit's best day yet. As with every big day for 133, however, it was costly, with the three deaths and Taylor's serious wounds. Taylor also came up short because, with the change of squadron commander from Thomas to Blakeslee and then to McColpin, and with Taylor unable to return to the squadron, his accomplishments were never submitted for a Distinguished Flying Cross.

On 1 August 1942 Harold Strickland turned 39 years old. To celebrate, he flew 3 hours and 45 minutes looking for bomber crews that might have survived landing in the Channel. Although Strickland saw no action, his squadron got one destroyed by Jim Gray and a probable by Bob Sprague. The last full month of duty in the RAF for Number 71 had begun. On the 8th, Strickland had a much sadder entry in his diary when he noted that his roommate, "Joe Helgason, Seattle, killed today in a practice attack on aerodrome gun post. Struck tree at 400 mph. Spitfire smashed into hundreds of pieces."[107] The new month brought no such action, good or bad, in 121 and 133 Squadrons, as they practiced, flew some convoy patrols, and made sweeps into France that were generally unchallenged.

A great deal of the talk around the mess during the early part of August centered on the impending transfer to the US Army Air Force. Most of the Eagles were looking forward to the move, primarily because it would almost triple their pay, but a number were having second thoughts. After all, they had become accustomed to the RAF, liked the way Fighter Command operated, and, most of all, hated to leave the Spitfire. Adding to the mixed emotions was the fact that, despite rumors of an impending transfer, nothing official had yet been received. Why was it taking so long when there were no US fighter units in England and the American B–17s were starting to show up in force? On 15 August, for example, Number 71 had flown escort for a group of the American bombers in one of their first large raids on France.

There were two problems to be overcome. The first was just how to transfer the Eagles to the American forces. There really was no mechanism in place for the transfer, which made the processs slow. Part and parcel of this problem was determining what rank the new Army Air Force pilots would hold. A second issue was the logistics that had to be worked out with the British. Would the Americans bring their Spitfires with them? If they did, who would maintain them and under what flag would they fly? What control, if any, would the British have over the aircraft? There are also unconfirmed accounts of a question about American payment to the British for the training received by the Eagles before they arrived in England and officially became members of the RAF. Working out all of these issues took time, so the Eagles waited.

A second item of discussion among the pilots in the summer of 1942 was the cancelled large operation that had precipitated their move to Gravesend in June. On 14 August movement began once again to the forward staging bases for the unknown but very big operation. Number 71 Squadron made the short flight to Gravesend, from which they flew their B–17 escort mission on the 15th. Number 133 had gone to Gravesend at the end of July, but on 14 August they moved again, to Lympne, where they settled into the familiar surroundings of Sir Philip Sasson's lovely country home. On the 17th, they too flew escort for more than 300 B–17s—a welcome reminder that the Americans were arriving in force. On the evening of 18 August each of the units was briefed on the upcoming "Operation Jubilee," a combined operation to cover an allied invasion of France at Dieppe. This was the first, and only, operation in which all three of the Eagle Squadrons participated at the same time. It was also their biggest operation, and the last of significance for both 71 and 121.[108]

"Operation Jubilee" was designed to be a reconnaissance in force to test both the German reaction to an invasion and the Allied planning for one. The attack was also intended to increase the Germans' fears of an assault on France and possibly force them to transfer forces to the west, thereby taking some pressure off the Soviets. Answers to numerous questions, ranging from the quantity and type of landing craft needed to mount the eventual invasions of France to the need for naval guns and air superiority, were also vital to the Allies. The attack was originally slated to be launched on 4 July, but bad weather had forced its postponement. Because the Allied Command believed that a large-scale operation against the mainland was still necessary, "Jubilee" was rescheduled for August.[109]

The role of the three Eagle Squadrons, and the respective wings to which they were attached, varied as the day went along, but was basically to maintain air superiority and prevent German air attacks on the assault forces. To a great many Eagles, the missions flown in support of Operation Jubilee were the most memorable of their tour in the RAF. Because it was such a significant operation for each of the Eagle Squadrons, it is instructive to briefly consider the day's action by each as well as some of the personal accounts of the fighting.

For Number 133, the action is described in the unit's History.

> Every Dog has his day—and on the 19th August No. 133 was the Dog! . . . The Squadron had been told to be at readiness at 0350 hours. . . . The Squadron finally took off at 0720 with orders to orbit Dieppe at 7,000 feet. Target was reached without incident, but the fun began soon after! F/Lt Blakeslee, D.F.C., P/O Baker and F/Sgt Alexander all had combats, as a result of which 2 F.W. 190's were destroyed, and another probably destroyed. We suffered no casualties. All returned and landed at 0820.
>
> They were ordered up again at 1015 with orders to fly top cover over Dieppe at 12,000 feet. Combats ensued immediately after the target was reached, the following claims being made: 1 Ju.88 and 2 F. W. 190's destroyed: 4 F.W. 190's damaged and 3 Do.217's damaged, the pilots being: F/Lt Blakeslee, F/Lt Brettell, P/O's Beaty, Wright, Gentile, Baker, Doorly, and Gudmundsen. As in the first patrol, our casualties were NIL. . . .
>
> A short time after, the Squadron was again ordered up with orders to orbit Dieppe as in the previous cases. Combats ensued in this patrol in which P/O Nelson probably destroyed a Do. 217, F/Sgt Alexander claimed a Do. 217 destroyed and F/Lt Blakeslee claimed a F.W. 190 as damaged. It was also noticed that the evacuation of troops was now in fairly full process. Bombers were dive-bombing both small and large boats, and 2 ships, one a destroyer, were seen to receive direct hits. All our aircraft landed safely at 1345.
>
> The Squadron took off for the fourth and last patrol at 1955, with orders to patrol the convoys returning from Dieppe. . . . No enemy aircraft flew over the convoy. . . .

All our aircraft . . . landed without further incident at 2055 hours.

A great ending to a "good day's work." . . . 6 DE-STROYED. 2 PROBABLES. 8 DAMAGED—For no losses !!!!![110]

"The Dieppe raid of Aug. 19th . . . was of course my most memorable day in the RAF," wrote Richard Alexander.

Since our arrival in Lympne, we had all been confined to base and were not allowed to make any outside telephone calls. We knew something big was afoot, but we did not know what until the evening of the 18th [when they were briefed]. . . . We took off [on the 19th] with orders to orbit Dieppe at 7,000 feet. . . . Four FW 190's carrying bombs approached us from the north. They were at about 1,000 feet, and flew directly below us, heading for the ships in the harbor. Blakeslee immediately called them in and we broke down and after them. I was flying Red Four to Eric Doorly. . . . Suddenly I observed two more 190's to the left and slightly below me. I closed on them, and fired one burst at long range. . . . I was able to close to within about 3 or 4 hundred yards, and by then was well lined up. I gave him two more bursts, and we both passed directly over the entire convoy in the harbor, at about 300 feet. . . . I was still firing, and observed good strikes in the fuselage, and on his port wing. Suddenly, his wing seemed to fall off, the aircraft exploded, and went directly into the water.

I continued to fly south, and . . . I saw three Ju 88's headed for the harbor . . . I fired one full deflection burst at the hindmost 88, and then came around to line up. I fired one more burst, observed strikes, and ran out of ammunition. . . . On the two missions that I flew for the day, I had destroyed a 190, destroyed a 217, and had damaged a Ju 88.[111]

LeRoy Gover, who was a member of 66 Squadron but joined Number 133 the day after Dieppe, wrote a very graphic account of the battle, which also was his most memorable combat experience while in the RAF:

> Our Squadron escorted twelve Hurri-bombers to Dieppe this morning at first light. . . . We all flew at sea level the entire mission. We took them in through flak that cannot be described. When you are within 100 feet of those big guns firing, concussion tosses you about to a large degree. There were hundreds of planes screaming through the sky. Dozens of dog fights going on. Planes plummeting to earth on fire. Pilots who had been shot down were in their dinghies. I saw nine or ten Spitfires just shooting hell out of a Jerry Dornier. We fought off attacks on the Hurricanes, but four were shot down by the shore batteries. We were attacked twice more by Messerschmitt 109's as we crossed back out over the coast of France. I got strikes on a Messerschmitt 109, but I was flying about 50 feet off the water and couldn't maneuver to finish him off. Three of our Spitfires were so badly shot up they were out of the fight, but did manage to fly back to England.
>
> There were five planes left in our Squadron for the second mission, and we went back across the Channel to shoot up any gun emplacements we came across. Seven Focke-Wulf 190's attacked us as we hit the French Coast. The only advantage we had was to out turn them. I got strikes on two . . . but did no real damage. We lost two more of our Spitfires. I was now out of ammo, so broke away and headed home.
>
> That afternoon, our Squadron, which now consisted of three aircraft, was detailed to fly close escort on 12 Bostons, who were to lay a smoke screen along the shore to cover the withdrawal of the commandos. We went in at sea level and two of the Bostons were shot down right in front of me. I was about 250 yards from shore and the German machine guns were spraying hell out of things. Large cannon shells were bursting all around, and cannon shells were hitting the water and shooting up tall columns of water. As the Bostons finished laying their smoke, two more were shot down. As I was now being shot up, I lost track of the other Bostons and do not know their fate. The beach was covered with fallen com-

mandos. About two miles out on the way home we were jumped by a gaggle of Focke-Wulf 190's. One was right on me and getting hits so I pushed full left rudder and his bullets struck the water beside me. He turned and shot my number two straight into the sea. Then the third man in our threesome was shot down, and I was now all alone. I weaved to beat hell and came home balls out. Saw three more pilots in the water in their little yellow dinghies. They sure looked lonely bobbing about in that mess.

Boats that had been sent in to pick up the commandos were leaving the beach with 3 or 4 commandos. Most all were dead on the beach or couldn't break out because of the terrible shelling directed at them. Then this evening I had the only aircraft available and it had so many bullet holes but was serviceable to fly. I was put on alert and sure enough a Jerry Junkers 88 came over and bombed the field. I had been scrambled after him, but the field defense guns brought him down, right near the mess, and I returned to base, and to bed, a very tired and lonely fighter pilot.[112]

"We were up at 3 AM, had breakfast and took off into the blackness from Gravesend," wrote Harold Strickland of the activity of Number 71. "Pete led the Squadron, Gus Daymond's flight was on his left. . . . Tommy Andrews led Blue flight, followed by Jim Clarke, myself and Brewster Morgan." The mission was to patrol the landing area to ensure British air superiority.[113] In the one encounter of the sortie, Strickland damaged an FW 190.

At 1045 Number 71 was airborne on its second sortie, again charged with flying cover for the invading force. "Enemy resistance was reaching its peak," recalled Strickland.

We encountered terrific flak . . . the destroyer-controller on the spot advised that the race track was captured and an emergency field near the town was available for crash landings. Assault boats were wrecked and burned on the beach.[114]

In the course of the mission, Peterson damaged a Ju 88.

The most action of the day for 71 Squadron was on the third sortie, which took off at 1316, about the time the evacuation was beginning. The Germans had put all their available resources into the attack at that time, hoping to inflict maximum damage on the retreating British and Canadian forces. When the Number 71 pilots arrived at Dieppe, an attack on the British convoy was underway by about 20 Ju 88s with a large fighter escort. Peterson immediately ordered the squadron into action and himself attacked a bomber that was beginning its run on the ships. He came at the enemy from astern and forced it to drop its bombs short of the target, but in the process was severely damaged by the tail gunner of the Ju 88. Moments after the enemy bomber crashed into the sea, Peterson himself was forced to leave his burning Spitfire. Oscar Coen and Mike McPharlin attacked another of the bombers and got a probable destroyed on it, but McPharlin was also forced to bail out of his badly damaged plane. Both Peterson and McPharlin were rescued and were back in action within a few days.[115]

On their final flight of the day, launched at 1715, 71 Squadron was detailed to cover the retreating convoy that LeRoy Gover spoke about. On this flight as well, they thwarted an enemy attack on the ships when they engaged a large flight of FW 190s, which promptly turned and retreated toward France upon sighting the Spitfires. After returning to Gravesend the unit prepared for a fifth sortie, which was not needed. The following day they returned to Debden, having flown 57 operational missions in support of Jubilee with no personnel losses.[116]

In contrast to Number 71, 121 Squadron saw the bulk of its action on the first flight of the day. They, too, had been ordered to patrol the beach at 5,000 feet and maintain cover over the landing and engaging force. They took off at 0840 with Number 19 Squadron and shortly after their arrival at Dieppe engaged a large force of FW 190s. In the ensuing melee, Selden Edner destroyed one of the Germans and Gilbert Halsey and Leon Blanding each got a probable destroyed. Don Smith damaged another FW 190. Although the enemy losses were something to celebrate, those to the squadron were not. Barry Mahon and Gene Fetrow were both shot down; James Taylor evidently had a mid-air collision with another Spitfire.

After being shot down, Barry Mahon had a ringside seat to all the action:

> I lay on my back in the dinghy and watched the tremendous air battle above me. It seemed like the entire battle was taking place right over my head with aircraft being shot down, parachutes coming out of the sky and explosions everywhere. It seemed like a giant Fourth of July display only much more tragic. I eventually drifted to shore, still confident that I would be rescued by the troops that were evacuating. To my surprise all the soldiers remaining had been captured and I joined their group after being led through a mine field to the loading station for the trucks.[117]

Fetrow, who also bailed out over the Channel, was fortunate not to have suffered Mahon's fate.

> Funny thing about it, the day before I got knocked down one of the guys at the base had a taxi accident and for his punishment he had to jump in this big pool as a demonstration, fully clothed, just like you would be coming out of an airplane. . . . They gave us all the equipment but they didn't show us how to use it, so I was watching this guy go through all this drill and the next day I was for real. When I bailed out I was 17 miles from England and only 5 miles from the Germans in France. My airplane was burning and it just came unglued so I had to get out. There were some commandos coming back out after getting shot up pretty bad and they saw me bail out but I didn't know that. I saw this ship coming toward me and I didn't know if it was a German or a British ship. And boy, when I saw the Union Jack flying in the breeze I said, "Man, I've got it made." They did have some trouble seeing me in that little dinghy with the big swells but I got picked up O.K. . . . A while later we picked

up another RAF pilot with a .38 calibre hole in his shoulder. I don't know how he ever got out of his plane. . . . Then we picked up a Free French pilot who had ditched a Spitfire, something you are never supposed to do.[118]

The second sortie of the day for 121 was airborne at 1130 but did not engage any enemy aircraft. Jim Daley was prepared to bail out when his engine quit, but it restarted and the unit returned to base with no engagements or casualties. The last flight took off at 1615 and patrolled Dieppe at 4,000 feet to cover the withdrawal. "Enemy aircraft were in and out of cloud taking pot-shots at our pilots but no serious attacks were made," reported the *Squadron Record Book*. With the exception of Julian Osborne, who had to bail out of his burning Spitfire over England, the rest of the squadron returned and were released at 1900, "having been in a state of super readiness since dawn."[119] Paul Ellington, who arrived at 121 Squadron just before the Dieppe raid, said of the day's events, "I stood around in shocked amazement at all the coming and going. . . ." The old hands earned their salt that day."[120]

For the whole day of 19 August, Numbers 71 and 133 each flew four missions and 121 flew three. In the process they accounted for nine German aircraft destroyed, four more probably destroyed, and 14 damaged. The cost to the three units was one killed and one prisoner of war, both from 121. This was the highest scoring single day for the units and marked them each as among the most effective squadrons in Fighter Command. For Number 133 the day was particularly momentous, for they led the Eagles in enemy aircraft shot down and, of possibly greater significance, emerged from the fighting with no losses—a sharp contrast to what seemed to be their usual lot.

Although losses to the total Allied force in Operation Jubilee were great, some of the needed lessons were learned. The overall lesson was that the Germans were unable to prevent an attack and landing on the mainland of France, even though they were apparently forewarned of the impending action and fully prepared for it. And though the operation did not cause Hitler to transfer any troops from the eastern front, the raid did demoralize some of the German leaders and it forced them to diversify their defenses along the coast of France. But Allied losses were indeed high. For example, about 5,000 Canadians embarked and 2,210 returned. Of those who did not make it back, 907 were killed, a large number of others died of wounds, and nearly 2,000 were taken prisoner. The British flew over 2,000 sorties during the day and lost 106 aircraft. The Germans' casualties on the ground are not known, but they lost only 48 planes destroyed and another 24 damaged. Certainly, the Allies would need to be better prepared for the major invasion that would come two years later.[121]

For both 71 and 121 Squadrons, the intense action of Operation Jubilee was the last they would see as members of the RAF. Immediately after their return to Debden, the members of 71 Squadron began taking physicals for the US Army Air Force and attention became focused on that event. Some action continued nonetheless. On 27 August, for example, the wing commander, Duke Woolley, and Gus Daymond each destroyed a German aircraft. On 31 August Bill Taylor was shot down over the Channel and, although he successfully bailed out, was never rescued. Number 121 likewise flew a number of normal missions but, aside from one Ju 88 shot down by Don Young, encountered few enemy aircraft. Increasingly, all three squadrons were called upon to escort Flying Fortresses of the USAAF on their bombing missions over France. Such missions often drew enemy fighters but they also proved to be a real challenge to leadership, which, for Number 133, proved terribly fatal.

ESCORT DUTY

Four problems plagued the fighter pilots while on escort duty. The first was making accurate rendezvous. Many bomber crews, relatively new to England, the war, and their airplanes, had difficulty being accurate, in either time or place, in joining up with the fighters. To the Fortress crews, being a few minutes late at the rendezvous point was not significant given a mission length of seven or eight hours and no shortage of fuel. So they did not consider delays in getting all the aircraft off the ground, building the formation, and climbing to their predetermined altitude to be significant. For a Spitfire pilot, however, always operating on the margin of fuel availability, two or three minutes was crucial.

The second problem appears in this entry from the *133 Squadron History:*

> Cover was, however, given to the bombers until they crossed the French coast on their way back, when, for some reason or other, the bombers began firing at their escort! This did not please the pilots at all, so they dived down to sea level and came back alone leaving the bombers to look after themselves.[122]

To many of the new, overeager, very young gunners in the Flying Fortresses, any fighter they saw had to be German; more than once, the British fighters had to break away to keep from getting shot down by the aircraft they were protecting. A large number of the Eagles in all three squadrons had this experience.

A third problem was one of discipline for the fighter squadrons themselves. Maintaining formation with the bombers regardless of the circumstances was a real challenge. One tactic the Luftwaffe often used was to attempt to lure the Spitfires away to engage in a dog fight and then attack the bombers in force. To fighter pilots accustomed to going after enemy fighters wherever and whenever they could be found, ignoring a nearby German squadron until they actually attacked the bombers was difficult indeed.

A final issue was that some of the pilots had difficulty taking the escort mission seriously. For many of the Eagles, escort duty soon became almost as boring as convoy patrol; complacency could easily set in, especially when the mission was simply a routine escort flight. Losses that should have helped focus attention did occur. On 6 September both Eric Doorly and Dick Gudmundsen were shot down over France on an escort mission with 133 Squadron. Doorly evaded capture with the help of the underground. Gudmundsen was killed. All the above factors, along with a final and most critical one, leadership, were to come into play for Number 133 on 26 September.

LEADERSHIP

As the war progressed, the three Eagle Squadrons gradually moved from having hand-picked British combat veterans such as Walter Churchill and Hugh Kennard as commanders, to being led by American officers. The first American to assume command of one of the units was Chesley Peterson, who took over Number 71 in November 1941. Others Americans who served as Eagle Squadron commanders were Carroll McColpin, Gus Daymond, Jim Daley, and Don Blakeslee. In addition to squadron commander, most of the flight leaders were Americans by 1942. A logical question is, How did the Americans stack up to the British as combat leaders? In a nutshell, very well. But to really answer this question, one must realize that there were two kinds of leaders to the fighter pilots of the RAF, as there no doubt are in most other air forces. First were the flying leaders, those men who inspired confidence in combat situations but who were seen as little else. The other type was the individual who not only had the unit's confidence in a flying and combat situation but who also inspired confidence, trust, and loyalty when the squadron was not flying. The two traits become clear in observations by squadron members.

"I remember Don Blakeslee well," said Jim Clark. "He was a superior leader because he always knew what to do in combat, he never got us lost, and he always got us back home."[123] This was a typical comment about Blakeslee. Edwin Taylor represented the view of many Eagles in saying, "Blakeslee was the best fighter pilot in the war."[124] His conduct while not in combat was often questionable, however, and he was relieved of command on one occasion. In that way he differed significantly from many of his British and American counterparts.

Art Roscoe saw the key traits of Chesley Peterson as quite different from those of Blakeslee.

> He seemed to have an attitude about him that inspired confidence in the pilots. He was always calm, cool, and collected and seemed to know what he was doing. You sort of felt that if it seemed right to him you knew it would be O.K. . . . Pete exemplified the right way of doing things and doing your job properly. He was also a good pilot . . . but without a doubt leadership qualities were more important than knowing how to pilot the airplane. Such qualities as decision-making in when to attack or is it right to attack . . . were more important than actually piloting the airplane. Many good leaders that I saw in the RAF . . . would make terrible landings, run into things on the ground, and that sort of thing . . . but you would follow them anywhere.[125]

LeRoy Gover added to these ideas about Peterson: "Pete was an excellent leader. He was a smart pilot, had courage, was very mature, and would see to it that he didn't lose people. He always thought about his people." Gover thought Carroll McColpin and Gus Daymond had the same characteristics.

> Mac was a fine leader because of his maturity, his ability to plan, his smooth flying techniques, and concern for his people. He would never use full power since that would cause the pilots at the back of a formation to fall behind. Gussie was the same way, just a super person in every way.[126]

The leadership traits of Peterson and McColpin, who were the only two active commanders of the Eagles to be promoted to general officer in the US Air Force, were learned from the British. While each of these Americans had the basics to be a great leader, they both watched closely just how the British operated and took to heart those characteristics they admired and believed were effective. "We had an advantage that many of the English squadrons did not have," reminisced Carroll McColpin.

> They [the RAF] picked their best people to lead us and form us into squadrons so we would be effective. They got us good squadron commanders and good flight commanders. . . . The British style of leadership was more loose than the American but you have to remember that the British were not fighting until their tour was over. They were fighting until they won or lost, were killed, couldn't take it any more, or the war was over. It was a long haul to them and so getting the job done was their emphasis.[127]

McColpin also talked about his ideas on being an effective leader.

> A leader first has to know what he is doing, or I should say his people need to believe he knows what he is doing. And if he does this and he does it right most of the time they will get that feeling. . . . I always tried to figure out the mission and the best way to get the job done and still get back. My theory was that you had a job to do and you did the job and lived to do more another day. . . . I never led any missions where we lost anybody, so they had confidence in me. . . . Pete [Chesley Peterson] was great at figuring out how to go about it. He would do it a little less flamboyantly than I did, as far as getting in and getting the job done and getting out, but he thought things out. Blakeslee was a hell of a pilot and a leader but he lost a lot of people. . . . I was a little older than a lot of them [Peterson was younger, however] and I didn't fool around. . . . I didn't go to the taverns and get drunk at night and I didn't fight with people and I didn't go out with girls. . . . I figured we were there to fight a war and it was a damn serious thing and I tried to train and find out as much as I possibly could of how to do it best. So I flew . . . more than anyone else in the outfit and always did. I think that if you have a serious guy who is doing the job as best he can and it turns out successfully, then you tag on to him.[128]

Chesley Peterson, Hugh Kennard, and Royce Wilkinson all agreed that these same characteristics of stability, thoughtfulness, planning, care for the men, and superior fighting ability were evident in most of the good leaders, American or British.[129]

MORLAIX

Given Carroll McColpin's views on his own responsibilities as a leader, the catastrophe that struck Number 133 Squadron on 26 September 1942 proved to be a devastating blow to him. On 23 September the unit, under McColpin's command, was moved from Biggin Hill to Great Sampford, a satellite base of Debden, to prepare for the ceremony transferring them to the USAAF, scheduled for 29 September. For a number of days preceding this move, the squadron members had been going to London in small groups and being sworn into the USAAF. By the time of the move to Great Sampford, McColpin was one of the few pilots who had not transferred to the American forces because he did not want to leave his squadron under another officer's command while he went to London. Nonetheless, on 25 September McColpin was ordered to London to make the change. In his absence, command fell to an Englishman, Flight Lieutenant Edward Brettell, who was competent but not particularly popular with the Americans. After giving Brettell a long briefing on leading the unit if there was a combat mission, McColpin departed for London.[130]

On the morning of the 26th, 133 flew to Bolthead and was briefed to fly an escort mission over France. Evidently, only Brettell and one or two others went to the mission briefing because the flight was supposed to be so routine—less than 150 miles from takeoff to target, with broken clouds and a 35-mile-per-hour wind from the south. But once in the air, things went poorly from the very beginning, as related in the *133 Squadron History*.

> At 1350 and after a very sketchy briefing, 12 aircraft of the Squadron took off together with 401 (Squadron) with orders

to make rendezvous with a formation of Fortresses in mid-channel approximately half-way between Bolthead and Morlaix. It is yet doubtful to know what happened but *some* Fortresses were seen after 45 minutes flying, during which time the Squadron had probably orbited the Bay of Biscay several times.

The mention of the Bay of Biscay is the key to the problems that followed. Unknown to the pilots of 133, the 35-mile-per-hour wind they were supposed to have from the south at their flight altitude was really nearly 100 miles per hour from the north; with the complete undercast, they were unknowingly being blown well down toward Spain while they searched for the B–17s. The 133 pilots were also unaware that the B–17s had arrived at the rendezvous point about 20 minutes early and had proceeded on without the fighters.

After about 15 minutes of flight, the combined squadrons lost radio contact with the ground control facility in England and were never able to talk with them again. Unknown to the pilots, they had been blown out of radio range by the monstrous tail wind. The last direction received by the fighters was to fly south to overtake the bombers, so they proceeded on course. After nearly 45 minutes they encountered a group of bombers coming back toward England from the south. The fighters joined up with the bombers and began to escort them back to home base. As fuel got to the critical point, Brettell requested permission to go down through the clouds and try to see where they were. Unfortunately, the entire squadron followed him down. George Middleton describes the decision:

We had flown south for a little over an hour, so, after flying back north for the same time we should have been over the English coast, and, spotting land through a small hole in the cloud, the C.O. waved good-by to the bombers and dove the twelve of us through it expecting to be near the landing strip we had used two hours before.[131]

The other fighter squadrons in the formation did not make this critical mistake. Once 133 descended, they did not have enough fuel to climb again.

The sight that greeted the Squadron below the clouds was startling. Not only did the area look unfamiliar, but when they flew toward a nearby city, they found themselves in formation over one of the most heavily fortified ports in France, Brest. Within a matter of minutes George Sperry, Brettell, Marion Jackson, Charles Cook, Middleton, and Gilbert Wright were shot down; all but Brettell would spend the rest of the war as prisoners. Brettell was one of the 50 prisoners shot for plotting and executing the "Great Escape." William Baker, Gene Neville, Leonard Ryerson, and Dennis Smith were all killed when they were shot down or ran out of fuel. Richard Beaty, having turned back about 50 minutes into the flight because of engine trouble, was prepared to bail out because of fuel starvation when he spotted the English coast and was able to crash land. He was critically injured but survived. Robert Smith bailed out over France but was able to evade with the help of the French underground and eventually returned to England through Spain with his squadron mate, Eric Doorly, who had been shot down three weeks earlier.

Of the twelve brand new Spitfire IX's that departed on the mission, none returned to their home base. The entire squadron had been wiped out. Two aircraft were also lost from 401 Squadron and one from 64 Squadron, the other two escort units on the mission. The Morlaix mission was the greatest tragedy to befall the Eagles, and one of the worst for the entire RAF. The unfortunate mission was an unneeded capstone to the history of Number 133, which had suffered an inordinate number of losses even without the Morlaix mission. Jim Goodson arrived in 133 Squadron on 26 September and he will never forget what he found.

The first time the war really came home to me was when I walked into the terribly silent barracks in 133 Squadron after the tragedy of Morlaix. There were all these little things laying around. I'll never forget seeing the half-written letter from someone to his mother and the rooms waiting for someone to return.[132]

LeRoy Gover, who had missed the mission because he was in London transferring to the AAF, added, "This is a sad place tonight around here. And it's raining hard."[133]

In London, Carroll McColpin, now a major in the USAAF, was shocked when he heard the radio tell of the loss of his squadron. He rushed back to Great Sampford but there was little he could do. Both American and British headquarters were besieged by the press for reports on what had happened, but information was sketchy. The initial reason for the disaster was given as wing icing.[134] "Alameda Pilot Shot Down, Nazi Prisoner," blared the Oakland *Post Enquirer* in six-inch headlines when it learned of George Sperry's fate three days after the mission. Stories about Sperry dominated the front page, as they did in the *Oakland Tribune*.[135] Determining the fate of some of the others shot down was not as easy. In October 1942 the RAF wrote to George Middleton's mother, saying that they believed he was a prisoner but only had German reports to go on. In that same letter, the RAF admitted, "the Spitfires ran short of petrol and the majority were forced to land in enemy occupied territory." It was not until 3 February 1943 that Carroll McColpin reported for certain that Middleton was alive and a POW.[136]

Many things went wrong with the Morlaix mission. The pilots of 133 Squadron should have all attended the mission briefing, a decision to abort the mission should have been made when the unit lost radio contact with the control facility in England much sooner than usual, and Brettell should have not allowed his squadron to follow him down through the clouds. The controllers at Exeter in England, having had no experience with fighter-escorted missions, failed to keep adequate control of the mission. Their plotting board only went as far as Brest, but no one said anything when the fighter squadrons went off the board and the control center no longer had any way of knowing where they were. Additionally, the mission was called on the spur of the moment without adequate planning.

But all of the Eagles involved single out two other factors in the mission. First, the weather briefing was hurried, incomplete, and gave an unexcusably inaccurate report on the winds at altitude. Had the wind report been accurate, it is safe to say the tragedy would never have happened. Second, Carroll McColpin was not leading the squadron on the mission. An experienced leader could have made all the difference. The official investigation of the disaster resulted in several changes in operating procedures, but that did nothing for the members of 133 who were gone. The *133 Squadron History* simply closes with the statement, "No further operational flying during the month."[137]

TRANSFER TO THE US ARMY AIR FORCE

From December 1941 to September 1942, progess in organizing the US Eighth Air Force was slow. Although many of the Eagles wondered just what was taking so much time, Chesley Peterson, as the highest-ranking American in the units, was in constant contact with the Army Air Force. He knew the US forces wanted the Eagles because they were operational units and the Eighth Air Force needed to become operational. The 22-year-old Peterson, who had never finished the US Army pilot training course, had many talks with General Spaatz, one of the legends of air power history. Peterson thought the situation was marvelous: the Eighth Air Force needed the Eagles, and most of the Americans wanted to transfer, but the RAF was not very keen on losing some of their operational units. The Eagles were in great demand.

A number of issues slowed the process of transferring the Eagles to the USAAF. One was the question of what rank the Americans would assume. Many of the Eagles were combat veterans who would be best used in leadership positions, but they had to have the rank to serve in those billets. Each of the Eagles was eventually interviewed to determine his qualifications and what he had done, and then a rank was assigned for each. A few, like Peterson, transferred as a lieutenant colonel, and McColpin, Daymond, and Daley, transferred as majors, went into leadership positions. The majority, though, transferred at a rank equivalent to their RAF rank, lieutenant or captain. The status of sergeant pilots was of particular concern. Since there was no such thing in the AAF, all the sergeant pilots had to be commissioned. Doing so, McColpin believes, went against the grain of many American officials, who felt they were forced to take these sergeants and make them officers.[138]

Second, none of the Eagles had graduated from an Army-accredited flying training program or had ever been awarded US pilot's wings. In the end, this matter was disregarded.

The third issue was the need to decide how the former Eagles would be employed. General Spaatz suggested that the Eagles transfer as individuals and go into his arriving fighter units as senior, experienced combat pilots. (Flight commanders in the Eagles would become squadron commanders in the US Forces, squadron commanders would become group commanders, etc.) This option was not acceptable to the Eagles or to Chesley Peterson, who believed it would not be good for the morale of Eighth Air Force fighter units to have new, outside leaders. In addition, the three Eagle Squadrons wanted to stay together as units. Peterson was forced to take the position that if the Americans could not transfer intact as individual squadrons then they were not going to transfer at all. There was, indeed, no way any of the Eagles could be forced to transfer. They had signed with the RAF for the duration of the war and could certainly choose to honor that agreement.[139] In fact, some negotiation was necessary to get the British to let the Americans out of that agreement. The negotiations brought up the issue of compensation for the British. After all, because the RAF had trained these pilots, weren't they to expect some reimbursement for their time and effort? There are rumors to the effect that the United States did pay something to the British, but no record of the matter exists and none of the key British or American officials I interviewed knew anything about payments being made.

Fourth, several of the Eagles believed there was some reluctance to take the Eagles into the US forces, or at least no hurry to get the job done. Carroll McColpin believes the American authorities definitely dragged their feet. Such on American attitude became evident to McColpin in spring 1942 when he, along with several other RAF members, was on a tour of the United States designed to cement American public opinion about the country's new British allies and stimulate the sale of war bonds. At one gathering, McColpin, standing near General Hap Arnold and Secretary of the Treasury Henry Morgenthau, overheard Morgenthau ask Arnold why he was being so slow in bringing the Eagles into the AAF. Arnold expressed surprise, because he assumed they had already been transferred. He then spied McColpin and asked him about the situation. Given Arnold's obvious concern, McColpin believes that Arnold's orders to get the Eagles transferred were being ignored at lower levels, partly because of bias against the squadron members.[140]

A final stumbling block concerned aircraft. Most Anglo-American negotiation focused on bombers, showing little initial concern about the availability of fighter aircraft. Without some agreement, the Eagles would have no aircraft to fly in the US forces because the United States would not have acceptable fighters available in England until very late in 1942. If the Eagles were to fly fighters in the Eighth Air Force, the planes were going to have to be Spitfires. In the end, the Eagle transfer was part of an aircraft exchange package that gave the United States 200 Spitfires in exchange for 200 P–51s to be delivered at a later date.[141] The Spitfires provided were model Vbs rather than the new IX model. If there had been any idea of giving the newer aircraft to the Ameri-

COURTESY OF DON YOUNG

A Spitfire with markings of the US Army Air Force.

cans it was squelched by the loss of so many new Spit IXs
by 133 Squadron on the Morlaix mission.[142]

The Fourth Fighter Group, which the Eagles were to
man, with its three squadrons, the 334th, 335th, and
336th, was actually established by a secret US War Department order dated 22 August 1942. This order listed
the real activation date of the units as 1 July 1942. It did
not mention the RAF squadrons, nor did it recognize
from where the pilots and aircraft would be obtained.[143]

By the first week in September, with arrangements
for the transfers agreed on, interviews were in full swing
for those Eagles who wanted to transfer, as most did.
They were sent into London in groups of two or three to
the American Army headquarters, where they normally
talked to a panel of two or three officers, often headed by
a general. A physical examination was also required to
ensure meeting AAF requirements. These physical requirements had changed since the American entry into
the war, so most of the Eagles who had been prevented
from joining the US Army Air Force earlier were now
able to pass the physical. Not all, however, were ready to
take the chance. Art Roscoe never did transfer out of the
RAF because he was afraid the eye problem that had
initially kept him out of the AAF would ground him if he
transferred.[144]

Following the interviews, the rest of the process went rather rapidly. Around the middle of September the Eagles were again called to London in small groups to be sworn into the American Air Force. They changed their rank, ordered new uniforms, tripled their pay, and, in most cases, returned to their RAF squadron and their Spitfires with British markings. The Eagles' reaction to their transfer varied from the simple note by Vinton Padgett, "On 15 September 1942, I, together with several other members of the Squadron, proceeded to London, where we were sworn in and commissioned in the US Air Corps," to Don Young's, "September 16, 1942 was a day to remember for me. I and other members of 121 Eagle Squadron transferred to the United States Army Air Corps."[145] On 23 September LeRoy Gover went "Down to Pen House at 9 A.M. Was sworn into the US Air Corps by Col. Ayling and then taken out to US Army Camp and given a bunch of papers to sign." The next day Gover wrote, "Well I'm in the Army now for sure. Back out to sign more papers and get 150 bucks for my uniform allowance. Then taken back into town where Lambert and I bought our uniforms."[146] The commissioning document was simply a letter to the individual, signed by the Adjutant General of the Headquarters of the European Theater of Operations, US Army:

1. The Secretary of War has directed the Theater Commander to inform you that the President has appointed and commissioned you a temporary _____ in the Army of the United States effective _____ . This appointment may be vacated at any time by the President and, unless sooner terminated, is for the duration of the present emergency and six months thereafter. Your serial number is _____ and you will rank from _____ .

2. This letter should be retained by you as evidence of your appointment as no commissions will be issued during the period of the war.

By command of Lieutenant General EISENHOWER[147]

Harold Strickland had a rather enjoyable transition from the RAF to the US Army:

> On the 15th of September 1942, with other Eagles, we were commissioned and sworn into the U.S. Army Air Force. I spent the next few days in London being fitted for my new U.S. uniform.
>
> Beginning on the 20th spent a few wonderful days as the guest of Roland J. Robinson and Mrs. Robinson [Robinson had been the first Intelligence Officer with Number 71 Squadron] at their delightful home, the Elms, on Spaniards Row. . . . For the duration the Robinsons held open house for the Eagles.[148]

On 23 September 121 Squadron moved to Debden to join Number 71 and 133 moved to Great Sampford, a satellite base of Debden. All the units were then in position for the transfer ceremony on 29 September. On that day the three Eagle Squadrons, 71, 121, and the remaining officers of 133, appeared together, for the first time in their history, to officially become squadrons of the US Army Air Force. The best account of the ceremony is in the *334 Fighter Squadron History*:

> At 1200 hours, the Air Chief Marshal Sir W. Sholto Douglas, KCB, MC, DFC, accompanied by Major General Carl Spaatz, DFC, DSC, Air Marshal Edwards, RCAF, and Brigadier General Hunter, DFS, DSC, and other officers arrived at Debden. . . .
>
> The party proceeded . . . to the Parade Ground where the squadrons were assembled in line in review order facing the flag staff in this order:
>
> 71st Squadron, Major G. A. (Gus) Daymond, DFC
>
> 121st Squadron, W. A. Williams, DFC (S/Ldr) [Major James Daley was acting commander during the changeover ceremony because Williams, as a British member of the RAF, could not transfer.]
>
> 133rd Squadron, Major C. W. McColpin
>
> The wing was under the command of W/C Flying R.M.B. Duke Woolley, DFC and BAR. . . .

COURTESY OF EDWIN TAYLOR

The Union Jack comes down while the Stars and Stripes go up at the transfer of the three Eagle Squadrons to the US Army Air Force. The background of the picture was blanked out by censors because it showed aircraft and airfield facilities.

As the party arrived on the grounds, the wing commander brought all to attention and General Salute was played. The squadrons were then inspected and an address was delivered by Air Chief Marshal Sir Douglas. In part, he said:

"We of fighter Command deeply regret this parting for in the course of the past 18 months, we have seen the stuff of which you are made and we could not ask for better companions with whom to see this fight through to a finish.

"It is with deep personal regret that I today say 'Goodbye' to you whom it has been my privilege to command. You joined us readily and of your own free will when our need was greatest.

"There are those of your number who are not here to-day—those sons of the United States who were first to give their lives for their country. We of the RAF no less than yourselves will always remember them with pride.

"The U.S. Army Air Forces' gain is very much the R.A.F.'s loss. The loss to the Luftwaffe will no doubt continue as before. . . . Of the 73½ enemy aircraft destroyed 41 have been claimed by the Senior Eagle Squadron No. 71—a record which I understand the other two squadrons are determined will not long remain unchallenged. Goodbye and thank you, Eagle Squadrons, and good hunting to you, Squadrons of 8th U.S. Air Force."

General Spaatz and General Hunter made brief talks and at their conclusion . . . the Stars and Stripes were hoisted . . . and the band played "The Star Spangled Banner." The three squadrons then marched past the reviewing stand. . . .

After lunch, the party proceeded to the vicinity of the watch office where three Spitfires with RAF markings and three with USAAF markings were drawn up. Officers of each squadron were drawn up in front of the aircraft. General Hunter then presented wings to the three squadron commanding officers, signifying that their commands were now part of the USAAF. The proceedings ended at 1500 hours.[149]

Just as the press had followed much of the Eagles Squadrons' formation and combat with such interest, so too they carried the story of the transfer. *Life* had several pages about the ceremony, including photographs of Sir Sholto Douglas and General Hunter presenting wings to Daymond, Daley, and McColpin. It carried some sobering words about the units for its readers as well.

Only four of the original 34 pilots were on hand. One hundred men were missing—killed in action or by accident, or prisoners of the Axis.[150]

The figure of 100 is too high but represents the idea of sacrifice that *Life* wanted to convey to its readers. *Time* echoed its sister publication (probably taking its similarly incorrect numbers from the same source).

In the first year of operations eight of them were killed, three were missing, one was taken prisoner. At the end of their second year of operations, when they lined up for the last time as pilots of the R.A.F. only four of Colonel Sweeny's originals were left. One hundred Eagles had been lost over enemy territory.[151]

Newspapers and magazines across America echoed these stories and the transfer was the occasion for a new rash of articles about individual Eagles and their accomplishments.[152] The British, too, were told of the accomplishments of the Eagles in a radio speech on BBC by "Robbie" Robinson, the member of Parliament who was the first intelligence officer of Number 71 Squadron. His long talk concluded with a moving tribute to his friends, the Eagles.

Now the first chapter of the Eagles' story is told. These Americans who came to fight in the Royal Air Force have gone to join the great Air Force sent here by their own country. They have changed from the blue of the RAF to the brown of the American Air Force. It is a slight change, little more than a nominal one, because while a man changes his dress and his uniform, he never changes his heart, and those stout-hearted fellows who came from America to fight for us a year and a half ago, still fight with us, alongside thousands of other American boys. As we see the planes in the sky, the American and the British squadrons, flying together, there is no telling which is which, nor does it matter. We think only, as we look up at them, that there go our boys, our British and American boys.

At this time of nominal parting, the Royal Air Force salutes the Eagles and wishes them good luck and God speed.[153]

Thus the three Eagle Squadrons ceased to exist. In their place were the 334th (71), 335th (121), and 336th (133) Squadrons of the Fourth Fighter Group, United States Army Air Force. The Eagles carried into their new organizations a great tradition of performance and bravery. In all, 244 American and 16 British pilots had served in the three units. Seventy-seven Americans lost their lives as Eagles and another 31 former Eagles were killed as members of the USAAF—a total of 108, or 44 percent of those who were members of the squadrons. Countless more had been killed in training and transit across the Atlantic. Five Englishmen who flew with the Eagle Squadrons were also killed during the war. Also not present at the transfer ceremony were 16 Eagle prisoners of war and a number who had transferred to Malta, Africa, and the Far East, as well as to other RAF squadrons.[154] (See appendix A.) A major chapter in the history of aviation had come to a close, for the Eagles were probably the last group that ever will volunteer and endure such sacrifice for a cause and a nation not their own.

6. AFTER THE EAGLE SQUADRONS

THE PERIOD FROM THE MIDDLE TO THE END OF
September 1942 is blurred in the history of the Eagles.
During that time, most of those who had decided to
transfer to the US Army Air Force did so and those who
had opted not to transfer moved on to other duties in the
RAF. Hugh Kennard probably captured the general feeling of the majority of Eagles when he wrote,

> When the American pilots were transferred to the USAAF
> late in 1942 there was some feeling of sadness at leaving the
> RAF, especially the Spitfire pilots. British Squadron Com-
> manders also viewed their loss with great reluctance. How-
> ever generally speaking the American personnel accepted
> that they should join their own Country's fighting forces,
> where they would, of course, enjoy the higher rates of pay. It
> was noted that those pilots who had achieved Flight Com-
> mander positions in the Eagle Squadrons were accepted by
> the USAAF as competent leaders and did in fact benefit by
> this when given USAAF ranks (usually Major).[1]

By then also, many former Eagle Squadron pilots had
joined other RAF units, either in England or in such
places as Malta or the Far East, some had returned to the
United States or Canada, a few were instructors at OTU,

a number were prisoners of war, and, of course, a large number had been killed. There were a few, however, who transferred from the RAF to the American forces in the months that followed, and some who made the move as late as the latter part of 1943.

Most of the active members of the three Eagle Squadrons completed the transfer in September, however, and continued flying as members of the Fourth Fighter Group of the Eighth Air Force, at least for a few months. General Spaatz' initial plan for the Eagles had been to fragment the units and put Eagles into many American units to provide experienced combat pilots. Although he agreed to shelving this plan in order to facilitate a smooth transfer, shortly after the Eagles moved into the US Army Air Force such transfers were initiated.[2] The three squadrons of the Fourth Fighter Group began to have fewer and fewer Eagles in their ranks, as illustrated by the fact that of the 81 aces in the Fourth, only 20 were Eagles.[3]

REALITIES OF THE US ARMY AIR FORCE

The continual loss of Eagles and the arrival of new pilots from the United States rapidly changed the character of the three Fourth Group squadrons until, by the early part of 1943, they were much the same as any other American fighter squadrons. And the Eagle heritage, kept alive for a time by the initial transfer to the USAAF as basically homogeneous units, also was rapidly lost as the number of former Eagles in American units continued to decline.

Two problems have since resulted from this personnel shift. First, it led to some confusion about who was and was not an Eagle. A very large majority of the pilots who served in the Fourth Fighter Group were not Eagles, but the title is often erroneously given to the Fourth and all its members. Although Eagles such as Don Blakeslee, Don Gentile, Jim Goodson, and Duane Beeson became some of the most famous fighter aces of the war while flying with the Fourth Fighter Group, there were very few Eagles in the Fourth by the end of 1943 and none at war's end.[4] So the second question concerns just what place the Fourth Fighter Group plays in the overall story of the Eagle Squadrons. In my opinion, little of the Fourth's history is relevant to that of the Eagle Squadrons. However, because some Eagles went on to such illustrious careers after joining the American forces, I will deal briefly with the Fourth and some of its pilots. I have considered the three RAF Eagle Squadrons as individual units because they had little in common during their tenure in Fighter Command. After transfer, however, the three squadrons made up one group of the Eighth Air Force and performed practically the same duty, so my focus here is on the Fourth Fighter Group, not the 334th, 335th, and 336th Fighter Squadrons.

Little changed on the surface for the former Eagles as they took their places as members of the Fourth Fighter Group. They still flew Spitfires, although they now carried the US star rather than the circles of the RAF, and the ground crews and support officers were still RAF. They were led by Raymond Duke Woolley, their RAF Group Commander, they still flew from Debden, they lived in the same quarters, and they ate at the same mess. Their day-to-day lives were essentially unchanged; they might well have still been in the RAF. Two significant items did change, however. First, their pay nearly tripled and the food became better. Second, they wore American Air Force uniforms and their social relationship with the British people changed dramatically. They were no longer "our boys" who were flying in the RAF. Rather, they were "Yanks" and subject to whatever reception the British offered the rest of the ever-increasing number of Americans in their midst.

As members of the RAF, the Americans had been paid just as any other British pilot was, about $86 per month as a pilot officer to $112 for flying officers. From this amount they had to pay for their mess bill, clothing, entertainment, and the like. As Robbie Robinson said, "They always seemed to be broke."[5] The change upon donning the uniform of the US Army was dramatic. The new US pilots received a minimum of $240 per month. And what a difference that made. As Don Ross put it; "We went from buses to taxis and from beer to scotch. Living got considerably better."[6] Each of the new US officers also got a free $10,000 life insurance policy, which, to John Brown and probably to some others, was more important than the monthly pay. (Members of the RAF did not have any service-sponsored life insurance plan).[7] They could afford steaks with all the trimmings and the many American dishes the Eagles had craved for so long.

The advantages in pay were, to some degree, offset by the changes in relations with the British people. Already in the fall of 1942, the characterization of US military personnel being "overpaid, oversexed, and over here" was beginning to be heard. This change in relations bothered many of the Eagles, especially those who had been part of the British scene as members of "the few" of the RAF for a considerable time. The former Eagles did have one advantage of wearing both RAF and US pilot's wings, the former over the right breast pocket, which gave the observant Englishman the cue that this was not the run-of-the-mill US airman. Nonetheless, gone were the free drinks at the bars, the theater tickets, most of the weekend invitations, and the like. Many of the Eagles agreed with Carroll McColpin that prices went up for Americans as their numbers increased, sometimes to twice what an RAF member had to pay.[8] Probably the most pronounced change was the decrease in openly expressed gratitude that Eagles like John Brown saw all over England earlier.[9] With such large numbers of Americans present, many an Englishman felt simply overwhelmed. After all, rather than fighting for Britain in its war for survival against Germany, the Americans were using England as a base to fight their own war with the Axis. Having already seen these changes taking place as Americans arrived in Britain during 1942, it is not surprising that many of the Eagles had very mixed feelings when the time came for their actual transfer.

In December 1941, the enthusiasm for joining the American forces had been very high among most of the Eagles. With the United States now in the war and desperately in need of trained pilots, the Eagles had sent their delegation to the US embassy on 8 December to ask for transfer out of the RAF to duty in the Far East. Much had changed for all three Eagle Squadrons between that "Day of Infamy" and the end of September 1942. As the time for their transfer approached, several factors combined to make many of the Eagles reluctant to move to the US forces.

First and foremost, many of the Eagles had embraced the comradery and esprit of the RAF. "While I welcomed the opportunity to put my experience and know-how at the disposal of my own country," remarked Jim DuFour, "I really did miss the comradery inherent in the RAF."[10] Even Jim Goodson, who was enthusiastic about transferring, thought he would miss the RAF. "We had a very sentimental attachment to that great flying force which had treated us so well," he said.[11] The Eagles were used to the customs and procedures of the RAF, were comfortable with the British, and believed in their system of operation. They had seen action in great quantities, downed more than 70 German aircraft, fought as part of an RAF wing, seen their fellows killed in combat, and generally become integral parts of the RAF.

Second, many of the Eagles had acquired a rather bad impression of the American airmen who had been sent to England, both as flyers and as potential combat officers. The problems with B–17 crews being late to rendezvous points, losing their way, and shooting at their escorts certainly contributed to the bad impression. Personal contacts with Americans in business and social settings were not much better. Both Chesley Peterson and Carroll McColpin recall that a group of American pilots were sent to observe the RAF operations in late September 1941. Several ended up in Number 71 Squadron with little idea of exactly why they were there or what they were to observe. McColpin remembered,

> They started talking like pursuit pilots and they were talking to someone who had been shot at every day and who didn't stand for that kind of stuff at all. The RAF pilots just sloughed them off. Then they found out that nearly all the Eagles had no former military experience and they didn't think we knew anything and so they weren't impressed by us and we didn't think much of them either. Some of these officers were to be our bosses when we transferred.[12]

Peterson observed that these American visitors "just sat around and put in their time waiting for a good excuse to go to the pub." In fact, they were so disinterested in learning about actual combat flying that Peterson sent them back to the US headquarters. "I'm sure they did not think much more of us [the Eagles] than we did of them," Peterson noted, "and that might have hurt our relations with some members of the American forces later on."[13] John Brown recalls the Americans snake dancing through downtown London with little regard for the feelings or customs of their English hosts[14]—people who had so readily welcomed the Eagles and for whom the Eagles had developed such high regard. Although these are isolated incidents, they illustrate the problem and help account for some of the Americans' attitude toward transferring out of the RAF.

A third significant factor had to do with airplanes. As the Spitfire had motivated many to join the RAF, so it tugged at their hearts as they considered leaving. The Eagles did not know just what aircraft they would fly in the US forces. Although there were several early rumors, most Eagles believed they would get the P–39 "Airacobra," or the P–40 "Tomahawk." Those few Eagles who had flown the P–39 had nothing good to say for it, and the British had turned down the P–40 as inadequate. "I did not want to transfer," wrote Leon Blanding. "The top US planes were the P–40 and the Bell 'Airacobra,' neither of which was any match for the

Me 109 or the FW 190."[15] Clearly, the flyers considered neither a reasonable substitute for the Spitfire.

An additional factor was the inexperience of the American forces. There were no American fighter units in Europe in September of 1942. The Eagles feared that entering a completely inexperienced service, especially if there was a chance of their being split up among new squadrons—which Peterson had argued against when negotiating with General Spaatz—would bring their combat flying to an end because their new units would do nothing but train for an unknown length of time. (That is, in fact, exactly what happened within a few months of the transfer.) Most Eagles had waited too long to get into combat to voluntarily take themselves out of it so soon. Robert Smith was reluctant to transfer for that very reason. "Our status in the RAF was unique and I felt the loss of an enviable identity with the RAF. I was transferring to a totally inexperienced military organization and wondered just what the future would bring."[16]

All of these elements combined to produce much less enthusiasm for transfer when the actual time came than there had been in late 1941. If they could have stayed in the RAF but received the American level of pay, many Eagles probably would have done so. Don Nee summed it up well when he wrote, "I was willing to transfer but I was also willing to stay in the RAF."[17] Reactions to transfer did vary, however. Ervin Miller characterized one extreme when he wrote, "There was no reaction as we had a free choice. I think most of us just accepted it as a matter of course. There was always the pay."[18] On the other hand, Roland Wolfe was "happy to get the extra money and be with US troops again."[19] Don Smith was also "happy to transfer to the US Army Air Corps, mainly for the money and benefits, since the job was still the same, fighting Germans."[20] But few were as enthusiastic as Don Ross, who said, "It was a great moment when I put on my USAAF uniform in London. . . . We painted US stars on our Spitfires."[21]

Several of the Eagles either did not transfer to the US Army Air Force at all or remained in the RAF for a considerable number of additional months. The Eagles who had previously transferred to Malta or Africa were quite late in making the move, partly because of a lack of desire and partly because of a lack of opportunity. Art Roscoe, as previously mentioned, remained with the British because he feared he would lose his flying status if he transferred. Jim Griffin, serving in the Middle East by the time of the transfer, also elected to remain in the RAF. "The US Army had their chance with me in 1940," said Jim Gray, "so I decided to stay in the RAF. I also didn't like the looks of the P–40 and the Spitfire was such a beautiful ship."[22] James Nelson also remained in the RAF, eventually retiring as a squadron leader.[23]

Leo Nomis, one of the group who transferred to Malta, was late in signing up with the American forces. Nomis and Art Roscoe had volunteered to go to Malta to avoid transfer because they were happy with the RAF and believed that the American forces were not organized and did not know how to properly employ fighter resources. "We were as foreign to the American service when we transferred as we had been to the British when we went into the RAF," observed Leo Nomis. "I think several were reluctant to transfer simply because they had established themselves in the RAF and didn't know how they would be accepted in the American forces or what their job would be. The RAF, on the other hand, was a known quantity."[24]. Other Malta- or Africa-based pilots, Reade Tilley, Douglas "Tiger" Booth, and Edward Miluck, also were quite late in deciding to transfer—and none came back to the Fourth Fighter Group when they did.

When the members of the Eagle Squadrons transferred to the US Army Air Force, they faced several uncertainties, not unlike those they had faced when they decided to join the RAF. First, as noted by Leo Nomis, they did not know just what the organization would be or how they would fit into it. After all, there were no American fighter squadrons in Europe in September of 1942. Second, they were uncertain until almost the last minute what rank they would have when they moved from the RAF. And while most were happy with their designation, a few did not believe they were treated fairly. A third concern was that, although they had transferred as complete squadrons, no one felt certain about just how long that arrangement would stand up. Fourth, they wondered what the attitude of their fellow American flyers would be toward them and their service in the RAF. And finally, even though they were able to take their Spitfires along into the American forces, most knew that it was only a matter of time until they would be equipped with an American fighter, a reality they faced with both anticipation and apprehension.

In many ways, the first three factors were inescapably intertwined. As previously noted, the initial US Army idea had been to split the Eagles up and send them to many new squadrons in command positions in order to best use their combat experience. Chesley Peterson would not accept that arrangement, both because he believed that most of the Eagles did not have the flying background, combat experience, or military training necessary to assume command of a squadron and because he carried an ultimatum from his fellow Eagles demanding that they either transfer as squadrons or not transfer at all.[25] When an agreement was reached that the Americans would be in squadrons made up of the existing Eagle units, they still did not know how the commanders would be selected, what their mission would be, or what experience level those who were picked to flesh out the squadrons to full American strength would have. Until the answers to these questions came—and the answers came fairly rapidly—the Eagles' concern was evident.

The key issue of leadership was handled very logically. Immediately after the transfer, each of the squadrons was commanded by an Eagle: 334 by Gus Daymond, William Daley in 335, and 336 by Carroll McColpin.[26] This command arrangement was soon changed as the number of Eagles in the three squadrons began to decrease. Daymond was replaced by Oscar Coen in March 1943 and in April the 334th got its first non-Eagle commander when Thomas Andrews assumed command. Not until July 1944 did the 335th get its first non-RAF-trained commander, while Bill Edwards was the last Eagle commander of the 336th, replaced after being shot down, also in July 1944.[27]

Initially, the Americans had named Colonel Edward Anderson, a regular US Army Air Force officer, to command the Fourth. At 39, he was too old to lead the unit continually in combat, so that chore fell to Wing Commander Raymond Duke Woolley, on loan from the RAF, who remained in charge of the flying of the entire Debden Wing. Chesley Peterson replaced Anderson as commander of the Fourth in August 1943 and, as the youngest colonel in the US Army Air Force, held the job through the end of the year. On 1 January 1944, Peterson, the last original Eagle remaining in the Fourth and long overdue transfer from the combat zone, was replaced by Don Blakeslee, also an Eagle. Blakeslee was to become a legend during his more than three years of almost continuous combat duty, earning a universal reputation as the "fighter pilot's fighter pilot." Because of their experience, former Eagles continued to serve as the commanders of the Fourth during most of the war.[28] This Eagle influence was not carried down to the squadrons, however, where most of the line pilots were non-Eagles by the end of 1943.

As mentioned briefly earlier, after much considerable consideration about rank, the decision was made that all the Eagles would be transferred as officers. The biggest problem in this regard was handling the sergeant pilots. The US Army, having stopped appointing sergeant pilots, had no place to put the Eagles who fell into that category. Although they had flying ability equal to the officers, the general opinion was that most were not officer material and many in the US Army questioned their training and ability to be effective commanders. In the end, the US Army Air Force was forced to take all the Eagles as officers, which was not popular in the eyes of the American commanders.[29] For the sergeant pilots remaining in the Eagle Squadrons by September 1942, the change was a big one, as related by Joe Bennett: "In the RAF I was a Sgt. Pilot making a little over eight pounds a fortnight. Upon transfer I was commissioned a 2nd Lt. on flying status getting $450 a month. This was about the same as an RAF Group Captain."[30]

Most of the Eagles had commissions in the RAF and simply transferred at their equivalent rank. A few were advanced in rank, however, because of their RAF position.[31] When Carroll McColpin was asked by his review board what rank he thought he should have at transfer he said, "general." The US general conducting the interview noted that he had spent eighteen years in the Army as a lieutenant and that a more reasonable rank for McColpin would be major. "I believe that some of the Eagles should have transferred at a higher rank than they were given," said McColpin years later.[32] With few exceptions, however, they were satisfied with their new ranks. Those who believed they were not given the proper rank thought their experience should have qualified them for a higher position. This issue was particularly vexing when new pilots arrived from the United States with little flying time and no combat experience, but higher rank that often made them unit leaders.

The issue of longevity in the new squadrons of the Fourth Fighter Group was more complex than it appeared to most of the Eagles. The ex-RAF pilots considered themselves fighter pilots ready to do their job for Uncle Sam just as they had for the King. However, they also became part of a huge force that was desperate for fighter pilots with combat experience. There were many places where the Eagles were needed and could make a greater contribution than they could in the air over France. By the end of 1942, as the Germans were starting to feel pressure from mounting combat losses on both the eastern and western fronts, the quantity and quality of aerial opposition over France was decreasing. A much greater need for the American Army was advice on combat, suggestions for training methods, evaluation of aircraft and staff decisionmaking by the combat-experienced Eagles.

To meet these more pressing needs, eight ex-Eagles departed the Fourth Fighter Group in early December for the United States, never to return to their old units. The group consisted of Carroll McColpin, Jim Daley, Michael McPharlin, Sam Mauriello, Harold Strickland, John Brown, Don Smith, and Ernie Beatie.[33] After arriving in the United States, Strickland recalled,

> We were interviewed for about two days by various USAAF Directors about fighter aircraft and tactics, weapons, guns, engines, etc. . . . Then . . . we reported to General Arnold . . . who wanted Mac and the group to visit several Air Force Bases for discussions about fighter aircraft then return to Washington by early February for debriefing and writing reports. . . . Our visits included the Bell Aircraft plant, Wright Field, Eglin Field (Army Air Force Proving Ground Command), McDill Field, Drew Field and Orlando (Army Air Force School of Applied Tactics). After returning to Washington and writing reports, I was assigned to the Fighter Test Section at Eglin Field as a test pilot.[34]

Another example of the ex-Eagles' experience being put to use appeared in the January 1943 edition of the Intelligence Service *Air Forces General Information Bulletin*. The Bulletin contained a four-page article titled "Tips from an Eagle Pilot" that included such advice as, "Air Discipline is one of the main secrets of not getting shot down," and, "Never fly straight and level in the combat area for more than three seconds." All pieces of advice were accompanied by a rather extensive elaboration of why the particular rule was important.[35] Given this general need for the experience of the Eagles, it took real effort for them to remain long in their squadron as active fighter pilots.

Unlike the British, who viewed combat flying as something that a pilot did until the war was over or he was captured, killed, disabled, or too tired to fly any more, the Americans had a 200-hour limit on the number of combat hours a fighter pilot could fly before he was sent back to the United States for other duties. Although some Eagles, such as Don Blakeslee and Don Gentile, got waivers to this rule, most fighter pilots did not and so were sent home after about 100 or 125 missions. For those flyers who had been in the RAF Eagle Squadrons for some time before their transfer, the 200-hour mark was already very close at hand when they joined US forces. A number of the Eagles flew very few missions with the Fourth before they were transferred for having too much combat time. At the same time, several Eagles, including Steve Pisanos, Howard Hively, Jim Goodson, Don Nee, and LeRoy Gover, joined their RAF squadrons rather late in the game and would fly well into 1944 with the Fourth.[36]

Some of the most diverse opinion from within the ranks of the Eagles concerns their reception by other Americans after becoming part of the US Army Air Force. Most thought that they would be welcomed with open arms by a service desperate for fighter pilots. Although many were, many more had a difficult experience. "I believe there was considerable bias against the Eagles when we were brought into the US service," said Carroll McColpin. "I know the Army dragged their feet on bringing us in at equal rank and that was one of the big hangups." One reason for the general bias, in McColpin's view, was that

the Eagles all had to be characters of some sort or another or they wouldn't have gone over there. They weren't run-of-the-mill college or high school kids. In a bunch of characters you get some pretty strong characters and we had them. They wouldn't knuckle under to the RAF control any more than they were ready to do so with the Americans. . . . They were of the opinion that there is a war going on and we are here to fight that and being shot at every day and to hell with this other stuff. . . . Many of the ones who stayed in the Fourth became identified as the hell raisers on the ground and this opinion seemed to follow some of the others.[37]

Another reason for the Eagles' less than warm welcome was the lack of any military training for many of them. Those who had come into the RAF through joining the RCAF had a very intense military training program before ever going to England. Ironically, these were the ones who were initially sergeant pilots, about whom the US Army Air Force had so much concern when deciding whether or not to commission them. For those who entered through the Clayton Knight Committees, however, the general rule was little or no military background, so these Eagles were often identified as a rough lot when it came to military qualities. Although they compiled an enviable record during the war, many were not promoted after the war's end for this reason, among others.

Hand in hand with the perceived deficiency in military training went the lack of having completed any US-approved pilot training program. Here again, the sergeant pilots who had come in through the RCAF were the only Eagles to have gone through a recognized pilot training program. The rest had whatever was available at the time, whether that was the RAF refresher programs given most Knight Committee entries or just the RAF OTU provided the early Eagles. This issue was not a major source of discrimination, but a number of Eagles believe it was a factor.

A final problem for the new members of the USAAF was well put by Don Smith.

I know that US Groups that were assigned to England had trained together and had a certain amount of pride in their groups and resisted having so-called outsiders come into their outfits and tell them how to win the war. They had their own ideas. I also think that some of them paid a big price for that experience.[38]

Roy Evans believes that envy contributed to the same resistance Smith notes. After all, these ex-RAF pilots had seen combat, had been in England during the dark days of the war, and had established a special relationship with the English people.

> I have the greatest respect for the Eagles not only for what we did but for the way we conducted ourselves. I know that there are and have been derogatory remarks around about the Eagles but I shade that with a little green coloring because we were entitled to wear two sets of wings . . . and I think that sometimes that green might show through. When I got back to the States I was insulted, I was snubbed . . . and I think it was because I was wearing that second set of wings.[39]

"There was some reaction to our privilege of wearing the RAF brevet on our right breast, but we coped and I think we wore those wings with pride," said Ervin Miller.[40]

On the other hand, Leon Blanding found his new comrades "respectful. These guys were eager for any help in surviving."[41] Roland Wolfe believed the Americans "were happy to have most of us although I'll admit we were on the rough side."[42] All in all, there seems to be about an even split among the Eagles in their perception of how the USAAF treated them. And while some of the Eagles were unsuccessful in their efforts to stay in the Air Force after the war or had less than completely satisfying military careers, many remained into the 1970s and were very successful. For example, Chesley Peterson, Carroll McColpin, and Don Ross all retired as major generals; LeRoy Gover, Don Blakeslee, Reade Tilley, Steve Pisanos, and Oscar Coen, among others, served full careers and retired as colonels.

ACTION WITH THE FOURTH FIGHTER GROUP

The accounts of the first operational missions of the Fourth Fighter Group read like a continuation of the activities of the RAF Eagle Squadrons. The people are the same, the leaders haven't changed, and their "American" Spitfires have the same numbers.

> On 2 October 1942, the three newly acquired squadrons took part in Circus 221. It was their first major mission under the Fourth Fighter Group. . . . With W/C Duke Woolley leading, the 334th squadron composed of Capt. Coen, Lts. Mills, Clark, Morgan, Care, Whitlow, Sprague, Anderson, Hively, McMinn, Priser, and the 335th squadron were engaged by a group of enemy fighters. . . . Major Oscar H. Coen, then Captain Coen, promptly engaged one E/A, an FW 190, and destroyed the machine. In another section of the sky, Lt. S. M. Anderson got on the tail of an FW 190. In a few seconds the E/A was spinning earthwards. W/C Duke Woolley and Lt. Clark also shared the credits of downing a FW 190 in this engagement. Lt. Morgan is credited with damaging another FW 190.[43]

Losses also continued in the same manner.

> On October 20 . . . two Spitfires of 334th Squadron were airborne on convoy patrol. Lt. Seaman . . . experienced engine trouble. His plane was seen to explode in mid-air; he was killed as it crashed into the sea.[44]

By the end of 1942 the Fourth Group had destroyed 8½ enemy aircraft but had lost 14 pilots.[45] Little seemed different from the early days of the three Eagle Squadrons. By that time, the character of the unit had begun to change with the increasing transfer of former Eagles. Through the end of 1942, however, the replacements were mostly non-Eagle transfers from the RAF so the Fourth was able to remain a largely RAF-trained unit. This filling of vacancies with RAF pilots was not the result of any desire to retain the Fourth as a unique RAF-trained unit but, rather, because US fighter pilot production had not yet reached the point where there were replacements. The ever-increasing number of American-trained pilots were being used to form new American fighter squadrons.[46]

During the first three months of their tenure in the USAAF, the three squadrons of the Fourth were the only operational American fighter units in Europe. Once again, the former Eagles received considerable press attention and visits from various Americans who were in England. And the US Army certainly made no effort to curtail either. "Shortly after the transfer," said Jim Goodson,

Dixie Alexander and I decided we wanted to make a "Rhubarb" [two-ship, low-level strafing flight] over France. We were a bit puzzled when we were told that we had to make a route that took us over Belgium as well as France. After the mission I found out just how much need there was for a good story about American fighters. Within 24 hours all the newspapers had an article on "the first US fighter raid over the continent." One article read, "At dawn today fighter planes of the US Eighth Army Air Force carried out daring low-level attacks on rail, road, and water transport in Northern France and Belgium, leaving behind them a trail of destruction." Dixie and I could hardly believe what our two planes were reported to have done.[47]

On 4 November Eleanor Roosevelt, the president's wife, went to Debden, along with General Hunter and Air Marshal Leigh-Mallory, to visit the group during her trip to England. The Americans obliged her by performing a Spitfire fly-by.[48]

All the Eagles who transferred to the American forces knew that they would not be able to keep flying their Spitfires forever, and it soon became common knowledge that the replacement would be the Republic P–47 "Thunderbolt." No one looked with any anticipation on the arrival of this "monster," but the day inevitably came. On 15 January 1943 the 334th went off operations to become the P–47 training unit for the Fourth Fighter Group. The first P–47s arrived the next day and were flying regularly by the end of the month, but not until 10 March did Chesley Peterson lead the first P–47 fighter mission in Europe. "Drinks that night were on

Pratt and Whitney and Republic," noted the operations record. The Fourth was declared operational in the P–47 on 10 April 1943, and flew their last mission in the Spitfire: the last vestiges of the group's British heritage were gone. On 15 April Don Blakeslee claimed the first German fighter shot down by a P–47; although the pilots lamented losing their beloved Spitfires, the "Jug" had begun to prove itself in combat.[49]

Day after day during the spring and summer of 1943 the members of the Fourth flew either escort or diversionary missions over France, hoping to engage the elusive Luftwaffe. There were occasional contacts and, when given the chance, the group's pilots took their toll of Germans. The losses, however, also continued. On 21 May, Brewster Morgan shot down an Me 109 but was then shot down himself and became a POW; Gordon Whitlow was lost to enemy aircraft the same day. But on 30 July the Fourth destroyed five enemy aircraft while losing one. The group continued to build its record, destroying eighteen German aircraft on 16 August while losing only Joe Matthews (who managed to evade his pursuers and return to England in late 1943).

Despite the daily combat missions, however, the score built by the Fourth during 1943 remained relatively low, compared to their eventual record, with 74 German aircraft shot down for the year. Most of those pilots who would end the war as well-known high scorers had not begun to emerge, with the exception of Duane Beeson who became an ace during the year, and Roy Evans and Don Smith, each accounting for four enemy aircraft. In fact, the 74 downed aircraft were spread among 43 different pilots, evidence that the Fourth was faithfully flying its assigned mission of bomber escort and not compromising that vital duty to hunt for enemy fighters, as some other groups were accused of doing.[50]

From the first time any of the pilots of the Fourth had seen the P–51, they had counted the days until they would get that aircraft. Not only was it very similar to their beloved Spitfire, but those groups who already had the Mustang were clearly demonstrating its superiority over anything the Luftwaffe had to offer. Chesley Peterson had flown the craft in the United States, and on the initial introduction of the Mustang in the European theater in late 1943, Don Blakeslee, Don Nee, and Bob Priser were sent to the 354th Fighter Squadron to provide some combat-experienced pilots to fly with the unit during its first missions. Their reports back to the Fourth simply added to the anticipation. Finally, on 14 February 1944, each of the squadrons of the Fourth received some P–51s to begin transition.

There were a number of problems with the new aircraft, and several pilots reported that the P–47, now being modified with a new propeller, was an equal to the P–51. Nonetheless, the Mustangs continued to arrive. On 28 February Major James Clark, an Eagle, led the group's first P–51 mission. Duane Beeson reported, "First show on Mustangs. VERY SWEET AIRCRAFT!"[51] Although problems continued, Don Blakeslee led the Fourth's first escort mission to Berlin on 4 March, in Mustangs, beginning the most productive period in the Group's history.

THE FOURTH BECOMES THE
TOP FIGHTER UNIT IN EUROPE

Although 1943 had been a year of less than spectacular productivity for the Fourth, the group's pilots had become accustomed to escort duty and performed it in a superior fashion. The situation, in both the Fourth Fighter Group and the war in general changed significantly in 1944, radically altering the fortunes of the unit. Of greatest significance was the arrival of the P–51. Unable because of the P–47's limited range to fly great distances from England, the Fourth had been forced to stay close to the bombers they were escorting. They could not go looking for the Luftwaffe; they could engage only those aircraft the Germans chose to send against the bombers over France. This situation was very similar to that faced by the Eagles during their days in the RAF.

After flying their Spitfires in the US Army Air Force for several months, the former Eagles of the Fourth Fighter Group flew the P–47 "Thunderbolt," more often called the "Jug" (above), until early 1944. By spring of 1944 the Fourth Fighter Group pilots were flying the P–51 (below), whose performance and great range made it an outstanding fighter.

The arrival of the P–51 allowed the Americans to go deep into Germany, where the Luftwaffe opposition was much greater than over France. It also allowed them to break off from the bombers and engage German fighters, knowing they would still have enough fuel to get back to England. For the first time, bands of American fighters could range Germany practically at will, looking for enemy aircraft to destroy both in the air and on the ground.

The experience level of pilots on the two sides of the war also became a factor by 1944. On the one hand, the pilots of the Fourth were gaining more and more experience in combat. Most of the Eagles had rotated out of the group, but there was a degree of stability so some experience remained. On the other hand, as the war came closer and closer to home on both the eastern and western fronts and the Germans continued to lose pilots and aircraft, they were able to provide less and less formidable opposition to the Allies with more poorly trained pilots and less reliable aircraft. Younger, less experienced pilots were being sent into combat as fuel and aircraft shortages curtailed flying training. By the end of 1944, the average American pilot had more combat time than his average German opponent had total flying time.[52] This combination of stronger forces on the Allied side and weaker ones on the German side made the enemy easier and easier prey for the American fighters ranging over Europe.

The lack of formidable opposition also allowed the US pilots to go after the Luftwaffe on the ground. Hundreds of German aircraft were destroyed as they sat on the ramp, all to become part of the total score of aircraft destroyed. This counting of aircraft destroyed on the ground is an emotional but critical point in any consideration of unit and individual records of the Fourth Fighter Group and the RAF Eagles against the Luftwaffe. If a pilot in the USAAF destroyed five German aircraft on the ground, he was an "ace," just as if he had shot them down. Some US pilots became aces without encountering an enemy aircraft in the air. In fact many of the high-scoring American fighter pilots got a number of their aircraft that way. In the RAF, every enemy aircraft claimed was shot down in air-to-air combat and verified by a witness or gun-camera film. Although the RAF had no real opportunity early in the war to go after aircraft on the ground, because of the formidable German opposition, claims of aircraft destroyed on the ground being counted as part of an individual fighter pilot's record would have been, and later in the war were, unacceptable to the British.

A final factor in the Fourth Fighter Group's impressive record was the reality of Germany's situation in the war. As the Allied bombing raids came further and further into Germany, the Luftwaffe had to counter them with all the aircraft they had, not only to try to minimize the damage wrought by the raids but also to maintain the political myth of the viability of the Third Reich. Often the Germans filled the skies with fighters to oppose bombing raids, providing a great increase in targets for the American pilots. The Germans' need to concentrate their fighters, as well as their maintenance problems and fuel shortages, led to great numbers of planes on the ground, where they proved to be easy targets for the new, long-range Mustang. The invasion of France in June of 1944 and the German effort to stop the Allied onslaught simply increased the number of targets available to the hungry pilots of the Fourth.

As 1944 began, Don Blakeslee took command of the Fourth from Chesley Peterson. Blakeslee's priority was simple—make the Fourth the most productive fighter unit Europe—and the unit wasted little time going after the objective. By the time they flew their first P–51 mission on 28 February, they had already destroyed 58 German aircraft. But the action was only beginning. With the combined advantages of the Mustang and the new mission into Germany, the Fourth destroyed a total of over 370 enemy aircraft, in the air and on the ground, in March and April. The high days were 5 April, when more than 80 enemy aircraft were destroyed or damaged on the ground, and 8 April, when the Fourth shot down 31 enemy aircraft, a record for the war.[53] The ground figure is significant because, although it was easier to destroy an aircraft on the ground than in aerial combat, every aircraft destroyed on the ground was one less that the Allied bombers and fighters had to face in the air.

By the end of April, the high-scoring Eagles of the unit had also begun to emerge, although most of the pilots contributed to the tally. Don Gentile got his total over twenty but crashed his aircraft making a low pass for newsmen and was sent home. Duane Beeson also got to the twenty mark but was then shot down and spent the rest of the war as a POW. George Carpenter, Jim Goodson, Jim Clark, and Don Blakeslee were among those who also had significant scores. The record was not achieved without cost. Besides Beeson, former Eagles Paul Ellington, Henry Mills, Selden Edner, Kenneth Smith, Kenneth Peterson, Raymond Care, and George Carpenter were all shot down and taken prisoner during the March and April action. Frank Boyles was killed, and Steve Pisanos was shot down but evaded, in an amazing adventure, eventually returning to his base at Debden six months later.[54] These losses considerably thinned the ranks of Eagles in the Fourth, and continued with Joe Bennett being shot down in May and Jim Goodson in June, both becoming POWs. By the time Don Blakeslee left the Fourth at the end of October 1944, there were practically no Eagles left on the rolls.

The action and productivity of the Fourth Fighter Group certainly did not end with the departure of the last of the Eagles. The unit continued in the thick of the war and, in the end, was responsible for 1,016 enemy aircraft destroyed, 550 of these in the air and 466 on the ground. Eighty-one of the pilots assigned to the Fourth, including twenty Eagles, were aces.[55] The record is impressive, but it does not tell the entire story of the men who transferred from the RAF in September 1942. A complete account of their contributions to the war would require recounting the history of many units. Unfortunately, the productivity of the Fourth Fighter Group and other units was partly offset by the additional Eagles killed and wounded in the cause of freedom. An increasing number also joined their fellow pilots as prisoners of war. Like the Eagles who served in the Fourth, those who saw duty elsewhere or who spent a portion of the war as prisoners deserve our attention.

EAGLES IN OTHER PLACES WITH THE RAF

While the three Eagle Squadrons existed, personnel continually moved into and out of the units. Although most of these transfers were among the three Eagle Squadrons, some members did transfer to other RAF squadrons both in the United Kingdom and, more commonly, overseas. Of the oversea destinations, the most common was Malta, but both Africa and Singapore also saw former Eagles piloting Spitfires on their airfields. German prisoner of war camps were the other most common location for pilots no longer with the Eagle Squadrons when they transferred to the USAAF. Sixteen Eagles had been taken prisoner, and theirs, too, are interesting, significant stories. As is true of the Fourth Fighter Group, a detailed story of these individuals is beyond the scope of this volume. Nonetheless, I will briefly consider these two groups to complete the record of the Eagle Squadrons.

Malta. Recalling his impressions of Malta, Leo Nomis said, "I have never been to a place before or since that had such a visible atmosphere of doom, violence, and toughness about it at first sight."[56] Although I can find no completely accurate record available of all those who at one time or another served on Malta, twelve to fifteen Eagles transferred there, most during the spring and summer of 1942.[57] Some, such as Reade Tilley and Douglas Booth, asked specifically to go there; others ended up on Malta after simply volunteering to be sent overseas from England. Although specific reasons for volunteering varied, those who went during the early spring of 1942 generally did so because they wanted more action against the Germans rather than the continual escort duty, patrols, and sweeps that were the fare of the Eagle Squadrons at that time. According to Reade Tilley,

> I volunteered because I didn't like the way we were flying over France at the time. We were using line astern formation . . . and were under orders not to follow the Germans when they dived through our formations because that was

what they wanted. With that formation you spent so much time making sure you didn't run into the guy ahead of you that you didn't have time to look for the Germans. . . . That was not my idea of air war. I also kept reading in the paper about all the action taking place in Malta and I thought, "What the hell am I doing here?" and so I volunteered. . . . Tiger Booth and I went down together on an aircraft carrier . . . the *Wasp*.[58]

The few who ended up on Malta in the summer of 1942 did not volunteer specifically for duty there but had simply asked to be posted overseas so they would not be in the United Kingdom when the transfer to the USAAF took place. "I didn't volunteer for Malta," said Art Roscoe.

I knew they were bringing the three Eagle Squadrons together at Debden and transferring them over to the US forces . . . and I was afraid that . . . the US forces would take me off flying because of my eyes. I didn't want to take a chance so I applied for posting and I got sent to Malta.[59]

Leo Nomis, who went to Malta with Art Roscoe, offers a further insight into why they decided to volunteer for oversea duty:

After the move to Russia for Number 71 was called off, Art Roscoe and I talked about what to do. Neither of us wanted to transfer to the USAAF at that time. . . . I didn't think they were organized at that time, there were no US fighter squadrons, and we didn't know what the Americans would do with us. We decided to apply for an overseas tour and see what happened and maybe figure it out after that. We talked to [Chesley] Peterson but he wouldn't let you transfer unless he wanted to get rid of you. He finally gave in since the word was that everyone would be transferred to the USAAF in September anyway. You didn't apply for where you wanted to go, you just went wherever they sent you. . . . We got our orders in three days and went to Scotland . . . where we were put on an aircraft carrier. . . . And then we were pretty sure we were headed to Malta.[60]

While there have been reports of a flight or even a squadron composed exclusively of Americans on Malta, such was not the case. A new pilot was assigned wherever he was needed, regardless of nationality. There were an inordinate number of Americans in 126 Squadron, but that was because the squadron commander, Squadron Leader Barton, thought the Americans were exceptional pilots and would go out of his way to get them posted to his unit. Often, he would even trade a pilot to get an American from another unit. Many of these pilots were not Eagles but simply Americans who had joined the RAF and were serving with other fighter units.[61]

Just what was it that made the tiny 9- by 17-mile island in the Mediterranean so critical to both the British and the Axis? As it has since the beginning of history, Malta's location largely determined its strategic importance. When the German and Italian invasion of Africa threatened Egypt and supplies of Middle East oil, Malta became critical. From it came the British ships and planes that harassed German shipping trying to reinforce German forces in Africa that, if they were successful, would open the entire oil-rich Middle East to Axis forces. Therefore, the British had to maintain the island at all costs, while the enemy became equally determined to conquer it. All the supplies for war, as well as food for the 280,000 inhabitants, had to be brought to Malta by sea. The vital aircraft, however, were flown in from carriers near Gibraltar. The loss of shipping to German submarine attacks was so great that the valuable aircraft and carriers could not be risked in a convoy through the waters of the Mediterranean to the island. The island was bombed almost daily, meaning the few defending fighters had to be repaired at night and serviced in the middle of bombing attacks. No wonder that the average tour length for a fighter pilot on the island was three months and that in 1942 the entire population of the island was awarded the George Cross for gallantry.[62]

Most of the pilots who went to Malta began their tours by flying off one of the aircraft carriers to deliver their Spitfires to the besieged island. Reade Tilley and Douglas Booth flew from the US carrier *Wasp*; Art Roscoe and Leo Nomis flew from the British carrier *Furious*. "None of us had ever flown a Spitfire off a carrier before," said Leo Nomis, "but we were told that was the way to get the airplanes to Malta so we did it."

> The carrier would get going as fast as it could into the wind and we would be as far back on the deck as possible. You gave the Spit full throttle and when the crew pulled the chocks you released the brakes and were off. I think that we were getting airborne in 30 or 40 feet. One interesting innovation was the use of part flaps for takeoff. In the Spitfire you either had full up or full down flaps, there was no middle position. For the carrier takeoff they put the flaps down and then held blocks of wood in them while they were put up. This held them part way down. After you were airborne you lowered the flaps and the wood fell out and you could then pull the flaps up. Real stone age stuff.[63]

Nomis failed to mention that at the time he and Art Roscoe took off their carrier was under submarine attack. "I looked off the port side where *Eagle* was steaming and . . . suddenly I saw four towering spouts of water go up from the *Eagle's* port side," Roscoe remembers. "Torpedo hits—we were under submarine attack. . . . As I passed over the bow of *Furious* I watched in horror as the creamy wake of a torpedo passed directly under my plane—a near miss on *Furious*." Tragically, the *Eagle* sank in less than ten minutes, taking with it more than 260 officers and men. The flight after leaving the carrier offered plenty of its own hazards since it was nearly 700 miles over open sea to Malta and the Spitfires carried no ammunition for their guns in order to save weight. The personal belongings of the pilots were stuffed into every little area of the fighter they could find since there was no other way to get them there. "When I finally got together with my belongings, everything was there except four cartons of cigarettes—smokes were in short supply like everything else," noted Art Roscoe.[64]

Spitfires take off from a carrier deck for the long flight to Malta.

Some of the frustration and challenge that went with trying to supply and defend Malta was evident in the fate of the 47 Spitfires flown into Malta off the US carrier *Wasp* on Fred Almos' first flight to the island.

> We brought in 47 Spitfires off the *Wasp* and two days later we only had six operational aircraft because they were just bombing the hell out of us. The next bunch of Spitfires that came in from the *Wasp* and the *Eagle* were armed and fueled and back in the air twenty minutes after they arrived in Malta. We were that short of planes. The Malta pilots just took over for those who ferried the Spits in. Because we had enough supplies and ammunition, in the next 48 hours I think we shot down about 220 German aircraft.[65]

Repairing damaged Spitfires also presented a challenge because spare parts, along with fuel and ammunition, had to be brought in by cargo submarine or by fast, small ships operating independently.[66]

Conditions on Malta were harsh to say the least. It was so hot that not only was the Spitfire flown without its canopy, but even eating and sleeping were difficult. Because of the nearly continuous air raids, everything had to be done underground. "The only reason all the machines and people on Malta weren't just blown away, was that everything important was either underground, or surrounded by thick, stone blast pens," recalled Art Roscoe. "All the aircraft were parked in 'J' shaped limestone blast shelters where only a direct hit would damage the aircraft."[67] Since all the food had to be brought in by hazardous convoy, submarine, or aircraft, the food supply was at a subsistence level and no more. When on alert, and that was most of the time, Art Roscoe recalls, "A tin plate of cold bully beef (canned corned beef), Italian style tomatoes, biscuits with jam, and hot tea was the fare." Meals after flying were not much better. "I used to get sick just going into the dining hall," said Leo Nomis.[68] But the pilots couldn't complain since the local population fared even worse.

> Malta food was Malta food. Bully beef gave us most of our meals. Served hot, it provided our breakfast; cold, it gave us our lunch; camouflaged, it served us for dinner. . . . Apart from goats' milk, which did not agree with any of us, the only milk we saw came out of tins.[69]

Bugs, skin diseases, and dysentery frequently affected aircrews. "You got ill as soon as you got there and were sick the entire time," recalled Leo Nomis. "The only thing that would take you off flying was sand fly fever when you got a temperature of about 106. Other than that, you flew."[70]

Sitting alert and flying were the continual fare of pilots assigned to Malta. Occasionally they got days off, but there was little to see other than the continual aerial

With facilities like this dispersal hut, at Takali Air Field in 1942, conditions on Malta were harsh indeed.

combat that raged over the island. There was no social life because, as Art Roscoe noted, "Just how one would date a girl on Malta, I never found out. There was no place to go, no way to get there, and nothing to do when you arrived."[71] Certainly, when a pilot had served his three months he was ready to go home.

One aspect of the flying in Malta that appealed to Reade Tilley was the tactics used by the RAF. Because of the Germans' and Italians' tremendous numerical superiority, the line astern formation used in England was not effective: it could not employ all the potential firepower of each flight.

> In order to survive, you couldn't possibly fly in line astern formation. We had to fly line abreast so each guy could cover each other's tail. We would fly far enough out, say 100 to 150 yards, so you didn't have to worry about running into anybody. We generally flew a four-ship formation although, on rare occasions, there would be more. . . . It was a hell of a fighting formation. [See illustration, p. 144.] There was no way anyone could sneak up on you. . . . The Germans used this formation against Malta just as they used it over

France, with the difference that the Germans often operated on a free-lance basis using two or four airplanes operating more or less independently. But for the Germans attacking Malta, the tables were turned since they were escorting the bombers and they had to stick close to them. They would send out a formation of fighters in line abreast ahead of the bombers to try to screw up our fighters. Our big concern was to stay away from their fighters because we needed to get the bombers and our ammunition was so short that we couldn't waste it on the fighters. . . . Radar was also critical, but it was often down for parts . . . but when it was working it was absolutely incredible and there were so few of us that it was a personalized thing—it was wonderful.[72]

When the time came for action, "A first alert would send a flight of four aircraft up for the initial intercept," wrote Art Roscoe.

Other flights of four aircraft would follow as scrambled, but the entire fighter force would never be committed to repulse a single raid. . . . Our main objective was to get at the bombers and try to break up the raid before it got to Malta. . . . As soon as we spotted the enemy formation, we tried to get in at least one pass at the bombers before the fighters knew we were there. . . . On the initial pass we tried to do as much damage to as many bombers as we could. A shot at one, a burst at another, going through their formation from rear to front. . . . As all this went on several times a day, the action was pretty continuous.[73]

The first Eagles to shoot down German aircraft over Malta were James Peck and Donald McLeod, who each got an Me 109 on 24 March. Most of the other Eagles stationed there also got several victories, with Reade Tilley earning the DFC for his seven shot down. But like elsewhere, perhaps more so, it was difficult to verify kills because there "seldom was a concerted squadron action—everyone was more or less on their own. If an enemy plane was seen to go in," wrote Art Roscoe, "who knew whose it was, you could only report the time and place, and then, no cine-guns." But, as Roscoe noted, "our job was to defend the island—not worry about big scores."[74]

The almost continuous air action resulted in scores of accounts of engagements between Eagles and their German adversaries. Reade Tilley recalls having to land and refuel during the heat of a battle, the ground crews demonstrating the "raw courage it took to conduct a 'bucket brigade' with five-gallon cans of aviation spirit while being strafed with explosive 20mm shells and tracers."[75] Leo Nomis, after having his guns jam, found himself flying wing-tip to wing-tip with an Me 109. Since any action by Nomis would have exposed him to being shot down by the German pilot, he decided to remain in formation and, in desperation, appeal to chivalry.

> Our gazes at each other had never faltered since the beginning of the predicament. . . . So, in a motion which I considered should explain everything . . . I pointed dramatically down at the port wing cannon with a gloved finger, then raised the finger and drew it across my throat. This, I figured, would indicate that my guns were jammed and therefore mercy could be accorded me. . . . The gesture did have an effect. The 109 pilot stared . . . and then in one lightening movement went onto his back and did the most rapid split-S I ever saw. . . . It was only when I was almost back to Takali that the truth of the farce hit me. I became weaker as I started to laugh because I could suddenly picture the 109 pilot, after he got home, telling the experience and saying that those Spitfire pilots must be either crazy or tougher than hell—they indicate by gestures what they are going to do to you before they shoot you down.

It was also on Malta that Art Roscoe was badly wounded but still managed to maneuver his mangled Spitfire into a position to shoot down his attacker.[76]

Although there is no record of how many enemy aircraft the Eagles assigned to Malta shot down, the number was certainly significant. As in the air war over the Channel and France, the Americans in the RAF had come to a place where they were needed and performed their duty willingly and admirably. They were seasoned fighter pilots when they arrived in Malta—as Reade Tilley said, "Malta was no place for the inexperienced pilot. He would get killed in no time at all."[77] And they left having endured some of the most fierce aerial combat of the entire war. As they did in the other places where they served, the Eagles who went to Malta brought credit to their unit and their country.

The Middle East, Africa, and Asia. By the middle of 1942 the need for pilots in North Africa had become crucial. The battle lines in Libya and Egypt had gone back and forth since the initial Italian invasion of Egypt in September 1940. The huge German offensive of spring 1942, led by the brilliant German Edwin Rommel, pushed the British back to within 60 miles of Alexandria, where they were able to hold at El Alamein. Some of the Eagles were thrust into this arena too.

"Many of the pilots from Malta were sent to the Western Desert," recalled Leo Nomis. "I made an unauthorized flight and so was sent to Number 92 Squadron, the punishment squadron, at Alamein. The living conditions were worse but the food was better."[78] Others who ended up at El Alamein or elsewwhere in the Middle East and North African area were simply volunteers for oversea duty. Harold Marting, Edward Miluck, Mike Kelly, and Charles Tribken, having asked to go to the Far East, had gotten as far as Durban, South Africa, when they were diverted to El Alamein. Other Eagles in the theater included Norman Chap, Edwin Bicksler, Jim Griffin, and Robert Mannix.[79]

The significant features of a tour in North Africa can be summed up in four words: food, housing, action, and escapes. These all varied during the fall of 1942 and problems were compounded by the continual movement of the battle lines after the October offensive that became known as the Battle of El Alamein. While the RAF pilots were stationed close to Alexandria they were able to get a respite from the primitive conditions of the front by going into town. "Hurried off to Alexandria . . . had a relaxing hot water shower, followed by a rub with a clean towel, then the usual lunch of prawns-mayonnaise, fried onions and sweet potatoes," wrote Edward Miluck on 3 November 1942. A little over a month later, Miluck found himself moving every few days as the line of battle continued to shift. On 11 December he was at Agedabia in conditions vastly different from those in Alexandria.

> We are in the middle of nowhere, surrounded by nothing. Water is so scarce that I hate to waste it even by sweating. Four of us share a tent, each one getting two pints of water daily, and to stretch it we use our "rotation ration" system, which involves a four-day period. Being first today, I took a cup of water and thoroughly washed my hands and face. When I had finished, Wally used the same cup of water to wash himself, then the other two had their turns. Mike Kelly was the last on washing, so he was first on shaving, still using the same cup of water. . . . Our toilet completed, the cup of water was strained and put into another canteen. . . . When the canteen is full—two pints—it is my turn to take a bath, which means that we get a bath once every ten days. When I'm through bathing, the water is still mine to wash my clothes. . . .
>
> The food has been so poor, we have considered eating Julius (the Squadron's pet goat). For a week it's been canned bully, hot or cold, three times a day, with soupy cold tea and hard biscuits. The water is worse than the food. Like drinking medicine, there is so much chlorine in it. Have been getting a little extra from a well down the road, but there is a dead Italian in it, so we don't use it for drinking. The army does, though.[80]

The different levels of action in England, Malta, and North Africa can be judged from the experiences of the Eagles who served in the latter two areas. Generally, those who served in Malta rate the flying there as much more hazardous and action-filled than that they did while in England. Those who flew in both Malta and North Africa generally had their most memorable experiences in North Africa. Leo Nomis offers a case in point. Once, flying over North Africa, out of ammunition and low on fuel after strafing enemy trucks and positions, his squadron suddenly encountered three Me 109s, led by the famous German ace Joachin Muncheberg. In the ensuing melee, in which the Spitfires seemed to Nomis like sitting ducks, almost every British aircraft was damaged and several were destroyed. To Nomis, the Germans' flying exhibition was a sight to behold. "It was frustrating to have empty guns in a dogfight but the way these pilots handled their aircraft and took constant advantage of speed and altitude, we wouldn't have gotten a shot at them anyway," wrote Nomis. "It is interesting to note that after that incident the Spitfire Wing was relieved of ground attack operations and relegated to escort cover for the fighter bombers."[81]

It was also in North Africa that one of the most publicized Eagle escapes from the Germans took place. Harold Marting, who had served in both 71 and 121 Squadrons, was shot down flying an RAF P–40 on 23 October 1942 and captured by the Italians. He was sent to Greece, made a daring escape, and evaded recapture for more than six weeks as he made his way back to Africa and eventually to Cairo, where he walked into a New Year's Eve party to greet Miluck and Tribken. "Marting walked in this evening, very casually, as if he had just been out for a drink. . . . What a New Year's Eve!" wrote Miluck. Marting's entire adventure was later chronicled in *American Magazine*.[82] Transferred to the USAAF in January 1943, Marting was killed in a plane crash in New York the following summer. Miluck and Tribken transferred in January as well; Leo Nomis joined the American forces in April.[83]

As in every theater where they fought, some Eagles lost their lives in North Africa. Robert Mannix and Norman Chap were both killed in November 1942. Mannix and his Hurricane were shot down during a strafing run. He had just been made a squadron commander a few weeks earlier.[84] Chap, also flying a Hurricane, found himself completely outnumbered by Me 109s. Unable to outrun them, he fought, but was eventually shot down. Edwin Bicksler was killed in a P–40 during an attack on German transport planes, shortly after he transferred to the USAAF.[85]

Although the entire Eagle contingent volunteered to go to the Far East to fight the Japanese the day after Pearl Harbor, and a number who ended up in North Africa and Malta had originally asked to go to Singapore, only two Eagles ended up in Asia as members of the RAF. Art Donahue had asked to leave Number 71 within a few weeks of the formation of that unit because, as a combat veteran, he did not want to spend the endless months he knew it would take to make the unit operational. After a number of months in other squadrons, Donahue had tired of the seemingly endless patrol missions, so he volunteered to be posted overseas. John Campbell, on the other hand, had requested to leave England shortly after his arrival in Number 121 Squadron because the climate aggravated a serious sinus condition. He left just before the unit's transition into Spitfires. "Had I known that we would soon be flying Spits," he said, "I might have put up with the sinuses and stayed with 121."[86]

Both Donahue and Campbell were assigned to 258 Squadron and, after a sojourn flying out of Gibraltar, arrived in Singapore on 29 January 1942, just seventeen days before it fell to the Japanese. Unable to be resupplied and suffering continual losses, the squadron became smaller and more fragmented, fighting in small groups against the vastly superior Japanese forces. Campbell was shot down on 28 February 1942. Along with several Englishmen, he evaded the Japanese for a time, but he was eventually captured on 20 March and remained a prisoner for the remainder of the war—the only Eagle to be a POW under the Japanese.[87] Donahue was seriously wounded on a strafing run against a number of Japanese river barges, an action for which he won the Distinguished Flying Cross, and was removed to Ceylon for recovery. He subsequently returned to England, where he lost his life trying to ditch his damaged aircraft in the Channel.

EAGLES AS PRISONERS OF WAR

Certainly the most difficult ordeal faced by any members of the Eagle Squadrons was that of those who were prisoners of war. At a minimum, most spent nearly three years as POWs; some spent nearly four. The list of Eagle prisoners of war began in June 1941 when Nat Maranz was shot down. (Although not still in one of the Eagle units at the time, Maranz had served in Number 71 Squadron.) It ended on 14 February 1945 with the downing of Roy Evans, then a lieutenant colonel in the USAAF, the 37th Eagle to become a POW.[88] Of this number, fourteen were taken prisoner while actually serving with one of the Eagle Squadrons. Those fourteen men are the subject here.

The first active member of an Eagle Squadron to be shot down and captured was William Hall of Number 71 Squadron, who became a prisoner on 7 July 1941. The list grew through 26 September 1942, when George Sperry, Charles Cook, Gilbert Wright, George Middleton, Edward Brettell, and Marion Jackson rounded out the list at fourteen after being shot down on the ill-fated Morlaix mission. Included in the number are William Nichols, William Geiger, Gilmore Daniel, Morris Fessler, William Jones, Leroy Skinner, and Barry Mahon, who were captured between September 1941 and August 1942. Among these men, accounts of their being shot down, their evasion and capture, their experiences while prisoners, and their escape or release would fill a complete volume. A few brief tales here can give some idea of the larger story.

Charles Cook, for example, was shot down over Brest on the Morlaix raid, captured, and transported along with George Sperry across France and Germany to Stalag Luft III near the Polish border. When the Germans began to move their prisoners west, away from the approaching Soviets, near the end of the war, Cook was suffering from a terrible infection in his hand and arm that had completely incapacitated him and caused the Germans to conclude that he would probably die. The Germans left him, after George Sperry and Marion Jackson had made him as comfortable as possible, for the Soviets to deal with. Fortunately, a British doctor treated him and, in Cook's opinion, saved his life. Cook eventually was moved by the Soviets across Poland and parts of Russia to Odessa, then to Istanbul, and eventually to Naples, where he finally was received into American ranks again.[89]

Barry Mahon was shot down during "Operation Jubilee," the costly invasion of France in July 1942. He sat in his dinghy in the Channel and watched the air battle for the rest of the day. Eventually he drifted to the French shore, was captured, and was transported to Paris. "I stayed in the car while my German captors went night clubbing," Mahon said. "They would occasionally bring some champagne or food out to my guard and myself and I really saw the night life of the city." Mahon was later turned over to the Gestapo for very harsh interrogation before ending up in Stalag Luft III with his Eagle compatriots.[90] William Geiger had wanted a career in the military and saw joining the RAF as a way to get a head start. When he was shot down in September 1941, one of the early Eagles to meet that fate, all his plans came to an end. The scars from his three-and-a-half years at Stalag Luft III have really never healed.[91]

Although no typical situation faced the Eagles who were shot down and captured, certain parameters could determine what their circumstances might be and the type of treatment they would receive. First, it was much better to be captured by the Luftwaffe than by the Gestapo. The former were airmen and tended to look on the fallen British pilots as comrades in a common vocation, albeit on the other side. Therefore, Luftwaffe handling of the captives was generally as good as could be expected; there are many stories of exceptionally good treatment for prisoners. The German system called for the Luftwaffe to get control of all captured airmen, but the German Army, the SS, or the Gestapo occasionally would find downed pilots and conduct a harsh, occasionally brutal interrogation of their RAF captives. In the end, however, all of the Eagle prisoners were turned over to the Luftwaffe and ended up in Stalag Luft III.

Second, with few exceptions, the downed airmen were not very successful at evading capture for any prolonged period of time. A number of those shot down were able initially to evade and make contact with the French, but most were either turned over to the Germans or decided to turn themselves in to prevent possible retribution toward the French. There were exceptions, however. Robert Smith, shot down on the Morlaix raid along with Cook, Jackson, Sperry, Brettell, Wright, and Middleton, managed to evade capture with the aid of the French underground. After being moved to Southern France, he was teamed with another downed pilot, fellow Eagle Eric Doorly, who had been shot down a few weeks earlier. The two, along with a few other evaders, eventually made their way to Spain by climbing over the Pyrenees in street shoes with no coats. After being put in Spanish jails, nearly starving and freezing to death, Smith, who had separated from Doorly, completed his amazing adventure by working his way back to England and returning to Debden. Doorly, too, was never captured and returned to fly with the USAAF.[92]

More typical are the experiences of Morris Fessler and Marion Jackson. Fessler was forced to put his Spitfire down in France in October 1941 after it was badly damaged during a strafing run on a locomotive. After landing, he recalls,

> I lit my plane on fire and then set off to evade the Germans. I was able to stay away from them and their dogs until about mid-afternoon when they finally gave up the search. I was near a farmhouse and watched it for several hours until late in the evening. I then decided to go to the door and see if I could get some help and food. The door was opened by a

woman in a long nightgown who was soon joined by the farmer, their daughter and two policemen who lived there. They fed me soup and some wine while we talked about my situation. They told me that if the Germans found out they had helped me they would certainly be killed as an example. I decided that I didn't want them all killed on account of me so I allowed them to turn me over to the German authorities.[93]

Marion Jackson, on the other hand, was in no condition to evade anyone when he crash-landed his new Spit IX after being hit over Brest.

The first thing I remember was being in a French farmhouse with a broken nose, a big hole in my head, two broken knees and an old woman dabbing something on my head that burned like hell. . . . One of the people around me was a little girl who spoke a little English. . . . I was able to communicate who I was and asked if they could hide me. The old lady refused because a few weeks earlier the people on a nearby farm had been caught sheltering a Canadian pilot and all the young people had been taken away to an unknown fate. . . . The German army came by soon and picked me up since I was in no shape to go anywhere. They took me to a military hospital in Brest where a doctor picked out the shrapnel, patched up my head, and gave me a shot for pain. The next day the British flight lieutenant in our squadron [Edward Brettell, the squadron commander of 133 on the Morlaix raid who would be executed by the Germans for his role in the "Great Escape"], who had ended up at the same medical center, and I were put on a freight train for Paris.

Jackson spent about eight weeks in the hospital, after which he was interrogated and finally sent to join his fellow prisoners at Stalag Luft III.[94] Also spending time in a hospital was Gilmore Daniel, the youngest Eagle and possibly the youngest POW at about age 17. He floated for 78 hours in his dinghy before being thrown onto the French beach and captured by the Germans. After regaining his strength at a hospital in St. Omer, he was sent to interrogation and eventually on to Stalag Luft III.[95]

The interrogation process for downed airmen was one to which the Germans devoted vast resources and from which they gained a significant amount of information. The master German interrogator, Hanns Scharff, believes he was successful in getting just about any information he needed from the captives with whom he talked. Many other interrogation officers were equally effective. The Germans' approach varied with both the interrogator and the prisoner, but generally focused on the rather helpless situation of the prisoner, convincing him that the Germans knew most of the requested information already and putting the prisoner in uncomfortable physical surroundings from which he could escape only by divulging the requested information.[96] No Eagle was severely tortured in order to obtain information.

Marion Jackson's experience is rather typical. After being released from the hospital, he was taken to the interrogation center in Germany for about ten days.

> They asked you all kinds of questions and really grilled you. Sometimes they mistreated you . . . but the only way that I was mistreated was being put in this little cell about five or six feet wide, ten feet long and about seven feet high . . . with an electric heater that was controlled from the outside. They would turn it up for a day or so and make the room like a Turkish Bath and then turn it off for a day or so and you would freeze.[97]

One of the amazing things to those who were captured was the amount of information the Germans already had both about them personally and about their organizations. When he first arrived in London, Charles Cook saw the complete investigation book that the Clayton Knight Committee made up on each applicant before accepting him for training.

It had where you were born, raised, family, where you went to school, the whole works. It cost them a lot of money. So when I'm a prisoner of war, here comes the German in there with a copy of the same thing. They paid somebody for them. . . . They came in there and told me all about myself. . . . Everybody who went through West Point, they had all the information on them too. You wouldn't believe the information they had on everyone. . . . They already knew that we had transferred to the USAAF . . . because on their bulletin board they had the English paper with the account of the entire transfer ceremony.[98]

Marion Jackson found the same degree of knowledge among his interrogators.

I would only give them name, rank and serial number. This went on for about three days and finally the interrogator told me they already had all they needed about me, and they did. I told them I was a Flight Lieutenant in the RAF and he said "You are not. You are a Captain in the American Air Force." [Since Jackson had transferred to the USAAF just before the Morlaix mission, the interrogator was correct.] He told me when I transferred, where I came from in California. He just knew everything about me. . . . They appeared to know a great deal about everyone.[99]

Hanns Scharff, in his book *The Interrogator*, says the Germans had extensive information on almost all British and American pilots. For those on whom they did not already have a file, they could build one in two or three days.[100] Morris Fessler's initial interrogator in France knew nothing about the downed Eagle. About three days later, when Fessler arrived at the interrogation center at Dulag Luft, near Frankfurt, he found they not only had a file on him (which he read) but also had a *Life* magazine that was only two weeks old and contained the full story of the Eagle Squadrons with pictures and information about each of the pilots.[101] When Roy Evans was shot down in 1945 he was confronted by scores of pictures from a photo album that belonged to LeRoy Gover. Gover had the photo studio located directly beneath the Eagle Club in London process his film and they evidently made duplicates of his pictures for the Germans. Gover and Evans believe the studio was run by the Germans for the purpose of collecting such information.[102]

Even those Eagles, like Fred Almos, who were not prisoners saw the extent of German knowledge about them.

> When I met the German interrogator at the Eagle Squadron Association reunion at Universal City I was introduced and said, "I'm glad to know you. . . . I know that you don't know me but I'm Fred Almos." He said, "Oh yes I do know you." "How could that be?" I asked, "since I've never met you before or seen you before?" He replied, "I know all about you." So the Germans had the finger on all of the members of the Eagle Squadrons.[103]

All of the serving Eagles who were captured ended up in the Luftwaffe camp at Sagan, in eastern Germany (now in western Poland), Stalag Luft III. It was from this camp complex that the "Great Escape" was made; prisoner innovation and organization were perfected to a degree probably unmatched in the story of POW experiences. While they were not all together, it appears the Eagles were a special interest group, as witnessed by a special sheet in the camp records with the Eagle insignia on it and the signatures of all the Eagle prisoners. A number of photos of groups of Eagles in the camp are part of the Stalag Luft III record.[104]

Living conditions at Stalag Luft III were a challenge in themselves according to Bill Geiger.

> One of the compounds at Stalag Luft III would hold about 2,000 men. They had long barracks with a hall down the center and rooms on either side with a communal toilet at the end of the hall. The rooms were about 18 feet square. We started out with about 8 men to a room but eventually got up to 12, so there was no such thing as privacy. There were some two-man rooms but they were very small. Bill Hall

Left to right, Charles Cook, Ben Mays, George Sperry, Henry Smith, and Burton Weil in Stalag Luft III prisoner of war camp.

and I had one for a while because we were some of the longest-time POWs. But as the camp became more crowded these rooms had four occupants. . . . In order to survive you had to learn to shut out all the noise that many people generate . . . a habit I have retained to this day. The compound itself was roughly square with a double barbed-wire fence and in between the fences were rolls of barbed wire, and there were guard boxes up above that. Inside the double fence was a death-fire area about 15 feet wide and you were not allowed to enter that area. If you crossed it they would shoot. If you accidentally kicked a ball into that area you could wave to the guard and he would let you go and pick it up, but they didn't want you in that area.[105]

The *Prisoner of War Bulletin* continues the description:

Light and electric lighting are reported to be adequate and each prisoner has at least two blankets. The sleeping mattresses are filled with wood fiber [which George Sperry recalled made the bed always lumpy]. . . . Some of the prisoners have succeeded in growing flowers, tomatoes and other vegetables in the sandy ground. . . . In each hut one or two wood-burning kitchen stoves make it possible for the prisoners to cook their own supplementary food, but the number of stoves thus available meets the needs of only a small proportion of the prisoners.[106]

Most of the food that the POWs got actually was sent in from abroad. "We got very little food from the Germans," remembers Bill Geiger.

We got potatoes and bread, but the rest of the food came from the International Red Cross. One man was supposed to get one parcel a week, but we seldom did. It was generally one parcel to two men, so we were often hungry. As I remember, a parcel contained a can of tuna, a can of Spam, and a can of corned beef. . . . There were some crackers, prunes or raisins, coffee, sugar, butter, a chocolate bar, some powdered chocolate, and powdered orange juice.[107]

George Sperry continued:

German issues of rations were mostly unappetizing. Jam was made of an unknown substance, maybe coal, sweetened with saccharine, while we had cheese made from some kind of fish and our coffee was roasted grain. All-in-all, not very appetizing.[108]

In addition to the food, the prisoners got some sports equipment through the Red Cross and the YMCA. Mail was infrequent, with a prisoner allowed to write three letters a month and about the same number coming into the camp. "We received no mail the last year because of the situation with the war," said Geiger. And despite the rather austere conditions under which the German guards lived, there was very little pilferage of the parcels. "If a German got caught taking things from one of the parcels," remembered Marion Jackson, "he would probably be sent to the Russian front as punishment."[109]

The prisoners also received plenty of news about what was going on in the outside world because the camp was well equipped with radios, both legal and illegal, and the prisoners listened to the BBC every day. Geiger remembered,

> The BBC would broadcast a program aimed at the POWs every evening and so we got the news just like we were sitting in the living room listening. We often knew more than the BBC because the guy who walked through the camp gate as a new prisoner had been shot down a week or so ago and had traveled through Berlin or Sweinfert and knew what had happened, the damage of the air raids, etc.[110]

But these things were not what the Eagle POWs considered the keys to surviving in the Camp. "There are two critical things involved in surviving as a POW," said Bill Geiger.

> The first was your ability to tolerate the loss of your freedom. The second was not knowing how long you would be there. More than about two years and you wondered if you would ever get out. A day seemed to be about two hours longer and a week seemed to have about 10 days in it . . . time just slowed down.[111]

Marion Jackson added keeping busy to the list. "The average guy would just lay around and let his hair and beard grow," he said. "Those people had a great deal more difficulty both as prisoners and when they got out than did those who were busy."[112]

Most activity in the camp focused on escaping. To facilitate escapes, there were prisoners engaged in everything from hand-printing documents that looked like they had been typed, to making false identification papers, clothes, maps, and other necessities, to actually digging the myriad escape tunnels. All this activity was coordinated by an escape committee, headed by a senior officer called "Big X." The committee decided who would try to escape, when, and how. For those who were successful in getting out of the camp, the penalty if recaptured was fourteen days in solitary confinement on bread and water, followed by movement to another compound within Stalag Luft III. The mass departure of the "Great

Escape," however, led to the execution of 50 of the participants, after which the attitude toward escaping became much more serious.

Schemes for escaping abounded. Marion Jackson was able to escape for about ten days by jumping from the roof of his cell house into a load of evergreen branches being hauled away from the camp.[113] Barry Mahon was going to try Jackson's method, but the Germans quit hauling the branches, so he had to look for another scheme. Eventually, Mahon and a number of others were able to leave a formation departing the camp for the prisoners' periodic delousing. His freedom was short also.[114] Nonetheless, the activity continued at all the camps throughout the war. Bill Edwards found escape committees and all the other activity of Stalag Luft III when he arrived at Stalag Luft I in July 1944.[115]

For most of those who were successful in getting out of the camp, it was just a matter of a few days before they were recaptured, often after having endured some rather tough circumstances. The reason was rather simple to George Sperry. "It was about impossible for the Americans to blend into the European society," he said. "Everything from looks to language made you stand out. A European, on the other hand, could blend into the society and this gave them a much better chance of successfully escaping."[116]

One of the important results of being a prisoner was the effect on the POW's military career after the war was over. The last five Eagles to be shot down while serving in 133 Squadron were actually classed as American pilots since they had transferred before the Morlaix mission. For them, as for any other long-term American POW, the consequence was one of losing time toward promotion and being behind the non-POW in rank when the war was over.[117] Most decided to get out of the Army after the war because they believed they could never catch up. Those who were downed earlier spent their time behind barbed wire as RAF officers, and their status was a matter of considerable question. "We all thought that we would be transferred to the American forces at the same time the other Eagles were transferred even though we were in prison," reminisced Bill Geiger.

> For some it didn't make any difference. But for Mahon, Skinner, and I it did because we were going to stay in the military. Chesley Peterson worked like a dog trying to get us transferred when the rest were but he was unsuccessful. After the war we were told by the US Army in London that transfer would be no problem but that the paperwork was in Washington, D.C. . . . After trying to get a straight answer in the Pentagon for about a week . . . we got with this one-star general who told us that we weren't going to get transferred. He said "We don't need any more flyers and we sure don't need any who haven't flown an airplane in over three years."[118]

Thus the dreams of a military career held by Geiger and Mahon came to an end.

The inmates of Stalag Luft III started their cold movement to the west, to escape the Soviet onslaught, on 27 January 1945. This was an extremely difficult march, for the weather was harsh and food and shelter scarce. "Our guards were now mostly old men *just pressed* into service with but a few of our regular officers and a few ever present S/S Nazi guards attached," recalls Jack Fessler. Intermixed with the marching were train trips in cattle cars with only minimum food and water. The huge column finally made its final stop on a large estate near Lubeck where, after several weeks, they were liberated by a group of Canadians.[119] Except for Edward Brettell, all of the Eagle POWs survived their ordeal. The scars that it left vary, as do the memories of the war as a whole. Although most missed the opportunity to become high-scoring pilots in the British and American forces, theirs is still a significant contribution both to the history and to the spirit of the Eagle Squadrons. They volunteered for a cause even though they knew the risks, and doing so ended up costing them several years of their lives.

7. THE EAGLE HERITAGE

MUCH HAS BEEN MADE OF MANY OF THE GROUPS OF MEN who have served in special circumstances and under special callings in war, and certainly the Eagles are no exception. In many ways, they are typical of young people the world over for whom a cause or an event catches the imagination, or generates the spark and circumstances that make a difference in their lives.

For the Eagles, I have tried to set the record straight on several fronts. First, they did not set any overall records for numbers of German aircraft destroyed by an RAF squadron, although they did lead Fighter Command in certain months, and they did form the nucleus of the Fourth Fighter Group, the highest-scoring American unit in the European Theater during World War II.

Second, they were not involved in the Battle of Britain as a group; only 7 individuals of the 244 Americans in the three units even flew in the Battle.

Third, they were but a small portion of the Americans who volunteered to fly for the RAF during World War II, although the identification *Eagle* has often been applied to all the Americans in the RAF and, in some quarters, all those who served in the Fourth Fighter Group of the US Army Air Force. Duty in Number 71, 121, or 133 Squadron was sometimes by request and sometimes by luck, but the only Eagles are the pilots who were in those units.

At the same time, their history is not very different from that of a number of other RAF squadrons during the early days of World War II, nor are the exploits of their members such that they stand out. The units are the subject of several books, some factual and some fabrications, but in them the stories of Eagle heroics have often overshadowed the Eagles' real contributions. Those contributions were much the same as the contributions of any Fighter Command squadron. Nonetheless, the Eagle squadrons stand out in the annals of military and aviation history because in many ways they were unique organizations.

As with so many significant events in history, circumstances played an important part in the Eagles' story; the young men who became Eagles found themselves in a unique situation. Since the first days of flight, young people have dreamed of being pilots and getting their hands on a "hot ship," be it the Sopwith Camel, the Spitfire, or the F–16. Aircraft are, after all, at the very high end of the technology scale, which helps to increase the motivation to be part of the elite group of flyers. But seldom have circumstances come together that could have made the realization of these men's dreams possible.

In normal times, most of the Eagles would have never had the opportunity to fly military aircraft, since almost all of them were either ineligible for entry into the US military pilot training program or had entered it and been eliminated. But times were not normal at the beginning of the 1940s. For this group of frustrated young men, willing to do about anything to get their hands on one of the hot aircraft of the day, there was a nation that had the airplanes and was desperate for pilots—Great Britain. There was also a recruiting system established for getting them into the RAF—the Clayton Knight Committee. Finally, the US government was, for the most part, willing to look the other way when the illegal recruiting was in progress. The Eagles were helped by what is a remarkable combination of circumstances by any measure.

But equally important was the nature of the individuals themselves. They were adventurous, absolutely consumed with flying, and willing to do about anything to fly the planes that the military had—nowhere else could they get behind the controls of the fastest aircraft available. With the US military option closed, the RAF became the logical alternative. Most Eagles also realized that the English had their backs to the wall and needed all the help they could get. For many, it was the desire to help that tipped the balance toward volunteering. But they could also foresee the United States entering the war and knew that if they did not act quickly the option of *flying* in combat might well disappear. In addition, a majority of them either understood before joining the RAF or saw after they became engaged in the war, that the British cause was worth dying for. They could have quit and gone home, but almost none did. They accepted the action they had taken and gave their all for it.

We should also remember that they were really volunteering for the unknown. They did not know what combat flying was all about or the full extent of the risk involved. Yet when the realities became apparent to them, they simply did what had to be done and took their chances. For many, in fact, it was that lure of combat, a venture into the unknown, that was part of the challenge of being a fighter pilot.

Most enjoyed walking down the streets of London and having the people look, the young ladies "ooh" and "ah," and the pub owners say "you don't pay for a drink in here, Yank!" And their scrapbooks abound with articles that appeared in their hometown newspapers extolling their actions against the Germans, praising their heroism. It has been thus with young men since time began. Flight and airplanes and a cause really motivated the Eagles.

The men who volunteered for the RAF, Eagles and non-Eagles, are sometimes accused of being mercenaries, a charge that was also leveled at the members of the Lafayette Escadrille in World War I and the Flying Tigers of China fame. If one takes the very parochial view that anyone who joins the military of a foreign country or fights in a war in which his or her own nation is not involved is a mercenary, then the Eagles, as well as the other groups mentioned, were mercenaries. If, on the other hand, a mercenary is defined as someone motivated by the desire or need for money to join a foreign military establishment or fight for an alien nation, then neither the Lafayette Escadrille nor the Eagles qualify, nor do those Americans who joined other squadrons of the RAF. After all, they were paid from about $45 to $100 a month, most of which was spent on subsistence. Any one of them could have bettered that pay in the United States. In fact, one of the reasons mentioned by so many Eagles for being glad to transfer to the American forces when the opportunity came was the significant increase in salary.

So it seems impossible to responsibly charge that the Eagles were mercenaries. The Flying Tigers are another story. Many of them were motivated by money, often a ten-fold increase over their US military pay—the money was one of the selling points in recruiting for the American Volunteer Group. Obviously, not all the Flying Tigers were so motivated, but the charge of mercenary can be leveled at members of that organization with much more validity than at the Eagles.

The Eagles, in fact, represented their country and its people in the war effort before the United States officially entered the war. Americans were hungry for news about the war in Europe, and most had strong feelings concerning the conflict, even though these thoughts were often tempered by a genuine fear of the United States becoming involved in the war. The tremendous amount of press coverage given all aspects of the war in Europe, and the Eagles in particular, reflects that spirit. So the three squadrons gave Americans some "homegrown" heroes at a time when they had precious few. Even if the

United States could not be in the war, the Eagles were, carrying the American flag to the besieged British.

The Eagles also served the United States well in the view of the British. For the Americans in the RAF, and the Eagle Squadrons in particular, were the forerunners of that large force of Americans that every Briton hoped would soon come to his country's aid in the struggle against Germany. Equally important, they provided a very positive presence—very different from that of many Americans who came later—as members of the RAF, accepting British ways and integrating themselves into the society as best they could. As long as there were Americans fighting for England, there was hope—and in war hope is precious. The ties that the Eagles formed with Britain have proved long-lasting: in 1986, then–Prime Minister Thatcher personally dedicated a memorial to the Eagles in Grosvenor Square in London, and the Eagles receive absolutely royal treatment whenever they return to their "other homeland."

The reaction of the US government to the Eagles was also instructive to both the US populace and the British. By choosing to ignore the legal restrictions against American citizens moving through a war zone, joining a foreign military, and even training openly in the United States, the government was making a statement whose meaning was not lost to people on either side of the Atlantic. The lack of any mass objection by the American public to having Americans in the RAF also helped encourage the British as they waited and hoped for the United States to enter the war.

Over the years, some people have played down the Eagles' contribution to the American military, but that contribution was significant. When the three Eagle Squadrons became the Fourth Fighter Group of the Eighth Air Force, months before there were American-trained and -equipped fighter squadrons in Europe, they helped provide the American press and people with the morale and confidence needed to sustain the effort that eventually led to the defeat of Germany. How ironic that a group of men who were not able to earn US Army pilot's wings through the established programs were among the first to wear those wings. They led all the American fighter pilots into battle and provided the nucleus for the overwhelming force that eventually dominated the skies over Europe.

It is ironic too that, among the flying units in World War II, the Eagles as a group, both while in the RAF and after transfer to the American service, were among those who made the greatest sacrifice for the cause of freedom, losing nearly half their men. Few other flying units lost so great a share of their personnel to the enemy over the course of the war.

When the circumstances, the people, and the nations involved are all put together, it is easy to realize that a group just like the Eagles will probably not be seen again in modern warfare. There will always be individuals ready to volunteer for causes just as the Eagles did, but it is unlikely that a situation like that the Eagles found themselves in will arise again. We should learn from history, however, and we can learn from the story of the RAF Eagle Squadrons. They volunteered to go fight in a war that was not their own; they stood up to be counted for the cause of freedom. Their story also demonstrates the power that flight has over individuals, for seldom in history has a group of men been so consumed by an aircraft—the Spitfire—and so willing to give up their way of life, their security, and, for nearly half, their freedom or even their lives in order to fly and fight in those hot ships. History is replete with examples of individuals who took risks and, in doing so, became examples for those who followed. The Eagles were such a group.

APPENDIX

A. EAGLE PERSONAL DATA

This accounting of the members of the RAF Eagle Squadrons is as accurate as is available in 1991. Several of the Eagles served in more than one of the three units. The squadron listed for a particular pilot is that with which he is most readily identified. Home state is that state with which a pilot is identified, not necessarily that from which he joined the RAF. The age listed reflects how old a pilot was when he officially became a member of the RAF, not when he signed with the Clayton Knight Committee, joined the RCAF, etc. Both education and occupation are those listed in the RAF records. No entry in one of these four colums means no information was available. No entry in the last column, however, means that the individual survived his military participation in the war. Those listed as KIA (killed in action) were killed on an operational mission against the Germans. KOAS (killed on active service) means killed in some other circumstance such as a training flight, accident, or the like. In these two categories, plus POW (prisoner of war), I have reflected the pilot's service at the time, with the exception of those who were either killed or captured on the Morlaix mission; they are classed as RAF since the unit to which they were assigned was Number 133 Squadron of the RAF, even though most had officially transferred to the USAAF before the mission.

The information in these rosters comes from several sources. James Gray provided "Eagle Squadron Pilots, Prisoners of War" and "Eagle Squadron Pilots Killed While Serving with the RAF," unpublished rosters; Edwin Taylor provided a "List of RAFVR Americans"; both also gave me considerable information in several telephone conversations and Jim Gray was kind enough to review the final roster. The other sources are "Eagle Squadrons" Folder, Air History Office, Ministry of Defence, London; Vern Haugland, *The Eagle Squadrons*, pp. 183–192, and *The Eagles' War*, pp. 226–228; Garry Fry and Jeffrey Ethell, *Escort to Berlin*, pp. 170–195; Personal Interviews and Eagle Squadron Questionnaires as listed in the Bibliography, and several conversations with Eagle Squadron members and their friends and relatives.

American Eagle Squadron Pilots

Name	Squadron	Home State	Age	Education	Occupation	WWII Fate
Alexander, James K.	71	MO	21	H.S.	Const.	POW (US)
Alexander, Richard L.	133	IL	25	H.S.+	Pro Athlete	
Allen, Luke E.	71	CO	23	H.S.+	Pilot	KIA (RAF)
Allen, Thomas W.	121	NC				
Almos, Fred E.	121	CA	19	H.S.+	Student	KIA (RAF)
Anderson, Newton	71	LA	30	College	Reporter	KOAS (RAF)
Anderson, Paul R.	71	CA				KIA (RAF)
Anderson, Stanley M.	71	CT	24	H.S.+		
Andrews, Thomas J.	71	KS	20	H.S.+	A/C Factory*	KIA (RAF)
Arends, William A.	133	ND	23	H.S.+		KOAS (RAF)
Atkinson, Roger H.	71	TX	20		A/C Factory	KIA (RAF)
Austin, Frederick C.	121	CA				KIA (RAF)
Ayer, John B.	71	ME	28			KIA (RAF)
Ayres, Henry L.	133	IN	20	H.S.	Race Driver	POW (US)
Baker, William H.	133	TX	21	H.S.+	Student	KIA (RAF)

* A/C Factory = Aircraft Factory

Name		State	Age	Education	Occupation	Fate
Barrell, Charles S.	133	MA	30	H.S.+	Planter	KOAS (RAF)
Bateman, Charles E.	71	MA	28	H.S.	Student	
Beatie, Ernest D.	121	GA	23	H.S.	Student	
Beaty, Richard N.	133	NY	21	College		
Beeson, Duane W.	71	ID	21	H.S.+	Student	POW (US)
Bennett, Joe L.	133	ID	24	H.S.+	Engineer	
Bicksler, Edwin H.	133	IN	21	H.S.+	Student	KIA (US)
Blakeslee, Donald J. M.	133	OH	22	H.S.	Chemical Wkr.	
Blanding, Leon M.	121	SC	22	H.S.+	Laborer	
Bodding, Carl O.	121	KS	27		Machinist	KIA (RAF)
Boehle, Vernon A.	71	IN	26	H.S.+	Elevator Co.	
Bono, Victor R.	71	CA	26	H.S.+		
Boock, Robert A.	71	IL				KIA (US)
Booth, Douglas E.	121	NY	21	H.S.	Student	
Boyles, Frank R.	121	NY				KIA (US)
Braley, Richard G.	133	CA	20	H.S.+	Student	
Brite, William O.	71	IN				KIA (US)
Brossmer, Robert V.	121	NJ	25	College	Banker	KIA (RAF)
Brown, Hugh C.	133	CA	21	H.S.+	Student	KIA (RAF)

American Eagle Squadron Pilots (cont.)

Name	Squadron	Home State	Age	Education	Occupation	WWII Fate
Brown, John I.	121	IL	21	H.S.+	Steel Mill	
Bruce, George R.	133	Canada*				KOAS (RAF)
Campbell, John A.	121	CA	19	H.S.	Pilot	POW (RAF)
Care, Raymond C.	71	IN	22	H.S.+		POW (US)
Carpenter, George	121	PA	25	H.S.+	Army Cadet	POW (US)
Chap, Norman R.	121					KIA (RAF)
Chatterton, Lawrence A.	71	NY	23	H.S.	Airlines	KOAS (RAF)
Clark, James A.	71	NY				
Coen, Oscar H.	71	IL	23	College	Teacher	
Cook, Charles A.	133	CA	24	H.S.+	Student	POW (RAF)
Cox, Forrest M.	121	IL	25	H.S.+	A/C Factory	
Coxetter, James G.	133	FL	23	H.S.+	Student	KOAS (RAF)
Crowe, Stephen H.	133	OH	21	H.S.+	A/C Factory	
Daley, William J.	121	TX	21	H.S.+	Clerk	KOAS (US)
Daniel, Gilmore C.	71	OK	15	H.S.	Student	POW (RAF)

* Though he was living in Canada, George R. Bruce was a US citizen.

Name		State	Age	Education	Occupation	Status
Daymond, Gregory A.	71	CA	19	H.S.+	Pilot	KOAS (RAF)
DeHaven, Ben P.	133	KY	25	H.S.+	Pilot	KIA (RAF)
Donahue, Arthur G.	71	MN	27	H.S.+	Pilot	
Doorly, Eric	133	NJ	20	H.S.+	Pilot	
Dowling, Forrest P.	71	TX		H.S.		
Downs, Bruce C.	121	TX	25	College	Engineer	
Driver, William R.	71	TN	22	H.S.	Car Factory	KOAS (RAF)
DuFour, John G.	71	CA	28	H.S.+	Salesman	
Dunn, William R.	71	MN	24	H.S.+	Military	
Durham, Joseph E.	121	AR	24	H.S.+	Golf Pro	
Edner, Selden R.	121	MN	22	H.S.+	Student	POW (US)
Edwards, Wilson V.	133	CA	22	H.S.+	Student	POW (US)
Eichar, Grant E.	133	IA	24	H.S.		KIA (RAF)
Ellington, Paul M.	121	OK		H.S.+	Army Cadet	POW (US)
Evans, Jack E.	71					KIA (RAF)
Evans, Roy W.	121	CA	27	H.S.	Railroad	POW (US)
Fenlaw, Hillard S.	71	TX	21	H.S.+	Clerk	KIA (RAF)
Fessler, Morris W.	71	CA	21	H.S.+	Pilot Tng.	POW (RAF)
Fetrow, Gene B.	121	CA	23	H.S.	A/C Factory	

American Eagle Squadron Pilots (cont.)

Name	Squadron	Home State	Age	Education	Occupation	WWII Fate
Fink, Frank M.	121	PA	21	H.S.+	Clerk	POW (US)
Florance, David R.	133	CA	28	College		KIA (RAF)
Flynn, John	71	IL	21			KIA (RAF)
Ford, William K.	133	TX				KIA (RAF)
Fox, Philip J.	121	NY				
France, Victor J.	71	TX	30			KIA (US)
Freiberg, Ralph W.	121	MN				KIA (RAF)
Galbraith, C. O.	71	CA	25	College	Eng. Tester	KOAS (US)
Gallo, Tony A.	133	CT	25	College	Reporter	KOAS (RAF)
Gamble, Frederick A.	121	TN	21	H.S.	Mechanic	KIA (RAF)
Geffene, Donald	71	CA	21	H.S.+	Playboy	POW (RAF)
Geiger, William D.	71	CA		H.S.+	Student	
Gentile, Donald S.	133	OH	23	College	Student	KOAS (RAF)
Gilliland, Jack D.	121	IL	18	H.S.	Student	POW (US)
Goodson, James A.	133	NY	27	H.S.	Pilot	
Gover, LeRoy	133	CA				

Name	No.	State	Age	Education	Occupation	Status
Gray, James A.	71	CA	22	H.S.+	Student	POW (RAF)
Griffin, James E.	121	NY	22	H.S.	Factory Wkr.	KIA (US)
Grimm, Chester P.	121	IL				KIA (RAF)
Gudmundsen, Dick D.	133					KIA (RAF)
Hain, Harry C.	133	KY	26	H.S.	Service St.	KIA (RAF)
Hall, William I.	71	VT	24	H.S.	Pilot	POW (RAF)
Halsey, Gilbert O.	121	OK				
Hancock, Fletcher	133	CA	21			KIA (RAF)
Happel, James R.	121	NJ				
Hardin, Charles A.	121					
Harp, Carter W.	133	GA			Pilot	KIA (RAF)
Harrington, James C.	71	NY				
Helgason, Joseph F.	71	WA		H.S.	Cycle Racer	KOAS (RAF)
Hively, Howard D.	71	OH		College		
Hobert, Robert D.	133	WA			Pilot	KIA (US)
Holder, Kenneth L.	121	CA	26	H.S.	Student	KIA (RAF)
Hollander, Walter J.	71	HI	20	H.S.+	Machinist	
Hopson, Alfred H.	71	TX	30	H.S.	Salesman	
Inabinet, William B.	71	SC	20	H.S.		KOAS (RAF)

American Eagle Squadron Pilots (cont.)

Name	Squadron	Home State	Age	Education	Occupation	WWII Fate
Jackson, Marion E.	133	CA	28	H.S.+	Bar Owner	POW (RAF)
Jones, William L. C.	121	MD	21			
Kearney, Jack L.	121	IL	21			
Kelly, Joseph M.	71	CA	18	H.S.	Electric Co.	
Kelly, William P.	121	NY				KIA (US)
Kennerly, Byron F.	71	CA	31	H.S.	Const.	
Keough, Vernon C.	71	NJ	28	H.S.	Parachutist	KOAS (RAF)
Kimbro, Karl K.	133	MA	27	H.S.+	Mining	
King, Coburn C.	133	CA	32	H.S..	Pilot	KIA (RAF)
Kolendorski, Stanley M.	71	NJ	25	H.S.		KIA (RAF)
Lambert, Donald E.	133	CA	25	H.S.+	Crew Chief	
Laughlin, Loran L.	121	TX	19	H.S.		KOAS (RAF)
Leckrone, Philip H.	71	IL	19	H.S.	Pilot	KOAS (RAF)
Loomis, Lyman S.	133	OH	29	H.S.+	Salesman	
Lutz, John F.	71	MO	21			KIA (US)
Lynch, John J.	71	CA	23	H.S.+	Instructor	

342

Name		State	Age	Education	Occupation	Fate
Mahon, Jackson B.	121	CA	20	H.S.	A/C Factory	POW (RAF)
Mamedoff, Andrew B.	133	CT	28	College	Pilot	KOAS (RAF)
Mannix, Robert L.	71	FL				KIA (RAF)
Maranz, Nat	71	CA				POW (RAF)
Marcus, Clifford H.	121					
Martin, Clarence L.	121	PA	26	H.S.	Carpenter	
Marting, Harold F.	71	IN				KOAS (US)
Mason, Earl W.	121	MN				KOAS (RAF)
Matthews, Joseph G.	133					
Mauriello, Sam A.	71	NY	32		Pilot	
Maxwell, George S.	71	MS				
Mays, Ben F.	71	TX	27	College	Pilot	KIA (RAF)
McCall, Hugh H.	133	CA	24	H.S.+	Salesman	KOAS (RAF)
McColpin, Carroll W.	133	CA	26	H.S.	Electrician	
McGerty, Thomas P.	71	CA	20	H.S.	Usher	KIA (RAF)
McGinnis, James L.	71	CA	29	H.S.	A/C Factory	KOAS (RAF)
McHan, Richard E.	121	CA	20	H.S.	Student	
McLeod, Donald W.	121	MA	27	H.S.+	US Navy	
McMinn, Richard D.	71	OK	22	H.S.+	Student	KIA (US)

American Eagle Squadron Pilots (cont.)

Name	Squadron	Home State	Age	Education	Occupation	WWII Fate
McPharlin, Michael G.	71	IL	24	College	Med. Student	KIA (US)
Meierhoff, Cecil E.	133	KS	21	H.S.+	Student	KIA (US)
Middleton, George H.	133	CA	24			POW (RAF)
Miley, Carl H.	133	OH				
Miller, Ervin L.	133	CA	27	H.S.+	Civil Service	
Mills, Henry L.	71	NY				POW (US)
Miluck, Edward T.	71	ND	22	H.S.+	Student	
Miner, Denver E.	133	WI	25	H.S.+	Clerk	
Mirsch, George E.	133	IL				
Mitchellweis, John	133	IL				KOAS (US)
Mize, Collier, C.	121	TX	25	H.S.+	Clerk	
Mooney, John J.	121	NY	20	H.S.	Driver	KIA (RAF)
Moore, Richard A.	71	TX	24	College	A/C Factory	
Morgan, W. Brewster	71	HI	23	H.S.+	Student	POW (US)
Morris, Moran S.	133	TX			Student	KIA (RAF)
Mueller, Robert S.	133					

344

Name						
Nash, Herbert T.	121	TX	26	H.S.+	Oil Fields	
Nee, Don D.	133	CA	23	H.S.+	Sales	
Nelson, James C.	133	CO	22	College	Bank Mgr.	
Neville, Gene P.	133	OK	23			
Nichols, William H.	71	CA	26	H.S.	Carpenter	KIA (RAF)
Nomis, Leo S.	71	CA	19	H.S.	Airport Wkr.	POW (RAF)
O'Brien, Lyman D.	121	TX	19	H.S.	Salesman	
Olson, Virgil W.	71	CA	27	H.S.+	A/C Factory	KIA (RAF)
Omens, Gilbert I.	133	IL	23	H.S.	Airline	KOAS (RAF)
Orbison, Edwin E.	71	OK	22	H.S.+		KOAS (RAF)
O'Regan, William T.	71	CA	25	H.S.+	Chem. worker	
Osborne, Julian M.	121	VA	23	College	Salesman	
Padgett, Cadman V.	121	MD	25	H.S.	Pilot	
Parker, Vernon A.	121	TX	28	H.S.	Salesman	
Patterson, Richard F.	121	FL			College	KIA (RAF)
Patterson, Robert G.	121	CA				POW (US)
Peck, James E.	121	CA	20	H.S.+	A/C Worker	KOAS (US)
Pendleton, Wendell	71	AK	22	H.S.+	Draftsman	
Peterson, Chesley G.	71	UT	21	H.S.+	A/C Factory	

345

American Eagle Squadron Pilots (cont.)

Name	Squadron	Home State	Age	Education	Occupation	WWII Fate
Peterson, Kenneth D.	133	AZ	20	H.S.+	Student	POW (US)
Pewitt, Robert L.	133	TX	21	H.S+	Student	KIA (RAF)
Pisanos, Steve N.	71	NJ	22	H.S.	Hotel Worker	
Potter, Eugene M.	71	IL	20	H.S.+	Reporter	KIA (US)
Priser, Robert L.	71	AZ	20	H.S.+	A/C Mechanic	
Provenzano, Peter B.	71	IL				KOAS (US)
Putnam, Hiram A.	133	TX				KIA (RAF)
Reed, Lawson F.	121	IA	28	H.S.+		
Robertson, Chesley H.	133	TX			A/C Factory	
Roscoe, Arthur F.	71	CA	19	H.S.	Student	POW (US)
Ross, Donald H.	121	CA	18	H.S.		
Ross, Gilbert G.	71	NM				
Ryerson, Leonard T.	133	MA	30			KIA (RAF)
Sanders, James M.	121	TN				
Satterlee, Dean H.	71	CA	24	H.S.+	Druggist	
Scarborough, Ross O.	71	CA	18	H.S.+	Mechanic	KOAS (RAF)

Name		State	Age	Education	Occupation	Status
Schatzberg, Seymour M.	133	TX				KOAS (RAF)
Scudday, Fred	133	NC	23	H.S.+	Student	KOAS (US)
Seaman, Anthony J.	71	PA				KIA (US)
Shenk, Warren V.	121	OH				
Sintetos, Nicholas D.	121	MO	20	H.S.	Merchant	
Skinner, Leroy A.	121	OK	22	College	Chemist	POW (RAF)
Slade, William C.	133	NY	25	H.S.+	Delivery	
Slater, John T.	121	KA	21	College	Med. Student	KIA (US)
Smart, Glen J.	133	NY				
Smith, Bradley	121	CA				
Smith, Dennis D.	133	MS	21			KIA (RAF)
Smith, Fred C.	121	TX				
Smith, Fonzo D.	121	ID	22	H.S.+	Army Cadet	POW (US)
Smith, Kenneth G.	121	DC				POW (US)
Smith, Robert E.	133	NY	22	H.S.	Student	
Smolinsky, Frank J.	121	CA				KOAS (US)
Soares, Walter G.	133	CA	22	H.S.+	Student	KOAS (RAF)
Sperry, George B.	133	CA	27	H.S.	Bank Clerk	POW (RAF)
Sprague, Robert S.	71					KOAS (US)

347

American Eagle Squadron Pilots (cont.)

Name	Squadron	Home State	Age	Education	Occupation	WWII Fate
Stanhope, Aubrey C.	121	NY	42	College	French AF	POW (US)
Stephenson, Andrew J.	133	CA				KOAS (US)
Stepp, Malta L.	121	CA	21	H.S.+	Furn. Sales	
Stewart, Hubert L.	71	NC	26	H.S.+	Dept. Store	KOAS (RAF)
Stout, Roy N.	133	MI	24	College	Pilot	
Strickland, Harold H.	71	LA	37	H.S.+		KOAS (US)
Taylor, Benjamin A.	121	OR			Student	
Taylor, Edwin D.	133	OK	23	H.S.+		KIA (RAF)
Taylor, James L.	121	IN	27		Accountant	KOAS (RAF)
Taylor, Kenneth S.	71		23		Machinist	KIA (RAF)
Taylor, William D.	71	MA	23	College	Brit.Navy	
Taylor, William E. G.	71	MD				KIA (RAF)
Teicheira, George	71	CA	21			POW (RAF)
Thorpe, Clifford R.	121				Student	
Tilley, Reade F.	121	FL	22	H.S.+	Pilot	KIA (RAF)
Tobin, Eugene Q.	71	UT	23	H.S.+		

348

Name	Unit	State	Age	Education	Occupation	Status
Tribken, Charles W.	71	NY	22	H.S.+	Guide	KOAS (US)
Tucker, Thaddeus H.	121	CA				KIA (RAF)
Vance, Fred R.	121					
Vosburg, Murray S.	71	CA	23	H.S.+	Rancher	
Wallace, Thomas C.	71	CA	23	H.S.		
Wallace, William R.	133	CA	22		Railroad	
Ward, Rufus C.	71	TX	29	H.S.		
Warner, John W.	133	WA	19	H.S.+	Student	KIA (RAF)
Watkins, Vivian E.	121	CA	31	H.S.+	Manager	KOAS (RAF)
Weir, Jack W.	71	CA		H.S.	A/C Factory	KOAS (RAF)
Whedon, Samuel F.	133	CA	21	H.S.+	Student	KOAS (RAF)
White, William J.	133	IL	20	H.S.+	Student	KOAS (RAF)
Whitlow, Gordon H.	71	WY	21	College		KIA (US)
Wicker, Walter C.	133	IL	17	H.S.	Student	KIA (RAF)
Willis, Donald K.	121	IN				
Wolfe, Roland L.	133	NE	23	H.S.+	Pilot	
Wright, Gilbert G.	133	PA	22	College	Policeman	POW (RAF)
Young, Donald A.	121	KS	22	H.S.+	Student	
Young, Norman D.	121	OR	25		Life Guard	KIA (RAF)
Zavakos, Frank G..	71	OH	24	H.S.+	Student	KOAS (RAF)

British Eagle Squadron Pilots

Name	Squadron	WWII Fate
Ambrose, Charles F.	71	
Bitmead, Ernest R.	71	
Brettell, Edward G.	133	KOAS (RAF)
Brown, George A.	133	
Churchill, Walter M.	71	KIA (RAF)
Gilbert, Humphrey T.	71	KOAS (RAF)
Johnston, Hugh A. S.	133	
Kennard, Hugh C.	121	
Meares, Stanley T.	71	KOAS (RAF)
Powell, Peter R.	121	
Scott, George W.	133	
Thomas, Eric H.	133	
Tongue, Reginald E.	71	
Wilkinson, Royce C.	121	
Williams, W. Dudley	121	
Woodhouse, Henry de C. A.	71	KIA (RAF)

Eagle Squadron Movements

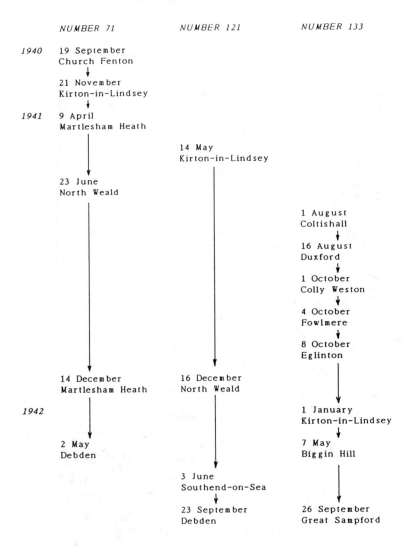

NUMBER 71   NUMBER 121   NUMBER 133

1940   19 September
Church Fenton
↓
21 November
Kirton-in-Lindsey
↓

1941   9 April
Martlesham Heath

14 May
Kirton-in-Lindsey

23 June
North Weald

1 August
Coltishall
↓
16 August
Duxford
↓
1 October
Colly Weston
↓
4 October
Fowlmere
↓
8 October
Eglinton

14 December   16 December
Martlesham Heath   North Weald

1942

1 January
Kirton-in-Lindsey
↓
7 May
Biggin Hill

2 May
Debden

3 June
Southend-on-Sea
↓
23 September
Debden

26 September
Great Sampford

All three Eagle Squadrons were deactivated 29 September 1942.

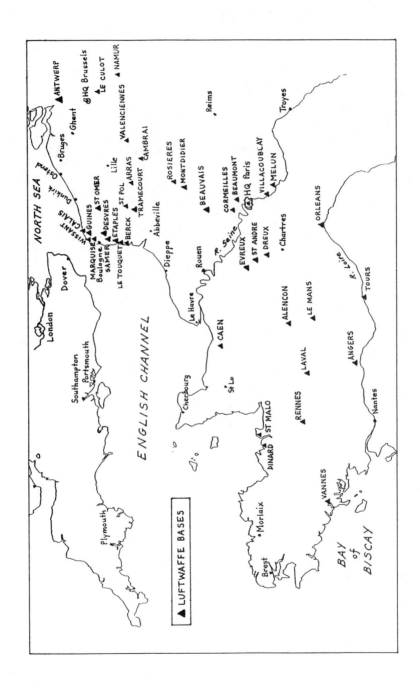

NORTH SEA

ANTWERP

GHQ Brussels

LE CULOT

NAMUR

Bruges

Ghent

VALENCIENNES

Reims

Troyes

Ostend

Dunkirk

Lille

CAMBRAI

ARRAS

TRAMECOURT

ROSIERES

MONTDIDIER

ST OMER

ST POL

BEAUVAIS

DESVRES

CORMEILLES

BEAUMONT

GHQ Paris

VILLACOUBLAY

MELUN

MARQUISE

GUINES

WISSANT

CALAIS

Boulogne

SAMER

ETAPLES

BERCK

Abbeville

LE TOUQUET

ORLEANS

Dieppe

Rouen

R. Seine

EVREUX

ST ANDRE

DREUX

Chartres

R. Loire

TOURS

Dover

London

Southampton

Portsmouth

Le Havre

CAEN

ALENCON

LE MANS

ANGERS

Plymouth

Cherbourg

St Lo

LAVAL

Nantes

RENNES

DINARD

ST MALO

VANNES

Morlaix

Brest

ENGLISH CHANNEL

BAY of BISCAY

LUFTWAFFE BASES

NOTES

CHAPTER 1

1. Letter, Donald Ross to the author, November 5, 1987. (Hereafter cited as Ross Letter.)

2. Interview, John Campbell with the author, Chula Vista, California, September 1, 1987. (Hereafter cited as Campbell Interview.)

3. Letter, Alida Scarborough Adams to the author, October 23, 1987. Mrs. Adams is Ross Orden Scarborough's sister. (Copy in author's files.)

4. Letter, LeRoy Gover to the author, October 15, 1987. (Hereafter cited as Gover Letter.)

5. Interview, Leo Nomis with the author, Pasadena, California, August 31, 1987. (Hereafter cited as Nomis Interview.)

6. Interview, Steve Pisanos with the author, San Diego, California, September 2, 1987. (Hereafter cited as Pisanos Interview.) Chesley G. Peterson, "Crash Landing," in Donald Robinson, *The Day I Was Proudest To Be An American*, Garden City, New York, 1958, pp. 125-129.

7. Interview, LeRoy Gover with the author, Palo Alto, California, September 10, 1987. (Hereafter cited as Gover Interview.)

8. Gover Letter.

9. One of the best sources for the development of aviation between World Wars I and II is C. R. Roseberry, *The Challenging Skies*, Garden City, New York, 1966. A delightful and valuable account of Americans and the airplane during the first half of this century is Joseph J. Corn, *The Winged Gospel*, New York, 1983.

10. Wesley Frank Craven and James Lea Cate, *The Army Air Forces in World War II*, Chicago, 1948, p. 41. This seven-volume series, completed in 1958, is the only comprehensive consideration of the use of air power in World War II. (Hereafter cited as Craven and Cate.)

11. Peter Wykeham, *Fighter Command*, London, 1960, pp. 64-65. (Hereafter cited as Wykeham.)

12. Wykeham, p. 62.

13. Craven and Cate, p. 86.

14. Craven and Cate, p. 89.

15. L. S. Stavrianos, *The World Since 1500*, Englewood Cliffs, New Jersey, p. 557.

16. Interview, Carroll McColpin with the author, Novato, California, September 8, 1987. (Hereafter cited as McColpin Interview.)

17. *The Sunday Times*, London, date unknown, p. 1.

18. *The Sunday Times*, London, date unknown, p. 2.

19. There are scores of volumes about the Battle of Britain. These include such standard books as Winston Churchill, *Their Finest Hour* (Boston, 1949); Volumes 1-3 of his *The Second World War* (London, 1948); William Shirer, *The Rise and Fall of the Third Reich* (London, 1964): Dennis Richards, *Royal Air Force, 1939-45* (London, 1953). An excellent little volume is the British Air Ministry, *The Battle of Britain* (New York, 1941). I also consulted Peter Townsend, *The Odds Against Us* (New York, 1987); Lee Kennett, *A History of Strategic Bombing* (New York, 1982); James Spaight, *The Battle of Britain* (London, 1941); Norman Gelb, *Scramble: A Narrative History of the Battle of Britain* (New York, 1985); Peter Wykeham, Fighter Command (London, 1960).

20. Letter, Charles Sweeny to the author, July 22, 1987. (Copy in the author's files.)

21. Letter, Jim Griffin to the author, November 5, 1987. (Hereafter cited as Griffin Letter.)

22. The Lafayette Escadrille is the subject of a number of books. The best is Philip M. Flammer, *The Vivid Air: The Lafayette Escadrille* (Athens, Ga., 1981). I also consulted Alan Clark, *Aces High: The War in the Air Over the Western Front, 1914-18* (London, 1973); Herbert M. Mason, *The Lafayette Escadrille* (New York, 1964); Bert Hall and John J. Niles, *One Man's War* (New York, 1980); Ralph Michaelis, *From Bird Cage to Battle Plane* (New York, 1943); Christopher Shores, *Fighter Aces* (London, 1975).

23. The Flying Tigers are among the most written about flying units of World War II. Among the many books on the subject are Ron Heiferman, *Flying Tiger: Chennault in China* (New York, 1971); Fourteenth Air Force Association, *Chennault's Flying Tigers* (Dallas, 1982); Anna Chennault, *Chennault and the Flying Tigers* (New York, 1963); Robert Lee Scott, *Flying Tiger: Chennault of China* (Garden City, 1959); Claire Chennault, *Way of a Fighter* (New York, 1949); Charles R. Bond and Terry Anderson, *A Flying Tigers Diary* (College Station, 1984).

24. Interview, Chesley Peterson with the author, Ogden, Utah, September 14, 1987. (Hereafter cited as Peterson Interview.)

25. For general information on the life of Colonel Charles Sweeny I have used Donald McCormick, *One Man's Wars: The Story of Charles Sweeny, Soldier of Fortune* (London, 1972); Ralph Michaelis, *From Bird Cage to Battle Plane* (New York, 1943); Herbert M. Mason, *The Lafayette Escadrille* (New York, 1964); Brian Kennerly, *The Eagles Roar* (Washington, 1979); Earl Boebert, "The Eagle Squadrons," *American Aviation Historical Society Journal*, Spring 1964, pp. 3-20.

26. Interview, Charles Sweeny with the author, London, March 20, 1988. (Hereafter cited as Sweeny Interview.)

27. Sweeny Interview.

28. Letter, Robert Sweeny to Vern Haugland, March 6, year unknown (used with permission of Charles Sweeny). Letters, Charles Sweeny to Vern Haugland, September 5, 1974, and June 24, 1980 (used with permission of Charles Sweeny). Eagle Squadron Association Address List, January 1987. (Copies in the author's file.)

29. Sweeny Interview.

30. Letter, Charles Sweeny to the author, July 22, 1987. (Copy in the author's file.)

31. Sweeny Interview. Telephone interview, Sir Harold Balfour with the author, London, March 24, 1988. Letter, Charles Sweeny to the author, July 22, 1987.

32. Letter, Charles Sweeny to Vern Haugland, September 5, 1974 (used with permission of Charles Sweeny). Competition between programs never became an issue because as the war progressed there were sufficient volunteers and the British sent a significant number of RCAF pilots to training centers around the United States. Although the entire plan was focused on the US there was apparently no American participation in the decision process.

33. Letters, Charles Sweeny to the author, July 22, 1987, and October 10, 1987.

34. *New York Sun*, October 9, 1940.

35. Sweeny Interview.

36. Earl Boebert, "The Eagle Squadrons," *American Aviation Historical Society Journal*, Spring 1964, p. 8. (Hereafter cited as Boebert, "The Eagle Squadrons.")

37. Peterson interview. Boebert, "The Eagle Squadrons," p. 8.

38. Sweeny Interview.

39. *New York Times*, October 9, 1940.

40. *New York Times, New York Sun, New York Herald Tribune, Washington Post, Baltimore Sun, Oakland Tribune*, October 9, 1940.

41. Sweeny Interview.

CHAPTER 2

1. Peter Kilduff, "Clayton Knight, No. 206 Squadron, RAF," *Cross and Cockade*, Spring 1967, p. 29. *The Oakland Tribune*, September 8, 1945. Also see Interview with Clayton Knight by Robert E. Hays, 8 March 1955, in file MS 766, Clayton Knight Papers, US Air Force Academy Library.

2. Interview, George Sperry with the author, Pleasanton, California, September 11, 1987. (Hereafter cited as Sperry Interview.) Boebert, "The Eagle Squadrons," p. 16.

3. RAF Narrative, *Aircrew Training, 1934-1942*, Air Historical Branch, Air Ministry, London, pp. 566-568. (Hereafter referred to as *Aircrew Training, 1934-1942*.) Air Publication 3233, *Flying Training*,

Air Ministry, London, 1952, pp. 77-79. Johnnie Houlton, *Spitfire Strikes* (London: 1985), pp. 7-8.

4. Clayton Knight with Thomas Fleming, *Aid To Victory*, unpublished manuscript, p. 2. (Hereafter cited as Knight, *Aid to Victory*.)

5. Knight, *Aid To Victory*, p. 6.

6. McColpin Interview.

7. William Stevenson, *A Man Called Intrepid*, New York, 1976, p. 345. C. Herman Pritchett, *The American Constitution*, New York, 1968, p. 766.

8. Federal Bureau of Investigation Report, John Edgar Hoover to Adolf A. Berle, Jr., Assistant Secretary of State, 29 January 1942, p. 3. National Archives, Washington, DC, file 800.00B Homer Smith. (Hereafter cited as FBI Report.)

9. Department of State Memoranda, August 31, 1940; June 21, 1941; June 23, 1941; July 3, 1941.

10. Knight, *Aid To Victory*, p. 8.

11. Knight, *Aid To Victory*, p. 11.

12. Clayton Knight Committee Questionnaire, National Archives, Washington, DC, file 800.00B Homer Smith.

13. Knight, *Aid To Victory*, pp. 11-12.

14. Interview Number Two with Charles Cook by the author, West Covina, California, July 2, 1989. (Hereafter cited as Cook Interview Number Two.) For further discussion of the German information issue see Chapter 7.

15. Letters, Clayton Knight Committee to James R. Heppel, June 7, 1941; July 29, 1941; September 18, 1941. National Archives, Washington, DC, file 800.00B Homer Smith.

16. Boebert, "The Eagle Squadrons," p. 9.

17. FBI Report, pp. 2-3.

18. *The Oakland Tribune*, August 28, 1940.

19. Letter, William H. Byington, Jr., Chairman of the Aviation League of the United States to Mr. J. C. Green, Chief Munitions Control, Department of State, August 19, 1940. National Archives, Washington, DC, file 800.00B Homer Smith.

20. Specifically, the allegations against Sweeny charged that he and a Colonel Wadell had made promises to pilots regarding employment in Canada that the Canadian government refused to honor, and that, although the individuals involved agreed to serve in Canada, they were actually being recruited to go overseas. The charges against Knight were substantially the same, but added the issue of an oath of allegiance and citizenship, and named Knight, Homer Smith, and Captain Ernest Benway, who was the Knight contact at the Hollywood-Roosevelt Hotel in Los Angeles, as the culprits. Letter, Pierrepont Moffat, American Legation, Ottawa, Canada to the Secretary of State, Washington, DC, August 15, 1940. National Archives, Washington,

DC, file 800.00B Homer Smith. Attached is the application for duty in the RCAF along with a questionnaire on health and personal data.

21. *Aircrew Training, 1943-1942,* p. 566.

22. Sweeny Interview. Letter, Charles Sweeny to the author, July 22, 1987.

23. Knight, *Aid To Victory,* pp. 16-17. Charles Sweeny denies the Knight account of the termination of his active recruiting in the United States. Sweeny Interview.

24. FBI Report, p. 2.

25. FBI Report, p. 3.

26. John DuFour answer to questionnaire, July 30, 1987. Interview, William Dunn witih the author, Colorado Springs, Colorado, 26 April 1990. (Hereafter cited as Dunn Interview.) William R. Dunn, *Fighter Pilot: The First American Ace of World War II* (Lexington, Kentucky, 1982) p. 30. (Hereafter cited as Dunn, *Fighter Pilot.*)

27. Letter, James E. Griffin to the author, August 1, 1987. (Hereafter cited as Griffin Letter Number 2.)

28. Richard Alexander answer to questionnaire, July 29, 1987. (Hereafter cited as Alexander Questionnaire.) Gilmore Daniel answer to questionnaire, July 28, 1987. (Hereafter cited as Daniel Questionnaire.)

29. Vernon Parker answer to questionnaire, August 3, 1987. (Hereafter cited as Parker Questionnaire.)

30. Letter, Ervin Miller to the author, November 5, 1987. (Hereafter cited as Miller Letter.)

31. Edward Miluck answer to questionnaire, August 1987.

32. "U. S. Fliers Aid British," *Washington Post,* August 20, 1940. This article is representative of dozens that appeared in papers nationwide.

33. Grover C. Hall, Jr., *1000 Destroyed: The Life and Times of the 4th Fighter Group* (Fallbrook Ca., 1978), p.14. (Hereafter cited as Hall, *1000 Destroyed.*) Paul Ellington answer to questionnaire, August 1987. Don Smith answer to questionnaire, August 1987.

34. Roscoe Interview.

35. Letter, George Carpenter to the author, August 24, 1987.

36. Interview, John Brown with the author, San Diego, California, 2 September 1987. (Hereafter cited as John Brown Interview.)

37. Campbell Interview.

38. Interview, William Geiger with the author, Pasadena, California, September 3, 1987. (Hereafter cited as Geiger Interview.)

39. Interview, Bill Edwards with the author, Colorado Springs, Colorado, September 16, 1987. (Hereafter cited as Edwards Interview.)

40. Peterson Interview.

41. Questionnaires, interviews, and letters cited above and below or in the bibliography.

42. Edward T. Folliard, "Eagle Squadron," *Washington Post*, April 2, 1941.

43. Sweeny Interview. Interview, Royce Wilkinson with the author, Minster, Sheppy, Kent, England, March 22, 1988. (Hereafter cited as Wilkinson Interview.) Letter, The Right Honorable Lord Martonmere, P.C., G.B.E., K.C.M.G., to the author, August 19, 1987. (Hereafter cited as Martonmere Letter.)

44. Peterson interview.

45. Interview, Reade Tilley with the author, Colorado Springs, Colorado, February 11, 1988. (Hereafter cited as Tilley Interview.) Charles Sweeny does not remember if Tilley called him or not but considers it very possible since he was periodically a liaison between the Americans flyers and the Air Ministry. Sweeny Interview.

46. Interview, Bert Stewart with the author, San Diego, California, October 15, 1988. (Hereafter cited as Stewart Interview.)

47. Griffin Letter.

48. Letter, Nancy Wicker Eilan to the author, March 1, 1988. Mrs. Eilan is Walter Wicker's sister.

49. George Carpenter answer to questionnaire, August 1987.

50. Gene B. Fetrow answer to questionnaire, September 1987.

51. Interview, Art Roscoe with the author, Hollywood, California, September 4, 1987. (Hereafter cited as Roscoe Interview.)

52. Edwards Interview.

53. Interview, William Geiger with the author, Pasadena, California, September 3, 1987. (Hereafter cited as Geiger Interview.)

54. H. H. Strickland, *War and Flight; Autobiography and Diary*, unpublished manuscript, pp. 2-3. Copy given to the author by Mrs. Pat Strickland. (Hereafter cited as Strickland manuscript.)

55. Strickland Manuscript, pp. 3-21.

56. Interview, Don Blakeslee with the author, Colorado Springs, Colorado, September 23, 1989. (Hereafter cited as Blakeslee Interview.)

57. Alfred Price, *Spitfire at War*, p. 76.

58. Leon Blanding answer to questionnaire, August 1, 1987.

59. Vern Haugland, *The Eagle Squadrons* (New York, 1979), p. vii. (Hereafter cited as Haugland, *The Eagle Squadrons*.)

60. "Eagles Switch to U.S. Army," *Life*, November 2, 1942, p. 40.

61. Wilkinson Interview.

62. Sweeny Interview. Martonmere Letter.

CHAPTER 3

1. *Liberty*, March 29, April 5, 12, 19, 26, 1941. Sweeny Interview. Biographical summaries, Andrew Mamedoff, Eugene Tobin, and Vernon Keough, Historical Archives of the Air Ministry, London.

2. Boebert, "The Eagle Squadrons," pp. 8-9.

3. Peterson Interview.

4. Stanley M. Ulanoff, *Fighter Pilot*, New York, 1986, pp. 76-78. Boebert, "The Eagle Squadrons," p. 9.

5. Biographical Summary, Philip Leckrone, Historical Archives of the Air Ministry, London.

6. Arthur G. Donahue, "Tally Ho!" *Saturday Evening Post*, May 3, 1941, pp. 12-13.

7. Arthur Donahue, *Tally-Ho!: Yankee in a Spitfire*, New York, 1941, pp. 26, 29, 48. This well-written book describes Donahue's experiences in the RAF. Biographical Summary, Arthur Donahue, Historical Archives of the Air Ministry, London.

8. Roscoe Interview.

9. *Squadron Operations Record Book, Number 71 Squadron*, Microfilm, Special Collections Division, US Air Force Academy Library. (Hereafter cited as *71 Record Book*.)

10. "Eagle Squadron of U.S. Fliers Will Aid Defense of Britain," *Salt Lake Tribune*, October 9, 1940.

11. "Eagle Squadron, RAF, Biographical Notes on Pilots of 'Eagle Squadron,'" Eagle Squadron File, Ministry of Defense, London. *71 Record Book.*

12. Air Ministry Bulletin No. 1928, *Formation of American "Eagle Squadron," The King Approves Special Badge*, Tuesday, October 8, 1940. Historical Archives, Air Ministry, London. The motto and description of the emblem were given to the author by Edwin Taylor and are in the author's files.

13. "U.S. Pilots Put British Planes Through Paces," *New York Herald Tribune*, October 14, 1940, p. 2.

14. *Life*, April 21, 1941, p. 51.

15. The best source on the CPTP is a short book by Patricia Strickland, the wife of Eagle Harold Strickland who worked as an administrator for the CPTP prior to enlisting in the RAF. It is titled *The Puttputt Air Force*, and was published by the Department of Transportation, Washington, DC, in 1971. It is unfortunately out of print and very few copies exist.

16. Interviews, Edwin Taylor with the author, San Clemente, California, August 27 and September 1, 1987. (Hereafter cited as Taylor Interviews.)

17. Ervin Miller biographical paper, Eagle Squadron Association files. (Copy in the author's files. Hereafter cited as Miller Biography.)

18. McColpin Interview. Nomis Interview. Interview, Marion Jackson with the author, Aptos, California, September 10, 1987. (Hereafter cited as Jackson Interview.)

19. Taylor Interviews.

20. Campbell Interview. Roscoe Interview.

21. Gene Fetrow answer to questionnaire, September, 1987. Robert Priser answer to questionnaire, August, 1987.

22. Taylor Interviews. Gover Interview. Nomis Interview. Interview, James Gray with the author, Dublin, California, 11 September 1987. (Hereafter cited as Gray Interview.)

23. Nomis interview. Most of my information about the RAF training program is from two documents. RAF Narrative, *Aircrew Training, 1934-1942*, Air Ministry, London, pp 463-485. RAF Monograph, *Anglo-American Collaboration in the Air War Over North-West Europe*, Air Historical Branch, Air Ministry, London, pp. 45-47, 63-67. The most complete study of the entire American pilot training program is Willard Wiener, *Two Hundred Thousand Flyers*, Washington, The Infantry Journal, 1945.

24. Peterson Interview.

25. Interview, Reade Tilley with the author, US Air Force Academy, Colorado, August 2, 1988. (Hereafter cited as Tilley Interview Number Two.)

26. Richard Alexander, *They Called Me Dixie*, Hemet, California, 1988, p. 83.

27. Tilley Interview. Blakeslee Interview.

28. Letter, Royal Canadian Air Force Casualties Officer to Mrs. V. Hammer, May 7, 1942. Copy in author's files.

29. Thomas A. Bailey, *A Diplomatic History of the American People*, New York, 1964, pp.713-718. C. Herman Pritchett, *The American Constitution*, New York, 1968, p. 766.

30. Telegram, Department of State, Washington, DC, to American Embassy, London, June 18, 1940. National Archives, Washington, DC, File 842.2311.

31. Memorandum, British Subject File, December 13, 1940. National Archives, Washington, DC, File 842.2311.

32. Certificate of Commissioning, RAF. Given to the author by Edwin Taylor. (Copy in the author's files.)

33. "State Department Not Looking Into American's Legal Status," *New York Times*, November 21, 1940. Several sources and a number of Eagles believe that the order to not interfere with the RAF recruiting effort in the United States came from President Roosevelt himself. I have been unable to find any documentation to either prove or disprove this theory, but it is certainly possible given the number of well-placed individuals who were involved with the Clayton Knight Committees and the very close relationship between President Roosevelt and Prime Minister Churchill. It is significant to compare the situation faced by the Eagles with that of the Flying Tigers. Because the latter were not becoming members of a foreign military as such, they did not risk the loss of their citizenship although the issue was still specifically addressed in the legislation that created the American Volunteer Group.

34. Letter, Senator Claude Pepper to Reade Tilley, Sr., February 19, 1941. Attached is a copy of Senate Bill S. 835. (Copy in the author's files.)

35. C. Herman Pritchett, *The American Constitution*, New York, 1868, pp. 767-768. US Code, Section 8, pp. 1059-1060.

36. McColpin Interview.

37. Pisanos Interview.

38. Jackson Interview.

39. Gray Interview.

40. Letter, H.A. Jones, Civil Liaison Officer, United Kingdom Air Liaison Mission, Ottawa, Canada to Morris Fessler, November 2, 1940. (Copy given to the author by Morris Fessler and is in the author's files.)

41. Cook Interview Number Two.

42. Miller Biography. Letter, Ervin Miller to the author, September, 1987.

43. Letter, Don Nee to Robert E. Hays, Jr., January 5, 1965. (Copy in the author's files. Hereafter cited as Nee-Hays Letter.)

44. LeRoy Gover Diary. (Copy in the author's files. Hereafter referred to as Gover Diary.)

45. Sperry Interview.

46. Interview, Robert Smith with the author, September 18, 1987, Alexandria, Virginia. (Hereafter referred to as Smith Interview.)

47. George Sperry, unpublished memoirs of his experience as an Eagle, given to the author by Sperry. (Copy in author's files. Hereafter referred to as Sperry Memoirs.) Miller Letter. Nee-Hays Letter. Strickland Manuscript, pp. 21-22.

48. Gover Diary.

49. Jackson Interview.

50. Smith Interview.

51. Telegram, Associated Press, New York, September 8, 1941. (Copy in the author's files.)

52. Carroll W. McColpin, "Sojourn of an Eagle," p. 4. (Copy in the author's files. Hereafter cited as McColpin, "Sojourn.")

53. Jackson Interview.

54. Sperry Memoirs.

55. Edwards Interview.

56. Miller Letter. Gover Diary. Campbell Interview.

57. McColpin Interview.

58. Taylor Interviews.

59. Nomis Interview. Gover Diary. Campbell Interview.

60. Geiger Interview.

61. All of the pilots arriving in England prior to June 1941 were sent to Uxbridge Depot. Due to overcrowding and the need for some ability to do military training, the RAF opened the reception center at

Bournemouth in the summer of 1941 and subsequent arrivals were sent there.

62. Roscoe Interview.

63. Pisanos Interview.

64. Miller letter.

65. Gover Diary.

66. Campbell Interview.

67. Sperry Memoirs.

68. Campbell interview.

69. Nomis interview.

70. Taylor interviews.

71. Sperry Memoirs.

72. *Aircrew Training*, pp. 497-500.

73. *Aircrew Training*, pp. 501-505.

74. Questionnaire completed by John Campbell, August 18, 1987.

75. Questionnaire completed by Donald Young, August 10, 1987.

76. Questionnaire completed by Ernie Beatie, July 28, 1987.

77. The Operational Training Units in January 1942 were: Number 51, Cranfield (Blenheim bomber); Number 52, Aston Down (Spitfire); Number 53, Llandow (Spitfire); Number 54, Church Fenton (Blenheim bomber); Number 55, Usworth (Hurricane); Number 56, Sutton Bridge (Hurricane); Number 57, Howarden (Spitfire); Number 58, Grangemouth (Spitfire); Number 59, Crosby (Hurricane); Number 60, East Fortune (Defiant); Number 61, Heston (Spitfire). *Aircrew Training*, p. 508.

78. Questionnaire, completed by Robert Priser, August 1, 1987.

79. *Aircrew Training*, p. 542.

80. Interview, Barry Mahon with the author, Hollywood, California, 4 September 1987. (Hereafter cited as Mahon Interview.) Jackson Interview.

81. Miller Letter.

82. *Aircrew Training*, pp. 542-543.

83. Questionnaire completed by Robert Smith, 11 August 1987.

84. Gray Interview. Peterson Interview.

85. Nomis Interview.

86. Gover Diary. Letter, LeRoy Gover to the author, August 2, 1988.

87. Dunn, *Fighter Pilot*, pp. 44-45. The most thorough information on the Hurricane is in Bill Gunston, *An Illustrated Guide to Allied Fighters of World War II*, Arco Publishing, Inc., New York, 1981, pp. 42-47.

88. Telephone interview, Bill Edwards with the author, February 18, 1988.

89. Wilkinson Interview.

90. Interview, General Johannes Steinhoff with the author, Colorado Springs, Colorado, July 29, 1988. (Hereafter cited as Steinhoff Interview.)

91. Edwin Taylor, unpublished manuscript, given to the author by Taylor. (Copy in the author's files.)

92. Roscoe Interview.

93. Jerry Scutts, *Spitfire in Action*, Squadron/Signal Publications, Carrollton, Texas, 1980. This is the complete book on the Spitfire and includes all the facts, figures and pictures to tell the story of the airplane.

94. Dunn Interview.

95. Roscoe Interview.

96. Tilley Interview.

97. The author examined an original Spitfire gunsight at the home of Reade Tilley on 11 February 1988.

CHAPTER 4

1. *Squadron Operations Record Book, Number 121 Squadron.* (Hereafter cited as 121 Record Book.)

2. *Squadron Operations Record Book, Number 133 Squadron.* (Hereafter cited as *133 Record Book.*)

3. Letter from Ervin Lloyd Miller to an unknown person, undated, copy in the author's files. Joseph Evans, Jr., "Eagle Squadron Asks 'Action' on Russian Front," *Herald Tribune* (New York), November 3, 1941. Sweeny Interview. Goodson Interview. Telephone Interview, Laddie Lucas with the author, London, March 24, 1988. (Hereafter cited as Lucas Interview.) Ervin Miller recalled that one group of sergeant pilots from the RCAF were assigned to a convoy going across the Atlantic by the Southern route when he came across in late 1941. "The poor chaps in the Southern convoy were torpedoed; one survivor was picked up but was again torpedoed. I met him a year later in the Eagle Club in London and he had just arrived. I've forgotten his name, I'm afraid." While there is no evidence that these pilots were to form a fourth Squadron, the story does agree with both Goodson's and Sweeny of what happened. In the November 3, 1941, *New York Herald Tribune*, an article about the Eagles noted, "A third Eagle squadron recently was posted to active duty with the RAF [that would be 133] while another is undergoing final training and a fifth is being formed." This is the only press account I could find referring to additional Eagle Squadrons.

4. *71 Record Book. 121 Record Book.* Basil Colier, *The Defense of the United Kingdom*, map 32. Dennis Richards, *Royal Air Force 1939-1945*, map facing page 164. John D. R. Rawlings, *Fighter Squadrons of the*

R.A.F. and Their Aircraft (London, 1976), pp. 175, 253, 271. (Hereafter cited as Rawlings, *Fighter Squadrons*.)

5. Taylor Interviews.

6. John Brown Interview.

7. Pisanos Interview.

8. Tilley Interview. Sperry Interview.

9. Taylor Interviews.

10. Taylor Interviews.

11. Examples of censorship are very evident in the letters sent home by LeRoy Gover. There are copies of several of these in the author's files.

12. Peterson Interview. "Parents Miss Lieutenant's Radio Talk," reference to Don Nee speaking from England, newspaper and date unknown. Copy in the author's files. Almos Interview.

13. *71 Record Book*.

14. Peterson Interview.

15. Peterson Interview.

16. *71 Record Book*.

17. Peterson Interview. Interview, Chesley Peterson with the author, San Diego, October 14, 1988. (Hereafter cited as Peterson Interview Number Two.)

18. *Washington Post*, "American Eagles Over Britain," October 23, 1940. *The Tribune-Sun* (San Diego), "Americans Will Fly as Unit in Fighting for England," October 22, 1940.

19. "U.S. Volunteer Flyers Saluted By Lady Aster," *Herald Tribune*, New York, December 6, 1940.

20. *71 Record Book*.

21. *Everybody's Weekly*, April 12, 1941, p 5.

22. Goodson Interview. Interview, Morris Fessler with the author, San Diego, October 14, 1988. (Hereafter cited as Fessler Interview.) Peterson Interview.

23. Martonmere Letter.

24. Cook Interview.

25. Taylor Interviews. Telephone Interview, Bill Edwards with the author, August 21, 1989.

26. Alfred Price, *World War II Fighter Conflict*, London, 1975, pp. 139-143. Blakeslee Interview. Tilley Interview.

27. Air Ministry Pamphlet ID/44/349, *Aircrew Training: Report on the Conference Held in the United Kingdom, January/February, 1942*. Ministry of Defense, Air Historical Branch Files, London, pp. 20-21.

28. Edwin Taylor, untitled notes. Copy in the author's files.

29. *Ten of My Rules for Air Fighting*, author unknown. Framed on the wall of the Air Historical Branch, Air Ministry, London. Taken on October 1, 1942 or 1943 from 61 OTU, Halsted.

30. James Saxon Childers, *War Eagles* (San Francisco, 1983), pp. 328-330. (Hereafter cited as Childers, *War Eagles*.) Interview, Fred

Almos with the author, San Diego, California, October 15, 1988. (Hereafter cited as Almos Interview.)

31. Peterson interview.

32. Sweeny Interview.

33. Wilkinson Interview. Peterson Interview Number Two.

34. *71 record Book*. Telephone Interview, Chesley Peterson with the author, November 10, 1988. Letters, W.E.G. Taylor to Vern Haugland, September 24, 1974, October 4, 1974. (Copies in author's files.) Rawlings, *Fighter Squadrons*, p. 175.

35. Wilkinson Interview. "Time Remembered: The Battle of Britain," newspaper and date unknown. Copy in the author's files.

36. *Everybody's Weekly*, London, April 12, 1941, p. 5.

37. Wilkinson Interview.

38. Peterson Interview Number Two. See Vern Haugland, *The Eagles War* (New York, 1982), pp. 215-222, for a complete explanation of the Kennerly fabrication.

39. Martonmere Letter.

40. Hall, *1000 Destroyed*, pp. 14-15.

41. Peterson Interview.

42. Geiger Interview.

43. Joe Durham answer to Eagle Questionaire. Martonmere Letter.

44. Stewart Interview.

45. *71 Record Book*.

46. *71 Record Book*.

47. *71 Record Book*.

48. H. H. Arnold, *Global Mission*, New York, 1949, p. 219. Interestingly, although Arnold makes a big story of the visit to the Eagles in his book, there is no mention of such a visit in his diary although the rest of the events of that particular day are documented in the exact order in which they occurred. The question obviously arises why Arnold wrote such a comment about the Eagles eight years later with aparently no documentation. Dairy of H. H. Arnold, Special Collections Division, US Air Force Academy Library.

49. Peterson Interview.

50. *71 Record Book*.

51. *71 Record Book*.

52. W. T. Yarbrough, "American Eagles Claw Germans to Celebrate Fourth of July," *New York World Telegram*, July 5, 1941. "American Air Unit Bags 3 Nazi Planes," *New York Times*, July 3, 1941. "Eagles to War," *Newsweek*, July 14, 1941, pp. 25-26. *71 Record Book*. Haugland, *The Eagle Squadrons*, pp.2-3.

53. Geiger Interview.

54. W. E. G. Taylor letter to Vern Haugland, October 4, 1974. (Copy in the author's files.)

55. Sweeny Interview.

56. *71 Record Book*.

57. Peterson Interview Number Two. Fessler Interview.

58. Gault MacGowen, "American Eagle Squadron Set For Air Action Against Nazis," *The Sun* (New York), March 19, 1941, p. 1.

59. J. Norman Lodge, "Eagle Squadron Shows Skill of Fighting Pilots," March 19, 1941, newspaper not identified. (Copy in author's files.)

60. "The New 'War Birds,'" *The Aeroplane*, March 28, 1941.

61. *The Illustrated London News*, March 29, 1941.

62. *71 Record Book.*

63. Fessler Interview.

64. Wilkinson Interview.

65. Stewart Interview.

66. Fessler Interview.

67. Interview, Roy Evans with the author, San Diego, California, October 13, 1988. (Hereafter cited as Evans Interview.)

68. Goodson Interview.

69. McColpin, "Sojourn," p. 9. Edwin Taylor, "Thoughts on the Eagles," undated manuscript given to the author by Edwin Taylor. (Copy in the author's files.)

70. Peterson Interview. Telephone Interview, Chesley Peterson with the author, November 10, 1988.

71. *New York Journal American*, November 2, 1941. "Eagle Squadron Leads R.A.F. in October Bag of Nazi Planes," *Herald Tribune* (New York), November 2, 1941. William H. Stoneman, "U.S. Airmen With British Fly Like Demons Eager for a Fight," *Chicago Daily News*, October 18, 1941. "Former Employer Calls Pilot 'Coolest' He Has Ever Known," *Oakland Tribune*, October 28, 1941.

72. Strickland Manuscript, p. 49.

73. "English, He Led the U.S. Eagles," *Daily Mail*, London, November 19, 1941.

74. Strickland Manuscript, p. 49. "Two More Eagle Flyers Win D.F.C. for Gallantry," *Herald Tribune* (New York), October 8, 1941. This article illustrates some of the problem the press had with differentiating between members of the Eagle Squadrons and Americans flying in any Squadron of the RAF. It identifies two Americans, Edward Alexander Morrison and James Haywood Little, as being Eagles and the first to win the D.F.C. Neither, however, was a member of an Eagle Squadron.

75. Peterson Interview Number Two. Bill Taylor's tenure as commander was really a political, rather than a merit, appointment since he had been part of the original Eagle Squadron agreement between Sweeny and the Air Ministry.

76. Wilkinson Interview.

77. *Time*, December 1, 1941, p. 23.

78. Peterson Interview.

79. Strickland Manuscript, p. 53.

80. McColpin Interview. Haugland, *The Eagle Squadrons*, p. 75.

81. Strickland Manuscript, p. 52.

82. Peterson Interview.

83. "U.S. Pilots in R.A.F. Eager to Come Home for Blow at Japan."

84. Peterson Interview.

85. Peterson Interview. Chesley Peterson taped answer to questionnaire. *71 Record Book. 121 Record Book.*

86. Telephone Interview, Carroll McColpin with the author, December 21, 1988. (Hereafter cited as McColpin Telephone Interview.)

87. Strickland Manuscript, p. 55.

88. Sweeny Interview.

89. Interview, Hugh Kennard with the author, London, March 24, 1988. (Hereafter cited as Kennard Interview.)

90. *121 Record Book.* Rawlings, *Fighter Squadrons*, pp. 175, 253.

91. Kennard Interview.

92. Wilkinson Interview.

93. Kennard Interview.

94. McColpin Telephone Interview.

95. Peterson Interview.

96. Kennard Interview.

97. Kennard Interview.

98. John Brown Interview.

99. James Griffin, "Flight to Martlesham," pp. 2-3. This article, in revised form, was published in *Air and Space*, as "Sea Serpents and Steel Forests," April/May 1988, pp. 30-31.

100. John Brown Interview.

101. Letter, Kenny John to the author, December 14, 1987. (Hereafter cited as Kenny John Letter. Copy in the author's files.)

102. Kenny John Letter.

103. Tilley Interview.

104. Taylor Interview.

105. Kenny John is a premier example of this relationship. In the late 1980s he played a key role in obtaining and rebuilding the Spitfire which now is on display at the San Diego, California, Air and Space Museum.

106. McColpin Telephone Interview.

107. Kennard Interview.

108. *121 Record Book.*

109. *121 Record Book.*

110. Wilkinson Interview.

111. McColpin Interview.

112. Wilkinson Interview.

113. John Brown Interview.

114. Cook Interview.

115. Taylor Interviews.

116. McColpin Interview.

117. Taylor Interviews.

118. *121 Record Book.*

119. Joseph S. Evans, Jr., "2nd Eagle Unit, Eager for Fight, To Get It Soon," *Herald Tribune*, New York, November 29, 1941.

120. Wilkinson Interview. Tilley Interview.

121. Kennard Interview.

122. Kennard Interview. Sweeny Interview.

123. John Brown Interview.

124. Sperry Memoirs, p. 16.

125. *133 Record Book.* Sperry Memoirs, p. 13.

126. *133 Record Book. Oakland Tribune*, September 29, 1941.

127. Sperry Memoirs, p. 16.

128. *133 Record Book.* Sperry Memoirs, p. 15.

129. *133 Record Book.*

130. Cook Interview.

131. Interview, Eric Doorly with the author, San Diego, October 15, 1988. (Hereafter cited as Doorly Interview.)

132. *133 Record Book.* Jackson Interview.

133. Telephone Interview, Edwin Taylor with the author, December 23, 1988.

134. Sperry Memoirs, pp. 14, 19.

135. Taylor Interviews.

136. Letter, George Sperry to Vern Haugland, March 3, 1975. (Used with permission of George Sperry. Copy in author's files.)

137. *133 Record Book.*

138. Telephone Interview, Edwin Taylor with the author, December 23, 1988. *133 Record Book.*

139. *133 Record Book.*

140. Letter, Air Historical Branch, Ministry of Defense, London, 13 November 1980. (Copy in author's files.)

141. Letter, Air Historical Branch, Ministry of Defense, London, 13 November 1980. Charley Gallagher, "Eagles over Eglinton," *Friends of the Eighth Newsletter*, June 1988, pp. 1-2. (Hereafter cited as Gallagher, "Eagles over Eglinton.") Sperry Memoirs p. 18.

142. Walter Wicker's Log Book provided by Nancy Wicker Eilan. (Copy in author's files.)

143. *133 Record Book.* Sperry Memoirs, p. 20.

144. Denver Miner Memoirs, undated, p. 5. (Copy in the author's files.)

145. Telephone Interview, Edwin Taylor with the author, December 23, 1988.

146. Letter, Walter Wicker to Walter Wicker, Sr., early 1942, provided by Nancy Wicker Eilan. (Copy in author's files.)

147. Gallagher, "Eagles over Eglinton," p. 2.

148. Sperry Memoirs, p. 21.

149. Gallagher, "Eagles over Eglinton," p. 2.

150. *133 Record Book*. Gallagher, "Eagles over Eglinton," p. 2. Telephone Interview, Edwin Taylor with the author, December 23, 1988. Sperry Memoirs, p. 22.

CHAPTER 5

1. *121* and *133 Record Books*. Telephone Interview, Edwin Taylor with the author, April 14, 1989.

2. Strickland Manuscript, pp. 56-59.

3. Tilley Interview.

4. Kennard Interview.

5. Harold Strickland's Diary. (Copy in the author's files. Hereafter cited as Strickland Diary.)

6. Sperry Memoirs, p. 34.

7. *133 Record Book*.

8. *121 Record Book*.

9. "Definitions of Fighter Operations," provided by Edwin Taylor. (Copy in author's files.)

10. Steinhoff Interview.

11. 4th Fighter Group Operational Slides, National Archives, Suitland, Maryland. (Hereafter cited as 4th Fighter Group Slides.)

12. "US Air Force Official Policy Concerning the Term 'Ace,'" The Alfred F. Simpson Historical Research Center, Maxwell Air Force Base, Alabama, October 20, 1975. (Copy in author's files.) Peterson Interview. Roscoe Interview. 4th Fighter Group Operational Slides. Those former Eagles listed as aces in the US Army Air Force include Don Gentile, Jim Goodson, Duane Beeson, Don Blakeslee, George Carpenter, Steve Pisanos, James Clark, Howard Hively, Joe Bennett, Raymond Care, James Happel, Kenneth Smith, Roy Evans, and Robert Nelson.

13. Tilley Interview.

14. Edwin Taylor, "Known but Unknown," unpublished manuscript. (Copy in the author's files.)

15. *71 Record Book*.

16. *Daily Routine Orders*, R.A.F. Station, Kirton Lindsey, Gainsborough, Lincolnshire, July 12, 1941. (Copy in the author's files.)

17. Edwards Interview.

18. Taylor Interviews.

19. Doorly Interview. Cook Interview.

20. *71, 121, 133 Record Books*.

21. US Army, Current Intelligence Section, "Interviews with 15 Pilots of Former Eagle Squadrons," December 17, 1942. This interview was with James Daley. Microfilm roll number A-1271, Office of Air Force History, Bolling AFB, Washington, DC.

22. Edwards Interview.

23. John Brown Interview.

24. McColpin Interview.

25. Taylor Interviews.

26. Roscoe Interview.

27. Quote from an unknown author. Copy in the author's files.

28. Taylor Interviews.

29. Gover Interview.

30. Interview, Don Young with the author, San Diego, California, October 14, 1988. (Hereafter cited as Young Interview.)

31. Interview, LeRoy Gover with the author, San Carlos, California, July 21, 1989.

32. Sweeny Interview.

33. John Brown Interview.

34. Mahon Interview.

35. Cook Interview. Telephone Interview, James Clark with the author, February 4, 1989. (Hereafter cited as Clark Interview.)

36. Taylor Interviews.

37. Miller Biography.

38. Mrs. Ervin Miller Memoir, undated. (Copy in the author's files.)

39. Denver Miner Memoir, p.2. (Copy in the author's files.)

40. John Brown Interview.

41. Cook Interview.

42. Evans Interview.

43. Sperry Interview.

44. McColpin, "Sojourn," p. 13.

45. John Brown Interview.

46. Memoir about Bert Stewart by an unknown author, undated. (Copy in the author's files.) The story was confirmed during the Stewart Interview.

47. Evans Interview.

48. Interview, Gene Fetrow with the author, San Diego, California, October 14, 1988. (Hereafter cited as Fetrow Interview.)

49. Strickland Manuscript, p. 63.

50. Sperry Memoirs, p. 37.

51. *121 Record Book*.

52. Campbell Interview.

53. *71, 121, 133, Pilot Roster*. (Copy in author's files.) Haugland, *The Eagle Squadrons*, pp. 121, 191.

54. Williamson Murray, *Strategy for Defeat: The Luftwaffe, 1933-1945* (Maxwell Air Force Base, Alabama, 1983), p. 134. (Hereafter cited as Murray, *Strategy for Defeat*.)

55. Steinhoff Interview. Murray, *Strategy for Defeat*, p. 134.

56. Letter, Leo Nomis to Vern Haugland, January 17, 1975. Used with permission of Leo Nomis. (Copy in the author's files.)

57. Steinhoff Interview.

58. Observations about the Me 109 cockpit are from the author's experience sitting in the cockpit of that aircraft at the Headquarters of the Confederate Air Force, Harlingen, Texas, February 25, 1988.

59. Headquarters, Confederate Air Force, 25 February 1988.

60. Much of the information in this section comes from the author's interview with General Johannes Steinhoff, a famous German ace in World War II who shot down 176 aircraft, most of them while flying the Me 109. While there are many books with large sections about the Me 109, I have relied primarily on Bill Gunston, *German, Italian and Japanese Fighters of World War II*, Arco Publishing Co., New York, 1980, pp. 58-63. I have also used conversations with various Eagle Squadron members, some of whom have talked at length with German pilots, and my own experience at the Confederate Air Force Headquarters, Harlingen, Texas.

61. Griffin Letter.

62. Telephone interview, author with Bill Edwards, 18 February 1988, Colorado Springs, Colorado. Letter, Jim Griffin to the author, August 1, 1987. (Copy in the author's files.)

63. Steinhoff Interview.

64. Steinhoff Interview. The source for most of my technical information on the Focke-Wulf FW 190 is Bill Gunston, *An Illustrated Guide to German, Italian and Japanese Fighters of World War II*, Arco Publishing, Inc., New York, 1980, pp. 24-28. Another excellent source for aircraft comparison is Alfred Price, *World War II Fighter Conflict*, London, 1975. The figures on the Focke-Wulf FW190 and the Spitfire are on pp. 106-107.

65. *133 Record Book.*

66. Telegram from the Chief of the Air Staff, Ottawa, Ontario, to Mrs. V. Hammer. (Copy in author's files.)

67. Letter from Squadron Leader E. H. Thomas to Mrs. Victor Hammer, April 29, 1942. (Copy in the author's files.)

68. Letter from the King of England to Mrs. V. Hammer. (Copy in the author's files along with other notes and letters pertaining to Wicker's death.)

69. "'Singing Lady' Carries on for Child Care—Son Died at Front," unidentified newspaper. (Copy in author's files.)

70. *Report of the Death of an American Citizen*, June 1, 1942 and June 23, 1942. (Copies in the author's files.)

71. Nancy Wicker Eilan, *A True Story of An American Family*, 1985, pp. 14-15. (Copy in the author's files.)

72. Graham Wallace, *RAF at Biggin Hill*, London, 1957, p. 223. (Hereafter cited as Wallace, *RAF at Biggin Hill.*)

73. *No. 133 (Eagle Squadron) RAF Squadron History*, p. 16. (Hereafter cited as *133 History*. Copy in the author's files.)

74. *133 History*, p. 16.

75. Cook Interview. Wallace, *RAF at Biggin Hill*, p. 225.

76. *133 History*, p. 19.

77. Edwin Taylor Manuscript. (Copy in the author's files.)

78. Steinhoff Interview.

79. *133 Squadron History*, p. 26. "133 Eagle Squadron Pilots Order of Joining Squadron." (Copy supplied by Charles Cook, in the author's files.)

80. *121 Record Book.*

81. Donald Young Biography Sheet. (Hereafter cited as Young Biography. Copy in the author's files.)

82. *121 Record Book.*

83. Tape sent to the author by Ernie Beaty, September 22, 1988. (Tape in author's files.)

84. *121 Record Book.* Young Biography.

85. *121 Record Book.*

86. *71 Record Book.*

87. Strickland Manuscript, pp. 67-69.

88. Letter from Leo Nomis to Vern Haugland, January 17, 1975. (Used with Leo Nomis' permission.)

89. John Brown Interview.

90. Leo Nomis Memoirs, pp. 9-11. (Copy in the author's files.)

91. Sperry Interview.

92. *71 Record Book.*

93. *71 Record Book.*

94. *71 Record Book.* Strickland Manuscript, pp. 78-79.

95. McColpin, "Sojourn," p. 9.

96. McColpin, "Sojourn," pp. 10-11.

97. Gover Diary.

98. Telephone Interview, LeRoy Gover with the author, September 5, 1989.

99. *71 Record Book.* Strickland Manuscript, p. 80.

100. Peterson Interview. *71 Record Book.* Strickland Manuscript, pp. 81-82.

101. *71 Record Book.*

102. Roscoe Interview.

103. Almos Interview.

104. Telephone Interview, Edwin Taylor with the author, January 24, 1988. Peterson Interview. Roscoe Interview. William Boehnel, "Eagle Squadron has Thrilling Flying Scenes," *New York World Telegram*, July 3, 1942. "Cinema-'Eagle Squadron,'" *Time*, July 13, 1942, pp. 86-87. "Eagles True and False," *Newsweek*, July 6, 1942, p. 59. "Movie of the Week: Eagle Squadron," *Life*, June 29, 1942, pp. 62-64.

105. *133 Squadron History*, p. 26.

106. Taylor Interviews. Telephone Interview, Edwin Taylor with the author, January 24, 1989.

107. Strickland Manuscript, pp. 84-85. Strickland Diary, p. 42.

108. *71* and *133 Record Books*. Strickland Manuscript, p. 85. Graham Wallace, *RAF at Biggin Hill*, London, 1957, pp. 227-229.

109. Winston Churchill, *The Hinge of Fate*, Boston, 1950, pp. 509-511.

110. *133 Squadron History*, pp. 27-28.

111. Letter, Richard Alexander to the author, October 8, 1988. (Copy in the author's files.) Richard Alexander, *They Called Me DIXIE*, 1989, pp. 102-104.

112. Letter, Lee Gover to the author, September 25, 1988. (Copy in the author's files.)

113. Strickland Manuscript, pp. 85-86.

114. Strickland Manuscript, p. 87. *71 Record Book*.

115. *71 Record Book*. Childers, *War Eagles*, pp. 84-86.

116. *71 Record Book*.

117. *121 Record Book*. Mahan Interview.

118. Fetrow Interview.

119. *121 Record Book*.

120. Letter, Paul Ellington to Dixie Alexander, August 25, 1974.

121. *71, 121* and *133 Record Books*. Strickland Memoirs, p. 88. Donald Young Biography, p. 12. Waller B. Booth, "The Other Side of Dieppe," Army, June 1979, pp. 48-49. Donald J. Webb, "The Dieppe Raid—An Act of Diplomacy," *Military Review*, May 1980, pp. 30-37.

122. *133 Squadron History*, p. 29.

123. Clark Interview.

124. Taylor Interviews.

125. Roscoe Interview.

126. Gover Interview. Interview, LeRoy Gover with the author, San Carlos, California, July 20, 1989. (Hereafter cited as Gover Interview Number Three.)

127. McColpin Interview.

128. McColpin Interview.

129. Peterson, Kennard, and Wilkinson Interviews.

130. McColpin Interview.

131. George Middleton Memoirs. (Copy in the author's files.)

132. Goodson Interview.

133. Gover Diary.

134. "American Eagles in U.S. Forces," *New York Times*, September 30, 1942.

135. *The Post Enquirer*, Oakland, California, September 29, 1942. *Oakland Tribune*, Oakland, California, September 29, 1942.

136. Letter, F. W. Trott, Royal Air Force Delegation, Washington, DC, to Mrs. G. H. Middleton, October 31, 1942. (Copy in the author's files.) McColpin Letter.

137. I used a number sources for information on the ill-fated Morlaix mission. Cook, McColpin, Jackson, Sperry, Smith Interviews. Sperry Memoirs. *133 Squadron History*, p. 30. *133 Record Book*. Vern

Haugland, *The Eagle Squadrons*, pp. 162-177. George Middleton Memoirs. 133 Squadron Folder, 12 July 1962, Air Historical Branch, Air Ministry, London.

138. McColpin Interview.

139. Peterson Interview.

140. McColpin Interview.

141. US Eighth Air Force Operational Records, *Records of Anglo-American Collaboration*, Record Group 18, National Archives, Washington Federal Records Center, Suitland, Maryland.

142. Gover Interview Number Three.

143. US War Department Secret Order AG 320.2, August 22, 1942. (Copy in the USAF Academy Library.)

144. Roscoe Interview.

145. Cadman Vinton Padgett Memoirs. (Copy in the author's files.) Young Memoirs.

146. Gover Diary.

147. Sample of Commissioning Letter in author's files.

148. Strickland Manuscript, pp. 91-92.

149. *334th Fighter Squadron History*, pp.1-3.

150. "Eagles Switch to U.S. Army," *Life*, November 2, 1942, pp. 37-38.

151. "New Wings for Eagles," *Time*, October 12, 1942, p. 70.

152. For example, see *Newsweek*, October 12, 1942, p. 28, and *The Illustrated London News*, October 10, 1942, p. 404.

153. Childers, *War Eagles*, pp. 336-337.

154. Gray Interview. Telephone Interview, James Gray with the author, October 1, 1989, and October 3, 1989.

CHAPTER 6

1. Letter, Hugh Kennard to the author, August 19, 1987. (Hereafter cited as Kennard Letter.)

2. Peterson Interview.

3. Garry L. Fry and Jeffrey L. Ethell, *Escort to Berlin*, New York, 1980, pp. 125-126. (Hereafter cited as *Escort to Berlin*.)

4. Telephone Interview, LeRoy Gover with the author, April 21, 1989. (Hereafter cited as Gover Telephone Interview.)

5. Martonmere Letter.

6. Donald Ross, Answer to Eagle Squadron Questionnaire.

7. John Brown, Answer to Eagle Squadron Questionnaire. John Brown Interview.

8. McColpin Interview.

9. John Brown Interview.

10. John DuFour, Answer to Eagle Squadron Questionnaire.

11. Goodson Interview.

12. McColpin Interview.

13. Peterson Interview.

14. John Brown Interview.

15. Leon Blanding, Answer to Eagle Squadron Questionnaire. (Hereafter cited as Blanding Questionnaire.)

16. Smith Interview.

17. Don Nee, Answer to Eagle Squadron Questionnaire.

18. Edwin Miller, Answer to Eagle Squadron Questionnaire. (Hereafter cited as Miller Questionnaire.)

19. Roland Wolfe, Answer to Eagle Squadron Questionnaire. (Hereafter cited as Wolfe Questionnaire.)

20. Interview, Don Smith with the author, San Diego, California, October 14, 1988. (Hereafter cited as Don Smith Interview.)

21. Donald Ross, Answer to Eagle Squadron Questionnaire.

22. Gray Interview.

23. Eagle Squadron Personnel Data for James Nelson.

24. Nomis Interview.

25. Peterson Interview.

26. Hall, *1000 Destroyed*, pp. 26, 283-285.

27. *Escort to Berlin*, pp. 128-129.

28. Peterson Interview.

29. McColpin Interview.

30. Joe Bennett Answer to Eagle Squadron Questionnaire. (Hereafter cited as Bennett Questionnaire.)

31. Pilot Officer to Second Lieutenant, Flying Officer to First Lieutenant, Flight Lieutenant to Captain, Squadron Leader to Major, Wing Commander to Lieutenant Colonel and Group Captain to Colonel.

32. McColpin Interview.

33. Strickland Manuscript, p. 94.

34. Strickland Manuscript, p. 95.

35. "Tips from an Eagle Pilot," *Air Forces General Information Bulletin*, Intelligence Service, US Army Air Forces, Washington, DC, Bulletin No. 8, January 1943. (Copy in the author's files.)

36. Order of Joining the Squadron, 71, 121, 133 Squadron. Internal Eagle Squadron Association List. (Copy in the author's files.)

37. McColpin Interview.

38. Don Smith Interview.

39. Evans Interview.

40. Miller Questionnaire.

41. Blanding Questionnaire.

42. Wolfe Questionnaire.

43. The detail in this account focuses on the 334th since it is taken from their Squadron History and they destroyed all the enemy aircraft on that particular mission. The 335th and 336th also participated in the mission. *334th Fighter Squadron History*, Fourth Fighter Group,

Eighth Fighter Command, p. 4. (Hereafter cited as 334th History. Copy in the author's files.)

44. *334th History*, p. 5.

45. *Escort to Berlin*, p. 7.

46. Telephone Interview, LeRoy Gover with the author, May 19, 1989. (Hereafter cited as Gover Telephone Interview Number Two.)

47. Goodson Interview. Also see James A. Goodson, *Tumult in the Clouds*, New York, 1983, pp. 66-69. (Hereafter cited as *Tumult in the Clouds*.)

48. Gover Diary.

49. *Escort to Berlin*, pp. 8-15. This volume contains the complete transcript of the operational diaries of the Fourth Fighter Group as well as almost any fact one could ask about the unit.

50. *Escort to Berlin*, pp. 131-133.

51. *Escort to Berlin*, p. 40.

52. Steinhoff Interview.

53. *Escort to Berlin*, pp. 135-144.

54. *Escort to Berlin*, pp. 156-159.

55. *Escort to Berlin*, pp. 125-127.

56. Nomis Interview.

57. As complete a list as I can make of Eagles who served in Malta includes Leo Nomis, Art Roscoe, Fred Almos, Reade Tilley, John Lynch, Douglas Booth, Donald McLeod, James Peck, Fred Scudday, Bruce Downs, Richard McHan, Hugh Johnston, Nick Sintetos, and Hiram Putnam.

58. Tilley Interview.

59. Roscoe Interview.

60. Nomis Interview.

61. Telephone Interview, Reade Tilley with the author, Colorado Springs, Colorado, June 12, 1989.

62. For an excellent account of the problems involved with the resupply of Malta see Dora Alves, "The Resupply of Malta in World War II," *Naval War College Review*, September-October 1980, pp. 63-72.

63. Nomis Interview.

64. Roscoe Interview.

65. Almos Interview.

66. Roscoe Interview.

67. Art Roscoe, "Reflections on Malta—Summer 1942," unpublished manuscript. (Hereafter cited as Roscoe Manuscript. Copy in the author's files.)

68. Roscoe Interview. Nomis Interview.

69. Paul Brennan, Ray Hesselyn, and Henry Bateson, *Spitfires Over Malta*, London, 1943, p. 63.

70. Nomis Interview.

71. Roscoe Manuscript, p. 6.

72. Tilley Interview. Always a student of tactics, Tilley went on to write a paper on the subject for new fighter pilots and continued to be an authority in this area throughout World War II. For a good summary of Tilley's concepts see Alfred Price, *World War II Fighter Conflict*, London, 1975, pp. 141-147.

73. Roscoe Manuscript, p. 8.

74. Roscoe Manuscript, pp. 9-10.

75. Frederick D. Claypool, "Oral History Interview of Colonel Reade Tilley, USAF Ret.," Seymour Johnson AFB, N.C., 15 August 1985, p. 17.

76. Nomis Interview. For the complete story of Roscoe's encounter see Vern Haugland, *The Eagle Squadrons*, pp. 122-123.

77. Tilley Interview.

78. Nomis Interview.

79. Interview, Edward Miluck with the author, San Diego, California, October 15, 1988.

80. Edward T. Miluck, "El Alamein Diary," unpublished manuscript, pp. 12, 29-30. (Hereafter cited as Miluck, "Diary." Copy in the author's files.)

81. Letter, Leo Nomis to the author, September 28, 1988.

82. Miluck, "Diary," p. 34. Edward Miluck, "Outline of Hal Marting Diaries on Eagle Squadron and Africa," given to the author by Edward Miluck. (Copy in the author's files.) Letter, Harold Marting to Lenore Marting, undated. (Copy in the author's files.) H. F. Marting, "I Escape," *American Magazine*, Date and edition unknown. (Copy of the article in the author's files.)

83. Nomis Interview.

84. Miluck, "Diary," p. 25.

85. Short biographies of Norman Chap and Edwin Bicksler by Jim Griffin. Sent to the author by Jim Griffin. (Copies in the author's files.)

86. Campbell Interview.

87. Campbell Interview.

88. The 37 Eagles who became prisoners during World War II are: Nat Maranz, William Hall, William Nichols, William Geiger, Gilmore Daniel, Jack Fessler, William Jones, John Campbell (a prisoner of the Japanese), Leroy Skinner, Barry Mahon, Cliff Thorpe, Edward Brettell (an Englishman), Marion Jackson, George Sperry, Charles Cook, Gilbert Wright, George Middleton, Brewster Morgan, Aubrey Stanhope, Fred Fink, Robert Patterson, Donald Ross, Paul Ellington, Henry Mills, Selden Edner, Kenneth Smith, Ken Peterson, Duane Beeson, Raymond Care, George Carpenter, Richard Alexander, James Goodson, Wilson Edwards, Henry Ayres, Fonzo Smith, James Gray, and Roy Evans.

89. Cook Interview. Also map of Charles Cook's route as a prisoner of war. Loaned to the author by Charles Cook.

90. Mahon Interview.

91. Geiger Interview.

92. Smith Interview. Doorly Interview.

93. Fessler Interview.

94. Jackson Interview.

95. Tape, Gilmore Daniel to the author, October 14, 1988. (Tape in the author's files.)

96. Raymond Toliver, *The Interrogator*, Fallbrook, California, 1978. (Hereafter cited as Toliver, *The Interrogator*.) This volume is a fascinating account of the experiences of one of Germany's most effective interrogators, Hanns Scharff, who told his story to Toliver. Although it contains little about the Eagle Squadrons, Scharff has lived in California since the early 1950s and has attended some of the Eagle Squadron Association reunions.

97. Jackson Interview.

98. Cook Interview.

99. Jackson Interview.

100. Toliver, *The Interrogator*.

101. Fessler Interview.

102. Gover Interview. Evans Interview.

103. Almos Interview.

104. The complete records of Stalag Luft III are located in the USAF Academy Library, Colorado.

105. Geiger Interview.

106. *Prisoners of War Bulletin*, "Prisoner of War Camps in Germany: Stalagluft III," pp. 7-8. Publication date and location unknown. (Copy in the author's files.)

107. Geiger Interview.

108. Sperry Interview.

109. Jackson Interview.

110. Geiger Interview.

111. Geiger Interview.

112. Jackson Interview.

113. Jackson Interview.

114. Mahon Interview.

115. Edwards Interview.

116. Sperry Interview.

117. Interview, A. P. Clark with the author, US Air Force Academy, Colorado, September 18, 1987.

118. Geiger Interview.

119. Morris W. Fessler, "Residences in Germany—POW October 28, 1941 to May 5, 1945," pp. 4-13. (Copy in the author's files.) Another excellent first-hand account of the movement of the Stalag Luft III POWs in the face of Russian advances is James A. Goodson, *The Last of the Knights*, Canterbury, Kent, England, 1990.

Selected Bibliography

Although this is not an all-inclusive list of materials used in the preparation of this book, I have made it rather extensive because none of the other books published on the Eagle Squadrons contains any type of documentation. I have divided this bibliography into sections that seem the most relevant to both the general reader and the scholar.

INTERVIEWS

All of the interviews listed were conducted by the author and the tapes are filed with the supporting material for this volume. I was impressed with the willingness of the people I asked to talk with me and with the candidness of their answers. I owe each of them my thanks.

Almos, Fred. San Diego, California, October 15, 1988.
Balfour, Sir Harold. Telephone interview, March 24, 1988.
Blakeslee, Don. Colorado Springs, Colorado, September 23, 1989.
Brown, John. San Diego, California, September 2, 1987.
Campbell, John. Chula Vista, California, September 1, 1987.
Clark, A. P. US Air Force Academy, Colorado, September 18, 1987.
Clark, James. Telephone interview, February 4, 1989.
Cook, Charles. West Covina, California, August 31, 1987.
_____ . West Covina, California, July 2, 1989.
Doorly, Eric. San Diego, California, October 15, 1988.
Edwards, Wilson. Colorado Springs, Colorado, September 16, 1987.
_____ . Telephone interview, February, 18, 1988.
_____ . Telephone interview, August 21, 1989.
Evans, Roy. San Diego, California, October 13, 1988.
Fessler, Morris. San Diego, California, October 14, 1988.
Fetrow, Gene. San Diego, California, October 14, 1988.
Geiger, William. Pasadena, California, September 3, 1987.

SELECTED BIBLIOGRAPHY

Goodson, James. London, England, March 23, 1988.

Gover, LeRoy. Palo Alto, California, September 10, 1987.

_____ . Telephone interview, April 21, 1989.

_____ . Telephone interview, May 19, 1989.

_____ . San Carlos, California, July 21, 1989.

_____ . Telephone interview, September 5, 1989.

Gray, James. Dublin, California, September 11, 1987.

_____ . Telephone interview, October 1, 1989.

_____ . Telephone interview, October 3, 1989.

Jackson, Marion. Aptos, California, September 10, 1987.

Kennard, Hugh. London, England, March 24, 1988.

Lucas, Laddie. Telephone interview, March 24, 1988.

Mahon, Barry. Hollywood, California, September 4, 1987.

McColpin, Carroll. Novato, California, September 8, 1987.

_____ . Telephone interview, December 21, 1988.

Miluck, Edward. San Diego, California, October 15, 1988.

Nomis, Leo. Sherman Oaks, California, August 31, 1987.

Peterson, Chesley. Ogden, Utah, September 14, 1987.

_____ . San Diego, California, October 14, 1988.

_____ . Telephone interview, November 10, 1988.

Pisanos, Steve. San Diego, California, August 31, 1987.

Roscoe, Arthur. Hollywood, California, September 4, 1987.

Smith, Don. San Diego, California, October 14, 1988.

Smith, Robert. Alexandria, Virginia, September 18, 1987.

Sperry, George. Pleasanton, California, September 11, 1987.

Steinhoff, Johannes. Colorado Springs, Colorado, July 29, 1988.

Stewart, Bert. San Diego, California, October 15, 1988.

Sweeny, Charles. London, England, March 20, 1988.

Taylor, Edwin. San Clemente, California, August 27 and September 1, 1987.

_____ . Telephone interview, January 24, 1988.

_____ . Telephone interview, December 23, 1988.

Tilley, Reade. Colorado Springs, Colorado, February 11, 1988.

_____ . US Air Force Academy, Colorado, August 2, 1988.

_____ . Telephone interview, June 12, 1989.

Wilkinson, Royce. Minster, Sheppy, Kent, England, March 22, 1988.

Young, Donald. San Diego, California, October 14, 1988.

QUESTIONNAIRES

I sent a questionnaire to each member of the Eagle Squadron Association in June 1987. I asked for both personal data concerning when and how they joined the RAF and such information as their feelings about combat, motivations for wanting to fly, etc. I received the following answers on the dates indicated. All of the questionnaires are in my files.

Alexander, Richard, July 29, 1987
Beatie, Ernest, July 28, 1987
Bennett, Joseph, August 18, 1987
Blanding, Leon, August 1, 1987
Booth, Douglas, August 5, 1987
Brown, John, August 24, 1987
Campbell, John, August 18, 1987
Carpenter, George, August 24, 1987
Clarke, Raymond, August 15, 1987
Daniel, Gilmore, July 28, 1987
Daymond, Gregory, August 5, 1987
DuFour, John, July 30, 1987
Durham, Joseph, August 31, 1987
Ellington, Paul, August 4, 1987
Fessler, Morris, August 13, 1987
Geiger, William, July 28, 1987
Goodson, James, August 18, 1987
Gover, LeRoy, August 13, 1987
Griffin, James, August 1, 1987
Hopson, Alfred, August 17, 1987
Jackson, Marion, August 5, 1987
Miller, Ervin, No date recorded
Miluck, Edward, November 5, 1987
Nee, Don, August 21, 1987
Parker, Vernon, August 3, 1987
Peterson, Chesley, August 25, 1987
Priser, Robert, August 1, 1987
Roscoe, Arthur, July 28, 1987
Ross, Donald, July 31, 1987
Smith, Donald, July 29, 1987
Smith, Robert, August 11, 1987
Taylor, William E. G., July 29, 1987
Tilley, Reade, August 17, 1987
Wilkinson, Royce, July 30, 1987

Wolfe, Roland, July 31, 1987
Young, Donald, August 10, 1987

In addition, I received taped responses, prompted by the questionnaire, from the following people:

Beatie, Ernest D.
Daniel, Gilmore
Peterson, Chesley

In November 1989, I sent a short biographical questionnaire to selected Eagles to determine their home state, age, education level and occupation when they joined either the RAF or RCAF. I received answers from the following individuals. The results of these questionnaires are reflected in appendix A.

Almos, Fred
Blakeslee, Don
Braley, Richard
Care, Mrs. Raymond
Coen, Oscar
Daniel, Gilmore
Fetrow, Gene
Geiger, William
Lambert, Donald
Morgan, W. Brewster
Nash, Herbert
Sintetos, Nicholas
Stanhope, Aubrey
Stewart, Hubert
Taylor, William E. G.

Additional information is available from Clayton Knight Committee Questionnaire, National Archives, Washington, DC, file 800.00B Homer Smith.

LETTERS, MANUSCRIPTS, MEMOIRS, REPORTS, AND TELEGRAMS

Copies of all of the documents cited are in the supporting files for this book unless otherwise noted.

SELECTED BIBLIOGRAPHY

Letters

Adams, Alida Scarborough, to the author, October 23, 1987.

Alexander, Richard, to the author, October 8, 1988.

Byington, William H., Jr., to J. C. Green, August 19, 1940. National Archives, Washington, DC, file 800.00B Homer Smith.

Carpenter, George, to the author, August 24, 1987.

Durham, Joe, to the author, October 2, 1987.

Eilan, Nancy Wicker, to the author, March 1, 1988.

Ellington, Paul, to Dixie Alexander, August 25, 1974.

HRH King George V of England to Mrs. V. Hammer, undated.

Gover, LeRoy, to the author, October 15, 1987; August 2, 1988; September 25, 1988.

Griffin, James, to the author, August 1, 1987; November 5, 1987.

Hopson, Alfred, to the author, January 8, 1988.

John, Kenny, to the author, December 14, 1987.

Jones, H. A., to Morris Fessler, November 2, 1940.

Kennard, Hugh, to the author, August 19, 1987.

(Clayton) Knight Committee to James R. Happel, June 7, 1941; July 29, 1941; September 18, 1941. National Archives, Washington, DC, file 800.00B Homer Smith.

Marting, Harold, to Lenore Marting, undated.

Martonmere, The Right Honorable, P.C., G.B.E., K.C.M.G., to the author, August 19, 1987.

Miller, Ervin, to the author, September, 1987; November 5, 1987.

_____ , to an unknown person, undated.

Moffat, Pierrepont, to Secretary of State, Washington, DC, August 15, 1940. National Archives, Washington, DC, file 800.00B Homer Smith.

Nee, Don, to Robert Hays, Jr., January 5, 1965.

Nomis, Leo, to the author, September 28, 1988.

_____ , to Vern Haugland, January 17, 1975.

Pepper, Claude, to Reade Tilley, Sr., February 19, 1941.

Ross, Donald, to the author, November 5, 1987.

Royal Canadian Air Force Casualties Officer to Mrs. V. Hammer, May 7, 1942.

Sperry, George, to Vern Haugland, March 3, 1975.

Sweeny, Charles, to the author, July 22, 1987; October 10, 1987.

Sweeny, Charles, to Vern Haugland, September 5, 1974; June 24, 1980.

Sweeny, Robert, to Vern Haugland, March 6, year unknown.

Taylor, William E. G., to Vern Haugland, October 4, 1974.

Thomas, E. H., to Mrs. Victor Hammer, April 29, 1942.

Trott, F. W., to Mrs. G. H. Middleton, October 31, 1942.

Wicker, Walter, Jr., to Walter Wicker, Sr., early 1942.

Manuscripts

Eilan, Nancy Wicker. *A True Story of an American Family.* Unpublished, 1985.

Knight, Clayton and Thomas Fleming. *Aid to Victory.* Unpublished and undated.

McColpin, Carroll W. "Sojourn of an Eagle." Unpublished and undated.

Miluck, Edward T. "El Alamein Diary." Unpublished and undated.

_____ . "Outline of Hal Marting Diaries on Eagle Squadron and Africa." Unpublished and undated.

Roscoe, Arthur. "Reflections on Malta-Summer 1942." Unpublished and undated.

Strickland, Harold H. *War and Flight; Autobiography and Diary.* Unpublished and undated.

Taylor, Edwin. "Definitions of Fighter Operations." Unpublished and undated.

_____ . "Known But Unknown." Unpublished and undated.

_____ . Manuscript. Unpublished and undated.

_____ . "Thoughts on the Eagles." Unpublished and undated.

Memoirs and Diaries

Fessler, Morris W. "Residences in Germany—POW October 28, 1941 to May 5, 1945." Unpublished and undated.

Gover, LeRoy. Diary. Unpublished and undated.

Griffin, James. Short Biographies of Norman Chap and Edwin Bicksler. Unpublished and undated.

Knight, Clayton, Papers (microfilm). Special Collections Section, US Air Force Academy Library. Note especially the interview of Knight with Robert Hays, 8 March 1955.

Middleton, George. Memoirs. Unpublished and undated.

Miller, Ervin. Biographical Paper. Unpublished and undated.

Miller, Mrs. Ervin. Memoirs. Unpublished and undated.

Miner, Denver. Memoirs. Unpublished and undated.

Padgett, Cadman Vinton. Memoirs. Unpublished and undated.

Sperry, George. Memoirs. Unpublished and undated.

Strickland, Harold. Diary. Unpublished and undated.

Taylor, Edwin. Untitled Notes. Unpublished and undated.

Young, Donald. Biographical Paper. Unpublished and undated.

Reports

Biographical Summaries, Andrew Mamedoff, Eugene Tobin, Vernon Keough, Philip Leckrone, Arthur Donahue. Historical Archives, Air Ministry, London. Unpublished and undated.

British Subject File, December 13, 1940. National Archives, Washington, DC, file 842.2311.

"Eagle Squadron, RAF, Biographical Notes on Pilot of 'Eagle Squadron.'" Historical Archives, Air Ministry, London, Eagle Squadron File.

FBI Report. John Edgar Hoover to Adolf A. Berle, Jr., January 29, 1942. National Archives, Washington, DC, File 800.00B Homer Smith.

Telegrams

Department of State, Washington, DC, to American Embassy, London. National Archives, Washington, DC, file 842.2311.

Associated Press, New York, September 8, 1941.

Chief of the Air Staff, Ottawa, Canada, to Mrs. V. Hammer, undated.

PERIODICAL AND NEWSPAPER ARTICLES

"Allied Air Forces." *Flying*, XXXI (September 1942), 146-48, 273.

Alves, Dora. "The Resupply of Malta in World War II." *Naval War College Review*, (September-October 1980), 63-72.

"American Air Unit Bags 3 Nazi Planes." *New York Times*, July 3, 1941.

"American Eagles in U.S. Forces." *New York Times*, September 30, 1942.

"American Eagles Over Britain." *Washington Post,* October 23, 1940.

"Americans Will Fly as Unit in Fighting for England." *The Tribune Sun* (San Diego), October 22, 1940.

Berry, F. Clifton. "Battle of Britain, 1940." *Air Force Magazine,* LXIII (September 1980), 114-119.

Boebert, Earl. "The Eagle Squadrons." *American Aviation Historical Society Journal,* IX (Spring, 1964), 3-20.

Booth, Waller B. "The Other Side of Dieppe." *Army,* (June, 1979), 48-49.

Boehnel, William. "'Eagle Squadron' Has Thrilling Flying Scenes." *New York World Telegram,* July 3, 1942.

Bulitho, Hector. "Tribute to the RAF." *Living Age* CCCLIX (December 1940), 324-326.

"Cinema-'Eagle Squadron.'" *Time* XL (July 13, 1942), 86-87.

Clemmens, Williams. "How Chennault Kills Japs." *Colliers,* CX (July 4, 1942), 58-60.

Conger, Beach. "Sweeny Recruit Gets to Paris, Can't Find a Unit to Fly With." *New York Herald Tribune,* March 2, 1940.

"Dominion's Squadrons." *Flying,* XXXI (September 1942), 142-144.

Donahue, Arthur G. "Tally Ho!" *Saturday Evening Post,* CCXIII (May 3, 1941), 12-13+.

"Eagle from Alfalfa Patch." *Time,* XXXVIII (December 1, 1941), 23.

"Eagle Squadron Leads R.A.F. in October Bag of Nazi Planes." *New York Herald Tribune,* November 2, 1941.

"Eagle Squadron of U.S. Fliers Will Aid Defense of Britain." *Salt Lake Tribune,* October 9, 1940.

"Eagle Squadrons." *Flying,* XXXI (September 1942), 145, 274.

"Eagle Squadrons Change Command." *The Illustrated London News,* CCI (October 10, 1942), 404.

"Eagles Go American." *Newsweek,* XX (October 12, 1942), 28.

"Eagles Switch to U.S. Army." *Life,* XIII (November 2, 1942), 37-38+.

"Eagles to War." *Newsweek,* XVIII (July 14, 1941), 25-26.

"Eagles True and False." *Newsweek,* XX (July 6, 1942), 59.

"English, He Led the U.S. Eagles." *Daily Mail* (London), November 19, 1941.

Evans, Joseph Jr. "Eagle Squadron Asks 'Action' on Russian Front." *New York Herald Tribune,* November 3, 1941.

_____ . "2nd Eagle Unit, Eager for Fight, To Get It Soon." *New York Herald Tribune,* November 29, 1941.

"Fighter Command." *Life,* X (March 24, 1941), 82-89.

"Fighter Command." *Flying,* XXXI (September 1942), 62-69.

Folliard, Edward T. "Eagle Squadron." *The Washington Post,* April 2, 1941.

"Former Employer Calls Pilot 'Coolest' He Has Ever Known." *Oakland Tribune,* October 28, 1941.

Frey, Royal D. "America's First World War II Ace." *The Airman,* XI (August 1967), 42-44.

Fry, Garry L. "Boise Bee: The Duane Beeson Story." *American Aviation Historical Society Journal,* XXIII (Winter 1978), 242-259.

Grant, J. Fergus. "British Commonwealth Air Training Plan." *Canadian Geographic Journal,* XXI (July 1940), 1-26.

Griffin, James. "Sea Serpents and Steel Forests." *Air and Space,* (April/May 1988), 30-31.

Haugland, Vern. "Eagles At Malta." *Air Force Magazine,* LXII (September 1979), 104-110.

"Keen American 'Eagles' Off on Patrol." *The Illustrated London News,* CXCVIII (March 29, 1941), 416.

Kennerly, Byron. "Combat Over Coventry." *Harper's Magazine,* CLXXXV (June 1942), 90-96.

_____ . "Squadron 71, Scramble!" *Harper's Magazine,* CLXXXIII (July 1941), 171-180.

Kilduff, Peter. "Clayton Knight, No. 206 Squadron, RAF." *Cross and Cockade,* (Spring, 1987), 29.

Lodge, J. Norman. "Eagle Squadron Shows Skill of Fighting Pilots." (Newspaper not identified), March 19, 1941.

MacGowen, Gault. "American Eagle Squadron Set For Air Action Against Nazis." *The Sun* (New York), March 19, 1941.

"Malta G. C." *Flying,* XXXI (September 1942), 68, 230, 234.

Marting, Harold. "I Escape." *American Magazine* 136 (August 1943), pp 34-35 ff.

McColpin, Carroll W. "A Jump Ahead of the Jerry." *Air Force* XXVI (February 1943), 7, 37.

"The Men Behind the Pilots." *The Illustrated London News,* CXCIX (August 16, 1941), 198-99.

"Movie of the Week: Eagle Squadron." *Life,* XII (June 29, 1942), 62-64.

"The New 'War Birds'." *The Aeroplane,* (March 28, 1941).

"New Wings for Eagles." *Time,* XL (October 12, 1942), 70.

O'Conner, Hugh. "Blood, Sweat and Glory." *American Magazine,* CXXXII (November, 1941), 9, 116.

Ohlinger, John F. "Hurricane Convoy." *Aerospace Historian,* XXVI (September 1979), 148-153.

Owen, Russell. "How the RAF Does It." *New York Magazine,* (June 7, 1942), 8-11.

"Paddy of the RAF." *New Yorker,* XVII (December 6, 1941), 31-43.

"The Pilots of the RAF." *New Yorker,* XVIII (March 14, 1942), 22-25.

Pinkley, Virgil. "The Four Horsemen." *Scholastic,* XLI (October 5, 1942), 2.

Post, Robert. "Four Miles Up—All Guns Going." *New York Times Magazine,* (December 1, 1940), 3, 23.

"The Preliminary Training of Cadets as RAF Pilots and Observers." *The Illustrated London News,* CXCVIII (March 22, 1941), 367-369.

Price, Clair. "On the Wing with the RAF." *New York Times Magazine,* (January 14, 1940), 12-13, 18.

"RAF Offensive." *Newsweek,* XIX (March 23, 1942), 32, 35.

"The RAF in the USA." *Scholastic,* XL (March 2, 1942), 28.

Ratley, Lonnie O. "A Lesson of History: The Luftwaffe and Barbarosa." *Air University Review,* XXXIV (March-April 1983), 50-65.

Reston, James B. "R.A.F.'s Tough Guy." *New York Magazine,* (December 15, 1940), 5, 22.

Reynolds, Quentin. "All Aircraft Returned Safely." *Colliers,* CVI (September 14, 1940), 11, 57-58.

_____ . "They Wouldn't Wait." *Colliers,* CX (August 22, 1942), 18-19, 46.

"Soldier of Fortune." *New Yorker,* XVI (December 21, 1940), 10-11.

"State Department Not Looking Into American's Legal Status." *New York Times,* November 21, 1940.

Stoneman, William H. "U.S. Airmen With British Fly Like Demons Eager for a Fight." *Chicago Daily News,* October 18, 1941.

Taylor, Samuel W. "Portrait of a Crew Chief." *Air Force,* XXVII (December 1944), 38-40.

Thompson, Craig. "Poland's Avenging Eagles." *New York Times Magazine,* (June 29, 1941), 4, 23.

Thruelsen, Richard. "Canada's Open Secret." *Saturday Evening Post,* CCXIII (February 1, 1941), 18-19, 35, 38.

Tobin, Eugene (as told to Robert Low). "Yankee Eagle Over London." *Liberty,* XVIII (March 29, April 5, April 12, April 19, April 26, 1941).

"Two More Eagle Flyers Win D.F.C. for Gallantry." *New York Herald Tribune,* October 8, 1941.

"U.S. Fliers Aid British." *Washington Post,* August 20, 1940.

"U.S. Pilots Put British Planes Through Paces." *New York Herald Tribune,* October 14, 1940.

"U.S. Volunteers Saluted By Lady Aster." *New York Herald Tribune,* December 6, 1940.

Webb, Donald J. "The Dieppe Raid--An Act of Diplomacy." *Military Review,* LX (May, 1980), 30-37.

"The Yanks of the Eagle Squadrons." *Airman,* IX (October 1965), 18-20.

Yarbrough, W.T. "American Eagles Claw Germans to Celebrate Fourth of July." *New York World Telegram,* July 5, 1941.

US AND BRITISH GOVERNMENT DOCUMENTS

There is an immense store house of information on the RAF in the Historical Archives of the Air Ministry in London. Much of this material is not well-cataloged and the researcher must spend a great deal of time trying to find all the documents on a specific subject such as the Eagle Squadrons. The same holds true for the National Archives in both Washington, DC, and Suitland, Maryland. Nonetheless, the very friendly and helpful people at all three locations make up for the time needed to search the records. The references here do not even scratch the surface of the material available.

Air Ministry Bulletin No. 1928. *Formation of American "Eagle Squadron", The King Approves Special Badge.* London: Historical Archives, Air Ministry, October 8, 1940.

Air Ministry Pamphlet ID/44/349. *Aircrew Training: Report on the Conference Held in the United Kingdom, January/February, 1942.* London: Air Historical Branch, Air Ministry, undated.

Air Publication 3233. *Flying Training.* London: Air Ministry, 1952.

Claypool, Frederick D. "Oral History Interview of Colonel Reade Tilley, USAF Ret." Seymour Johnson Air Force Base, North Carolina, August 15, 1985.

Daily Routine Orders. RAF Station Kirton Lindsey, Gainsborough, Lincolnshire, July 12, 1941.

Eagle Squadron Personnel Data forms, Special Collections Section, US Air Force Academy Library.

Fourth Fighter Group Operational Slides. Washington National Records Center, Suitland, Maryland: Box 634, Record Group 18, Entry 7.

"Prisoner of War Camps in Germany: Stalagluft III." *Prisoners of War Bulletin.* Publication location and date unknown.

RAF Monograph. *Anglo-American Collaboration in the Air War Over North-west Europe.* London: Air Historical Branch, Air Ministry, undated.

RAF Narrative. *Aircrew Training, 1934-1942.* London: Air Historical Branch, Air Ministry, 1942.

Squadron Operations Record Book, Number 71 Eagle Squadron. Microfilm, Special Collections Section, US Air Force Academy Library.

Squadron Operations Record Book, Number 121 Eagle Squadron. Microfilm, Special Collections Section, US Air Force Academy Library.

Squadron Operations Record Book, Number 133 Eagle Squadron. Microfilm, Special Collections Section, US Air Force Academy Library.

334th Fighter Squadron, 4th Fighter Group, 8th Air Force. *History of the 334th Fighter Squadron.* Microfilm, Office of Air Force History, Bolling Air Force Base, Washington, DC.

335th Fighter Squadron, 4th Fighter Group, 8th Air Force. *History of the 335th Fighter Squadron.* Microfilm, Office of Air Force History, Bolling Air Force Base, Washington, DC.

336th Fighter Squadron, 4th Fighter Group, 8th Air Force. *History of the 336th Fighter Squadron.* Microfilm, Office of Air Force History, Bolling Air Force Base, Washington, DC.

"Tips from an Eagle Pilot." Air Forces General Information Bulletin. Washington, DC: Intelligence Service, US Army Air Forces, Bulletin No. 8, January 1943.

"U.S. Air Force Official Policy Concerning the Term 'Ace'"
The Alfred F. Simpson Historical Research Center, Maxwell Air Force Base, Alabama.

U.S. Air Force Operational Records. *Records of Anglo-American
Collaboration.* Washington Federal Records Center,
Suitland, Maryland: Boxes 634, 1142, Record Group 18,
Entry 7. 1142.

US Army Current Intelligence Section. "Interviews with 15
Pilots of Former Eagle Squadrons." December 17, 1942.
Microfilm, Office of Air Force History, Bolling Air Force
Base, Washington, DC.

US War Department Secret Order AG 320.2, August 22,
1942. Special Collections Section, US Air Force Academy
Library.

BOOKS

There are innumerable books on World War II, air power in
general, fighter aircraft, pilots' reminiscences, and the like. I
have listed and commented on only those I found to be particularly useful or that contain a reasonable amount of material
about the Eagle Squadrons.

Alexander, Richard L. *They Called Me Dixie.* Hemet, California:
Robinson Typographics, 1988.
Interesting first-hand account of an Eagle's experiences
during World War II. Contains many human interest stories as well as details of combat.

Bond, Charles R., and Terry Anderson. *A Flying Tiger's Diary.*
College Station: Texas A and M Press, 1984.
A very thorough and well-written diary of service with
the American Volunteer Group.

Bowyer, Chaz. *Fighter Pilots of the RAF, 1939-1945.* London:
William Kimber, 1984.
Short chapters on individual fighter pilots. Chapter 15 is
on Chesley Peterson.

Brennan, Paul, Ray Hesselyn, and Henry Bateson. *Spitfires Over
Malta.* London: 1943.

British Air Ministry. *The Battle of Britain.* New York: Garden
City Publishing Co. Inc., 1941.
The official Air Ministry Record of the Battle of Britain.

Chennault, Anna. *Chennault and the Flying Tigers.* New York:
Paul S. Eriksson, Inc., 1963.

A very friendly biography of Claire Chennault by his wife.

Chennault, Claire Lee. *Way of a Fighter: The Memoirs of Claire Lee Channault.* Edited by Robert Holtz. New York: G. P. Putnam's Sons, 1949.

Childers, James Saxon. *War Eagles.* San Francisco: Eagle Publishing, 1983. (Reprint of a 1943 edition.)

A very sympathetic account written by a US Army officer who lived with Number 71 Eagle Squadron during 1942. Contains stories about almost every member of that Squadron including combat, life in the unit, and off duty activities. This edition also contains an account of the fate of each member of the unit, complete roster of the members, and pictures of most.

Churchill, Winston. *The Second World War.* 6 vols. Boston: Houghton, Mifflin and Company, 1949.

One of the standard and most readable of the large histories of World War II. Especially strong on British and American cooperation.

Clark, Alan. *Aces High: The War in the Air Over the Western Front, 1914-1918.* London: Weidenfeld and Nicolson, 1973.

A good history of the use of aircraft during the First World War. Chapter 8 is about the Lafayette Escadrille.

Corn, Joseph. *The Winged Gospel.* New York: Oxford University Press, 1983.

American's romance with aviation from 1900. A thorough and delightful account of attitudes, views of aviation and aviators as well as the development of the industry. A must for the development of aviation between World Wars I and II.

Craven, Wesley Frank, and James Lea Cate. *The Army Air Forces in World War II.* Washington, DC: Office of Air Force History, 1983.

The standard and most thorough work on the subject.

Donahue, Arthur G. *Tally-Ho!: Yankee in a Spitfire.* New York: The MacMillan Company, 1941.

The memoirs of an Eagle who was one of the first Americans to fly with the RAF during World War II. Especially valuable for the views of the times and the action as it happened since Donahue wrote the book while he was actively flying with the RAF.

Dunn, William R. *Fighter Pilot: The First American Ace of World War II*. Lexington: The University of Kentucky Press, 1982.

An interesting first-hand account of fighter operations in World War II and subsequent. Focus on the actions in which the author took part with the subtle aim of substantiating his claim to having been the first American ace in the War, a deed accomplished while flying with the RAF as an Eagle.

Flammer, Philip M. *The Vivid Air: The Lafayette Escadrille*. Athens: University of Georgia Press, 1981.

The standard and most factually complete history of the Lafayette Escadrille. Contains a complete bibliography and extensive notes.

Fourteenth Air Force Association. *Chennault's Flying Tigers*. 2 vols. Dallas: Taylor Publishing Company, 1982.

The official history of the 14th Air Force commissioned by the veterans of that unit. Includes not only narrative but pictures, biographies, insignia, aircraft, and about any other thing you would care to know. Volume 2 is all pictures.

Fry, Garry L. *Debden Eagles, the 4th Fighter Group in World War II*. Edited by Kenn C. Rust. (City unknown): Walker-Smith, Inc., 1970.

A brief historical summary of the Americans at Debden beginning with the Eagles and going through World War II. Good pictures compose a large portion of the book. Gives a good feel for the units.

Fry, Garry L., and Jeffrey L. Ethell. *Escort to Berlin*. New York: Arco Publishing, Inc., 1980.

All you ever wanted to know about the Fourth Fighter Group. Includes complete operational logs, facts, and statistics ranging from missions flown to records of individual pilots and complete personnel rosters. Excellent pictures of personnel, aircraft, and action.

Galland, Adolf. *The First and the Last*. London: Methuen and Co., Ltd., 1955.

An excellent account of the war from the German perspective written by the most famous Luftwaffe pilot of the war.

Gelb, Norman. *Scramble: A Narrative History of the Battle of Britain*. New York: Harcort, Brace, Jovanovich, 1985.

Goodson, James A. *Tumult in the Clouds.* New York: St. Martin's Press, 1983.

A well-written, first-hand account by an Eagle and one of the leading American aces of World War II. Focus is on individuals in both the Eagles and the Fourth Fighter Group with numerous human interest and combat accounts.

_____ . *The Last of the Knights.* Canterbury, Kent, England. 1990.

Gunston, Bill. *Allied Fighters of World War II.* New York: Arco Publishing, Inc., 1981.

Contains a brief history, color pictures, and complete facts and figures about every significant Allied fighter aircraft in World War II.

_____ . *German, Italian and Japanese Fighters of World War II.* New York: Arco Publishing, Inc.,1980.

Contains a brief history, color pictures, and complete facts and figures about every significant Axis fighter aircraft in World War II.

Hall, Grover C., Jr. *1000 Destroyed.* Dallas: Morgan Aviation Books, 1946.

A comprehensive history of the Fourth Fighter Group with a brief chapter on the Eagle Squadrons. This volume is one source for the myth that all the pilots of the Fourth were Eagles. It is also focused on Don Blakeslee as the key to the success of the Fourth. Many good first-hand accounts of battles and daily life.

Hansell, Haywood S., Jr. *The Air Plan that Defeated Hitler.* Atlanta: Higgins-McArthur/Longino and Porter, Inc., 1972.

The comprehensive story of AWPD–1 by one of the architects of that plan.

Haugland, Vern. *The Eagle Squadrons.* New York: Ziff-Davis Flying Books, 1979.

The first book about the Eagles written under the auspices of the Eagle Squadron Association. This rather brief volume is primarily composed of first-hand stories about individuals with a heavy emphasis toward combat.

_____ . *The Eagles' War.* New York: Jason Aronson, 1982.

The second of a planned three volumes on the Eagles. Repeats much of the material in *The Eagle Squadrons* but continues the story through the end of World War II. Most of the volume is devoted to adventures of Eagle Squadron members after they became members of the Fourth Fighter Group. Emphasis is on first-hand accounts and combat.

Heiferman, Ron. *Flying Tigers: Chennault in China.* New York: Ballantine Books, 1971.

A very general account of the American Volunteer Group and the China-Burma-India theatre of operations.

Hollon, Eugene. *History of Preflight Training in the AAF, 1941–1953.* Maxwell Air Force Base, Alabama: US Air Force Historical Division, 1953.

Kelly, Terence. *Hurricane and Spitfire Pilots at War.* London: William Kimber, 1986.

An interesting composite of stories about these two aircraft and the men who flew then in the various theaters of World War II. Contains only one chapter about the Eagles.

Kennerly, Byron. *The Eagles Roar: Air Combat with the American Eagle Squadron in World War II.* Washington, DC: Zenger Publishing Company, 1979. (This is a reprint of a 1942 original.)

Written by one of the original Eagles who was sent home by the RAF, this exciting volume is a complete fabrication of action in which the author never participated. While it gives a flavor of the environment and the action it is completely unreliable.

Mason, Herbert M. *The Lafayette Escadrille.* New York: 1964.

McCormick, Donald. *One Man's Wars: The Story of Charles Sweeny, Soldier of Fortune.* London: Arthur Barker Limited, 1972.

An interesting biography of one of the great soldiers of fortune of the 20th century. Participated in almost every war from the Spanish-American through World War II. Had the original idea of the Eagle Squadron and was their first honorary commander.

Michaelis, Ralph. *From Bird Cage to Battle Plane.* New York: Thomas Y. Crowell, 1943.

Murray, Williamson. *Strategy for Defeat: The Luftwaffe, 1933–1945.* Maxwell Air Force Base, Alabama: Air University Press, 1983.

One of the most comprehensive volumes available on the history of the German Luftwaffe.

Peterson, Chesley. "Crash Landing" in Donald Robinson. *The Day I Was Proudest To Be An American.* Garden City, New York: 1958.

Price, Alfred. *Spitfire at War.* New York: Charles Scribner's Sons, 1974.

_____ . *World War II Fighter Conflict.* London: MacDonald and Jane's, 1975.

Particularly valuable on the specifics of various fighter aircraft flown by both the Allies and the Axis during World War II and the tactics they used. Contains the details of British formations and a good account of Reade Tillley's ideas on tactics.

Pritchett, C. Herman. *The American Constitution.* New York: 1968.

RAF Monograph. *Anglo-American Collaboration in the Air War over North-West Europe.* London: Air Historical Branch, Air Ministry, (no date).

A very complete volume on the entire scope of negotiations that led to the Eighth Air Force coming to England.

Rawlings, John D. B. *Fighter Squadrons of the R.A.F. and Their Aircraft.* London: 1976.

Includes the complete history of every fighter squadron in the history of the RAF. Very useful.

Richards, Denis. *Royal Air Force, 1939-1945.* London: Her Majesty's Stationary Office, 1974.

A long and detailed history of the RAF in World War II.

Roseberry, C. R. *The Challenging Skies.* Garden City, New York: Doubleday and Company, 1966.

One of the best sources for the development of aviation between World Wars I and II.

Scott, Robert Lee, Jr. *Flying Tiger: Chennault of China.* Garden City, New York: Doubleday and Company, Inc., 1959.

A friendly account of Channault and the American Volunteer Group.

Scutts, Jerry. *Spitfire in Action.* Carrollton, Texas: Squadron/Signal Publications, 1980.

The most complete book on the Spitfire. Includes all the facts, figures and pictures to tell the complete story of the airplane.

Shirer, William. *The Rise and Fall of the Third Reich.* London: 1964.

The standard work on Hitler and the Third Reich.

Smith, Leslie. *Development of AAF and USAF Training Concepts and Programs, 1941-1952.* Maxwell Air Force Base, Alabama: USAF Historical Division, Air University, 1953.

Spagnuolo, Mark M. *Don S. Gentile: Soldier of God and Country.* East Lansing: College Press, 1986.

A very friendly and complementary biography of Don Gentile who was an Eagle and one of the leading aces of the Fourth Fighter Group. Interesting reading although often too complimentary and not completely accurate.

Spaight, James M. *The Battle of Britain, 1040.* London: Geoffrey Bles, 1941.

Stevenson, William. *A Man Called Intrepid.* Hew York: Harcourt, Brace, Jovanovich, 1976.

A well-written and fascinating account of British spies during World War II. A must on the subject of espionage.

Strickland, Patricia. *The Putt-putt Air Force.* Washington, DC: Department of Transportation, 1971.

The story of the civilian pilot training program and the war training service from 1939 to 1941. Focus is on the evolution of training civilians to fly and the impact the program had on our ability to produce pilots in World War II.

Toliver, Raymond F. *The Interrogator.* Fallbrook, California: Aero Publishers, 1978.

The experiences of Hanns Scharff, the German who many called the master interrogator, as told to Raymond Toliver. One of the best books available on the subject of interrogation of Allied prisoners during World War II. Particularly valuable for the detail on interrogation methods and the results.

Toliver, Raymond F. and Trevor J. Constable. *Fighter Aces of the USA.* Fallbrook, California: Aero Publishers, 1979.

Lists all the top aces in US flying history. Contains a short paragraph about each. The best source on the subject.

Townsend, Peter. *The Odds Against Us.* New York: William Morrow and Company, 1987.

Ulanoff, Stanley M. *Fighter Pilot.* New York: 1986.

Wallace, Graham. *The RAF at Biggin Hill.* London: 1957.

An interesting history of the air base at Biggin Hill complete with both battle accounts and stories of everyday life and colorful personalities.

Wiener, Willard. *Two Hundred Flyers: The Story of the Civilian-AAF Pilot Training Program.* Washington, DC: The Infantry Journal, 1945.

A complete coverage of the various civilian contract bases used by the Army during World War II. Contains a brief coverage of location, type of training, changes, contractor and those who were trained at the bases.

Wykeham, Peter. *Fighter Command.* London: Putnam, 1960.

Excellent on the history of the RAF Fighter Command. Especially good on aircraft requirements and developments.

INDEX

INDEX OF SUBJECTS

THE AUTHOR

Philip D. Caine retired from the US Air Force in 1992 as a brigadier general. His final assignment was at the Air Force Academy, where he was a Permanent Professor and the Deputy Commandant for Military Instruction. He did much of the research and writing for this book while assigned as a Senior Fellow at the National Defense University. A Distinguished Graduate of the Reserve Officer Training Corps, General Caine holds both MA and PhD degrees in history from Stanford University. He was a command pilot with more than 4,500 hours of flying time, having served flying tours with both Air Training Command and Air Defense Command. General Caine also served as Acting Chief of Project CHECO in Vietnam, Professor and Acting Head of the History Department at the Air Force Academy, and Professor of International Studies at the National War College. He lives in Monument, Colorado.